BEFORE CANADA

McGill-Queen's Studies in Early Canada / Avant le Canada

Series Editors / Directeurs de la collection : Allan Greer and Carolyn Podruchny

This series features studies of the history of the northern half of North America – a vast expanse that would eventually be known as Canada – in the era before extensive European settlement and extending into the nineteenth century. Long neglected, Canada-before-Canada is a fascinating area of study experiencing an intellectual renaissance as researchers in a range of disciplines, including history, geography, archeology, anthropology, literary studies, and law, contribute to a new and enriched understanding of the distant past. The editors welcome manuscripts in English or French on all aspects of the period, including work on Indigenous history, the Atlantic fisheries, the fur trade, exploration, French or British imperial expansion, colonial life, culture, language, law, science, religion, and the environment.

Cette série de monographies est consacrée à l'histoire de la partie septentrionale du continent de l'Amérique du nord, autrement dit le grand espace qui deviendra le Canada, dans les siècles qui s'étendent jusqu'au début du 19ᴱ. Longtemps négligé par les chercheurs, ce Canada-avant-le-Canada suscite beaucoup d'intérêt de la part de spécialistes dans plusieurs disciplines, entre autres, l'histoire, la géographie, l'archéologie, l'anthropologie, les études littéraires et le droit. Nous assistons à une renaissance intellectuelle dans ce champ d'étude axé sur l'interaction de premières nations, d'empires européens et de colonies. Les directeurs de cette série sollicitent des manuscrits, en français ou en anglais, qui portent sur tout aspect de cette période, y compris l'histoire des autochtones, celle des pêcheries de l'atlantique, de la traite des fourrures, de l'exploration, de l'expansion de l'empire français ou britannique, de la vie coloniale (Nouvelle-France, l'Acadie, Terre-Neuve, les provinces maritimes, etc.), de la culture, la langue, le droit, les sciences, la religion ou l'environnement.

BEFORE
CANADA

*Northern North America
in a
Connected World*

EDITED BY

ALLAN GREER

McGill-Queen's University Press

Montreal & Kingston • London • Chicago

ISBN 978-0-2280-1920-6 (cloth)
ISBN 978-0-2280-1921-3 (paper)
ISBN 978-0-2280-1955-8 (ePDF)

Legal deposit first quarter 2024
Bibliothèque nationale du Québec

Printed in Canada on acid-free paper that is 100% ancient forest free
(100% post-consumer recycled), processed chlorine free

This book has been published with the help of a grant from the Canadian Federation for the Humanities and Social Sciences, through the Awards to Scholarly Publications Program, using funds provided by the Social Sciences and Humanities Research Council of Canada.

Funded by the   Financé par le
Government   gouvernement
of Canada   du Canada

Canada Council   Conseil des arts
for the Arts   du Canada

We acknowledge the support of the Canada Council for the Arts.
Nous remercions le Conseil des arts du Canada de son soutien.

McGill-Queen's University Press in Montreal is on land which long served as a site of meeting and exchange amongst Indigenous Peoples, including the Haudenosaunee and Anishinabeg nations. In Kingston it is situated on the territory of the Haudenosaunee and Anishinaabek. We acknowledge and thank the diverse Indigenous Peoples whose footsteps have marked these territories on which peoples of the world now gather.

Library and Archives Canada Cataloguing in Publication

Title: Before Canada : northern North America in a connected world / edited
    by Allan Greer.
Names: Greer, Allan, editor.
Series: McGill-Queen's studies in early Canada ; 8.
Description: Series statement: McGill-Queen's studies in early Canada / Avant
    le Canada ; 8 | Includes bibliographical references and index.
Identifiers: Canadiana (print) 20230476635 | Canadiana (ebook) 20230476686 |
    ISBN 9780228019206 (hardcover) | ISBN 9780228019213 (softcover) | ISBN
    9780228019558 (PDF)
Subjects: LCSH: Canada—History—To 1763 (New France)
Classification: LCC FC300 .B44 2024 | DDC 971.01—dc23

CONTENTS

Figures

Preface and Acknowledgments

This book consists of a series of studies that probe the distant past of Canada in the centuries and millennia that preceded its organization into a nation-state. It owes its origin to an interdisciplinary conference held at McGill University in October 2019 at a time, just before the outbreak of a global pandemic, when scholars could safely assemble in person to exchange ideas. I'd like to thank all those involved in organizing that event: Maxime Dagenais, Mike Davis, Sam Derksen, Helen Dewar, Fannie Dionne, Renée Girard, Nathan Ince, Mike LaMonica, Sandra-Lynn Leclaire, Brad Loewen, and Carolyn Podruchny. Thanks also to Joshua Piker of the *William and Mary Quarterly*. For their generous financial support, gratitude is due to the Wilson Institute for Canadian History, Daniel Boudin and McGill-Queen's University Press, as well as McGill's Department of History, Canada Research Chair in Colonial North America, Canada Research Chair in Scottish-Canadian History, and McGill Institute for the Study of Canada.

At McGill-Queen's University Press, I'd like to thank skilled and helpful acquisition editors Philip Cercone and Jonathan Crago, as well as copy editor Shelagh Plunkett. Ciel Haviland did a great job of preparing the manuscript.

BEFORE CANADA

Canada before Canada

ALLAN GREER

The title of this book, *Before Canada*, situates our subject in both space and time: it concerns the northern portion of the North American continent, roughly corresponding to the territory of modern Canada but prior to the establishment of the nation-state. What follows are ten studies representing the perspectives of archaeologists, historians, and literary scholars, some working on the Indigenous past, others on European visitors and colonizers, still others on the interactions of Indigenous and Europeans. Temporally, coverage extends from the Pleistocene to the early nineteenth century. *Before Canada* highlights recent research on this fascinating and very protracted period; it also challenges some prevalent understandings of the Canadian past. Current historiography tends to presuppose the condition of modernity and to accept the nation-state as the natural framework of history; it is inclined to find meaning in earlier centuries to the extent that they seem to lead towards a national future.[1] The contributors to *Before Canada* avoid the teleology of national history as they examine Indigenous trade and migration, Atlantic fishing operations, missionaries, and empires, all on their own terms and not as precursors of a modern territorial polity. In thus freeing themselves from the constraining hold of the modern and the national, they speak for something more than a simple extension of the temporal range of scholarship: they imply a different mode of apprehending the past.

In common parlance, the term "Canada" designates two quite different things. On the one hand, it can mean a set of governmental institutions, laws, and policies that seem to define a sovereignty-exercising state, and on the other, it can refer to the physical space – the soil, waters, mountains, plains, and forests – claimed by that state. In keeping with the first, political, definition, the word Canada evokes images of a flag, a constitution, a map with clearly defined borders; we may think of passports and citizenship, laws that apply equally and uniformly (within the limits allowed by federalism) across the national territory. To that extent, our view of Canada reflects the dominant view of an international order composed of independent sovereign states claiming all the world's land surface (except Antarctica). It is an idealized and simplified picture of the world, for we know that state sovereignty is limited by the role of international agencies and multinational corporations, undermined by the global power of the United States, challenged internally by ethnic and regional movements. In the specific case of Canada, First Nations land claims and assertions of sovereignty (not to mention those of many francophone Quebeckers) conflict with the ideal of full, complete, and uniform territorial sovereignty. The common tendency to conflate Canada-as-physical-space and Canada-as-state makes for distorted history. It literally naturalizes the nation-state, subsuming nature under the claims of a political sovereignty that only took shape recently. It also obscures previous ways of organizing people and spaces, whether Indigenous or colonial-imperial. The fact that the Canadian state emerged in the nineteenth century as a settler-colonial entity makes the tendency to naturalize the nation-state and read its logic back into earlier eras all the more problematic.

Canada as sovereign territorial state is a very recent (and never fully realized) entity, a "young country" as the cliché has it. However, there is another "Canada" that underlies and predates this legally constructed political space: the land itself, together with its flora, its fauna, and its peoples. When we think of the Precambrian rocks of the Canadian Shield, as old as any portion of the earth's surface, or when we think of ancestral Indigenous peoples settling the emergent land and developing cultures here during the late Pleistocene, or when we think of European fishers establishing regular trans-Atlantic links with Atlantic Canada well before the Spanish had even heard of Mexico and Peru, then Canada doesn't seem so young. There is an enduring material reality to Canada and there is also a continuous human presence stretching back into the mists of time, for its lands have been populated essentially since the last glaciers melted.

Some will ask whether the concept of "Canada" has any real meaning in such a long temporal context, or is it simply a projection into the past of a political space formed in recent times by means of legislation, international negotiation, and railroad construction? Without claiming that this "Canada before Canada" formed a fully coherent geographical entity and without attempting to colour precisely within the political borderlines traced over the course of the nineteenth century, I would say that, yes, the concept of an ancient and enduring northern space is a meaningful one. The diverse regions lying between the Arctic, the Pacific, and the Atlantic Oceans and roughly bounded to the south by a very fuzzy approximation of the current border with the United States, did indeed share, over the millennia and the centuries, a number of similarities, affinities, and connections, notwithstanding their obvious differences. They all underwent a primordial experience of being scraped and crushed by the greatest ice sheets in the world. And over thousands of years of glacial retreat, these same lands were subject to the upheavals of rushing waters, massive floods, and shifting coastlines as the ice melted and the depressed surface of the earth rebounded.[2] During successive Ice Ages stretching back millions of years, this ancient version of "Canada" connected the Americas to the eastern and western extremities of Eurasia, which is why northern species of flora and fauna tend to have more similarity to the plants and animals of Europe and Asia than do those of southern parts of the Americas.[3] Long after the land connection between Siberia and Alaska had been broken by the rising waters of the Bering Sea, peoples such as the ancestral Dene and the ancestral Inuit, as well as technologies such as the bow and arrow, continued to arrive from Asia.[4] Even in the (by this timescale, comparatively recent) early modern age of global contacts, Canada functioned as something of a gateway where Europe met North America. Looking at matters from a long-term perspective, we can then discern vast northern spaces joining the Americas, Europe, and Asia and, because it corresponds roughly to the territory of a contemporary nation-state, we might as well refer to this "Canada before Canada" by the shortened form, "Canada." Of course, that term is a glaring anachronism in a pre-1867 context. (The word seems to be a misunderstood and awkwardly pronounced Iroquoian term that the French applied, first to the region around Quebec City and later to the whole St Lawrence valley). However, as long as we keep in mind its anachronistic and spatially imprecise qualities, the label "Canada" can serve as useful shorthand for the more correct but cumbersome phrase, "roughly the northern half of North America, excluding Alaska."

As is well known, this half-continent has long been the home of hundreds of Indigenous societies that, over the millennia, developed distinct languages, cultures, and ways of deriving a living from the different regions of the land. And yet, as chapters in this volume by John W. Ives, Adrian Burke, and Christian Gates St-Pierre demonstrate, these societies never lived in local isolation: instead, they undertook astonishing journeys, either to migrate definitively or to exchange goods and ideas with distant peoples. From early times, people in eastern Canada were also in regular contact with European mariners: first the Vikings making their way from Iceland to Greenland to Newfoundland around the year 1000[5] and then fishers arriving in the late fifteenth and through the sixteenth century from England, France, Portugal, and the Basque country. (See chapters by Jack Bouchard and Brad Loewen.) The winds and currents of the North Atlantic tended to favour a northerly sailing route, and so, along with the Caribbean, this part of the Americas was the first to be touched by the currents of the "first globalization." Transatlantic voyaging intersected with existing Indigenous trade networks, and, as a consequence, objects of European origin – copper pots, iron blades, glass beads – soon made their way deep into the interior.[6] These sixteenth-century contacts and long-distance exchanges seem to confirm a defining feature of Canada, observable over the very long term, as a space of global interconnections.

Lightly touching the Atlantic littoral at first, the French and the English eventually hatched plans to take over, plans that began to have serious effects in the seventeenth century. That century saw the formation of small colonies – English in Newfoundland, French in the Maritimes and the St Lawrence valley – and more extensive imperial networks of trade and alliance stretching out into the continent from bases on the St Lawrence and on Hudson Bay. The pattern of early empire formation here diverged from that of the Caribbean, which saw Indigenous peoples exterminated to make way for the establishment of slave plantation societies; it was also unlike the Latin American pattern typified by decisive conquest and the subjugation of Indigenous societies as tribute payers and labourers. There were more affinities with the English North American colonies that became the United States in that the latter developed on settler-colonial lines, colonists seizing and occupying more and more territory and progressively eliminating the Indigenous presence over most of the land. However, for two centuries, the Canadian version of settler colonialism was much more spatially limited than its "American" counterpart, directly affecting fairly small enclaves within a vast territory that was still dominated, demographically and politically, by First Nations. Even in the nineteenth and twentieth centuries, settlement by agricultural colonists remained constrained by climate and topography to only a tiny percentage of Canada's surface.[7] Through the long centuries of the European invasion, most of Canada felt the effects of imperial-commercial penetration and resource extraction rather than literal settler colonization.[8]

Here then is another feature that sets Canada apart from most other parts of the Americas: it was the site of early and exceptionally prolonged European imperial penetration, an Indigenous space progressively infiltrated by the ramifying webs of empire. Unconquered and politically independent Indigenous nations were drawn into the alliance system of New France or into the trading circuits of the Hudson's Bay Company. The expanding range of traders, missionaries, and soldiers of European origin, accompanied as they were by imported products and deadly pathogens, had a profound impact on Indigenous peoples across Canada far in advance of intruding settlers and territorial states. Scholars have noted the way that many First Nations succeeded in manipulating European commercial/imperial intrusions to their own advantage, but there is no denying the disastrous effects of the epidemics, violence, and intensified warfare that commonly accompanied an imperial presence. Across the Great Lakes in the seventeenth century, through the Hudson Bay drainage in the eighteenth, and into British Columbia in the early nineteenth century, it was a commercially inflected form of empire rather than settlement colonies per se that projected power across the land and disrupted Indigenous existence. The destabilizing effects of trade and war opened opportunities to enhance imperial influences, though it rarely led to the establishment of real colonial jurisdiction. The transformation of space, in Henri Lefebvre's terms, was far from absolute: imperial space expanded into, rather than in place of, Indigenous space.[9]

Other parts of the Americas had their borderlands of ambiguous control in the early modern period: the contested southern cone of South America, the Southwest borderlands north of Mexico, areas surrounding Russian posts in Alaska, to take three examples.[10] What made the Canadian case special are the extent and the duration of this "edge of empire" dispensation. For the longest time, European empire in northern North America was almost all "edge," with quite small centres of full colonial control. Empires, French and English, gained footholds here at a very early stage and the British maintained their ascendancy until long after colonists across most of the Americas had secured formal independence from European powers. The Age of Empire persisted in Canada, not only in the international realm, where sovereignty remained partial and qualified well into the twentieth century, but also internally, in that the pretention to rule Indigenous territories across the North took forms that seem more "imperial" than colonial or national. Down to the present day, the Canadian government still exercises sovereignty over more than half the territory it claims using practices of rule more associated with empires than with nation-states.

Big, ice-scoured, and globally connected, Canada-before-Canada was for thousands of years the scene of momentous developments, not all of them equally visible in the record of artifacts and documents. For at least four centuries, it became a site where thinly extended European empires interacted with independent Indigenous nations. Yet the historical profession seems interested in only the narrowest temporal slice of that very long timeline, as though the history of Canada were scarcely more than the history of the territorial state and its immediate colonial antecedents.

HISTORIOGRAPHY OF CANADA

Periodization is never innocent, argues Kathleen Davis; instead, it partakes of what she calls "the politics of time."[11] Writers of sixteenth-century Europe tended to denigrate the medieval past as chaotic, "feudal," and "superstitious" as they struggled to construct a new order based on the legal concept of sovereignty. At the same time, and not just coincidentally, they portrayed the Americas and other overseas territories as similarly benighted and disorganized. In this way, Davis contends, they justified powerful states domestically, the seizure of territories abroad, and the imposition of colonial slavery: all this rested on a basic equation of a dark European past with a dark Indigenous present. Our enduring sense of a watershed separating the Middle Ages from the Renaissance, according to Davis, derives from a program to rationalize administration and realize sovereignty, both domestically and in the Americas:

"the space of transition out of a 'feudal' past was theorized in relation to the challenges of colonial administration."[12] Davis's analysis of the politics of time in the European setting alerts us to the need to reflect on traditions of periodization in our own field.

Canadian history has traditionally been divided into distinct temporal compartments, pre-Confederation and post-Confederation. A third period, "pre-contact," was sometimes invoked; it provided an implicit starting point for pre-Confederation history by defining everything that happened before European explorers arrived as Other. Though it encompassed thousands of years of time, "pre-contact Canadian history" was something of an empty signifier since it concerned Indigenous peoples and the discipline usually treated them as "people without history." "Contact," it was thought, marked the point where Canadian history began, for it was then that recognizable historical actors appeared on the scene (read: white men); equally important and not unrelated, it was then that written documents began to appear and such textual sources were seen as a fundamental requirement for historical scholarship. (Even more than historians, the courts and the legal profession have made a fetish of "contact" as a primordial temporal boundary.) The pre-contact era was best left to archaeologists and anthropologists, specialists trained in the study of "primitive peoples." If "pre-Confederation" suggests the quality of a prelude, interesting to the degree that it leads towards something more significant, the double-pre of "pre-contact" implies a before so alien that it hardly sheds any light on later developments.[13]

Since the late twentieth century, many researchers have fruitfully breached the traditional dividing lines. Historians of the nineteenth century regularly violate the pre-Confederation/post-Confederation boundary. Bruce Trigger's work, which insistently situated European contact in a longer-term history of the Wendat and other eastern First Nations, stands out as an early challenge to the assumption that history begins at the time of "contact."[14] More recent research in Indigenous history routinely declines to treat the arrival of Europeans as a watershed moment.[15] Furthermore, some scholars dispense altogether with European-derived conceptions of linear time and explore the use of Indigenous temporalities to build Indigenous history.

And yet the tripartite periodization that slices the history of Canada into pre-contact, pre-Confederation, and post-Confederation eras has not disappeared: far from it. Even though these divisions do not necessarily constrain research, they still retain a hold on historical thought at a deep level and shape the metanarrative we present to students, notably at the introductory level. One only has to look at the way the subject is organized into pre- and post-Confederation components in post-secondary survey courses and introductory textbooks to get a sense of the enduring potency of the traditional temporal divisions.[16] Course titles like "Beginnings to 1867" leave one guessing as to when those "beginnings" occurred, but other institutions provide explicit starting points – either 1500 or 1600 or "the Age of Discovery" – for their pre-Confederation surveys. Professors and textbook authors are visibly working hard to develop a more inclusive, less colonialist Canadian history, one that accords greater prominence to Indigenous peoples, but they remain hampered by a tradition of periodization originally shaped by the colonialist assumption that Indigenous peoples exist outside history and therefore beyond the purview of the historian. Moreover, with the nation-state defining the parameters of the field, developments prior to 1867 tend to be configured as a colonial prologue, diverse regions assembled together only by virtue of a confederation that has not yet occurred. Though most history departments offer pre- and post-Confederation surveys, some divide at 1885 rather than 1867 and some offer a trio of courses, subdividing the post-Confederation period at the time of World War II, these latter variants reflecting a general tendency, worrying to some,[17] to privilege the very recent past.

The "telescoping of time" is not limited to Canadian history; it seems to be a general phenomenon within the historical discipline, and that in turn reflects a more general disinterest in the past within contemporary culture.[18] There is nothing wrong with contemporary history per se, except insofar as it comes to dominate the field almost to the exclusion of longer temporal perspectives. When the depth of vision extends no further back than a century and a half, one sees only versions of modernity, which can easily give rise to the delusion that modern Canada arose out of some dark and alien condition that has nothing to tell us about ourselves and our world. To the extent that the field is defined by a modern nation-state, the danger is that settler sovereignty and modernity itself can be naturalized. The oft-repeated ontological assertion that "Canada was/is a liberal project" makes sense within a modern setting but not otherwise; indeed the phrase "liberal order" sometimes seems to function as a synonym for modernity.[19] The blinkers imposed by a foreshortened Canadian history make it hard for the field as a whole to take account of the early modern centuries when Canada (in the geographical sense) was mostly Indigenous and when extensive European empires, along with small, and not particularly "liberal," European settlements, were making their presence felt; needless to say, those blinkers allow few glimpses of the hundreds of centuries when Canada was exclusively Indigenous. Consequently, Ian McKay's call for "a liberal-order reconnaissance [that] would aim to see our present-day politics afresh, to make the familiar unfamiliar, to destabilize the conventional first-order apprehension of our own world,"[20] tends to be frustrated by mainstream Canadian history's reluctance to look beyond the familiar world of modernity.

"Modernity," write Daniel Smail and Andrew Shryock, "like Europe in its heyday, is full of itself. The time has come to provincialize it."[21] One aim of this collection is to decentre the modern period in Canadian history, to "provincialize" it in something like the way Dipesh Chakrabarty provincializes Europe. In his book, *Provincializing Europe*, Chakrabarty notes the way that historical scholarship on India and other parts of the non-Western world has been shaped by false universals and a vision of historical evolution derived from Europe's particular experience.[22] Following Smail's and Shryock's proposal to provincialize modernity, we aim to interrupt the now-entrenched tendency within the historiographical mainstream to equate "Canada" and modernity and to study it in isolation from everything that went before. While the authors of the chapters that follow may not necessarily subscribe to the historiographical views set forth in this Introduction, their essays all serve to illustrate the value of a long view of Canada's past. They also demonstrate how much can be gained by mobilizing the intellectual resources of multiple disciplines.

SPEAKING ACROSS DISCIPLINES

Other disciplines have done a much better job than history in probing Canada's deep past. This would be an opportune moment to acknowledge the enormous contribution of geography, and especially of the school of historical geographers that flourished in the second half of the twentieth century, to our understanding of the subject. In addition to offering a fine series of specialized studies, the geographers organized an important multi-disciplinary synthesis, the *Historical Atlas of Canada* (1987).[23] The first volume of that monumental work covers the period from the Pleistocene to the end of the eighteenth century, integrating the findings of geology, archaeology, and history, as well as the work of professional geographers. The spatial breadth and the temporal depth of the atlas are noteworthy, as are its multidisciplinary nature and its policy of integrating history and so-called "prehistory." In all these respects, the *Historical Atlas* prefigures *Before Canada* and even if much of its substantive content is no longer current, this work continues to inspire us.

One of the purposes of this volume and the conference that preceded it was to promote dialogue across disciplinary lines among researchers interested in Canada-before-Canada. Our shared object of study invites and requires the attention of scholars with diverse training and a variety of angles of vision. When confronting the distant past, we historians are frequently reminded of the severe limitations imposed by our habit of relying on documentary sources, with all their biases in favour of the European, the male, and the powerful. Without doubt, we would benefit from more collaboration with the archaeologists, geographers, art historians, and others who "read" the records of material artifacts, landscapes, and images. Experts in the analysis of texts, whether they work in literary or religious studies, also have a major role to play in the enterprise of coming to terms with other centuries.[24] Last but not least, we all have much to learn from Indigenous oral histories and from the academic discipline of Indigenous studies.[25]

Between history and archaeology in particular, a deep gap in academic cultures persists, arguably the product of the way the two disciplines arose in nineteenth-century North America to study, respectively, "primitive" and "civilized" peoples. (Archaeology had a different vocation in Europe and the Middle East, where its prime focus was initially classical antiquity.)[26] History, when it first gelled as an academic profession, was an inquiry mainly focused on the origins and progress of nations, focusing particularly on wars and constitutions and generally emphasizing the role of great men in pressing on the forward march of civilization. State, empire, and sovereignty were the main vessels of history, narrative its favoured mode of presentation. Even when history writing was not visibly telling a story, it was usually addressing a shared underlying metanarrative. Debates, for example, about whether Charles V was an early modern monarch or the last medieval emperor presupposed an agreed upon chronological framework. Particular events, personalities, and institutions, situated in time and place, became meaningful in the context of a broad sweep of progressive change. Conceived in Europe and exported to overseas settler societies, this approach to the study of the past was never intended to apply to colonized (or colonizable) peoples. Because they were seen as culturally and intellectually stagnant and because they supposedly lacked the requisite institutions of state sovereignty, the latter were considered "peoples without history." (Lord Durham wanted to extend this epithet to French Canadians as well as Indigenous peoples.) Such societies needed to be studied, not by historians but by scientists.

Small wonder that North American archaeology was so often conducted, in its early days, under the auspices of museums of natural history where ancient spear points and human skeletal remains would be displayed next to dinosaur bones, mineral samples, and stuffed animals. The emphasis was on objects and on the light these shed on material processes, especially subsistence practices. Unlike the archaeologists excavating Jericho or Troy, those working on Canadian sites had no literary texts to guide (or mislead) them, and so they could say little about politics, events, intellectual developments, or beliefs. But then, their field was organized in the nineteenth century around the premise that the "primitive peoples" who inhabited pre-Columbian America, belonged to essentially static societies lacking the progressive thrust of advanced, history-making peoples. That being the case, many researchers had no compunction about removing objects and human remains without the permission of their descendants, for they imagined they were investigating a generic ancient "humanity" disconnected from local Indigenous communities.[27]

These are the divergent disciplinary traditions of history and archaeology, both structured to a significant degree around racist and colonialist assumptions. Of course, times changed and so did scholarship, leading to fundamental re-orientations in both fields. In our own time, great efforts are underway to decolonize the two disciplines by subjecting their methodological and interpretive ways to searching critique, by listening to Indigenous voices, and by welcoming Indigenous scholars into their ranks. And yet, the mutual isolation of the two disciplines, profoundly colonialist in its origins, persists. History and archaeology now find themselves on opposite sides of the "two cultures" divide, a term coined half a century ago by C.P. Snow to describe the divergence that had developed between scientific and humanistic modes of thought.[28] Though archaeology maintains strong connections with anthropology, a discipline where literary and humanistic tendencies are by no means absent, its predominant orientation tends in the direction of geomorphology, chemistry, biology, linguistics, dental science, and, increasingly, genetics. The payoff for this scientific turn in enhanced precision and expanded scope is undeniable. On the other hand, the aspiration to impersonal objectivity may not encourage self-reflexive habits of mind on the part of practitioners who are, after all and no matter how rigorous their methods, socially situated human beings. Meanwhile, even as they do their best to read evidence "against the grain," historians remain addicted to documentary sources that, on the whole, reflect a European and an elite viewpoint and that limit the temporal range of their inquiries.

History–archaeology crossover does occur in studies of what historians call the early modern period, where the techniques of the two disciplines visibly complement one another,[29] but I think both disciplines would benefit from greater interaction. Such exchanges might encourage historians to extend their chronological horizons; why should they not play a part, for example, in the debates and discussions currently roiling the world of "prehistory" over the early peopling of the Americas?[30] Frequenting archaeologists might also encourage them to incorporate the evidence of material objects into their research as an alternative to an exclusive reliance on texts.[31] For its part, archaeology might even have something to learn from history, including the latter discipline's generally skeptical response to all claims to "factual" and fully objective knowledge. Perhaps even more than their colleagues in other fields, historians tend to be acutely aware of the intellectual history of their own discipline, an awareness that fosters a certain self-reflexivity.[32] Finally, the historian's fondness for narrative as a device for integrating dispersed findings into a continuous sequence and for discussions framed within a metanarrative, may be of interest to archaeologists, if only to improve communications with the general public.

In addition to the various academic disciplines mentioned so far, Indigenous oral traditions also reach back into ancient times. The Arikara scholar Roger Echo-Hawk argues that the stories of his people draw on collective memory reaching back as much as 40,000 years into the past.[33] As to the *adawx*, ancestral stories recited by Tsimshian clan heads on the northern coast of British Columbia, anthropologist Jay Miller writes, "Beginning in a stark and wet world that is obviously postglacial, the most ancient adawx therefore span at least ten thousand years."[34] Stories from peoples of the Pacific Northwest often feature ancestral figures combining human and animal aspects; recorded versions of these accounts speak of migrations, battles, and primordial claims to territories, all set in a specific landscape of named places. In some narratives, mention is made of floods, earthquakes, or landslides, some of which have been corroborated and dated by geological and archaeological research.[35] Such external corroboration helped convince the Supreme Court of Canada to accept the evidence of Indigenous oral history in support of land claims in the famous Delgamuukw decision of 1997.[36] And yet, as anthropologist Julie Cruikshank and others have insisted, oral tradition is a meaningful discourse within the context of a specific Indigenous culture and is not to be judged valid or invalid on the basis of outsiders' research. By the same token, it should not be treated as a storehouse of extractable data to be appropriated from their original context and plugged into academic accounts.[37] The work of Marianne and Ronald Ignace on the *Secwépemc* people stands as an exemplary study that brings together oral tradition, linguistic analysis, archaeological research, and historical documentation in a particularly successful Indigenous history.[38]

A GLANCE AHEAD

In "After Beringia: The Archaeology of Indigenous Social Networks," Adrian L. Burke and Christian Gates St-Pierre review the evidence for long-distance connections between the peoples of eastern Canada over the course of millennia. Pooling their respective expertise – Burke is a specialist in lithic materials while Gates St-Pierre focuses more on pottery and bone implements – they show how objects discovered far from their point of origin provide indications of circuits of travel, trade, and social interaction. Thus, pots from southern Ontario made their way hundreds, if not thousands, of kilometres north into the boreal forest while Onondaga chert (a flint-like stone) from the Niagara escarpment was distributed all across the eastern woodlands where it was shaped into blades and tools. In reviewing this evidence, the authors offer a helpful lesson to non-specialists in the techniques of archaeological investigation and the ways in which archaeologists interpret these material clues to gain a sense of how people lived and thought in the distant past. Drawing on the insights of anthropology and other disciplines, they argue that the exchange of objects followed a logic of reciprocity designed to create and reinforce positive relations between societies. Thus, the presence in southern Ontario of seashells from Long Island or copper from Lake Superior indicates the existence not of impersonal trade links but of social ties connecting different peoples. "Some of these exchange and interaction networks," they note, "lasted for generations and point to sustained social interaction networks between culturally and linguistically distinct groups."

Archaeologist John W. Ives works on the West and his evidence comes not only from stone and ceramic artifacts but also from leather and other organic materials that have survived intact for surprisingly long periods of time. Mountain glaciers in the Yukon, as they melted and receded, have rendered up long lost objects buried under the ice centuries ago, including a 1,400-year-old moccasin. Ives also found preserved leather footwear dating from the thirteenth century in caves overlooking Great Salt Lake in the dry environment of Utah. Astonishingly, the style of these moccasins in the Great Basin nicely resembles the one that emerged from the Yukon ice, as well as moccasins that continue to be made by northern Dene people to this day. Ives has used these clues, along with linguistic evidence, to trace and date the long southward migration of Dene people from the Northwest Territories, by way of Alberta, all the way to the plains of the Southwest, where they formed the Apache and Navajo societies. The Dene migration had been triggered initially by a volcanic eruption in the Yukon that had covered their homeland with a thick layer of ash. Like Burke and Gates St-Pierre, Ives demonstrates the importance of long-distance connections linking Canada-before-Canada to other parts of the North American continent. Since some ancestral Dene seem to have migrated from Siberia into northern Canada long before they set out on their southward trek, this chapter also highlights ancient links with Asia.

Jack Bouchard brings a historian's perspective to intercontinental connections, in this case the maritime networks that spanned the Atlantic as early as the fifteenth century, linking a greater "Newfoundland" to Europe as well as to other points around the circum-Atlantic. Viewed against the backdrop of a long-term European reconnaissance of the Ocean Sea that had taken sailors and fishermen to the coasts of Africa, the Canaries, the Azores, and Iceland, the "discovery" of northeastern North America seems less like a new beginning and more like the culmination of a century-long maritime expansion. Portuguese, Spanish, French, and English vessels began visiting the shores of Newfoundland, Labrador, and the Maritimes around the year 1500, and they soon established a seasonal fishery that solidified a regular connection across the North Atlantic. The Iberian powers sponsored projects of colonization here, but these proved abortive. The pattern that emerged instead, based as it was on fishing and later fur trading, was one of a regular European presence without colonization or imperial rule.

The Basques, a people with ancient roots in the coastal borderlands where France and Spain meet, are among the most intriguing actors in the North Atlantic fisheries that connected Canada to Europe in the early modern period. Because they did not attempt to establish a colonial empire – indeed, they actively opposed colonization on some occasions – they have not been well known to historians. Brad Loewen is one of the scholars working to shed light on the history of Basque whaling and fishing by means of archaeological research, supplemented by historical documentation and linguistic analysis. Increasingly, attention is turning to the relations that developed between these European mariners and the Indigenous peoples of the Atlantic region. In his chapter, "Sea Change: Indigenous Navigation and Relations with Basques around the Gulf of Saint Lawrence, c. 1500–1700," Loewen places the spotlight on a particular piece of technology, the sea-going *txalupa*, a small vessel that was used to carry out the work of the fishery, but that was frequently passed on to Indigenous partners. Thanks to the *txalupak* (plural of *txalupa*) that they acquired, Mi'kmaq, Innu, Inuit, and Iroquoian people were able to travel freely across open waters whose winds and waves could easily destroy their traditional canoes. This enhanced mobility opened up numerous commercial opportunities and enabled the Mi'kmaq of Cape Breton Island to cross the Cabot Strait and establish themselves in Newfoundland.

While thousands of unheralded vessels traversed the seas in pursuit of codfish and whales, a much smaller number of voyages carried officially sponsored explorers seeking lands to colonize and/or a maritime route to Asia. A chapter by the literary scholar Mary Fuller examines this sixteenth-century European reconnaissance of the northwestern Atlantic as both a textual and a cartographic phenomenon. At the heart of her study is an English map of the world, the Molyneux globe, together with the exploration narratives compiled by Elizabethan scholar and colonization promoter, Richard Hakluyt. Where eastern Canada is concerned, the globe provides a good deal of geographic detail, informed as its makers were by the reports of English, French, and Portuguese explorers. It also displays a number of blank spots and fanciful touches that can be traced to more or less fictitious travel books by imaginative writers such as the Venetian, Nicolo Zeno. Fuller's meticulous research shows us how mapping served to disseminate up-to-date geographical knowledge but also to promote national claims to territory and precedence and to fuel fantasies of wealth and power.

Among the coastal Indigenous peoples with a very long experience of contact with these fishers and explorers were the eastern Inuit. The Inuit were able to incorporate the iron blades, glass beads, and wooden boats from Europe into their way of life without ever accepting European pretentions to control them or claim their territories; indeed their consistent feistiness intimidated Basque, French, and English visitors and forced them to bend to their demands. Lisa Rankin offers us a wide-ranging account of the Inuit migration from the Bering Straits to the eastern Arctic and their subsequent expansion down into Labrador at about the time that European fishers and whalers began frequenting that coast. Her chapter also shares the findings of her recent archaeological excavations at Snack Cove in southern Labrador. The evidence she uncovered there of relatively large houses strewn with luxury objects of European origin leads her to conclude that charismatic leaders arose here to organize the gathering of hides and oils for trade. Enriching themselves through their control of commercial networks linking French and Basque whaling and sealing stations to Inuit communities far to the north, these entrepreneurial individuals enjoyed high status within a traditionally egalitarian society.

For at least a century, the European presence on the coasts of Canada was entirely maritime. Fishers and whalers, especially the Basques, as well as royally authorized explorers, mastered the sea lanes of the North Atlantic, but they scarcely ventured inland. Indeed, many actively opposed colonization, forcing Samuel de Champlain to fight his way into the St Lawrence when he founded Quebec in 1608. Even after establishing their colony, however, the French still tended to treat New France as a maritime realm, according to

Helen Dewar. Her chapter, "Corridors of Jurisdiction: The Role of Aquatic Spaces in Sovereign Claims-making in New France (1600s–1620s)," examines the way French sovereignty was constructed in the early seventeenth century, highlighting the crucial role of the admiral of France, Henri de Montmorency. Montmorency was determined to extend his control over shipping and trade, both in France and overseas; thus, empire formation and the consolidation of monarchical power in Europe operated as interlocking, mutually reinforcing processes. Through the activities of a reinvigorated admiralty, the early Bourbons consolidated their hold over France even as they built an empire in North America. As the French began to penetrate into the heart of the continent, they passed from a maritime to a riverine environment where, as Dewar points out, sovereignty and jurisdiction were construed differently, both by the Europeans and by Indigenous peoples.

The aquatic theme continues in a chapter by the French literature specialist, Katherine Ibbett. She draws attention to the perilous nature of travel on the St Lawrence and its tributaries with their plunging rapids and their cycles of freeze and thaw: canoes occasionally capsized and people could, and did, drown. The Jesuit Paul Lejeune was one of those who fell into the water and came close to perishing, only to be rescued just before he went down for the last time. In "Saved from the Waters: The Drowning World of Paul Lejeune," Ibbett closely examines the missionary's copious writings, showing how much importance he attaches to that story and to similar ones featuring the near-death experiences of Indigenous people swallowed up by the river. Linking these incidents to references to baptism, the Jesuit's narrative infuses them with religious meaning; by suggesting symbolic associations with the sacrament of baptism, Lejeune manages to find hopeful signs of mass conversions to come. Katherine Ibbett's sensitive analysis of these passages from the *Jesuit Relations* reminds us of just how much can be learned from an informed close reading of familiar texts.

The next chapter takes a new look at a venerable topic in Canadian history, the fur trade. In "Debt, Liquor, and Violence in the Fur Trade," Allan Greer and Samuel Derksen highlight the neglected story of credit relations connecting Indigenous hunters and Euro-Canadian traders. Over the course of three centuries and all across the continent, they find that commerce rarely took the form of direct barter; instead, traders typically advanced goods on credit and then waited to be repaid in furs at the end of the season. However, since the traders' capitalist accounting practices did not correspond exactly to Indigenous customs of reciprocity, they frequently resorted to pressure and manipulation to secure prompt payment. Alcohol was usually offered as a reward to induce Indigenous people first to take on debt and then to discharge it. When the balance of power allowed, traders – especially those associated with the North West Company – also used violent coercion to achieve these ends. Indigenous peoples were certainly not helpless victims – indeed they shaped the culture of exchange and pushed back against manipulative traders – but the expanding fur trade nevertheless exposed them to the demanding ways of global capitalism.

Finally, Christopher Parsons' essay, "Maple, Beaver, and New Roots for a Global Early Canada," has the longest temporal sweep of all, moving as it does from the present to the deep geological past to the period of New France and then back again to the twentieth century. He begins by examining modern attempts, expressed in art, literature, and scholarly writing, to define a Canadian national identity on the basis of the country's landscapes, its flora and fauna. At the heart of these efforts literally to ground nationhood in the natural environment, Parsons discerns a basic delusion: the notion that nature is static and that Canada's plants and animals are peculiar to this country alone. In fact, he maintains, the natural world has always been in motion, with species migrating and expanding across and between continents. Examining the cases of the beaver and the sugar maple, emblematic Canadian species, he shows that both came from Eurasia and thus early French visitors found them reassuringly familiar, rather than strange and exotic. Viewed from this very wide temporal and spatial perspective then, maple and beaver seem to symbolize global connections rather than national distinctiveness.

Before Canada presents readers with a sampler of topics and approaches currently under investigation in this vast field of scholarship. It makes no claim to exhaustive treatment of Canada-before-Canada: how could it when the subject is infinitely varied and the lines of possible inquiry virtually limitless? Work is underway in various disciplines and in a variety of areas including religion, race formation, women, art and architecture, slavery, Indigenous languages, and science. Beyond these subjects stand a thousand and one other potentially rewarding avenues of research. I wish they could all be represented in these pages, just as I wish we had more content on Western Canada and the Arctic to counterbalance the chapters focused on the Atlantic and the St Lawrence, but even if this book were expanded to multiple volumes, "full coverage" would remain an elusive goal.

For similar reasons, *Before Canada* offers no concluding chapter: this diverse collection of studies, touching on so many centuries and regions and following a multiplicity of methods and disciplinary practices, simply cannot be summed up in the way that a single-authored monograph with a coherent argument can. Scholarship in the field tends to be centripetal with lines of inquiry pointing in many different directions. Perhaps that very diversity is the strength of the volume and the point of this collective exercise. That said, I will venture the claim that the foregoing chapters, taken together, do highlight the interest of a deep and wide approach to the long-term history of northern North America. I hope they will serve to stimulate further explorations.

ACKNOWLEDGMENTS
Special thanks to Brad Loewen for his helpful feedback and suggestions.

NOTES
1 See, for example, Cole Harris's insistence on deriving national meaning from the history of Pre-Confederation Canada: *The Reluctant Land*, xv–xvi.
2 Dyke, "An Outline of North American Deglaciation," 373–424; Dalton, et al., "An Updated Radiocarbon-Based Ice Margin Chronology."
3 See the chapter in this volume by Christopher Parsons, as well as Pielou, *After the Ice Age*; Wynn, *Canada and Arctic North America*, 1–32.
4 Blitz, "Adoption of the Bow"; McGhee, *Ancient People of the Arctic*; Fagan, *The First North American*, ch. 3, ch. 8; Raghavan et al., "Genetic Prehistory"; Friesen and Mason, "Pan-Arctic Population Movements," 673–92; Maschner and Mason, "Bow and Arrow in Northern North America," 133–8.
5 Fitzhugh and Ward, eds, *Vikings*; Hansen, *The Year 1000*, 22–36; Kuitems et al., "Evidence for European Presence."
6 Turgeon, "The Tale of the Kettle"; Birch and Williamson, *The Mantle Site*, 149–51; Ramsden, "Sixteenth-Century Contact," 227.

7   See *Historical Atlas of Canada*, vol. 2, *The Land Transformed*, plate 5.
8   Greer, "Settler Colonialism and Empire"; Greer, "Settler Colonialism and Beyond."
9   Lefebvre, *The Production of Space*.
10 See Herzog, *Frontiers of Possession*; Barr, "Geographies of Power"; Hämäläinen and Truett, "On Borderlands."
11 Davis, *Periodization and Sovereignty*.
12 Ibid., 11. Cf., Dussel, "Eurocentrism and Modernity."
13 See Wolf, *Europe and the People Without History*; Smail and Shryock, "History and the 'Pre.'"
14 Trigger, *The Children of Aataentsic*; Trigger, *Natives and Newcomers*.
15 Some examples: Binnema, *Common and Contested Ground*; Simpson, "Looking after Gdoo-Naaganinaa"; Ignace and Ignace, *Secwépemc People, Land, and Laws*.
16 These observations derive from a survey of courses listed by the following Canadian university and college history departments for the 2019–20 academic year: Simon Fraser, Fraser Valley, Thompson Rivers, Athabasca, Calgary, Saskatchewan, Regina, Winnipeg, Manitoba, Lakehead, Waterloo, Wilfrid Laurier, Brock, Windsor, McMaster, Ryerson, Trent, Queen's, Université de Montréal, McGill, Université du Québec à Montréal, Université du Québec à Trois-Rivières, Université Laval, and Memorial. The majority of institutions offer a pair of Canadian history survey courses following the pre-/post-confederation convention. Likewise, the most popular textbooks also come in two volumes, dividing at 1867. Bumsted, *The Peoples of Canada*; Conrad, Finkel, and Fyson, *History of the Canadian Peoples*, vol. 1, *Beginnings to 1867*. One encouraging development worth noting: the latest edition of the Conrad, Finkel, and Fyson textbook comes with expanded coverage of the period prior to the sixteenth century.
17 Greer, "Canadian History"; Thomas Peace, "What Does Canadian History Look Like? Impressions from the Periodical Room," *Active History*, 26 May 2014, http://activehistory.ca/2014/05/what-does-canadian-history-look-like-impressions-from-the-periodical-room/; Robert Englebert, "Where has Pre-Confederation History Gone? The CHA and the Changing Contours of a Discipline," *Active History*, 2 June 2015, http://activehistory.ca/2015/06/where-has-pre-confederation-history-gone-the-cha-and-the-changing-contours-of-a-discipline/.

18 Bennett, *History Matters*, ch. 3, "Who's afraid of the Distant Past?"; Neuschel, "History and the Telescoping of Time."

19 The phrase "liberal order" was initially introduced in a thoughtful and open-ended essay by Ian McKay, but others sometimes treat it as an all-purpose incantation that serves to exclude from view regions and periods not deemed liberal or modern. McKay, "The Liberal Order Framework."

20 Ibid., 630.

21 Smail and Shryock, "History and the 'Pre,'" 713.

22 Chakrabarty, *Provincializing Europe*.

23 *Historical Atlas of Canada*, vol. 1, *From the Beginning to 1800*. Other important works in historical geography include Harris, *The Seigneurial System in Early Canada*; Clark, *Acadia;* Heidenreich, *Huronia*; Ray, *Indians in the Fur Trade*.

24 Some examples: Anderson, *The Betrayal of Faith*; Radisson, *The Collected Writings*, 2 vols; Ouellet, *La Relation de voyage en Amérique (XVIe - XVIIIe) siècles*.

25 For an Australian attempt to bring Indigenous perspectives on the past into conversation with academic historians and archaeologists, see McGrath and Jebb, *Long History, Deep Time*.

26 Trigger, *A History of Archaeological Thought*, 40–79.

27 On the removal of skeletal remains without the permission of a nearby descendant community, see Roy, *These Mysterious People*.

28 Snow, *The Two Cultures and the Scientific Revolution*.

29 See, for example, Trigger, *Children of Aataentsic*; Turgeon, *Une histoire de la Nouvelle-France*; Pope, *Fish into Wine*; Nassaney, "The North American Fur Trade in Historical and Archaeological Perspective."

30 Erlandson, Graham and Bourque, "The Kelp Highway Hypothesis"; Fagan, *The First North Americans*; Stone, "The Lineages of the First Humans," 170–2; Raff, *Origin*.

31 The turn to "material culture" history is, of course, already well underway. J.R. McNeill even wonders whether the discipline as a whole has passed "peak document": McNeill, "Peak Document and the Future of History."

32 Which is not to suggest that archaeology is epistemologically naive. While much work in the field seems positivist in approach, there is also a strong current of critical theoretical reflection in the discipline. See, for example, Pinsky and Wylie, *Critical Traditions in Contemporary Archaeology*; Hodder, *Theory and Practice in Archaeology*.

33 Echo-Hawk, "Ancient History in the New World."
34 Miller, "Tsimshian Ethno-Ethnohistory."
35 Teit, "Tahltan Tales"; McMillan, "When the Mountain Dwarfs Danced"; Hall, "Paleoenvironments, the Tsini'Tsini Site, and Nuxalk Oral History"; Harris and Kii7iljuus, "Tllsda Xaaydas K'aaygang.Nga"; Martindale, "Methodological Issues."
36 Dickason, *Canada's First Nations*, 337–8.
37 Cruikshank, "Oral Tradition and Oral History." See also, Cruikshank, *The Social Life of Stories*; Vansina, *Oral Tradition as History*.
38 Ignace, *Secwépemc People, Land, and Laws*.

1
———

After Beringia: The Archaeology of Indigenous Social Networks

ADRIAN L. BURKE AND CHRISTIAN GATES ST-PIERRE

INTRODUCTION

Before Canada/Kanata, there was Denendeh, there was Mi'kma'ki. There was a continent of rivers, lakes, and islands that were all named: Nagwichoonjik (Mackenzie River), Weenipagamiksaguygun (Lake Winnipeg), Tiohtià:ke (Montreal Island), and countless others. The mountains and the valleys also had names, Katahdin and Okanagan. Before Canada there was a land with many peoples, a diversity of societies and languages that had prospered and grown since the end of the last glaciation. How did these societies organize themselves on the vast landscape that was to become Canada? How did they interact and cohabit and make this place their own? To reconstruct this long-term human history, we can study First Nations' oral history, toponymy, and cartography as well as the written descriptions of early European travellers and missionaries to North America. Archaeology can also help by providing a long-term perspective on inter-group exchanges and interactions over several thousand years. All of these sources of diverse and divergent knowledge can help us to understand how these societies interacted and created the Indigenous geography and geopolitical framework of a huge territory that would one day become Canada.

In this chapter we focus on the contribution that archaeology can make to understanding the pre-contact, socio-political landscape of the geographic area known today as eastern Canada and northeastern USA. We provide archaeological examples of how different societies in the past interacted over large distances, demonstrating that these groups had extensive knowledge about their neighbours and groups beyond, and maintained extensive social relations with each other, in some cases despite having very different languages, social and political organizations, and cultural traditions. We begin with the premise that Indigenous groups in pre-contact Canada were not isolated from their neighbours. Our chapter is separated into three parts where we examine: (1) how archaeologists identify and interpret past social interactions and relations, (2) archaeological examples of these past interactions, and (3) why Indigenous groups maintained these extensive social networks. We conclude with our perspective as archaeologists for what this tells us about Canada-before-Canada on a human social and political scale.

ARCHAEOLOGY AND PAST SOCIAL INTERACTIONS

Archaeologists, anthropologists, historians, and geographers know that First Nations communicated and interacted with each other prior to European contact. These interactions took many forms, for example trade, diplomacy, collective rituals, and conflict (figure 1.1). In archaeology, the distribution of similar forms of stone arrowheads or decorative styles in pottery over thousands of square kilometres is a first indication that groups exchanged ideas, know-how, personnel, objects, and raw materials. In this chapter we focus on exchange as it is a highly visible and ubiquitous example of intergroup interactions in the archaeological record. Archaeologists working in North America have accumulated extensive evidence for the long-distance movement of materials and ideas prior to European contact.[1] This primarily takes the form of artifacts that are preserved in the archaeological record (e.g., stone tools, pottery, ornaments, pipes, pigments, seashells, copper). These concrete examples of the human movement of materials are studied in detail by archaeologists using comparative analyses, statistics, and state-of-the-art techniques borrowed from chemistry, physics, biology, geology, and materials science (commonly referred to as archaeological sciences or archaeometry).[2] Archaeologists can empirically demonstrate the movement of these materials – and the ideas associated with them – over tens and hundreds of kilometres, from the place

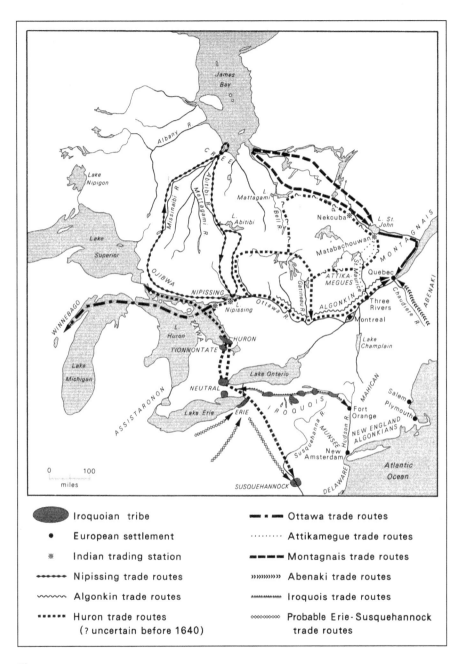

Figure 1.1
Map of eastern Canada showing Indigenous travel and trade routes.

of their extraction and/or manufacture, to the final resting place in a village or campsite that the archaeologist excavates. Using these modern tools, archaeologists now have a more accurate point of origin for many of the non-local materials they find on ancient sites.

Objects and raw materials of course do not travel on their own, they are carried by people who have to negotiate a series of social interactions and relationships, often across cultural and linguistic borders. While archaeological science may help us to understand the point of origin (a quarry and workshop) and the point of final deposit (archaeological site), it is not so helpful in understanding what motivated people to exchange these materials and objects. To get at the underlying economic, social, or political motivations we need to look to other disciplines such as oral history, anthropology, ethnohistory, economics, geography, and political science. Sadly, we do not have the space here to examine in detail these varied approaches, but we will return to this question at the end. For the moment, suffice it to say that among pre-state societies without market systems or currencies, exchanges of material goods and possibly of personnel are generally regulated by the principle of reciprocity.[3] The oral history, anthropology, and ethnohistory of North America strongly suggest that reciprocity was indeed the basis for most of the exchanges of materials and objects we see in the archaeological record. From this perspective, the exchange of raw materials, tools or personal ornaments is not based on a transaction where the cost is calculated solely on the basis of supply and demand or distance travelled or even what is in fashion. Because the value ascribed to what is received or given does not follow formalist economic models based on a "market value," it can vary from one interaction to the next. Moreover, there is no currency with a set value pegged to any standard.[4] The exchange of an object is therefore grounded on the expectation of reciprocity. This reciprocity can be immediate or delayed and creates a connection between the two actors. As such, any transaction requires a pre-existing social relationship or the creation of a new relationship.

From an archaeological perspective it is worth noting that the majority of materials and objects that we find on sites that were obtained through exchange from afar are not essential to a group's survival. By this we mean that in almost all cases a group will have a local source of stone for example that is perfectly adequate for making all the stone tools necessary for survival. However, despite this potential autonomy it is hard to find an archaeological site in North America where the stone tools do not include materials from outside a group's territory and which were obtained via exchange with neighbouring groups. In some cases, like copper from Lake Superior, it is possible to see a technological advantage in obtaining this material for making certain tools, but Indigenous groups survived for millennia without it (just fine). In addition, some objects that were exchanged, such as shell beads from the Atlantic Coast, must have carried symbolic value. In this case it is difficult for an archaeologist to ascribe an "exchange value" to these materials since they were not essential to daily survival. On the other hand, they most certainly possessed "value" in terms of reciprocity between trading partners. It is not possible for us to establish what the "value" of objects and materials might have been in any contemporary economic sense. Fortunately, this is not essential to our discussion. For this chapter it is important to retain that exchanges took place millions of times between people in pre-contact North America. These exchanges were largely based on the principle of reciprocity; they were underwritten by pre-established social relationships between groups and individuals, and were sustained by the raw materials and objects in circulation. The artifacts that archaeologists find are simply the material embodiment of this reciprocity and the social networks that were created through millions of meetings and interactions in what was to become Canada.

INDIGENOUS NETWORKS IN EASTERN NORTH AMERICA

In the process of peopling new, previously unoccupied territories, the first inhabitants of northeastern North America maintained contact with their areas of origin to the South and West.[5] There is limited evidence of exchange during this early period referred to as the Paleoindian period (ca. 12000–10000 BP).[6] Paleoindians seem to have been able to obtain everything they needed during their annual rounds, which could cover huge territories spanning hundreds of kilometres. But far from being isolated, these small bands of hunter-fisher-gatherers had to maintain contact with other groups in order to ensure their biological and cultural survival in a new continent. The Bull Brook site in eastern Massachusetts, dated to 12300 BP, is an excellent example. At this large aggregation site, two groups seem to have come together, one that used a territory extending to the West as far as the Hudson Valley of

New York and another that used a territory to the north in Maine and New Hampshire.[7] These territories are inferred through the identification of the stone tool raw materials used by the occupants of the site (figure 1.2). Groups almost certainly shared parts of their annual territory, which can be seen as a form of exchange and reciprocity. Aggregation allowed for the sharing of strategic information and the establishment of political alliances, sometimes sealed by means of a marital union between members of two different bands.

As people gradually occupied all of eastern North America and populations grew, social interaction networks naturally evolved and underwent significant transformations during the subsequent periods of the pre-colonial history of Canada and the USA. Thus, from about 7000 to 3000 years BP, Indigenous networks integrated new types of raw materials into extensive, continental-scale exchange networks. Well-known materials were extensively exchanged such as Onondaga chert from southern Ontario and western New York, and new materials were incorporated into these exchange networks, such as copper from Lake Superior and marine shell from the Atlantic seaboard. Projectile points, knives, awls, needles, fishhooks, beads, arm bands, and other objects were made of copper in the Upper Great Lakes and have been found in large quantities at many archaeological sites in eastern Canada and USA.[8]

Thousands of non-local stone and copper artifacts were recovered from archaeological excavations at the Morrison and Allumettes Islands sites in the Ottawa River Valley that were occupied between 6,100 and 5,500 years ago.[9] Figure 1.3 shows the geologic and geographic source of some of the materials identified at these sites. While the Archaic period occupants of Morrison and Allumettes Islands managed to supply most of their daily needs within twenty kilometres or less of the site (small circle in figure 1.3), they also found it necessary to maintain long-distance exchange and interaction networks that brought them materials from the Upper Great Lakes, Southern Ontario, Montreal, and Northern New England. Considering the vast distances separating these two sites from the different sources of raw materials exploited – the sources of native copper are located more than 800 kilometres away as the crow flies, for example – this type of network must have involved middle-men.[10] Indeed, the Indigenous populations of the time, though nomadic, could have hardly travelled the hundreds of kilometres separating the source of each of the raw materials they used on a regular basis.

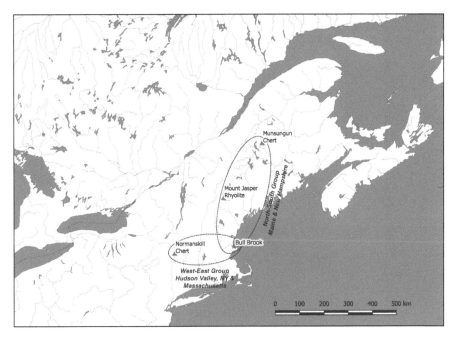

Figure 1.2
Location of the Bull Brook Paleoindian site (star) and the proposed territories of the
two groups that met and camped at the site. Quarries are indicated by triangles. One
group used the quarries of chert and rhyolite located to the north in what is today
Maine and New Hampshire, while the other group used chert from the Hudson Valley,
New York, to the west.

The example of the circulation of native copper throughout Eastern North
America is particularly striking. Approximately 6,000 years ago, Indigenous
groups around western Lake Superior started mining and extracting copper
in its natural mineral state in the form of nuggets and veins of pure metallic
copper.[11] They extracted hundreds of kilos of copper and produced thousands
of tools, weapons, and personal decorative items (figure 1.4). These were
widely traded among Indigenous groups. The raw material was also traded
as can be seen at Morrison and Allumettes Islands where many tools such as
points, awls, and fishhooks were made on site by local Ottawa Valley Indigenous people from copper nuggets. Archaeologists believe that Morrison and
Allumettes Islands actually served as workshops where large quantities of

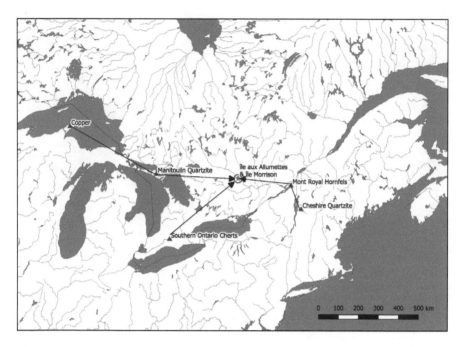

Figure 1.3
Location of the Île aux Allumettes and Île Morrison Archaic period sites (star) in
the Ottawa River Valley and the source of different raw materials and tools found at
the site (triangles). The arrows indicate the most likely travel routes. The small circle
has a radius of 20 km, which represents the local territory exploited on a daily or
weekly basis.

copper items were made, in part for trade purposes. This unusual material
with its reflective qualities and reddish colour also had symbolic value for
many Indigenous groups in Eastern North America and was highly sought
after during the historic period.[12]

This extensive network was almost entirely dismantled in the St Lawrence
lowlands between 4500 and 4000 years B P. Exotic materials such as Onondaga
chert and native copper ceased to circulate there. Local, low-quality materials
such as quartz and hornfels were used instead. At the same time, new types
of lithic artifacts similar to those made in other regions to the south appeared
in the St Lawrence River valley, such as narrower types of projectile points.
This could be the result of a sudden and perhaps brutal arrival of foreign pop-

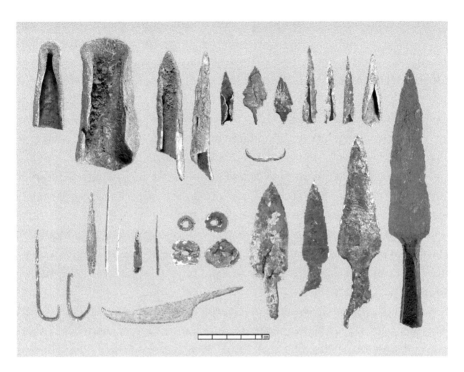

Figure 1.4
A small sample of copper artifacts recovered from the Île aux Allumettes Archaic site in the Ottawa River Valley showing the diversity of ornaments, tools, and weapons that were manufactured and exchanged.

ulations seeking new territories to the north as a consequence of an overall population growth that prevailed at the time. These newcomers would have either expelled or assimilated local populations, which of course represents a completely different kind of social interaction, one that also occurred in the past. Some authors even suggest that this migration may represent proto-Iroquoian people moving into northern latitudes, thus explaining their presence on territories that were almost entirely surrounded by Algonquian peoples at the time of European contact.[13] While this hypothesis has to be taken seriously, it must be considered with caution, as pushing historical ethnicities this far back in time is now acknowledged to be far more difficult and problematic than once thought.[14]

Whatever the explanation for this dismantling, it did not last: Onondaga chert and other materials made a comeback at the onset of the third millennium BP. However, the network in which they circulated took a new form. Often referred to as the Meadowood interaction sphere by archaeologists, it was a network in which participants also shared a common set of ideas, technologies, and funerary rituals.[15] This interaction sphere, or sphere of influence, covered an immense territory extending from the Great Lakes to the Maritime Provinces (figure 1.5). Stone tools, polished slate bird figurines, copper beads, and marine shell beads were exchanged among very distant and different Indigenous communities. But this was not a rigid nor a homogeneous network: instead, it contained many examples of regional variations. For example, some artifact types, such as blades made of Onondaga chert, are ubiquitous throughout, but regional variations are often present towards the periphery and are expressed through the use of local raw materials as substitutes for more exotic materials.[16]

Chert is very much like flint in that it is made up of microcrystalline quartz. This means that it can be worked to produce tools with very sharp edges. Outcrops of limestone containing nodules of Onondaga chert run across southern Ontario and upstate New York and provided ample supplies of chert for trade over a vast region. Thousands of tools made of Onondaga chert were produced between 3000 and 2500 years BP and exchanged as part of the Meadowood interaction sphere. They stand as a conspicuous example of a material that was highly sought after and exchanged over large distances. The most common product was a bifacially worked blade or knife, often referred to as a cache blade (figure 1.6). These finely crafted blades are very thin and were probably produced by part-time specialist flintknappers living in communities near the chert outcrops in the Niagara region.[17] The blades are in fact so ubiquitous and numerous that at times they suggest a shared value approximating a currency. Onondaga chert may have had symbolic value as well to many groups since it is often found as burial offerings, and at times the blades are sacrificed by burning or breaking ("killing") them prior to burial. Onondaga chert is closely associated with the Iroquois creation story of Teharonghyawago and his twin brother Tawiskaron.[18]

The succeeding Middlesex interaction sphere, which lasted from about 2500 to 2200 years BP and had a slightly smaller geographic span, illustrates the diverse levels of participation by different communities even further (figure 1.5).

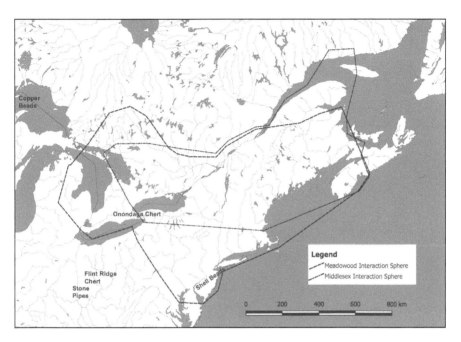

Figure 1.5
The Meadowood and Middlesex interaction spheres. The polygons show the
approximate maximum extent of each interaction sphere. The major raw materials
that circulated within these interaction spheres are shown.

This network was one in which populations maintained their local or regional
identities and preferences but shared similar burial customs including cre-
mation of the deceased, the ashes of whom were buried with large amounts
of exotic offerings, sometimes in circular earth mounds.[19] Many exotic materials circulated in this network, such as copper beads, large knives made of
Flint Ridge chert from Ohio and tubular smoking pipes made of flint clay
from Ohio and Illinois.

Although the Meadowood and Middlesex interaction spheres needed to be
highly structured in order to function and to last for centuries, they were also
highly flexible and do not appear to be under the leadership or control of any
specific groups or individuals. On the other hand, it is likely that some middlemen positioned themselves in order to accumulate trade goods and gain
economic and social prestige.[20] These networks allowed each group or population to freely adapt and adjust their level of participation according to their

Figure 1.6
Onondaga chert bifacial cache blades recovered from the Early Woodland
(Meadowood) period Lambert site in Saint Nicolas, Quebec, near Quebec City.
The 109 blades shown here are part of a group of 180 blades that were intentionally
burned as part of a burial ritual.

own needs and strategies, while maintaining regular contact with near or far
neighbours within a large-scale interaction network.

An even larger network emerged around 2200 years BP and lasted for several centuries (figure 1.7). Centred in the US Midwest but covering most of
the eastern United States and adjacent parts of Canada, the Hopewell interaction sphere included the circulation of raw materials and finished products
over amazingly vast distances, such as mica from the Appalachians, obsidian
from Wyoming, and shark teeth, whelk, and turtle shells from the Gulf of
Mexico.[21] It is possible that these three temporally successive and geographically overlapping interaction spheres (Meadowood, Middlesex, and Hopewell) actually represent an enduring network that gradually evolved through
time but persisted, cross-cutting archaeological cultures and periods as centres
of influence moved from one region to another.

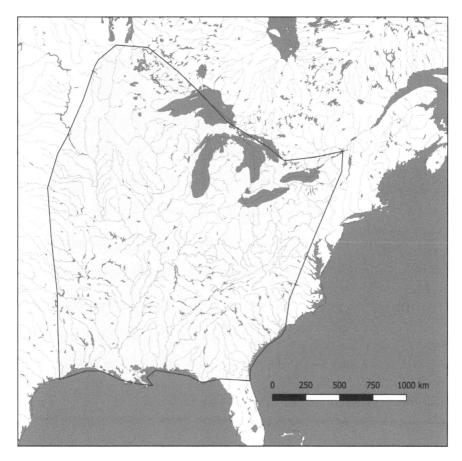

Figure 1.7
The Hopewell interaction sphere. The grey hachured area shows the maximum extent of this interaction sphere which included many regional cultural manifestations that were independent and distinct but which participated in this vast network that was centred primarily on the Ohio and Havana (Illinois) Hopewell centres.

The reasons for the demise of the Hopewell culture and interaction sphere remain somewhat enigmatic. What is more certain however, is the fact that it was the last of its kind. None of the subsequent networks to appear in Indigenous northeastern North America that archaeologists can identify ever attained the same geographic extent or the same level of eclecticism in the goods and materials traded. The interaction networks that archaeologists observe during the next centuries were more limited in geographic scale.

However, they were no less important for the participant's well-being and possibly to their survival. For instance, between 1000 and 800 years BP, Indigenous groups that archaeologists believe to represent proto- or ancestral Iroquoians in southern Quebec and Ontario maintained close relations with their cousins in New York State. This is visible through resemblances in the way these different groups made and decorated their pottery.[22] However, there was a shift from this north–south axis of interaction and communication to an east–west axis in the same area a few centuries later, from 800 to 650 years BP, as indicated by changes visible in ceramic decorative styles.[23] Although contact with southern populations never completely ceased, the new east–west preference in interregional interactions lasted until the arrival of the first Europeans in the St Lawrence River valley in the sixteenth century.[24] Recent social network analyses applied to ceramic collections has revealed that St Lawrence Iroquoians served as brokers or middlemen between the Huron-Wendats of Ontario and the Haudenosaunee of New York, until this pan-Iroquoian socio-economic network was dismantled following the dispersion of the St Lawrence Iroquoians at the end of the sixteenth century (figure 1.8).[25] Another archaeological indication of east–west contacts and exchange between Iroquoian nations at that time is the presence of stone beads on St Lawrence Iroquoian sites that were made using steatite from a geological source located in pre-contact Huron-Wendat country.[26]

The confederacies that were established by the Huron-Wendats, the Neutral, the Petun, the Haudenosaunee, and possibly the St Lawrence Iroquoians, represent another level of interaction, perhaps more political and diplomatic than economic in nature.[27] However, the socio-political alliances and reciprocal relations defining confederacies would have fostered and facilitated economic exchanges with trade acting as a lubricant allowing such confederacies to run smoothly and endure.

Iroquoian populations also maintained socio-economic relations with their Algonquian neighbours. For instance, it is well known that the Huron-Wendats were regularly trading maize in exchange for hides and meat with northern Algonquian tribes such as the Nipissing. Likewise, a branch of the Weskarini Algonquians from the Ottawa Valley, created after the inclusion of St Lawrence Iroquoian refugees, so frequently traded with the Huron-Wendats that they often needed to overwinter at or near the latter's villages and became better known by their Huron-Wendat name: the Onontchataronon.[28] As a

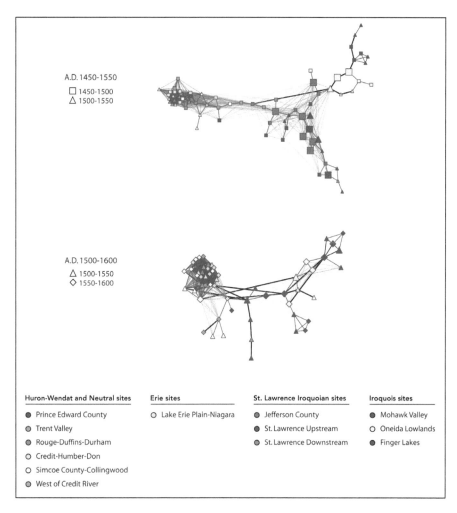

Figure 1.8
Visualization of a social network analysis (SNA) applied to Huron-Wendat, Haudenosaunee (Iroquois) and St Lawrence Iroquoian sites based on decorative attributes
on ceramic vessels. The St Lawrence Iroquoians (indicated by red, blue, and orange
squares and triangles) occupy a central position in the network (*top*), indicating their
role as social brokers until their dispersal at the end of the sixteenth century (*bottom*).
Note how the Huron-Wendat sites (*to the left*) seem to constitute a tight and dense
network compared to the more diffuse networks of the Haudenosaunee (*to the right*)
and St Lawrence Iroquoians.

matter of fact, the French described the Huron-Wendats as the "granary of the Algonquians."[29] These regular trading activities may explain the surprisingly frequent discovery of pre-contact Huron-Wendat ceramics in Algonquian archaeological sites from the eastern subarctic. Contrary to a common assumption, it may not be the pots that were the subject of trade but most probably their content, for example maize or nuts or oils.

Socio-economic interactions between Iroquoians and Algonquians took another form in the St Lawrence Estuary. The shores and islands of the St Lawrence Estuary east of Tadoussac were visited by St Lawrence Iroquoians from the Quebec City area during the winter, when harp seals (*Pagophilus groenlandicus*) are present in large numbers during the whelping and breeding season, before they migrate back to the Arctic. For their part, ancestral Innu spent the winter hunting caribou (*Rangifer tarandus*) in the hinterland, moving to the coast during the warm season to fish salmon (*Salmo salar*), at a time when the St Lawrence Iroquoians were back in their villages (this was before the Innu became sedentary and settled near coastal trading posts).[30] Despite the existence of inherited family hunting territories, most Innu perceived territory as something that was not possessed *per se* but as something that was inhabited, used, walked, lived, and sometimes shared.[31] By no means should this be interpreted as if the Innu have no rights on the land but simply that those rights are based on the idea that the Innu belong to the land they still inhabit, not the idea that the land belongs to them in a Western perspective. This is a perception that was shared by many, if not most, Indigenous peoples in North America but that was misunderstood by the first Europeans, which contributed to massive land dispossessions.[32] The archaeological case presented here seems to support the idea that sharing a territory without ceding it was also conceivable in pre-contact times.[33] Whether it implied some sort of economic compensation or reciprocity is not known, but there were clearly some exchanges taking place as can be seen by the movement of stone tool raw materials and ceramics.

Our final example comes from the Maritime Peninsula, a region that includes most of the state of Maine, the regions of Gaspé and Bas-Saint-Laurent in Quebec, and the provinces of New Brunswick and Nova Scotia (figure 1.9). This is the traditional territory of the Penobscot, Passamaquoddy, Wolastoqiyik (Maliseet), and Mi'kmaq. By studying the exploitation and circulation of stone tool raw materials over the past 3,000 years, it is possible for archaeologists to reconstruct how the Wolastoqiyik created an extensive social network that extended up and down the St John River (Wolastoq).[34] The use of different quarries of chert located in Maine, Quebec, and New Brunswick correspond to the traditional annual hunting and fishing territories of small family bands, these combining to form a larger territory we can refer to as the upper St John Wolastoqiyik. These families were in turn connected to the larger extended territory of the Wolastoqiyik First Nation encompassing the entire St John River valley from its source in Quebec and Maine to its mouth on the Bay of Fundy (figure 1.9). This Wolastoqiyik network was connected to neighbouring First Nations in the St Lawrence Estuary and the Bay of Fundy through the exchange of stone tools and ceramic pots and pipes.[35]

To summarize, archaeologists have material evidence for long distance exchange and interaction between Indigenous communities going back thousands of years. These networks were maintained by the exchange of various raw materials and objects that are visible archaeologically and are underwritten by social relationships based on reciprocity. Some of these exchange and interaction networks lasted for generations and point to sustained social interaction networks between culturally and linguistically distinct groups. Networks were also established and maintained within groups through various processes, not all of which were economic in nature, such as the acculturation of war captives or refugees, the aggregation or coalescence of regional communities, and the creation of political alliances and confederacies.[36] Most, if not all of these socio-economic networks were also flexible, dynamic, and subject to change, calling to mind a cloud that can vary in size, shape, and content through space and time. Moreover, the examples provided above demonstrate that Canada's Indigenous peoples were never isolated and could always establish, join, modify, leave, or maintain various kinds of interaction networks that functioned at different participation levels and geographic scales. In this regard, sedentary horticultural populations were no less integrated than their mobile, hunter-fisher-gatherer neighbours, although the interaction networks they participated in seem to have been less extensive, at least in terms of the distances covered. Indeed, recent research on pre-contact Iroquoian societies has been particularly dynamic in this regard, taking advantage of the new methods, techniques, and scales of analysis that have emerged in this field of research (figure 1.8).[37]

Figure 1.9

The Wolastoqiyik (Maliseet) Nation social network just prior to and during the early colonial period. The use of specific kinds of chert to make stone tools helps to define three different extended family groups that occupied the upper St John River valley: Munsungun-Aroostook in Maine, Témiscouata-Madawaska in Quebec and New Brunswick, and Tobique in New Brunswick. These three groups formed a closely related, upper St John River valley Wolastoqiyik division of the Wolastoqiyik Nation. They were in constant contact and interaction with Wolastoqiyik groups occupying the middle and the lower St John River valley. These Wolastoqiyik in turn traded with Mi'kmaq groups in the Bay of Fundy for multi-coloured cherts and copper which made their way back up the St John River valley via Wolastoqiyik social networks. The upper St John River valley Wolastoqiyik maintained relations with Indigenous groups in the St Lawrence Estuary, including the St Lawrence Iroquoians on Île Verte, as is evidenced by the presence of chert from the three different upper St John River quarry sources on sites in the estuary.

WHY MAINTAIN EXTENSIVE SOCIAL NETWORKS?

The reader may ask what the purpose of trading raw materials and tools or ornaments is if they are not really essential to survival or if a group can easily find a local substitute. Our archaeological, anthropological, and "economic" interpretation is that the exchange of these objects is not the primary driver of these social networks; they functioned as the lubricant rather than the currency of exchange. To maintain a relationship based on reciprocity between two partners from different villages or nations it was important to exchange material goods, as well as information and, probably, ritual actions. We have archaeological proof that these relationships were maintained over large distances and for many generations. The creation of an extensive social network that criss-crossed the continent was essential for sharing the land and avoiding conflict. Diplomacy had its place, but it was often preceded and accompanied by exchanges of goods. Social networks allowed different villages or nations to maintain relationships with various neighbours at the same time, thus reducing tensions and allowing for the exchange of information and sometimes people. As the continent became increasingly populated, Indigenous groups found many ways to keep communications open. In addition, it is possible to reduce risk to a group by maintaining such extensive social networks so that if there is a catastrophe or a bad year it is possible to get help and support from neighbours or simply share resources and territory.

On the other hand, we have no wish to dismiss more conventionally "economic" motives driving exchange in the past. People were probably strongly motivated to obtain a raw material like copper or Onondaga chert because it was a superior material for making tools. Seal oil from the estuary and Gulf of St Lawrence may have been highly prized for its taste, as no doubt were nuts from trees further south. It was important to exchange for tobacco or shell beads with a neighbour because these materials, essential to rituals, could not be found locally or easily substituted. Thanks to the extensive networks that these groups participated in, people would have known about these "exotic" materials and foods and would have made an effort to obtain them. In some cases the goods exchanged, such as maize for deer hides, might even prove crucial for the survival of the groups involved, especially during periods of food shortage. But the necessary prerequisite was an established relationship with a neighbouring group, a relationship that was based on reciprocity and was seen as first and foremost a social connection. In some cases, a person wanting to trade might even adopt another as a fictive brother or sister.[38] Once this relationship was in place, it was also important to maintain it, which is one of the reasons that we see some archaeological materials such as shell beads or Onondaga chert knives on a recurrent basis. What is striking in the archaeology of North America is how some of these exchange and interaction networks persisted in time over many generations and over a vast geographic area. To maintain such an enduring intergenerational network would have required regular and predictable meetings. It is worth noting that a network such as the Meadowood interaction sphere lasted at least 500 years (twenty to twenty-five generations) and covered an area of approximately 850,000 kilometres squared (figure 1.5). For comparison, the Hudson's Bay Company, which historically covered an equally vast territory, has lasted, with the full backing of a royal charter, the British Empire, and wealthy financiers, only 350 years.

CONCLUSION

Extensive social interaction networks linking communities and nations were in place by at least 6,000 years ago in the area that is known today as eastern Canada and northeastern USA. They persisted over generations and over large distances. These social/trade networks were sustained and underwritten through regular interaction and the exchange of goods, raw materials, people, and ideas. Networks came and went over the centuries and millennia, expanding and contracting, and eventually fading or being replaced by other networks.

These networks point to the complex political geography of northeastern North America and the extensive and ongoing socio-political negotiations that underpinned the relations between various Indigenous nations and confederacies. At the time of European contact and colonization, these networks represented a cultural geography and geopolitical map that was well emplaced and into which European powers would have to insert themselves. These social networks created an Indigenous geopolitical landscape that clearly structured intergroup interactions during the colonial period and had a direct impact on the success or failure of many European ventures in Canada. Before they could establish their own networks, Europeans had to learn about the right way to participate in these pre-existing interaction networks, which had functioned in various forms and scales for thousands of years before Canada.

NOTES

1 Baugh and Ericson, *Prehistoric Exchange Systems in North America*; Nassaney and Sassaman, *Native American Interactions*; Wright, *A History of the Native People of Canada*, vol. 1.

2 López Varela, *The Encyclopedia of Archaeological Sciences*; Malainey, *A Consumer's Guide to Archaeological Science*.

3 Mauss, *Essai sur le don*; Sahlins, *Stone Age Economics*.

4 But see the interesting case of wampum in the seventeenth century, Ceci, "The Value of Wampum"; Lainey, *La "Monnaie des Sauvages."*

5 Tankersley, "A Geoarchaeological Investigation."

6 Burke, "Paleoindian Ranges in Northeastern North America"; Meltzer, "Was Stone Exchanged?"

7 Robinson et al., "Paleoindian Aggregation and Social Context at Bull Brook."

8 Halsey, "Without Forge or Crucible"; Martin, *Wonderful Power*.

9 Clermont and Chapdelaine, *Île Morrison*; Clermont et al., *L'île aux Allumettes et l'Archaïque supérieur dans l'Outaouais*.

10 Burke, "La provenance des matières premières lithiques"; Chapdelaine and Clermont, "Adaptations, Continuity and Change."

11 Martin, *Wonderful Power*.

12 Fox et al., "Where East Met West"; Martin, *Wonderful Power*.

13 Byers, "The Eastern Archaic"; Clermont, "The Origin of the Iroquoians"; Clermont and Chapdelaine, *Pointe-du-Buisson*, 4; Chapdelaine, "Le site Jacques à Saint-Roch-de-Richelieu."

14 Hu, "Approaches to the Archaeology of Ethnogenesis"; Jones, *The Archaeology of Ethnicity*; Tremblay, "Culture et ethnicité en archéologie"; Chrisomalis and Trigger, "Reconstructing Prehistoric Ethnicity."

15 Clermont, "Le Sylvicole inférieur au Québec"; Farnsworth and Emerson, *Early Woodland Archaeology*; Spence et al., "Cultural Complexes of the Early and Middle Woodland Periods"; Taché, *Structure and Regional Diversity*.

16 Chrétien, "Les lames de cache du site Lambert"; Taché, *Structure and Regional Diversity*.

17 Granger, *Meadowood Phase Settlement Pattern.*

18 Williamson, *Legacy of Stone.*

19 Clermont, "Le Sylvicole inférieur au Québec"; Farnsworth and Emerson, *Early Woodland Archaeology*; Rutherford, "Reconsidering the Middlesex Burial Phase"; Spence et al., "Cultural Complexes of the Early and Middle Woodland Periods."

20 Abel et al., "The Williams Mortuary Complex"; Taché, *Structure and Regional Diversity.*

21 Braun, "Midwestern Hopewellian Exchange"; Carr and Case, *Gathering Hopewell*; Dancey, "The Enigmatic Hopewell of the Eastern Woodlands"; Charles and Buikstra, *Recreating Hopewell*; Seeman, "The Hopewell Interaction Sphere"; Streuver and Houart, "An Analysis of the Hopewell Interaction Sphere."

22 Clermont, "The Meaning of Early Late Woodland Pottery"; Gates St-Pierre, "Iroquoians in the St Lawrence River Valley"; Morin, "Early Late Woodland Social Interaction"; Petersen and Sanger, "An Aboriginal Ceramic Sequence f or Maine."

23 Dodd et al., "The Middle Ontario Iroquoian Stage"; Gates St-Pierre, "Iroquoians in the St Lawrence River Valley"; Tremblay, "A Middle Phase for the Eastern St Lawrence Iroquoian Sequence"; Williamson, *Legacy of Stone.*

24 Loewen and Chapdelaine (eds), *Contact in the 16th Century*; Warrick and Lesage, "The Huron-Wendat and the St Lawrence Iroquoians."

25 Hart et al., "Effects of Population Dispersal"; Hart et al., "An Analysis of Network Brokerage."

26 Baron et al., "Characterization and Origin of Steatite Beads."

27 Chapdelaine, *Le site Mandeville à Tracy*; Chapdelaine, "L'analyse spatiale et le tissu social"; Gates St-Pierre, "Iroquoians in the St Lawrence River Valley."

28 Fox, "Ethnogenesis in the Lower Great Lakes"; Pendergast, "The Ottawa River Algonquin Bands"; Pendergast, "Quelques notes sur la bande Algonquine Ountchatarounounga."

29 Tooker, *An Ethnography of the Huron Indians, 1615–1649*, 25; Trigger, *The Children of Aataentsic*, 166.

30 Castonguay, "Les impératifs de la subsistance chez les Montagnais."

31 Lacasse, *Les Innus et le territoire Innu Tipenitamun*; Mailhot and Vincent, "Le droit foncier Montagnais."

32 Greer, *Property and Dispossession.*

33 Gates St-Pierre, "Iroquoians in the St Lawrence River Valley"; Plourde and Gates St-Pierre, "Les phocidés du secteur de l'embouchure du Saguenay."

34 Blair, "Ancient Wolastoq'kew Landscapes"; Burke, "Lithic Procurement and the Ceramic Period Occupation of the Interior of the Maritime Peninsula"; Holyoke, "Late Maritime Woodland Lithic Technology in the Lower Saint John River Valley."

35 Burke, *Lithic Procurement and the Ceramic Period Occupation*; Burke, "La provenance des matières premières lithiques"; Tremblay, "La connexion abénaquise."

36 Birch, "Coalescent Communities"; Birch, "Social Institutions and the Differential Development"; Birch and Hart, "Social Networks and Northern Iroquoian Confederacy Dynamics"; Chapdelaine, "L'analyse spatiale et le tissu social"; Fenton, *The Great Law and the Longhouse*; Lynch, "The Iroquois Confederacy and the Adoption"; Ramsden, "Becoming Wendat"; Ramsden, "The Use of Style in Resistance"; Starna and Watkins, "Northern Iroquoian Slavery"; Snow, *The Iroquois;* Tooker, "Northern Iroquoian Sociopolitical Organization"; Tooker, "The League of the Iroquois"; Trigger, *The Children of Aataentsic;* Trigger, "Prehistoric Social and Political Organization"; Tuck, "The Iroquois Confederacy"; Viau, *Enfants du néant et mangeurs d'âme.*

37 Birch, "Coalescent Communities"; Birch and Hart, "Social Networks and Northern Iroquoian Confederacy Dynamics"; Hart et al., "Effects of Population Dispersal"; Hart et al., "An Analysis of Network Brokerage"; Jones and Creese, *Process and Meaning in Spatial Archaeology*; Miroff and Knapp, *Iroquoian Archaeology and Analytic Scale.*

38 Trigger, *Children of Aataentsic.*

2

Ways of Becoming: The Apachean Departure from the Canadian Subarctic

JOHN W. IVES

Were one to ask after prominent Indigenous personages from North America's historic past, many Canadians and Americans would certainly name Sitting Bull and Crazy Horse. Soon after those choices one might very well hear names of prominent Apache leaders such as Geronimo and Cochise enter the conversation. Members of a wider public are often surprised to learn that Navajo and Apache peoples of the American Southwest and southern plains share close language and genetic ties with Canadian Dene or Athapaskan speakers. These ties were first recognized by mid-nineteenth century philologists including Horatio Hale, who documented the links between Pacific Coast Dene speakers such as the Hupa and Alaskan and Canadian Dene speakers, as well as by William W. Turner, who saw that the Navajo and Apache languages were clearly related to Canadian Dene languages.[1]

How this situation came to be is certainly one of the remarkable stories in the human history of the Americas, with links to the very earliest Indigenous late Pleistocene presence in North America, a mid-Holocene crossing of the Bering Sea, and a more recent dispersal of Dene speakers from the north in the wake of a cataclysmic volcanic eruption just over a millennium ago. These events would make the Athapaskan or Dene language family the largest (in geographic scope) in North America, with representatives extending from the north slope of Alaska and the Bering Sea, to Hudson Bay, and south to California, the Sierra Madres, and northern Mexico (figure 2.1).

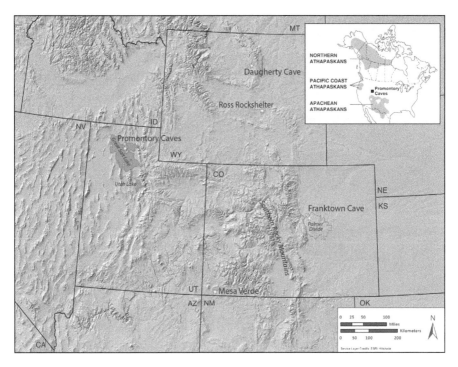

Figure 2.1
A map showing the distribution of sites mentioned in the text in interior western North America. The inset shows the three main geographic areas in which Dene or Athapaskan speakers lived in the nineteenth century.

DEEP TIME AND THE DENE PAST

Dene heritage in North America has complex genetic, language, and archaeological roots. Working with Indigenous communities and using both modern and ancient DNA (aDNA) samples, geneticists have reached a degree of consensus on the original peopling of the Americas.[2] Although the rather few aDNA and modern genetic samples inspire caution, geneticists posit that the founding population for the Americas took shape when a truly small group (perhaps as few as 300 individuals) became isolated either in Siberia or the Bering Land Bridge (linking Asia and the Americas during glacial periods, in a world known to scientists as Beringia).[3] Between roughly 18,000 and 22,000 years ago that founding population split into two groups, one termed "Ancient Beringian" and one ancestral to all Indigenous populations in the Americas. Between 17,500 and 14,600 years ago, the latter group then split into northern and southern lineages with the southern lineage becoming dominant in the United States, Central and South America. The northern lineage became ancestral to Haida, Tsimshian, Tlingit, Algonquian, Salishan, Wakashan, and Kutenai language families or isolates – in short, virtually all of the northern First Nations today in Canada. It was also ancestral to Dene (Athapaskan) communities, who would come to dominate the entire western subarctic.

Inundation of the Bering Land Bridge at the end of the Pleistocene did not end traffic between Siberia and North America: there is both genetic and archaeological evidence for extensive interaction across the Bering Strait during more recent, Holocene time (the last 11,700 years). Here, the Dene past began to diverge from that earlier northern lineage heritage. Genetic studies established that a subsequent Paleo-Siberian lineage took shape in central Siberia roughly 6,500 years ago.[4] Flegontov et al. proposed that Paleo-Siberian arrivals who would also be ancestral to Dene and Tlingit speakers entered Alaska from Siberia just after 5,000 years ago. This lineage later contributed anywhere from 5 to 25 per cent of their genome to modern Dene and Tlingit populations, with that proportion having been higher (up to 40 per cent) for pre-contact Dene individuals from the last millennium in Alaska. Sikora et al. suggested an earlier time frame for this Siberian incursion, between 9,000 and 5,500 years ago.[5]

The mid-Holocene was already known to archaeologists as a particularly fluid time frame in circumpolar human history: widely separated archaeological assemblages from Alaska to Greenland share remarkably similar material culture, among them evocative sculpted art forms, mid-passage slab hearths in linear houses, small leaf-shaped projectile points, microblades, and specific burin and concave sidescraper forms appearing rapidly across the Arctic just after 5,000 years ago. Several regional expressions of these archaeological assemblages – Denbigh Flint in Alaska, Pre-Dorset in Western Arctic Canada; Independence I in Ellesmere Island and northern Greenland, and Saqqaq in remaining Greenland – were united under a single archaeological concept, the Arctic small tool tradition (ASTt).[6] There are clear links for ASTt origins to central Siberia, with Syalakh-Belkachi archaeological expressions there, present from roughly 6,000 to 4,000 years ago. These Siberian connections were affirmed by whole genome aDNA studies of a ~4,000 year old Saqqaq individual from Greenland.[7] The AST t phenomenon reflects a rapid spread of ancestral Esk-Aleutian language speakers along the high Arctic littoral beginning 4,800 years ago.

The mid-Holocene time frame becomes especially interesting from the perspective of linguistics. Edward Vajda has put forward a Dene-Yeniseian hypothesis, testing it with rigorous historical linguistic methods, that would link Yeniseian languages of central Siberia (the last surviving example being Ket) with Dene, Eyak, and Tlingit languages in North America; they would all be part of a language macrofamily that emerged in Siberia about 6,500 years ago.[8]

It is apparent from the genetic evidence reviewed above that Dene-Yeniseian speakers must also have been among those who entered Alaska from Siberia about 4,800 years ago but proceeding instead toward the interior via the Yukon River.[9] A speech community ancestral to Dene, Eyak, and Tlingit speakers took shape as these Siberian populations encountered earlier and more numerous northern lineage peoples along an interior frontier in Alaska.[10] The new arrivals interacted with northern lineage Indigenous ancestors who shared in a "Northern Archaic" lifeway featuring generalized large and small game hunting as well as fishing conducted in boreal forest settings.

The linguistic and genetic data thus suggest that a proto-Dene-Eyak-Tlingit speech community was created with the arrival of Dene-Yeniseian language and detectable Siberian gene flow but with a preponderance of northern lineage North American participants. Soon thereafter, Tlingit would split from Athapaskan-Eyak, and roughly 3,000 to 3,400 years ago, Eyak split from Athapaskan. In the interval from 2,700–2,200 years ago, the proto-Dene speech community itself began to diversify across the western subarctic. As the diversification of the proto-Dene speech community proceeded, the Pacific Coast Athapaskan or Dene speakers departed the north. They would become the Hupa, Tolowa, Wailaki, Upper Umpqua, and other Dene speakers ranging from southern Washington to northern California. Linguists conclude that this differentiation began prior to AD 500.[11]

This brings us to the principal subject matter of this chapter – the departure of Apache and Navajo ancestors from the Canadian subarctic, which both linguists and geneticists believe began just over a millennium ago.[12] Both late Pleistocene, northern lineage heritage, and later mid-Holocene Siberian heritage would follow Dene ancestors southward just over a millennium ago.

There, many people of southern lineage genetic heritage would join Apachean ancestors in nascent Apachean communities.

Apachean ancestors thus have some of the most complex and intriguing human histories in the Americas, weaving together both founding Native North America genetic lineages from the Pleistocene with mid-Holocene Siberian genomes and languages featuring unique properties. After considering the factors involved in this last diaspora, I will explore the remarkable archaeological record of the Promontory caves as an indication of Apachean presence at a midpoint between subarctic origins and ultimate southern homelands (figure 2.2).

THE TRIGGER FOR APACHEAN DEPARTURE
FROM CANADA

Human migrations involve push and pull factors: negative conditions in a homeland region, which for Dene speakers was someplace in Alaska and the Yukon, and conditions perceived as more positive elsewhere. Beginning in the 1970s, evidence began accumulating for a massive volcanic catastrophe that had emanated from the Mount Churchill-Bona massif at the Alaska-Yukon border.[13] First thought to be a single eruption in which the wind shifted direction, earth science research eventually revealed that there had in fact been two events yielding the White River ash falls: a north lobe of ash (White River ash north, WRAN), running along the Alaska-Yukon border, was deposited roughly AD 300, while a massive east lobe of ash (WRAe), stratigraphically visible as far as Great Slave Lake, had been deposited in a second, more recent eruption.[14] Jensen et al. subsequently detected WRAe in Greenland ice cores where that event has now been dated to the winter of AD 852–3.[15]

There is a provocative coincidence between the White River events and Athapaskan dispersal: WRAN was deposited in a time range when linguists suspect that Pacific Coast Athapaskans moved southward (prior to AD 500), while WRAe corresponds to linguistic and genetic estimates of when Apachean speakers began their divergence (ca. AD 800–1000). Leaving aside the more poorly understood WRAN event and Pacific Coast Athapaskan departure from the north, I here focus on the implications of WRAe. It is important to grasp the sheer scale of this massive event. It ejected roughly forty-seven cubic kilo-

Figure 2.2
Top, the view from Promontory Cave 1, with Cody Sharphead screening deposits; *bottom left*, Aileen Reilly recovering a bison limb from a multispecies bone bed at her feet in Cave 1; *bottom right*, Bruce Starlight, Tsuut'ina elder and ceremonialist, conferring with Ives over moccasins during one of his visits to Promontory Point.

metres of debris into the northern hemisphere atmosphere, with visible ash over an area of one million square kilometres. That ash is cryptically detectable as far away as Ireland and northern Germany. Lerbekmo referred to this as one of the largest Plinian eruptions during the Holocene,[16] calculating an eruptive column height of about forty-three kilometres: we should not underestimate the awesome spectacle this would create for people quite far removed from the more immediate impacts of the eruption. While the scope and duration of impacts have been debated, there is a core zone in which compressed ash deposits of five to twenty centimetres extend over an area of roughly 200,000 kilometres squared in the Yukon and Northwest Territories. The ash is composed of tiny to microscopic shards of obsidian, the sharpest of all natural substances, with a range of terrible respiratory and abrasive effects for both terrestrial and aquatic organisms. It is difficult to imagine that this could have had anything other than serious impacts over a few seasons, years, or perhaps decades for a region that would normally have sustained no more than three or four regional marriage isolates (groups of several hundred persons each).[17]

Recent, comprehensive research has shown that wRAe created a mosaic of impacts for vegetation, terrestrial animals, and aquatic ecosystems with significant consequences extending for a decade to perhaps a few human generations.[18] There was a partial genetic replacement of southern Yukon caribou populations in this very time range.[19] Bunbury and Gajewski reported a variety of aquatic impacts at lakes 100–200 kilometres downwind from the volcanic source, from negligible in one more distant case to decades, and perhaps a century of recovery in other more proximal cases.[20] In fine scale sampling (one millimetre intervals) of a sediment core from the Yellowknife area (1,400 kilometres downwind of the vent), Hutchinson et al. concluded that lake conditions and freshwater diatom communities were significantly affected for a year following the wRAe event, with subsequent partial recovery.[21]

The most recent research clarifies that the west-to-east axis of the heaviest wRAe impacts fell directly across the Yukon and Liard Rivers, thereby affecting salmon and other freshwater fish runs and downstream aquatic systems. Similarly, wRAe fell across both year-round woodland caribou habitat and critical winter range for migratory Barren Ground caribou.[22] These were both important resources for Dene ancestors over a vast region. Moodie et al. argued that the White River eruption figures in a number of Dene oral traditions, particularly to do with copper and the Copper Woman.[23] Coupled with human health considerations (such as pre-existing respiratory conditions fostered by frequent use of indoor fires for cooking and heating) and a multitude of other implications (such as fuelling forest fires at a much larger scale than the recent past), it seems likely that wRAe caused significant disruption in the region for one to two human generations, as ecosystems recovered.

wRAe is coincident with significant technological change: prior to that ash fall, the perishable artifacts being recovered as the consequence of climate change and melting, high altitude ice patches in Alaska, the Yukon and the

Northwest Territories indicate that darts and spear-throwers provided the only form of propulsive weaponry.[24] After wrae, spear-thrower technology virtually disappears, supplanted by the bow and arrow as directly evidenced by the recovery and dating of both bows and nocked arrows.[25] A Yukon ice-patch bow dating from just after wrae was made of coastal maple. Shifts in the use of obsidian sources strongly suggest an intensified relationship between the interior Yukon and coastal Tlingit areas, quite likely the consequence of interior Dene ancestors moving southwestward away from the wrae vent. Native copper use and trade in the region also began in the wake of wrae.[26] To the east, long-standing trade in a regional Northwest Territories tool stone, Tertiary Hills Clinker, was disrupted by wrae.[27] So many well documented natural and cultural shifts are difficult to explain by coincidence alone.

wrae impacts would *not* have needed to affect a large number of people to set in motion the southward movement of Apachean ancestors. Genetic evidence strongly suggests that the initial proto-Apachean population was relatively small, created by founder effects.[28] wrae had severe enough consequences more than sufficient to have triggered initial Dene population movements to the south and east. If so, this event would provide one temporal boundary for Apachean migration, roughly 1,100 years ago.[29]

Linguistic evidence supports the genetic perspective regarding a small founding Apachean population. By the time they reached south central Alberta, people from a boreal forest environment would begin encountering decidedly unfamiliar plants, animals, and things for which names would be required: maize, tobacco and pipes, rattlesnakes, cacti, turtles, antelope, lizards and turkeys, for example.[30] Dene languages are inherently conservative and strongly resist borrowing terms, one solution to such a problem. Instead, they are internally creative, nominalizing verb stems in unique ways. Maize reached the north in historic times, for instance, and across that vast area we see a number of ways it was named, ranging from "big flour berry" to "horses' teeth." Not so in the Apachean languages, where maize is universally known as "enemy" or "alien" food – telling us much about the ambiguous sociopolitical circumstances in which maize was first encountered.[31] This pattern of having just one or two neologisms for plants, animals, and things holds for many of these novel encounters, suggesting that the original proto-Apachean speech community was both relatively compact and had cohesive naming practices, just as the genetic evidence would suggest.

THE INCENTIVE

Rather little is known about what then must have transpired for Apachean ancestors. The reason for this lies with the nature of most subarctic archaeological records. Apart from the extraordinary Yukon and NWT ice patch records mentioned earlier, boreal forest soils are typically acidic. That acidity rapidly destroys all the organic artifacts people used (in many Dene cases, the *great* majority of material culture) and the faunal residues that inform us about economy. Moreover, Dene ancestors over almost the entire western subarctic did *not* make pottery, a flexible and additive technology that can more freely express style and cultural identity. Instead, the boreal forest archaeological record is usually reduced to stone tools and their manufacturing byproducts (stone flakes and fragments). In the western Canadian subarctic case, these are rather generic. Stone arrow tips in northern Alberta and British Columbia, for instance, are very difficult to distinguish from contemporaneous northern plains forms.[32] Thus, while much of interest can be inferred from stone tool technology in the western subarctic, the remaining archaeological record is poorly suited to exploring the cultural identities of the past.

We are not, however, completely handicapped in exploring potential next steps in the migration process. In this regard, it is helpful to consider the historic end point of Apachean presence in the American Southwest and southern plains that the Spanish encountered as early as the *Entrada* of 1540. Francisco Vazquez de Coronado and his lieutenants were much impressed by highly mobile Plains people, writing:

> After seventeen days of travel [across vast plains, the Llano Estacado, with bison always in sight], I came upon a rancheria of the Indians who follow these cattle. These natives are called *Querechos*. They do not cultivate the land but eat raw meat and drink the blood of the cattle they kill. They dress in the skins of the cattle, with which all the people in this land clothe themselves, and they have very well constructed tents, made with tanned and greased cowhides, in which they live and which they take along as they follow the cattle. They have dogs which they load to carry their tents, poles and belongings.[33]

Soon after, many of those called *Querechos* would be known to the Spanish as Navajo and Apache peoples, many of them engaging in the extensive trade of bison products (e.g., dried meat, hide, leather clothing, bison scapulae hoes) for Puebloan products (e.g., maize, turquoise, fine ceramics). Could a bison-focused economy have provided the incentive for proto-Apachean speakers to have left the southern subarctic, crossing the aspen parkland ecotone, and entering the northern plains? The plains had a unique appeal. By the historic period, every major language family nearby had representatives living on or seasonally visiting the plains, including the Kutenai, Salishan speakers, the Numic Northern Shoshone and Comanche, the Tanoan Kiowa, Caddoan speakers, the Algonquian Cheyenne, Arapaho, Cree and Saulteaux, the Siouan Lakota, Dakota, Nakoda, Crow and Hidatsa, the Dene Tsuut'ina, Lipan and Ndee (Plains Apache) peoples, and, more recently, the Métis. Historic Plains societies featured highly productive economies with communal bison hunting, as did earlier cultures known to archaeologists as Old Women's, Avonlea, Besant-Sonota, Pelican Lake, McKean, and Oxbow phases or complexes on the northern plains.

Many northern Dene speakers were accomplished communal hunters, particularly of caribou and sheep. The other meaningful direction of flight from WRAe impacts would be into northeastern British Columbia and northern Alberta. In the Peace, Athabasca, and Slave River drainages of those regions, wood bison were present in appreciable numbers until the early nineteenth century height of the fur trade.[34] Dene peoples hunted wood bison individually and communally.[35] Any Apachcan ancestors approaching the southern subarctic and aspen parkland ecotone would be likely to encounter overwintering plains bison, seeking shelter from the severe winter conditions of the open plains.[36] Dene ancestors would not be strangers to this species. Given the scale of communal bison hunting that went on in the late prehistoric aspen parkland and northern plains, Apachean ancestors would rapidly become aware of how successful this livelihood could be, providing for both daily needs and trade surpluses. Plains societies also had rich and dramatic ceremonial lives. These factors would be meaningful "pulls."

This connection with bison can be extended forward in time and space. Earlier research showed that central plains bison populations detectably diminished by the AD thirteenth century, while southern plains bison populations began to flourish, perhaps as the consequence of cooler Little Ice Age conditions that might have improved forage.[37] Cooper found that large bison kills were concentrated in the heartland of communal bison hunting (southern Alberta, southern Saskatchewan and Montana) from AD 500–1700 but were absent from the central and southern plains from AD 500–900. By AD 900–1250, moderate to large bison kills began to appear on the central and southern plains; from AD 1250–1700, large bison kills took place in New Mexico and Texas.[38] If we were to be looking for a motive force drawing Apachean movement southward, the shifting state of late prehistoric bison abundance certainly fits the bill.

A SEARCH IMAGE

Sapir used four key words (maize, spoon, to broadcast seed, and insomnia) to reveal the northern origins of the Navajo language.[39] Maize we have already seen; the raw material for "spoon" for Navajo and Apache people is the husk of a gourd, but the word itself derives from horn – the mountain sheep horn used for spoons in the Dene north. (Figure 2.3a illustrates a spoon made from bison horn, the substance commonly employed for spoons in plains settings.) The verbal construction to "broadcast seed" derives from movement of particulate matter over a surface, such as snow drifting, and the Navajo word for insomnia, where sleep drifts away from the person desiring it, is a usage connected with a canoe gliding over water in the Dene north.

At the end of this engaging article from a master scholar comes a remarkable insight.[40] Much anthropological literature at this time was concerned with the definition of culture areas in North America and culture element trait lists that characterized those areas. Writing in that vein, Sapir argued that in seeking Navajo (and by extension, Apachean) origins, we should expect four cultural "strata": a fundamental northern layer, similar to that of Dene in the Mackenzie basin; a pre-equestrian plains adaptation; an initial Southwestern influence, from relatively simple non-Puebloan cultures of the Southwest; and a second, strongly Puebloan influence. Today, we would be more inclined to rephrase this to say that Apachean ancestors were once boreal forest hunter-gatherers, that they then entered the "dog days" bison hunting world of the northern plains. Farther south they interacted with somewhat more sedentary and sometimes horticultural societies, such as ones we would today refer to as Fremont, and then finally, Apachean ancestors entered Southwestern and southern plains worlds where, in profoundly creative episodes of ethnogenesis, they would make their homes.

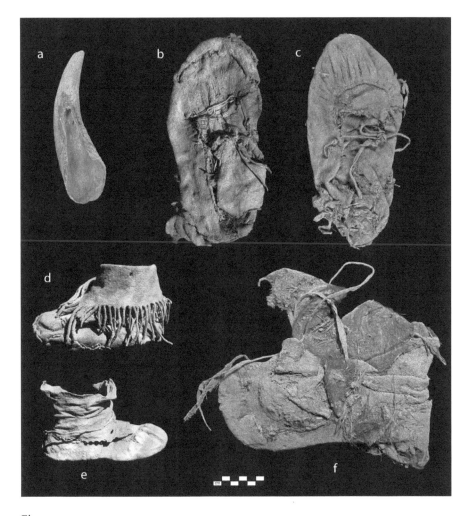

Figure 2.3

a) A bison horn spoon (UMNH 42B01 9501) from Steward's Promontory Cave 1 collections; b) a finely made, quill decorated BSM 2 (Bb) moccasin, UMNH 42B01:10241, radiocarbon dated to 784 ± 28 ^{14}C yr B.P. (OxA-18162); c) a BSM 2 (Bb) moccasin, UMNH.A.2011.18 42B01:FS173, radiocarbon dated to 706 ± 25 (OxA-25183); d) a BSM 2 (Bb) child's moccasin with fringed ankle wrap, UMNH 42B01:10055, radiocarbon dated to 784 ± 28 ^{14}C yr B.P.; e) a BSM 2 (Bb) child's moccasin, with higher ankle wrap, UMNH 42B01:10065 radiocarbon dated to 757 ± 23 ^{14}C yr B.P. (OxA-23921); f) a Promontory Cave 1 moccasin (UMNH.A.8011.18, FS-42B01.801.1) with bison fur lining and ankle wrap.

Sapir gives us a search image that more recent genetic and linguistic evidence allows us to refine. The earth science, genetic and linguistic evidence we have reviewed would suggest that just over a millennium ago the WRAe eruption triggered the movement of one or a few ancestral Dene groups on the order of a few hundred people, away from the high impact zone created by the ash fall. It could be that small groups displaced from the immediate impact area continued southward on this great journey, or it could be that a ripple effect was created in which those temporarily displaced groups affected ancestral Dene groups farther to the south and east, detaching them from the southern subarctic fringe or the Aspen parkland ecotone. Some combination of both eventualities is also conceivable.

While the initial proto-Apachean population was small, it clearly did not remain so, experiencing great growth by the time Apachean peoples had reached their southern destinations. While the plains bison hunting lifestyle had its own exigencies, the archaeological and historical records show that these societies could experience tremendous success. It could be that an initial proliferation of ancestral Apachean populations was fuelled by adopting that lifestyle in and near the heartland of communal bison hunting in North America: southern Alberta and Saskatchewan and Montana.

Yet, we would also expect burgeoning populations to employ familiar group forming principles guided by specific kin relationships. In other research I have pointed to evidence that kin principles shifted as Dene speakers moved southward, placing greater emphasis upon exogamous marriage practices that would facilitate the incorporation of others in nascent Apachean groups.[41] In this connection, we need to recall the substantial shift that geneticists see in Apachean genetic signatures: Dene speakers both north and south feature high frequencies of mitochondrial (mt)DNA haplogroup A (particularly haplotype A2a), which is heavily dominant (80 to 100 per cent) in the north. In some western Apache and Navajo communities, mtDNA haplogroup A frequencies fall to levels of just 50 or 60 per cent while haplogroups B and C (southern lineage mtDNA absent in the north but common in the Southwest) rise significantly.[42] Because mtDNA is inherited exclusively from our mothers, this means a large number of women were entering Apachean society. Navajo oral traditions strongly reinforce the genetic perspective. Many Navajo clans are adoptive, founded by maternal ancestors with ties to specific Puebloan sites or other language groups.[43] It is likely therefore, that dramatic growth in Apachean populations resulted both from successful adoption of new life-ways and recruitment of many new members who would take up Dene language but bring with them ideas and material culture from their previous life.

We would expect these groups to continue employing kin principles that had been successful for millennia, featuring a combination of small local groups of twenty-five to fifty persons moving widely over the landscape, at-tuned to the seasonal availability of resources, from time to time coalescing in larger gatherings of a few hundred people in which information could be shared, spouses found, friendships renewed, and games could be played. Apachean migration has sometimes been imagined as a wave or vector of peo-ple favouring exclusive routes west of the Rockies, along the east side of the Rockies and the foothills, or the high plains. It seems much more likely, how-ever, that their movement southward would reflect small group infiltration of all of these settings, with periodic coalescence, and subsequent dispersal. Many of these themes are explored in Navajo oral traditions.[44]

By the time the thirteenth century dawned, nascent Apachean groups would have found themselves travelling in one of the more turbulent times in the human past in western North America. Rapid change had been affecting the more sedentary societies of the eastern Great Basin and Puebloan world. Some of this change was precipitated by profound eleventh-, twelfth-, and thirteenth-century droughts that had seriously impacted maize horticulture; some of this change reflected significant cultural reorganization of these so-cieties.[45] In the eastern Great Basin, Fremont peoples had during the medieval climatic optimum engaged in settled village lifestyles supported by maize hor-ticulture. The twelfth-century drought ended that capacity, with communities returning to lakeside foraging activities reliant on wild plant and animal foods. The distinctive signs of overarching Fremont material culture (specific rock art and ceramic styles, evocative figurines, a peculiar form of moccasin, long-standing basketry styles) would vanish after a significant regional drought from AD 1276–99. Massive change was afoot in the American Southwest too. The later thirteenth century, for example, saw the abandonment of the elab-orate cliff dwellings of Mesa Verde and the movement of many people from those communities to the northern Rio Grande pueblos, where, by the time of Spanish contact, they would regularly interact with Apachean ancestors. Southwestern scholars have more generally documented a retraction of Puebloan peoples into fewer, larger centres at this time.[46]

These trends would have created challenges for Apachean ancestors. Schwindt et al., amongst other authors, felt that the northeastern periphery of the Puebloan world was becoming an increasingly dangerous place in the thirteenth century.[47] For Apachean ancestors, this would mean moving through landscapes with ambiguous socio-political circumstances. On the other hand, as more sedentary societies retracted from the larger landscape, there were increasing opportunities for Apachean and Numic hunter-gatherer societies to infiltrate the larger Southwestern regions. It was not only the case that bison hunting opportunities apparently increased on the southern plains: the new presence of large Puebloan communities along the northern Rio Grande, at the plains periphery, would provide the basis for intensive interaction between settled Puebloan communities and Apachean ancestors. Strategies ranged from the friendly enclavement of Jicarilla Apache groups, to the raiding activity more common farther to the south (something about to be reinforced by the Spanish reintroduction of the horse).[48]

Thus, a search image is critically important for two reasons. First, as any survey of nineteenth- and early twentieth-century photographs in western North America shows, Dene speakers had a particular cultural genius for accepting and re-purposing useful ideas and material culture from neighbouring communities. Whether towards the northwest coast, in the Pacific northwest, on the plains or in the American Southwest, Dene peoples rapidly assimilated practical and ceremonial material culture from adjacent societies all the while retaining their language identities in a *highly* conservative fashion. This of course creates the most challenging of circumstances for archaeologists, who are reliant upon material culture for indications of cultural identities in the past. Secondly, archaeological records do not always comply with the facets of the past about which we may be curious. Archaeological records rich in stone tools and faunal remains, while informative about many aspects of the past, do not serve well in tracing cultural identities. For instance, while some archaeologists are attracted to shifts in forms of projectile point technology (for arrow or dart tips) as reflecting past ethnic or language identities, there is considerable evidence that these forms can have regional or even broader scope, encompassing many identities.

Ideally, archaeologists might hope to find material culture traces of those northern and plains phases reflecting Apachean origins along potential migration pathways, in tandem with the adoption of material culture typically encountered in those midpoint and southern homes. In practice, this is very often prohibitively difficult. This is a conundrum for which there is no simple solution – *unless* we should encounter an archaeological record of unparalleled richness greatly expanding the field of material culture against which we could evaluate our search image.

THE PROMONTORY CAVES

One of Sapir's contemporaries, noted twentieth century anthropologist Julian Steward, had in fact explored just such an archaeological record in the same 1930s timeframe as Sapir wrote his Navajo origins article. Steward would go on to become best known for an influential perspective on cultural ecology. Early in his career, however, he conducted considerable archaeological research, most notably in the Promontory Caves of Utah.[49] Steward was seeking the earliest Indigenous occupation of these caves, but early evidence in these particular instances was scant. Instead, he encountered one of the richest *late* period archaeological records ever discovered in western North America, which he termed the Promontory Culture. He recovered 250 pieces of footwear (245 of which were leather moccasins), mittens, basketry, cordage, many and varied gaming pieces, a complete range of stone and bone tools (from hunting weaponry to hide processing), pottery, items of adornment, indications of ceremonial life (such as rock art and incised tablets), all in the midst of extensive midden deposits of animal bone, hide, hair, and animal dung.[50] Steward concluded that this record had been created by an intrusive northern hunting population with plains and subarctic ties; they lingered long enough on Promontory Point to begin assimilating material culture and ideas from surrounding, late Fremont neighbours. He strongly suspected that they were an ancestral Apachean group.

Curiously, Steward's conclusions elicited little further interest. There even grew to be a perception of a "Promontory Problem" especially with respect to the nature of the pottery found in the caves and at other eastern Great Basin sites, ignoring the incredibly rich perishable artifacts from the caves.[51] In some respects, Steward's later theoretical pursuits made him the author of this situation: interest in cultural ecology and the economic basis of life would eventually lead to a commitment among many Great Basin specialists to human behavioral ecological approaches to archaeological data. Seeking cultural identities is not a core activity in these paradigms. However that may be, Steward's remarkable Promontory cave collections attracted little further attention until our project group took a renewed interest in them.[52]

INTERPRETING THE PROMONTORY RECORD

What did Steward see that caused him to suspect the presence of Navajo or Apache ancestors? From extensive work with Shoshone, Gosiute, Ute and Paiute, and other Numic speakers, Steward had a firm grasp of material culture across the Great Basin; there was little indication of Numic presence in the Promontory Culture materials, although these groups would inhabit the region in the centuries to follow. The focus on large game hunting, particularly of bison and antelope, along with intensive hide processing and a high frequency of implements connected with that work, confirmed a completely different economy from the occasional large game hunting, small game capture with nets, harvesting of wild seeds, and use of wetland resources characteristic of typical Great Basin archaeological cultures. Above all else, the many moccasins he knew were completely out of character for the region. Steward could call upon the excellent early work of Gudmund Hatt, who had censused North American footwear, and was familiar with the leather moccasins of the Canadian north.[53] The Promontory moccasins were constructed in a distinctive manner, in which a single lower sole piece was folded upwards towards a vamp or upper (figure 2.3, b–f).[54] The two were joined with a seam creating a round, puckered toe. There might be an additional tongue piece above the vamp; there could also be an ankle wrap with laces. Curators today refer to these as Bata Shoe Museum (or BSM) 2(Bb) style moccasins. These moccasins were made principally of finely tanned bison leather, often with the fur turned inward for a lining. Sewing levels varied, but often moccasins were made by artisans with very good or in some cases exquisite sewing skills (figure 2.3b in particular). Moccasins were sometimes further decorated with red ochre applications, use of bird or porcupine quill wrapped cords to cover the toe seam, and occasional instances of porcupine quill decoration. Moccasin construction patterns as well as sewing and decorative techniques definitely *did* signal cultural identity in the historic past.

The Promontory style moccasins were unlike the unusual and less well-made Fremont or hock moccasins occasionally found at surrounding Fremont sites, or the hide and fibre sandals found in a broader arc across late period interior North America. Nor were they like the BSM 4 style moccasins common in the plains region historically. Instead, Steward could see that the Promontory moccasins were very like moccasins that Tsimshian, Tlingit, and Canadian Dene made. It was also true that this style of moccasin was common among Algonquian speakers of the eastern subarctic. There is no reason, however, to suspect that subarctic Algonquian speakers were in the vicinity of the northeastern Great Basin and every reason to think that Apachean ancestors must have at least been nearby if they were ever to make their rendezvous with the Spanish by 1540. Moreover, a well-preserved moccasin has been recovered from the Gladstone ice patch in the Yukon, situated within the zone that would have been heavily impacted by the White River Ash east eruption. Constructed in the same basic form, that moccasin yielded a calibrated date of AD 558–663 (1430 ± 40 radiocarbon years).[55] This moccasin came from a northern Dene homeland region, pre-dating the Promontory moccasins by some seven centuries.

In our more recent work, we have continued to find moccasins and moccasin fragments and have been able verify more of Steward's earlier conclusions. We have amassed more than 140 accelerator mass spectrometry (AMS) radiocarbon dates as part of renewed work on the Promontory record. The ninety-five Promontory phase dates in Cave 1 range from 662–886 ^{14}C yr BP, with median calendric dates extending from AD 1220–1321.[56] Bayesian modelling of all these AMS dates from Cave 1 affirms that the Promontory Cave 1 occupation lasted from roughly AD 1248 to AD 1290. These dates indicate that both the onset and end of the Promontory Culture occupation, which accumulated so much cultural debris, were abrupt. The Cave 1 occupation took place as a series of visits in different seasons over just one or two human generations, from groups of roughly thirty-five people.[57]

We have made a distinction between "northern" and "southern" perishable artifacts found in the caves that could be directly dated.[58] "Northern" artifacts were dominated by moccasins, reflecting a clear discontinuity with previous Fremont footwear and having demonstrable ties to the subarctic world. "Southern" artifacts were characteristic of the northeastern Great Basin and included basketry, matting, looped rawhide sandal-like footwear, juniper bark rings, and cane arrow shaft parts. Steward had argued that the Promontory Culture reflected an intrusive population that arrived prior to the end of the Fremont interval and persisted afterward, having had time to assimilate some distinctively southern cultural elements. We concur, finding that while there was overlap between the northern and southern elements, Bayesian modelling reveals that northern elements tend to precede the southern elements in time.[59] This finding is consistent with expectations for an intrusive population assimilating northeastern Great Basin traits during the course of the Promontory phase occupation.

The Promontory moccasins have also afforded unique insights into the demographic structure of the cave population.[60] Moccasin length can be accurately related to foot length, which in turn is a precise index of stature until roughly eleven to twelve years of age, a perspective that can be verified with Boasian era anthropometric data. There then exists a gray zone in which it is more difficult to distinguish adolescent males from adult females. Beyond this, very large moccasins are assumed to be those of adult men. A high proportion (just over 80 per cent) of the Promontory moccasins were worn by children and adolescents. There is undoubtedly a discard bias for adults, particularly adult males, who would be more likely to leave worn out moccasins behind at various off-site locations. Nevertheless, the high numbers of children and adolescents are striking and strongly suggests a thriving population. This would be consistent with the large game hunting success evident in the abundant faunal remains present in Cave 1.

Coming to this site with the benefit of another nine decades of advancing archaeological techniques, our current research discovered other evidence, in addition to the moccasins, suggestive of northern and plains ties for the Promontory cave inhabitants. The emphasis on stone scrapers and bone fleshers (for removing residues from hides) and beamers (for removing hair from hides, copious quantities of hair being present in the cave deposits) is consistent with the high-quality leather being produced by the cave inhabitants but is uncharacteristic of Fremont assemblages (figure 2.4a). In and of itself this would not be conclusive, but there is one specific stone tool type that is unknown in Fremont assemblages but has a long history in subarctic assemblages. These semi-lunar and crescentic forms are known as *chi-thos* or tabular bifaces and are specifically used in the final softening of hides (figure 2.4b). They remain in use today among Dene women processing hides in traditional manner. The Promontory moccasin makers were decidedly specific in their raw material choices for leather, with the great majority (87 per cent) coming from female bison, as determined by aDNA sexing of leather samples.[61]

In yet more recent findings, we have discovered four instances of intricate plat sinnet weaving in the Cave 1 assemblages (figure 2.4c).[62] In both Dene and Algonquian traditions of the subarctic, such weaving is used in moccasin and legging garters, mitten strings, and birch bark basket handles. This form of manufacture is otherwise unknown in the Great Basin. There is also a lattice-like object of heavy leather strongly resembling a dog travois basket, a traditionally Plains mode of burden transportation (figure 2.4d).[63]

Both our search image and Steward's conclusions would suggest that the Promontory cave inhabitants resided there long enough to begin absorbing material culture traits from surrounding late Fremont peoples. Yanicki argues persuasively that the Promontory cave ceramics were in fact inspired by a Fremont variant known as Uinta Gray, common to the east of Great Salt Lake, something that would suggest Fremont influence, along with the likelihood that Fremont women may well have been entering the Promontory cave population.[64] Basketry is not common in the Promontory cave deposits, but a few instances are identical to longstanding Great Basin forms that persisted into the Fremont era, such as the half rod and bundle construction example in figure 2.4e, with similar implications.

In Steward's era, faunal remains were not retained for the study of diet and economy, with only a casual sample of specimens taken for museum collections. Many of the stained bones scattered at the Cave 1 and 2 peripheries are very likely Steward's discards. This left doubt in the mind of some Great Basin researchers as to whether Steward's emphasis upon large game hunting (of bison in particular) might have obscured more important small mammal and waterfowl remains as well as evidence for wild seed harvesting and processing. Our modest testing program, of less than three cubic metres of deposits, yielded more than 30,000 whole and fragmentary faunal remains, dominated by bison, antelope, deer, sheep, and elk. Small mammals and birds are rare, most wild seeds present were likely introduced by rodents, and ground-stone milling tools for seed processing are almost completely absent.[65] While our faunal analysis remains underway, it is clear that Minimum Number of Individual (MNI) values we can calculate for large animals in the entire Cave 1 contents will almost certainly number in the hundreds. The Promontory cave

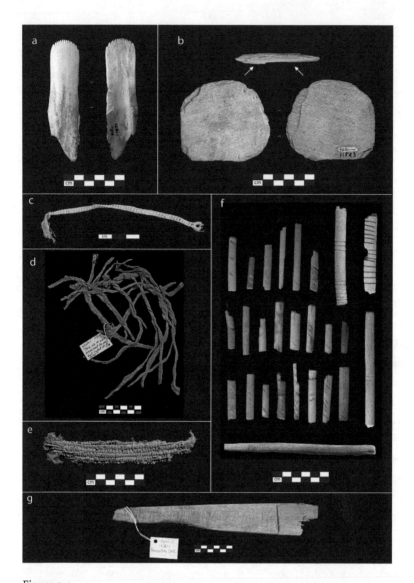

Figure 2.4

a) A finely made bone flesher from Promontory Cave 1 (UMNH 42Bo1 10306); b) a *chitho* or tabular biface (UMNH 42Bo5 11523) from Promontory Cave 5; c) UMNH 42Bo1 FS 210, a strand of intricate four-strand plat sinnet of a type known across the Canadian subarctic but unknown in the Great Basin apart from Promontory Cave 1 examples; d) UMNH 42BO1 11595, a lattice-like heavier leather construction, a probable dog travois basket fragment; e) a close-coiled, half rod, non-interlocking stitch, bundle stacked foundation basket fragment dating to 694 ± 24 ^{14}C yr BP (OxA-28441, UMNH 42Bo1 FS 1098, calibrated to AD 1275–1385 [2]) from our Promontory Cave 1 excavations; f) scored cane dice and decorated sticks, among the many Promontory gaming pieces; and g) the limb of a discarded Promontory Cave 1 juniper bow (UMNH 42Bo1 11602.2, perhaps scored to remove or affix a composite backing (b, d, and g).

occupants were prodigiously successful hunters of bison and other large game. A small sample (less than fifty centimetres squared) from a much larger burned bone feature yielded more than 6,500 fragments, with an MNI of twenty-two large mammals, nine of which were bison. Even more intriguing was the fact that these burned bones had abundant evidence of accelerants in the form of valuable fats and greases.[66] This seems highly suggestive of feasting as the cave inhabitants would undoubtedly have known how to crush and boil bones to extract the greases used in making pemmican had they chosen to do so.

The possibility of feasting aligns very well with the diversity and abundance of gaming pieces in the Promontory caves. The gaming pieces include cane dice, beaver and porcupine incisor dice, hoops and darts, bone hand game pieces, counting sticks, a shuttlecock, and a ball (figure 2.4f).[67] There are 177 scored cane dice, with projections for the entire cave deposits running into the thousands. Dice games were commonly played by women and their frequency may be suggestive of gaming within or among domestic groups. The many other forms of gaming pieces, on historical and oral tradition grounds, are highly suggestive of externalized interactions. Gaming is often accompanied by gambling, which historically, in interactions with outsiders, could involve high stakes (such as slavery for oneself or family). The wide array of gaming pieces affirms two things: first, the Promontory cave inhabitants were familiar with a variety of games from much of western North America, apparently unlike their Fremont neighbours. Second, gaming is known to be an effective way of mediating new relationships in ambiguous socio-political circumstances: it does require its own fluency even where different languages would be involved, both for an understanding of how to play and certainly for the stakes involved.

Other evidence makes it clear that the Promontory cave inhabitants had avenues of communication ranging far afield in western North America. There is an abalone shell pendant, for example, which must have come from the Pacific.[68] A great majority of the obsidian in the caves comes from the Malad source 100 kilometres to the north in Idaho, a location likely within the seasonal ambit of the cave inhabitants. Malad obsidian has an interesting temporal pattern that parallels general trends in Apachean movement. It was traded quite widely throughout all of prehistory. Its presence on the central and southern plains peaks in the fourteenth century, however, and then falls

away as obsidian sources in New Mexico and Arizona become more important.[69] Perhaps the most striking example occurs with rock art. Promontory
Cave 1 has instances of late Fremont art, typical of the eastern Great Basin.
More than a thousand kilometres away, near Canmore, Alberta, the Grotto
Canyon pictographs involve a panel with virtually identical rock art – far out
of place in southwestern Alberta (figure 2.5).[70] Precisely what this means is
not entirely clear, but the Grotto Canyon panel occurs in an area we could
fully expect Apachean ancestors to have passed by. It could reflect sojourning
Fremont ancestors moving far afield to seek alternative homes in that turbulent thirteenth century or perhaps Apachean ancestors with detailed knowledge of such art making a return journey northward. However it may be, there
was clearly some form of traffic between the northeastern Great Basin and
southwestern Alberta.

There is also evidence of a purposeful human migration behaviour: scout-
ing. Using carbon isotope data, Metcalfe et al. showed that a remnant fragment
of a Promontory Cave 1 ankle wrap came from a bison that had lived 800 kilometres or more to the south (Arizona) or southeast (eastern Colorado or beyond).[71] An ankle wrap is the one portion of a moccasin least apt to wear out;
someone had apparently scavenged leather for this ankle wrap that had come
to Promontory Cave 1, where it was attached to a moccasin with leather from
the Great Salt Lake region.

BEYOND PROMONTORY

The Promontory caves reflect one, unusually clear instance of an intrusive
population with northern and plains ties. In many respects, however, it is likely
the high fidelity of the preservation involved that makes for such a singular
record. The search image developed earlier would suggest that we should expect many instances of ancestral Apachean populations infiltrating pathways
toward the American Southwest and southern plains. There are indeed other
occurrences of Promontory-related artifacts where there is superior preservation at scattered sites in Wyoming, Colorado, Arizona, and New Mexico.[72]
Ross Rockshelter and Daugherty Cave in Wyoming each have a moccasin
made in the Promontory style; Daugherty Cave also featured incised stones
and scored cane dice like Promontory. Franktown Cave on the Palmer Divide

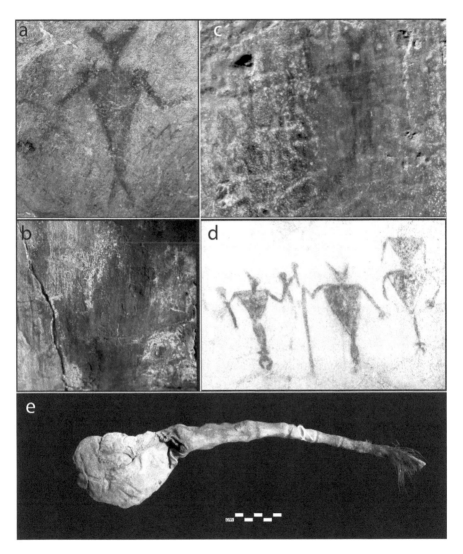

Figure 2.5
Ochre rock art figures from Promontory Cave 1 and Grotto Canyon, Alberta: a) One of the pictographs from Promontory Cave 1; b) a second more elaborate Fremont rock art figure from Promontory Cave 1; c) a pictograph figure from Grotto Canyon, near Canmore, Alberta; d) a line of figures from Grotto Canyon, Alberta, with three likely rattles near the figure on the left; e) UMNH 42Bo1 10233, a buffalo tail rattle from Promontory Cave 1.

south of Denver has a complete child's moccasin in the same style, fragments of others, a fringed legging fragment resembling one from Promontory, a ceramic sherd difficult to distinguish from Promontory examples and a gaming hoop.[73] These sites all fall in locations where one could legitimately expect to find other, small groups moving southward.

Yet more intriguing are the instances of Promontory moccasins in the Mesa Verde area, once the home of Puebloan people but subsequently part of Dinetah, the heartland of the Navajo world. Dene ancestors have long been suspected of introducing leather footwear to the southwestern world. Fewkes reported a Promontory moccasin fragment (and possible gaming hoop) from Spruce Tree house at Mesa Verde, and in nearby Johnson Canyon, Osborne reported a pair of Promontory moccasins recovered alongside a heavy composite bow (a technology a number of archaeologists suspect Apachean ancestors introduced to the Southwest) (figure 2.4g is a portion of a Promontory Cave 1 bow).[74] We have also noted Promontory style moccasins yet farther south, from Aztec Ruin and the vicinity of Otowi Pueblo in New Mexico, and Montezuma's Castle in Arizona. All of these instances come from within lands that ultimately became the homelands of Navajo and Apache peoples. Effectively then, there is a trail of similar moccasins extending along likely pathways for Apachean movement extending from northeastern Utah and Wyoming through Colorado and into the Southwest.

CONCLUSIONS: ON RELEVANCE

I close with two lines of thought about the relevance of archaeological research. First, in more and more cases, archaeologists are "relinquishing the inception" of research as Dent aptly phrased it, where Indigenous communities set the agenda for topics they wish to see explored.[75] Our research has been of a different yet related character, reflecting a situation in which we are drawing to the attention of Dene communities the existence of remarkable collections made nine decades ago, providing information we can supplement with modern methods and insights. One of the most gratifying aspects of our work over the last two decades has been interaction with Dene communities from across western North America in community-driven Dene language conferences, Dene migration workshops (2009 and 2017), a moccasin making workshop at the 2009 Canadian Indigenous Languages and Literacy Development Institute (CILLDI, University of Alberta) session, in reviewing collections with Mescalero and Chiracahua community members, and the Dene Reunification gathering held at Tsuut'ina First Nation in Calgary in October of 2019 (this last meeting drew more than 500 Apache, Navajo, Pacific coast, and Canadian Dene representatives). We have also been pleased to bring together Dene representatives with Northwest Shoshone representatives in whose traditional territory the Promontory caves today lie (figure 2.2c).

One cannot help but be struck by the power held by both the artifacts we find and the places in which we are so privileged to conduct fieldwork. For all of us, but especially for First Nations people, the moccasins strike a chord – perhaps because we can so clearly sense an individual from the past in the highly skilled stitching, the imprint of a foot, or the mending of a hole. We have also been deeply moved to hear Tsuut'ina and Shoshone voices during blessings and ceremonies conducted in Promontory Cave 1, decades and even centuries since this last happened. In all these contexts, we see how these artifacts, sites, and findings can assist Dene peoples in an underlying desire to reacquaint communities long apart from each other and to express a Dene language identity.[76]

Second, with respect to the certainty of our findings, archaeologists generally face a "black box" conundrum: human activities have taken place in the past, unrecorded or unobserved, leaving behind residues from which we must infer the nature of those activities, knowing that there are many ways that both natural and cultural causes can leave us with "false positives" or "false negatives" in making our inferences. Although in practice it often does not, this fundamental situation should encourage intellectual humility. Very many aspects of the Promontory and related archaeological records align closely with the search image developed in earlier passages, so that our research group *does* feel that these records are our best indications of midpoints in an Apachean transit from Canada to the southwest and southern plains – one that was at such a large scale and so remarkable a phenomenon that it must have left definable traces. That said, we do make a conscious effort to entertain alternative scenarios. It could be that these records reflect a greater polyethnic phenomenon, including but not restricted to Apache and Navajo ancestors. Or, it could be that some of these instances reflect the shift of Tanoan-speaking Kiowa populations from Fremont villagers to the fully Plains people they would become.[77] Yet, even a Kiowa dimension would involve Apachean presence. Kiowa and Ndee ("Kiowa Apache") oral traditions state that they had been associated for as long as both groups could recall, including their movement southward from the Yellowstone and Black Hills regions to the east of Promontory.[78]

Introspection in this spirit leads to some important underlying issues. In the climatic and social instabilities of that turbulent thirteenth century, we should expect to find the seeds of socio-economic and socio-political orders that would characterize the following centuries until early Spanish and French documentation began. By then, some ancestral Apachean populations were going "against the grain" in fascinating ways. Having left the most abundantly watered region of North America, ancestors of Navajo and Western Apache groups were infiltrating available, highly arid landscapes of the greater Southwest, taking up mixed economies, with some maize horticulture along with hunting and foraging activities. Once sheep and goats had been introduced, a pastoral dimension flourished in their economies.[79] To the east, groups like those ancestral to the Jicarilla Apache established a pattern in which they "overwintered under the eaves" of the northern Rio Grande Pueblos, bringing Plains products (dominated by bison hides, clothing, dried meat, and scapulae hoes) that they would exchange for Puebloan goods (maize, beans and squash, various obsidians, turquoise, and polychrome ceramics).[80]

Apachean ancestors were not alone in creating a new order of interactions: Ute, Paiute, and Caddoan speakers were also doing so. Some Puebloan peoples themselves began to make forays onto the plains.[81] Seen in this light, the Promontory and related records suggest that the underlying form of these more widespread Plains–Puebloan interactions was being established by the thirteenth century, irrespective of the specific cultural identities that might have been involved at individual archaeological sites. These processes, and Dene expansion in particular, reflect an epic story in western North America, one that would leave the American Southwest and southern plains forever changed by newly arriving peoples – with more than a few lessons for the present-day world.[82]

ACKNOWLEDGMENTS

The many members of our Apachean Origins research group, including colleagues Joel Janetski (Brigham Young University) and Sally Rice (University of Alberta), are deeply grateful to George and Kumeroa Chournos for their support and assistance in working in the Promontory caves, which they have protected from the looting ravages suffered by so many Great Basin sites. I thank staff members of the Natural History Museum of Utah (Glenna Nielson-Grimm, Kathy Kankainen, and Michelle Knoll) for their tremendous assistance in working with Steward's 1930s Promontory collections, and the Museum of Peoples and Cultures, Brigham Young University (Paul Stavast, director) for assisting with and housing our more recently excavated materials until they were united with Steward's collection at the Natural History Museum of Utah. I have been grateful for collaborations with Sally Rice (emerita professor, Linguistics, University of Alberta), Beth Shapiro (University of California-Santa Cruz, UC-SC Paleogenomics Lab) and Duane Froese (Canada research chair, Earth & Atmospheric Science, University of Alberta). My research has been supported by SSHRC Standard Research Grant 410-2010-0480 and SSHRC Insight Grants 435-2012-0140 and 435-2019-0593, as well as by funding from the Landrex Distinguished Professorship. Bruce Starlight (Tsuut'ina First Nations), Patty Timbimboo (Northwest Shoshone), and Henrietta Stockel (Mescalero) have been extraordinarily helpful in our efforts to work with Dene and Northwestern Shoshone communities.

NOTES

1 Hale, "United States Exploring Expedition," vol. 6; Turner, "The Apaches." Athapaskan is a word of Cree derivation that came to be a scholarly convention. Most speakers of "Athapaskan" languages identify with cognate terms related to "Dene" (e.g., Dineh, Ndee, Dindje) with an underlying meaning of "person" or "the people." Throughout, I will preferentially use the term Dene but do occasionally use the term Athapaskan because it is so deeply embedded in the literature.

2 Willerslev and Meltzer, "Peopling of the Americas," provides a concise summary of the current genomics literature.

3 E.g., Fagundes et al., "How Strong Was the Bottleneck"; Tamm et al., "Beringian Standstill," e829; Waters, "Late Pleistocene Exploration," eaat5447.

4 Flegontov et al., "Palaeo-Eskimo Genetic Ancestry"; Fortescue and Vajda, *Mid-Holocene Language Connections*, 453–79.

5 Sikora et al., "Population History of Northeastern Siberia."

6 Cf. Friesen, "Pan-Arctic Population Movements"; McGee, "Paleoeskimo Occupations"; Powers and Jordan, "Human Biogeography."

7 The human populations behind AST t expressions have been known by the inappropriate name "Paleo-Eskimo," but are now being termed Paleo-Inuit; for the Saqqaq genome, see Gilbert, "Paleo-Eskimo mtDNA."

8 Vajda (see Fortescue and Vajda, *Mid-Holocene Language Connections*) has found 130 reliable cognates (words of similar phonetic form and meaning identified through strict application of the comparative method) between the Siberian and North American languages; he has also elucidated an uncommon morphological pattern in which Dene-Yeniseian languages feature an inventory of verb stems whose meaning is inflected by several prefixing positions (with a number of prefixes again sharing both form and meaning). See also, Vajda, "A Siberian Link"; Vajda "Dene-Yeniseian."

9 Fortescue and Vajda, *Mid-Holocene Language Connections*, 453–68.

10 See Anthony, *The Horse, the Wheel*, 102–19, on the significance of persistent frontiers between archaeological entities that are often created at the terminus of migrations. Such frontiers can exist over centuries, marking stable distinctions between speech communities. These language boundaries were not necessarily impermeable. People might move freely across such frontiers, although there can be strong expectations about conforming to material culture or language norms on opposite sides of a frontier. The AST t-Northern Archaic frontier appears to illustrate this phenomenon, which in some ways, repeated itself later in Apachean prehistory (cf. Ives, "Dene-Yeniseian, Migration," 325–9; Ives, "Seeking Congruency"; Ives and Janetski "Ways of Becoming").

11 E.g., Krauss and Golla, "Northern Athapaskan Languages," 68; Snoek et al., "Linguistic Relationships," 16, 23–4.

12 Krauss and Golla. "Northern Athapaskan Languages," 68; Achilli et al., "Reconciling Migration Models."

13 Derry, "Later Athapaskan Prehistory"; Lerbekmo, "The White River Ash"; Workman, "The Cultural Significance"; Workman, *Prehistory of Aishihik-Kluane Area*; Workman, "The Significance of Volcanism."

14 Lerbekmo, "The White River Ash"; Reuther et al., "Revisiting the Timing"; Robinson, "Extending the Late Holocene."

15 Jensen et al., "Transatlantic Distribution"; Mackay et al. "The 852/3 CE Mount Churchill Eruption."

16 Lerbekmo, "The White River Ash."

17 Gordon, "The White River Ash Fall" and Doering et al., "A Multiscalar Consideration," differed with this interpretation, arguing that the timing of Dene population movements and the WRAE event was coincidental, a perspective difficult to sustain with the limited evidence they provide and the demonstrably massive consequences of the second White River eruption.

18 See Kristensen et al., "Identifying and Sourcing Pyrometamorphic"; Kristensen et al., "The Movement of Obsidian"; Kristensen et al., "Environmental and Hunter-Gatherer Responses"; Kristensen et al., "Power, Security, and Exchange" for many of the details following.

19 Kuhn et al., "Modern and Ancient DNA."

20 Bunbury and Gajewski, "Post-Glacial Climates."

21 Hutchinson et al., "Diatom Ecological Response."

22 Kristensen et al., "Environmental and Hunter-Gatherer Responses."

23 Moodie et al., "Northern Athapaskan Oral Traditions."

24 Kristensen et al., "Power, Security, and Exchange."

25 Andrews et al., "Alpine Ice Patches"; Hare et al., "The Archaeology of Yukon."

26 Kristensen et al., "The Movement of Obsidian."

27 Kristensen et al., "Identifying and Sourcing Pyrometamorphic"; Kristensen et al., "The Movement of Obsidian."

28 Achilli et al., "Reconciling Migration Models"; Mahli et al., "Native American mtDNA"; Mahli et al., "Distribution of Y Chromosomes"; Monroe et al., "Exploring Prehistory." When small populations break away from larger populations a genetic "bottleneck" is created because the group breaking away reflects less genetic variability than the larger parent population. When geneticists and medical researchers find noticeably reduced genetic variability, they infer that a founder effect involving small population fissioning has occurred. This has consistently been the conclusion geneticists reach for the ancestral Apacheans.

29 Notably, Flegontov et al. ("Paleo-Eskimo Genetic Legacy," 11) found no evidence of Inuit genetic ancestry among Apachean ancestors, consistent with a departure from the north *after* WRAE *with* Paleo-Siberian heritage but *prior* to Inuit expansion (known archaeologically as Thule) across the Canadian high Arctic, now known to have taken place in the AD thirteenth century.

30 Ives, "Seeking Congruency," 37–8.

31 See Sapir "Internal Linguistic Evidence"; Ives, "Seeking Congruency," 37–8.

32 Ives, "Alberta, Athapaskans," 280–1; Ives, "Early Human History"; Peck and Ives, "Late Side-Notched Projectile Points," 185–9.

33 Coronado to King Charles, 20 October 1541, quoted in Hammond and Rey, *Narrative of the Coronado Expedition*, 186.

34 Ives, "Alberta, Athapaskans," 270–5; Olson and Janelle, *The Ecological Buffalo*, 14, 54.

35 E.g., Goddard, "The Beaver Indians," 214, and various Dunne-za (Beaver Dene) stories concerning bison in that publication.

36 Ives, "The Prehistory of Northern Alberta." In this respect, wood bison and plains bison ranges overlapped at the aspen parkland ecotone; there is also the prospect that a "mountain" bison hybrid of wood and plains bison had a range extending into Utah along the Rockies and foothills, as per Olson and Janelle, *The Ecological Buffalo*, 14, 54.

37 E.g., Creel et al., "A Faunal Record"; Dillehay, "Late Quaternary Bison"; Huebner, "Late Prehistoric Bison Populations."

38 Cooper, *Bison Hunting*.

39 Sapir, "Internal Linguistic Evidence."

40 Ibid., 235.

41 Ives, *A Theory of Northern Athapaskan Prehistory*; Ives, "Developmental Processes"; Ives, "Dene-Yeniseian, Migration"; Ives, "Seeking Congruency," 37–8.

42 Mahli et al., "Native American mtDNA"; Mahli et al., "Distribution of Y Chromosomes"; Monroe et al., "Exploring Prehistory."

43 See, for example, Brugge, "DNA and Ancient Demography"; Brugge, "When Were the Navajos?" and Zolbrod, *Diné bahane`*, regarding Navajo creation oral traditions.

44 Zolbrod, *Diné bahane`*, especially passages concerning the gathering of the Navajo clans, 281–335.

45 See Benson et al., "Possible Impacts" and Mensing et al., "Extended Drought," on droughts. For social implications, see Kintigh and Ingram, "Was the Drought"; Kohler et al., "The Better Angels"; Mills, "Multiscalar Perspectives"; Robinson et al., "Dendrochronological Dates," and Schwindt et al., "The Social Consequences."

46 E.g., Mills, "Multiscalar Perspectives"; Robinson et al., "Dendrochronological Dates."

47 Schwindt et al., "The Social Consequences," 89.

48 E.g., Eiselt, *Becoming White Clay*; Spielmann, "Late Prehistoric Exchange"; Spielmann, "Coercion or Cooperation"; Vehik, "Conflict, Trade."

49 Steward, *Ancient Caves*.

50 See Steward, *Ancient Caves*; also Ives, et al., "A High Resolution"; Ives et al., "Promontory Revisited"; Yanicki and Ives, "Mobility, Exchange."

51 Ives, "Resolving the Promontory."

52 Steward was prescient on the timing and nature of the Promontory occupations with respect to Fremont, far in advance of the advent of radiocarbon dating. I would be remiss, however, if I did not mention a darker side to Steward's work. Steward later became a US government witness arguing *against* Ute and Paiute land claims. In this, he was opposed by other anthropologists, including Alfred L. Kroeber, Robert Heizer, and Omer C. Stewart; the Ute and Paiute claims were upheld by the Indian Claims Commission despite Steward's testimony to the contrary. See Kerns, *Scenes from the High Desert*, 382 and Pinkoski, "Julian Steward."

53 Hatt, *Moccasins and Their Relation to Arctic Footwear*.

54 See Ives et al., "The Promontory Moccasins" for details concerning the following passages.

55 Hare et al., "The Archaeology of Yukon," 125.

56 Ives et al., "A High Resolution"; Ives et al., "Promontory Revisited," 60–70.

57 Hallson and Lakevold, "Predicting Group Size."

58 Ives et al., "A High Resolution Chronology."

59 Ibid., 631–2; Ives et al., "Promontory Revisited," 62–6.

60 Billinger and Ives, "Inferring the Age Structure."

61 Shirazi et al., "Ancient DNA-Based Sex."

62 Goldberg et al., "The Local and the Distant," 165–6.

63 Ibid., 169–70.

64 Yanicki, "Follow the Women."

65 Rhode, "Archaeobotanical Investigations."

66 Ives et al., "Promontory Revisited."

67 Yanicki and Ives, "Mobility, Exchange."

68 Steward, *Ancient Caves*, 40–1.

69 E.g., Hughes et al., "Investigating Dismal River."

70 Lints et al. "Art in the Time of Promontory Cave."

71 Metcalfe et al., "Isotopic Evidence."

72 Ives et al., "The Promontory Moccasins," 91–2.

73 Gilmore et al., "Franktown Cave, Colorado."

74 Fewkes, *Antiquities of the Mesa Verde*, 51; Osborne, *The Wetherill Collections*,
    74–7; Yanicki and Ives, "Mobility, Exchange," 160–1. Apachean ancestors have
    been suspected of introducing composite bows (i.e., bows strengthened by the
    use of other backing materials) to the American Southwest (e.g., Kohler et al.,
    "The Better Angels," 449). The earliest known composite bow in the larger re-
    gion is in fact the sinew-backed bow fragment that Steward (*Ancient Caves*,
    17–18) discovered in Promontory Cave 1.

75 Dent, "Community-Sourced Archaeology."

76 See also, Coates, "Walking into New Worlds."

77 Ortman and McNeil, "The Kiowa Odyssey."

78 Mooney, "*Calendar History*, 247–8.

79 Campbell, "Na'nilkad nee na'niltin."

80 Eiselt, *Becoming White Clay*.

81 Clark and Speth, *Living and Dying on the Periphery*.

82 Cf. Altschul et al., "To Understand How Migrations." In this vein, it was not
    surprising to learn while writing this chapter that the first Indigenous person
    to travel to the International Space Station would be Captain Nicole Aunapu
    Mann, a Wailaki member of the larger community of Pacific Coast Atha-
    paskans mentioned earlier. One of her early tasks was to use the Canadarm to
    capture a cargo supply vessel approaching the space station. See NASA biogra-
    phy for Nicole Aunapu Mann, "Astronaut Biography: Nicole Aunapu Mann,"
    accessed 9 January 2023, pdf available at https://www.nasa.gov/astronauts/
    biographies/nicole-a-mann/biography.

3

The Newfoundland Fisheries in an Early Atlantic World, 1400–1550

JACK BOUCHARD

Buried in the Bibliothèque nationale de France is a remarkable manuscript. Catalogued as Ms.Fr. 24269, it is a handwritten sailing guide from the 1540s, a fairly routine catalogue of techniques used to calculate latitude and distances.[1] Most of the text is unremarkable, but several folios at the end are taken up by a pair of unexpected additions: two dual-language vocabularies, word lists compiled to aid mariners and merchants travelling to new colonial outposts in the Atlantic. These were not atypical tools in the sixteenth century, but it is unusual for them to have survived in manuscript form. The first vocabulary is for the *langaige de guynée,* the second for the *langaige du bresil.* The vocabulary for the *langaige de guynée* includes a variety of words in Kru (from present day Liberia) and their French equivalents. The vocabulary for the *langaige du bresil* likely represents Tupi, and Norman traders were known to voyage to the coasts of Brazil in the early sixteenth century.[2] Together they represent some of the earliest evidence for Norman interactions with communities in West Africa and South America and the ethnographic knowledge accumulated in this process.

These two handwritten vocabularies are joined in the manuscript by a third, seemingly unrelated and unique text. At the bottom of the penultimate page, taking up half of the leaf, are two paragraphs written in a dense and hurried hand. Bearing the title *Pour la Terre Neufve,* the text constitutes a brief personal note about Newfoundland and its fisheries.[3] The text of the paragraphs describe, perhaps as a memory-aid, how to recognize when one has

arrived off the coast of Newfoundland and where the author has stored his
fishing boats over the long winter. It includes descriptions of birds, the Grand
Banks, Renews Harbour, and the kinds of marks used by fishworkers to identify their boats.[4] This description of *Terre Neufve* is an invaluable text. Brief
as it is, it is perhaps the only surviving description of the early sixteenth-
century fisheries and their environment from the unmediated perspective of
a mariner who worked there. Yet it is the physical and conceptual position of
Terre Neufve in the book, relative to the Brazilian and Guinea vocabularies,
which is most striking. The note about *Terre Neuvfe* follows directly from,
and is almost embedded within, the languages of Brazil and Guinea. As we
page through the manuscript, we can see the author's thoughts move from
Guinea to Brazil to Newfoundland, so that the harbour at Renews forms one
point in a maritime network and lived experience which had brought the
Norman mariner to the estuaries of West Africa and the dense forests of
Brazil. The final page of the book tellingly includes a sketch of a ship, presumably the boat which had taken our mariner-author to all three spots, the
tool which would link colonial operations in North America, South America,
and West Africa. A century later these same places would be bound together
in the oceanic trades which drove life and death in the Atlantic, as salt cod
from Newfoundland fed enslaved peoples from west Africa who laboured in
the American tropics. This is an essential triptych of Atlantic history, the great
and terrible engine of the eighteenth-century economy, represented here hundreds of years earlier than we typically expect.[5]

What the BnF manuscript suggests is that at least one European in the early
sixteenth century saw Newfoundland and its fisheries not as an isolated endeavour but as a place connected to and bound up with a wider emerging Atlantic world. What I hope to make clear in this essay is that our Norman
mariner was not alone in that worldview. During the first half-century of sustained European activity in the northwest Atlantic, the formative period for
the Newfoundland fisheries, European mariners, merchants, navigators, and
statesmen were shaped by their experiences elsewhere in the Atlantic basin.
That had profound consequences for why, when, and how the fishery developed but also for how modern historians and archaeologists should research,
write, and teach about the topic. We must see *Terre Neufve* as our rouenais
mariner did, as one place in an emerging constellation of sites for contact, exchange, and exploitation in the Atlantic basin.

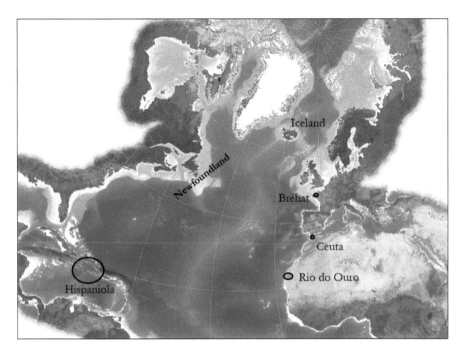

Figure 3.1
Map of Atlantic basin showing locations mentioned in text.

In the first half of the sixteenth century, European mariners developed a major commercial fishery in the northwest Atlantic, the Newfoundland fishery.[6] The actions of these early voyagers formed a permanent European presence in the region, establishing a vector for European colonization of North America and for the exploitation of its resources. Scholars, educators and even the public are used to imagining the Newfoundland fisheries as a starting point for many kinds of history – of transatlantic fishing, of empire in North America, of the fur and whale trades of Canada.[7] Where better to begin our stories of the New World than in the New Found Land? The very name is so forward looking – it is "redolent of late-medieval promise" as one author has put it.[8] Nonetheless, I would suggest that we should instead see the early Newfoundland fisheries as a kind of end point instead of a beginning. The northwest Atlantic was a place where different strands of Atlantic history met and were woven together by a diverse group of maritime actors: the late medieval expansion of commercial fisheries, the Iberian conquest and colonization of islands, the European search for new sources of food and resources in a widening Atlantic basin. As much as we still treat the year 1492, or 1497 in the north, as an historical inflection point, all of these histories stretched back much further and encompass much broader spatial histories. The rise of a multinational fishery at Newfoundland was a culmination, or even just a waystation, in these historical trends.[9]

Rethinking our starting points means that historians of early Newfoundland must engage more with Atlantic history.[10] Most studies of sixteenth-century Newfoundland limit transatlantic frameworks to connections between Newfoundland and Europe. Far less has been done to compare the early European experience in the northwest Atlantic to similar activity in the Caribbean, Brazil, mainland Americas, or Africa. Newfoundland was one of the four major European projects in the Americas in the early sixteenth century, alongside the Caribbean, New Spain, and Brazil. It was likewise concurrent with expanding Portuguese trade in West Africa and Luso-Castilian settlement of the mid-Atlantic archipelagoes. It is therefore worthwhile to consider both comparisons and connections between these different sites of colonization.[11] It is particularly important to read Newfoundland against an *early* Atlantic.[12] The preponderance of historical work remains focused on the post-1600 Atlantic basin, but the ways in which Europeans interacted with the Atlantic basin from roughly 1400–1550 were distinct from what came later. Far from the mature, integrated Atlantic system and economy of the seventeenth and eighteenth century, the early Atlantic was much more fragile, dynamic, and multipolar. By the time Zuan Caboto reached Newfoundland in the summer of 1497, Europeans had already been investigating and settling the Ocean Sea's many corners for several centuries.

What I wish to demonstrate in this essay is the need to view Newfoundland with a very broad and inclusive lens, to read it against what was happening elsewhere in the early Atlantic, and in so doing to answer two questions. First, what experiences in the Atlantic basin shaped how Europeans interacted with Newfoundland and its waters? Second, when and where do we begin our narrative of the Newfoundland fisheries? To answer these two questions, I will consider how the early Atlantic world influences our choice of narrative starting points, of how we see histories and histories-that-may-have-been, and of the connections and legacies of fishing in the wider Atlantic basin. As we move through these perspectives, we will see the Newfoundland fisheries as being connected to a much wider and much longer Atlantic history than we often recognize.

STARTING POINTS

In the late summer of 1415 a well-armed expeditionary force, led by Portugal's King João I, descended on the city of Ceuta in what is today northern Morocco. Centuries earlier the Portuguese had completed their phase of the long Reconquista, and a new wave of imperial expansion was beginning. The Portuguese crown envisioned a leap across the sea to the northern coast of Africa, beginning with Ceuta and encompassing all the Kingdom of Morocco. To facilitate this endeavour, Portuguese navigators and merchants would soon begin moving down the western coast of Africa and into the mid-Atlantic Ocean in a series of exploratory and trading voyages. These acts of navigation, exchange, and colonization soon took on a life of their own and became the leading edge of European expansion into the Atlantic basin. The successful capture of Ceuta in 1415 legitimized the new Portuguese expeditions, compelling more and more voyagers, settlers, and warlords to head south and west. Within a decade they would begin settling the Azores and Madeira archipelagos in the mid-Atlantic. By the 1430s ships had rounded Cape Bojador and were at Cabo Verde and the Guinea Coast, and thereafter the first *feitoria* trade posts would be planted on the West African shore. Soon Castilian adventurers would follow suit, attacking and seizing the Canary Islands in a series of brutal wars. The capture of Ceuta marks the start of a new phase of first Portuguese and later Castilian overseas expansion into the eastern Atlantic basin.[13]

Hundreds of miles to the north, a different kind of overseas expansion was taking place. In 1415 the king of England, Henry V, declared a ban on all English fishing vessels sailing to Iceland.[14] This followed earlier complaints from Denmark that English ships were fishing off the coast of the island. This would soon spiral into a dispute, often a violent one, between English, Danish, and Hanse mariners over the fishing grounds. The ban of 1415 is some of the earliest evidence that an offshore commercial fishery was operating in Icelandic waters and that it was being prosecuted by foreign mariners rather than the island's inhabitants. By the second decade of the fifteenth century largely anonymous mariners were travelling the long distance between England and Iceland in search of preservable fish, mainly cod, even if that meant defying the Danish crown.[15] Their actions pushed the limits of state power to control maritime space but, in exchange, allowed fishworkers to ruthlessly exploit valuable fish stocks along the Icelandic coast. We know, however, that Iceland was far from the only commercial fishery experiencing growing pains in 1415, and similar disputes would soon overtake fishworkers in the Irish Sea, North Sea, Algarve, and elsewhere. The Icelandic dispute was broadly representative of the growth of new commercial, oceanic fishing operations across the eastern Atlantic basin.

Out of these two strands of European activity would arise a permanent European presence in the northwest Atlantic. In the first instance was a sustained, state-backed effort to seize control of territory, especially islands, for integration into a new commercial network. This is the effort which produced colonies in the Canaries and Madeira, which led to the foundation of trade posts at Arguim and da Mina, would see a series of continuous wars across Morocco. Concurrently, there was a parallel and often invisible effort by European mariners to seize and exploit new coasts and open waters in the eastern Atlantic. By the end of the fifteenth century they had blanketed the eastern Atlantic from northern Norway to the Sahara with commercial fisheries. Both of these processes would shape how Europeans interacted with Newfoundland and the northwest Atlantic and allowed for the creation of a commercial fishery in the early sixteenth century. We cannot separate what came later at Newfoundland from these events; I would therefore argue that the history of European activity at Newfoundland should be traced back to 1415.

Of course, Newfoundland did not appear suddenly on the map in 1415. Newfoundland as an island and human space has existed for eons. Human presence in the region goes back thousands of years, and archaeologists have uncovered evidence of thriving Indigenous societies on Newfoundland which long predate 1415. For the Beothuk, Mi'kmaq, and their predecessors the fall of a North African city or expansion of fishing at Iceland meant little.[16] We now know that Norse mariners had reached "Vinland" four centuries before the capture of Ceuta and briefly established an outpost on the island. In the long arc of history the Vinland settlement was a flash-in-the-pan moment, but it did form an early if brief connection between the two sides of the north Atlantic.[17]

The sustained European presence from the fifteenth century onward was nonetheless something different. The formation of a permanent European presence in the northwest Atlantic, embodied in the cod- and whale-fisheries of the sixteenth century, was a distinct historical development with far-ranging consequences. Part of this involved the creation of New-found-land, a space of European occupation and activity which replaced Vinland and various Indigenous conceptions of geography in the northwest Atlantic. To that end, the year 1497 has long held pride of place as the starting point for our collective narrative of European activity at Newfoundland. In June of that year Zuan Caboto, in the service of a group of Bristol merchants and the English crown, made landfall somewhere in the northwest Atlantic, probably on the east coast of Newfoundland. The information they brought back, soon amplified by Portuguese expeditions, led directly to continuous European visits and a thriving fishery.[18] Caboto and his English masters never quite spoke of a Newfound*land* – they described new-found-islands for the most part – but it represents for many historians the moment when Newfoundland, Canada, the fisheries, all appear in the European consciousness for the first time.[19] Even so, Caboto's encounter with the northwest Atlantic and the sudden appearance of Newfoundland in the European imagination, was just one moment amongst many in a century of exploration, exchange, and conquest. If we focus too much on 1497 we are liable to lose this perspective and lose sight of the longer history of European expansion into the Atlantic.

VISIONS OF NEW-FOUND-ISLANDS

We may also lose sight of histories that might-have-been, alternative visions of the northwest Atlantic which were shaped by European experience in the fifteenth century. Europeans came to Newfoundland for fish from the earliest years of the sixteenth century, but it was not clear to them that harvesting food was to be the sole European preoccupation with the region. After all, at the heart of the northwest Atlantic were islands – Newfoundland, Cape Breton, Prince Edward, Anticosti – and islands were well familiar to the inheritors of Ceuta.

In the summer of 1511, Spanish authorities set their sights on exploiting a new opportunity in the western Atlantic. The colonial project in the Caribbean was still in its infancy and the European presence in the Americas faced a multitude of futures. Castilians had not yet made the leap to Terra Firme, and most of their activity centred on the seas and islands of the western Atlantic basin. Now a world of islands lay to the north of the Caribbean, recently explored by the English and Portuguese and already well-known to Breton mariners who could be hired to pilot ships there. It would be here that new island colonies, a New Hispaniola, could be founded – unless of course the Portuguese managed to found a New Madeira first.

The very idea of a permanent Iberian colony, along Caribbean lines, in the northwest Atlantic seems laughable: the bleak, cold, thin-soiled, rocky, sparsely populated island of Newfoundland could never be tropical, densely settled Hispaniola. Yet we know that in 1511 the Spanish crown did have such designs on the northwest Atlantic. That year the crown tasked Juan de Agramonte, a Catalan navigator, with a reconnaissance of the coasts, islands, and waters far to the north of the Caribbean. The navigator was to take a fleet of ships to the northwest Atlantic, a space which the Spanish conceded might already fall under Portuguese jurisdiction, to learn "the secret of Terra Nova [*el secreto de Tierra Nueva*]."[20] A warrant granted by the crown in 1511, which survives in an archive at Simancas, explicitly authorized Agramonte that any islands he found were to be "settled in our [the crown's] name, as has been done in the said island of Hispaniola."[21] The patterns of imperial territorial claims, forcible seizure of island spaces, land distribution, and intensive agriculture which marked emerging Caribbean settlements (and which themselves had a much older lineage) were to be transplanted to the subarctic Atlantic.[22]

Agramonte's dream of a New Hispaniola was nonetheless not an isolated ambition.[23] In 1499 the Portuguese crown had tasked João Fernandes with recreating the colonization of Madeira in the northwest Atlantic, so long as he found appropriate islands. In it the crown rewarded Fernandes for his "effort to seek out and discover at his own expense some islands lying in our territory" by granting him "the governorship of any island or islands, either inhabited or uninhabited, which he may discover and find anew, and this with the same revenues, honours, profits and advantages we have granted to the governors of our islands of Madeira and the others."[24] That same language was repeated in 1520, in letters patent which gave the aristocrat-turned-navigator João Fagundes authority to plant a colony as if it were a new Madeira. The king of Portugal granted extensive letters patent to Fagundes, authorizing him to explore and lay claim to whatever islands and lands he could find, and the text of the letters indicates that Fagundes had already sailed in the region.[25] Most importantly, the royal letters patent specify the terms by which Fagundes could exercise power: "which lands and islands we give and grant him [Fagundes] the governorship in the same form and manner that we have granted the governorship of our islands of Madeira and the rest."[26] In the eyes of the Portuguese crown, Newfoundland was to become the Madeira of the north.

Why did so many Europeans envision a New Hispaniola or a New Madeira, rather than a New Found Land? The first Europeans to reach the northwest Atlantic were more excited by the presence of islands than anything else. The very earliest English record related to Caboto in 1497 referred to "the new Isle," while that same year reports sent to Venice and Milan spoke of "*ixole nova*" and "*insula nova*" respectively.[27] Agramonte saw the northwest Atlantic through the lens of the Caribbean, expecting to find new islands which could be settled and exploited. Fernandes and Fagundes saw the region through the lens of Portuguese activity in the mid-Atlantic, from the Azores to Madeira to Cabo Verde. Both groups brought experiences and expectations with them. Chief amongst these regarded the importance of islands and insular environments. Lessons from the mid-Atlantic and Caribbean argued for the need to seize and settle islands and to turn them into sites of agricultural and mineral production. Such a system had, after all, been brilliantly successful (from the Iberian perspective) at places like Madeira, the Canaries, and Hispaniola.

The fifteenth and early sixteenth centuries were marked by consistent and far-ranging engagement with insular spaces by European mariners, settlers, and state actors. At Madeira, the Azores, and Cabo Verde Portuguese expeditions had found valuable, uninhabited archipelagos to turn into thriving colonies. In the Canaries, and then in the Caribbean, Castilians found inhabited islands to be forcibly subjugated, settled, and ruthlessly exploited. In the many islands of the North Atlantic – Iceland, the Faroes, Shetland, the Hebrides, Lofoten, Orkney – the many coastal communities of northern Europe had found important centres of food production and exchange.[28] From the perspective of Portugal, Castile, or England around 1500, we can see that Newfoundland fits into a wider pattern of island-centred encounters and colonization. As John Gillis has pointed out, islands held a particularly strong hold on the late fifteenth-century imagination of many Europeans, and islands were seen as crucial to the early development of the Atlantic world.[29] Gillis and Stefan Halikowski Smith have described fifteenth and sixteenth century Europeans as possessed by "insulamania," a manic obsession with islands, that approached a series of utopian projects (including Thomas More's fictional island *Utopia*) for their development.[30] So powerful was this mania that it

spawned an entire literary genre in sixteenth century Venice. *Isolario*, a kind
of atlas and geographical treatise devoted entirely to the islands of the world,
were drafted and printed by several different authors in that city.[31] Portuguese
and Castilian experience had largely been on tropical and temperate islands
in the mid-Atlantic and Caribbean, shaping an assumption that Atlantic islands were meant to have a mild climate and fertile soil. As of 1511, after all,
almost the total of Iberian experience on islands spaces had been in temperate,
resource-rich archipelagos. Geopolitics was interpreted through the lens of
access to Atlantic archipelagoes and wishful thinking about insular climates
at the turn of the sixteenth century.

Such thoughts about island spaces rested upon a basic assumption that the
northwest Atlantic would be an extension of the Iberian Atlantic, either a Por-
tuguese- or a Castilian-controlled space, rather than an open fishery. This fit
an established fifteenth-century pattern of Portuguese and Castilian overseas
expansion, and there was every expectation that it would carry over to the
north Atlantic. Many of the earliest European visitors to the northwest Atlantic
were Iberian, and many of the earliest fishworkers as well. Iberian languages
are written on the landscapes of Newfoundland and Labrador, and in the sixteenth century the Portuguese "Terra Nova" was widely used as a name for
the fisheries. Some maps from the early sixteenth century show the Caribbean
and the northwest Atlantic together as Iberian – variously Castilian or Portuguese – spaces in a new imperial framework.[32] The attempts to create a New
Hispaniola or a New Madeira reflected these assumptions.

The early attempts to explore and settle the islands of the northwest Atlantic
could not be disentangled from a wider Atlantic experience. The Corte Real
brothers, who are responsible for putting the northwest Atlantic squarely on
the European map at the turn of the sixteenth century, were themselves from
an Atlantic lineage. Their family had settled in the Azores during the fifteenth
century, shock-troops in the Portuguese quest to seize and settle the insular
mid-Atlantic. Their father may even have helped the Danish crown re-explore
Iceland and Greenland in the 1470s.[33] Azoreans are known to have worked
with Bristol merchants and the Portuguese crown to outfit some of the first
voyages to the northwest Atlantic – Labrador is said to have been named after
one of them, João Fernandes the *lavrador* (farmer-settler). Decades later, when
the Portuguese crown licensed João Fagundes to plant a colony at Terra Nova,
it would be Azorean settlers who were to be transported across the sea.[34] From

one Atlantic island to the next, colonization begat colonization. This pattern held true more broadly. If Zuan Caboto had gained his maritime experience in the Mediterranean, his Bristolian crew had certainly sailed the northern Atlantic. The Ango family of Dieppe, which dispatched several voyages to the northwest Atlantic in the first decades of the sixteenth century, was also outfitting voyages to the Levant, Atlantic coastal cities, even Sumatra.[35]

As a permanent European presence coalesced in the northwest Atlantic, routes to and from Newfoundland were shaped by wider Atlantic currents and events. The Saintongeois mariner Jean Alfonse noted that the Azores were "halfway along the route between Newfoundland and Portugal," perhaps implying that ships leaving Lisbon or Porto stopped at the Azores en route to the fishery.[36] When navigators like Giovanni Verrazano or Estevão Gomes explored the northwest Atlantic, they started in the Caribbean, moving from one colonial project to the other.[37] When John Rut's 1527 expedition to Newfoundland fell apart, he sailed south to the Castilian Caribbean to find safety, instead of taking the trade winds home to England.[38] Mariners, merchants, and colonists reached Newfoundland from other parts of the emerging Atlantic world, not from Europe alone.

The dream of Agramonte in 1511 reminds us that the creation of a European presence at Newfoundland did not happen spontaneously but was shaped by decades of experience in every corner of the Atlantic basin. It was also, importantly, something which was in flux and contingent. Newfoundland was not fated to be the site of a major commercial fishery. Amongst the earliest European reactions to encountering the northwest Atlantic was a desire to recreate Madeira or Hispaniola, not Iceland. We can see why they failed to realize those dreams – climate, ecology, and economics would always be acting against them – but that does not mean we should overlook the many futures Agramonte and others saw for Newfoundland at the start of the sixteenth century.

FAR-FLUNG FISHWORKERS

What put an end to the dreams of island colonies in the northwest Atlantic were the actions of largely anonymous fishworkers who sailed to Newfoundland even as Agramonte, Fagundes, and others were debating its future. The waters around Newfoundland in the early sixteenth century were worked by thousands of like mariners, most of whom are entirely unknown to history, who came from across Europe. Most came from marginal coastal communities across Europe's "frayed Atlantic edge," small outports and villages which otherwise would play no part in the grand narrative of Atlantic history.[39] They were not so different from the likewise anonymous English fishworkers whose daring voyages to Iceland in 1415 had spurred complaints from Denmark. In the early Atlantic there was still room and opportunity for them to create new spaces beyond the reach of empire and to find solutions to the widespread problems of food insecurity which plagued their homes.

In the winter of 1514, a group of monks living on the northern coast of Brittany created a record which laid out their grievances against the residents of the small outport of Île-de-Bréhat. The short but fierce complaint has survived in written form, a record of how one community saw the changing face of fish production in the early Atlantic. The official cause of the complaint was that the men of the Île-de-Bréhat were failing to pay the required fees when they brought in catches of sea fish. But the text also alludes to the fact that the fishworkers were venturing to fish along "the coast of Brittany, Terra Nova (*la Terre-Neuffve*) and Iceland, amongst others (*que ailleurs*)."[40] One small community was dispatching ships across the Atlantic Ocean, up to Iceland, and all along Europe's coast. In pursuit of food and security, which so many parts of Europe lacked in the early sixteenth century, these fishworkers ventured far afield to many different places.

The men of Bréhat had good reason to turn to the sea in the fifteenth century. From the mid-fifteenth century onward, European populations began to grow significantly, part of the slow recovery from the mid-fourteenth century disasters of plague, war, and famine. By the early sixteenth century population growth problems, especially in urbanized areas, had become acute. Things were made worse by repeated cycles of conflict, from the numerous Anglo–French conflicts to the systematic Habsburg–Valois wars. The climate anomaly known as the Spörer Minimum lasted from roughly 1430 to 1550, plunging the northern hemisphere into a sharp, deep downturn in temperatures.[41] Northwest Europe was suddenly colder, wetter, and more tempestuous than in previous centuries, putting added strain on food production. Agricultural production was disrupted even as it was needed most, and many of the early mariners to visit Newfoundland must have sailed from ports hard-pressed by population growth and poor harvests. Together these different pressures led to widespread problems of food insecurity. The vast biological resources of the eastern Atlantic were an easily accessible solution. Marine food could be produced in large quantities, preserved, and shipped across time and space to alleviate hunger and malnutrition in northwest Europe and the Mediterranean. This was why the men of Bréhat were sailing so far afield in pursuit of fish.

What did *que ailleurs* look like to these fishworkers? It encompassed a wide world of other New-found-lands, some far beyond European waters. Sailing south from Lisbon in 1501, the ship carrying the famed navigator Amerigo Vespucci to the Americas passed close by the coast of Africa. Before picking up the trade winds, Vespucci's crew worked their way along a barren stretch of coast where the white sands of the Sahara met the open expanse of the Atlantic Ocean. It was here, as he remarked in a later letter, "in which coast we made our fishery, for a sort of fish which is called *pargos*, staying there three days."[42] Vespucci had likely stopped at the Rio do Ouro, a point on the Saharan coast where the oceans produced a rich ecosystem that provided an abundance of fish well-suited to catching and preservation.[43] Vespucci was not the only captain to make use of the fishing grounds along the coast of Saharan Africa. A half century later an anonymous Portuguese mariner, in a surviving letter, described stopping at the same spot en route to the *feitoria* on São Tomé island. Like Vespucci he found good and plentiful fish, stating that "And near this coast, if it seems good and the sea is calm, in the span of four hours, with net or with only long, thin lines with all manner of hooks attached, which are dropped into the sea, they catch as many fish as they have need, because they cannot lower many ropes into the sea, that immediately on all of their hooks they find fattened fish and some big ones and some small ones."[44] Like Vespucci, the anonymous mariner caught and salted fish along the Saharan coast before heading on his way to other parts of the Atlantic basin.

There is in fact quite abundant evidence for not merely stopover fishing but a regular, seasonal commercial European fishery along the coast of Saharan Africa.[45] As early as the 1450s a Venetian observer wrote that "All along this coast we find a great fishery [*grandissima pescaria*] and no end of diverse and excellent fish."[46] By the 1500s residents of Lisbon knew that at the Rio do Ouro "There is here a great fishery."[47] In the 1550s the Saintongeois navigator and geographer Jean Alfonse gave special mention of the fishery in his new

geographical treatise of the Atlantic. He advised his readers that along the
Saharan coast "And all this coast is low-lying, sandy, and along it there is a
great fishery for all sorts of fish. And here come ships out of Andalusia and
Portugal to the fishery."[48] In a different work he described nearby Arguim Bay
as "a good port filled with good fishing."[49] In the 1550s an English traveller
stated that "Seuen or eight leagues off from the riuer del Oro or Cape de las
Barbas, there vse many Spaniardes and Portugals to trade for fishing, during
the moneth of Nouember."[50] That fishworkers were drawn to this patch of
coast is not surprising. The cool Canary Current coursed southward along
the coast, enriching the waters with resource-rich upswells much as the cold
and southbound Labrador current would at Newfoundland. A wide variety
of species – porgy, dogfish, mullet, tuna, and others – were dry-salted or pick-
led in barrels to be brought back to Lisbon, Seville, and elsewhere. The voyage
was long and arduous, probably a month out and back, and required navigating the tricky Cape Bojador. Mariners nonetheless made the long round
trip every year, exploiting seasonal cycles of fish migration to provide a steady
stream of salt-cured fish for markets in southern Iberia. We also know that
there were sealing operations along the Saharan coast, especially in Arguim
Bay. Portuguese mariners sought seals for the leather which could be made
from their skin and the oil from their fat.[51] So successful were Portuguese ships
that by 1494 Castilians were trying to cut in on the action, prompting heated
negotiations which led to a Treaty of Tordesillas to manage the claims.[52]
Columbus himself and his crew had visited the Rio do Ouro fisheries, and his
famous ships were manned by fishworkers.[53] By the time that Vespucci sailed
south to the Americas, fishing was already closely associated with the dry,
sandy Saharan coast.

Whereas most fifteenth-century fisheries were associated with a place already inhabited by Europeans, at Rio do Ouro fishing took place entirely removed from any permanent European settlement. Although nearby Arguim
Bay had a small *feitoria*, the Rio do Ouro would not see a European colony
until the nineteenth century. The terrain was too inhospitable, the opportunities for exchange too paltry, and the climate too harsh to justify a year-round
presence. This was not the initial plan, for the first Portuguese voyagers to the
Rio do Ouro had come not for fish but for trade. The very name River of Gold
reflects an aspiration that the waterway would lead Europeans towards the
gold-bearing trade routes of the Sahara.[54] Along the Sahara coast the Por-

tuguese found itinerant Idzagen communities which were willing to trade, and it was on the banks of the Rio do Ouro that the first recorded purchase of sub-Saharan African slaves by Portuguese slave-traders took place. As would be the case at Newfoundland a half-century later, the dreams of commerce never materialized: the Idzagen had little to offer and less interest in a permanent Portuguese presence. As Portuguese mercantile interests moved elsewhere, fishworkers filled the vacuum. In so doing, Iberian mariners were able to maintain a permanent European presence in a region which was otherwise overlooked and abandoned by the emerging Atlantic empires. Here on the long coast between powerful Morocco and the vibrant Senegambian delta, fishworkers carved out a niche for themselves which endured across the sixteenth century. Nearly the same process would take place in the northwest Atlantic in the early sixteenth century. The earliest expeditions to Newfoundland explicitly sought trade, but by the 1510s few merchants saw any point in investing in commercial ventures in the region.[55] As Caboto, Corte Real, and others failed to find worthwhile opportunities, they left space for fishworkers to establish themselves instead.

Saltfish production, commercial fishing, seasonal rhythms, sealing, the failure of trade, a lack of European settlements, a rugged and inhospitable coast: the Rio do Ouro is so fascinating because it has so much in common with Newfoundland but in a completely unexpected setting. It certainly seemed this way to contemporaries: at the end of the sixteenth century a French author remarked, "In Galicia … they have Caravels and sail as far as Cap Blanc in Africa to fish for dogfish and mullet and other fish which they salt and dry in the sun, just as one makes saltcod at *Terre Neufves*."[56] One Spanish author even thought that the Portuguese had come to Morocco in the fifteenth century specifically to find *bacalao*, codfish, a food associated with Newfoundland.[57] Yet we must realize that the Rio do Ouro fisheries were considerably older. Whereas clear evidence of a fishery in the northwest Atlantic dates to around 1505, as early as the 1450s Portuguese fishworkers were systematically fishing the Saharan coast. In the long run, connections between the far north Atlantic and the tropics would be more explicit: by the seventeenth century Basque whalers were hunting their prey off of Brazil, having carried their experience from Labrador southward.[58] At the same time, the Newfoundland fisheries would increasingly rely on salt taken from the Cabo Verde archipelago, and merchants would resell their catch in the Caribbean. At the dawn of the sixteenth century, however, the connections were limited primarily to parallel processes of European mariners establishing permanent fisheries on far-off coasts. From the perspective of the Rio do Ouro, familiar elements of the early history of Newfoundland seem like they were borrowed from African experiences or at least developed in different locations simultaneously. If we wish to de-centre and rethink the story of Newfoundland, paying more attention to the fifteenth-century history of places like the Rio do Ouro is a good place to start.

Before there was Newfoundland there was the Rio do Ouro, and before fishworkers went west to find their catch they went south. By 1514 they were sailing in many directions at once, north to Iceland and west to Newfoundland as well as south to Africa. As Vespucci and the men of Bréhat could attest, European fishworkers engineered a revolution in maritime food production over the course of the fifteenth century, one which reached a culminating point in the first half of the sixteenth century. These were multinational, complex, and highly capitalized oceanic fisheries which focused on the conversion of pelagic species into preserved foodstuffs. Though each fishery followed its own history and served particular slices of the European population across the board this expansion was marked by similar patterns: more intensive fishing by more ships, a focus on pelagic species, a focus on preserving fish for export over long distances, and the use of increasingly sophisticated financial and organizational techniques.[59] This process long predated the first encounters with Newfoundland, so that by 1514, when the monks of Beauport put their complaints to paper, the eastern Atlantic basin was already blanketed with commercial fisheries by European mariners. From Norway in the north to the Sahara in the south, from as far west as Greenland and as far east as Russia, Europeans sought food on the Ocean Sea.

Compared to Newfoundland (at least before the 1550s) many of these fishing operations were quite large. In 1535 an English official reported "600 sail" of fishing ships operated in Ireland.[60] By the 1570s it was reported that 600 Spanish fishing ships alone visited southwest Ireland every year, a fleet double the size of that at Newfoundland.[61] The Irish Sea fisheries were especially important for Basque fishworkers, often those from the same communities which dispatched ships to the northwest Atlantic.[62] By the 1560s the North Sea herring fleet may have numbered 700 ships, double the size of the Newfoundland fleet but comprised of much smaller craft.[63] By the early 1520s English sources make reference to an "Iceland fleet" which returned each year.[64] In 1528 a count of merchant ships in England was undertaken by the crown, which showed that East Anglian towns possessed 150 ships dedicated to the Icelandic trade.[65] Such operations flooded the cities of northwest Europe and the Mediterranean with preserved fish, so that in the marketplace dried cod from Shetland or Iceland competed directly with *bacalao* and *morue verte* from Newfoundland. Crucially, this far-ranging fishwork of the fifteenth century built up a layer of practical, vernacular knowledge about the sea, fish, and the fish trade which was essential for success in the northwest Atlantic.[66] The hundreds of ships that plied the waves of southern Ireland or the Algarve developed techniques, standards, and deep pools of practical skills which were applied to the cod-rich waters of Newfoundland after 1505. There would be no Newfoundland without these other fisheries.

The exploitation of fish stocks in the northwest Atlantic took place in a context of thriving, expanding commercial fishing across the seas – offering both a template and sources of competition which shaped the worldview of the first mariners to visit Newfoundland. The successful creation of a commercial fishery in the northwest Atlantic was predicated on the relative ease with which techniques and technology from the eastern Atlantic could be adapted at Newfoundland. The fifteenth century saw the refinement of commercial fishing as an industrial enterprise. Basic techniques for catching and preserving fish were honed in places like the Irish Sea, the Algarve, and Iceland. The dry-salting of codfish had been practiced in Ireland and elsewhere before 1500 and proved highly effective in the northwest Atlantic. The shipboard brining of cod in barrels to make a "wet" cured fish, known as *morue verte* in France where it was most popular, was an established technique for quickly preserving cod by the fifteenth century.[67] The growth of fishing at Newfoundland was predicated on the existence of an already-robust salt industry in the Bay of Biscay, which had developed in tandem with growing fishing operations before 1500. Fishing at Newfoundland did not require specially built ships, so that vessels could be outfitted for the fishery with relative ease. The size of ships varied considerably, and it was not uncommon in the early sixteenth century for vessels of only sixty tons burthern to make the transoceanic crossing. This allowed for great flexibility, as merchants could move ships in and out of the fishery without having to worry about reconfiguring them before or after each season.

Above all, Newfoundland benefitted from the growth of an experienced, knowledgeable maritime labour pool along the coasts and rivers of northwest Europe in the fifteenth and early sixteenth century. Newfoundland crews were typically recruited locally and within kin networks, exploiting the close-knit bonds of coastal communities and their shared knowledge about sailing and food.[68] Fishwork itself required skill and rewarded experience but was not a specialist industry. Fish were caught and processed using relatively simple tools: metal hooks, handlines, knives, and barrels. This stands in contrast to alternative industries like the Basque whaling industry, which required considerably more specialized equipment and infrastructure and which employed specialists like harpooners or flencers.[69] Instead, individuals passed in and out of the Newfoundland cod trade, even if a core of dedicated mariners maintained hard-won knowledge about the fishery over generations.[70] One mariner might serve a season at Newfoundland and never return; another might work the waters of the northwest Atlantic for several decades straight. This was the great strength of the Newfoundland fishery: it allowed for flexibility, competing with and drawing from other maritime endeavours across the Atlantic basin.

The rise of a commercial fishery at Newfoundland before 1550 was the capstone of the new fishing landscape and ensured that sixteenth-century consumers had access to a wide variety of marine food from across the Atlantic basin. The new, sixteenth-century fishing system can be seen in the outfitting of two caravels in Seville in 1563.[71] Part of the *Carrera de Indias*, they were outfitted using the city's ample and sophisticated provisioning infrastructure. The ships were loaded with smoked sardines from Galicia (eight thousand), dry-salted cod (*bacalao*, twenty-four dozen), and porgies (fifteen dozen). The sardines were purchased from Andrés Cotanda, a Valencian merchant; the *bacalao* from the French merchant Martin Sáez; the porgies from the Portuguese resident Vicente Yáñez. Thus each of Iberia's major fish sources were represented on the same ships: sardines from the local fisheries, cod from Bretons or Normans in the north Atlantic (Newfoundland or Ireland), porgies from the Portuguese in northwest Africa. This was typical of how Europeans interacted with the Atlantic Ocean in the sixteenth century, drawing simultaneously on multiple sources of food and resources.

ATLANTIC NEWFOUNDLAND

The experiences of 1415, of Ceuta and Iceland, hang over the different moments in Newfoundland's history which I have highlighted above. The descendants of Iberian conquerors who stormed Ceuta, seized Madeira and founded Arguim were those who dreamt of a New Hispaniola and New Madeira in the northwest Atlantic. The fishworkers who sailed to Iceland in 1415 were a first wave of European mariners who intensified and ruthlessly exploited the bountiful waters of the Atlantic, from the Rio do Ouro to *Terre Neufve* and *que ailleurs*. This fifteenth-century legacy was also very real to our anonymous Norman mariner whose text opened this chapter. On the Guinea Coast and in Brazil he was following in the wake of Portuguese navigators, traders, and colonizers who had first reached the region in the mid-fifteenth century as part of their post-Ceuta expansion. At *Terre Neufve* he met and worked alongside fishworkers whose parents and grandparents had worked the fisheries of the eastern Atlantic. What these moments and connections stress is the way in which the early Newfoundland fisheries were embedded in a history of the early Atlantic which was far-ranging and dynamic.

Such experiences cut both ways. European activity at Rio do Ouro, Iceland, Ceuta, Brittany, and elsewhere were not merely legacies but ongoing experiences which shaped and were shaped by Newfoundland in real time. Rising activity in the northwest Atlantic drew mariners, ships, and capital away from other fisheries. The failed colonial experiments in the northwest Atlantic were quickly abandoned as more enterprising opportunities appeared in the Caribbean, mainland Americas, West Africa, and beyond. In turn, the success of the fishery in the northwest Atlantic drew ships, mariners, and capital away from other trade routes. In 1560 an English mariner returning from a voyage to West Africa remarked that he had sailed for twenty-eight years as a mariner. During his long tenure he had served on ships to "the Newe Fownde land, Russia and other places."[72] His view of Newfoundland, then, was shaped by a lifetime of sailing between different corners of the Atlantic and Arctic, linking them with European ships. Certainly, his experience would have resonated with the anonymous mariner in Rouen who penned his note *pour la terre neufve*. This then is an essential point: we must see that Newfoundland arose out of an early Atlantic world but also remained embedded in it. It was created out of the widespread experiences and legacies of European activity on the Atlantic Ocean which stretched back to 1415. Yet it was also an active and evolving node within these new networks and histories, shaped by and shaping events elsewhere, a point where many strands of history were woven together.

These twisting histories, routes, and legacies of the early Atlantic ultimately led to the waters of Newfoundland. More than anything, this chapter points to the experiences Europeans brought with them to Newfoundland and how those experiences may have shaped their actions. This is why, as I have argued, we should see Newfoundland as a culminating, rather than a starting, point – those who made a fishery were building on deeper processes of maritime expansion and food production. The history of the Newfoundland fisheries does not end in the mid-sixteenth century, of course. Indeed, the 1540s and '50s marked a kind of turning point, the moment of expansion and acceleration of fishing activity which would bring the fisheries to their height within a few decades.[73] Yet if we wish to understand the origins of a European presence in the northwest Atlantic, we must pay closer attention to the earliest years of European arrival and realize that it was something unique and contingent. It was not clear what Newfoundland's place in the Atlantic was going to be to Europeans of the early sixteenth century – a new Hispaniola? Iceland? Rio do Ouro? Madeira? Atlantic Newfoundland was something that had to be created, not found, in a tempestuous early sixteenth century. Mariners at Newfoundland drew on experiences at Ceuta and Iceland but connected their ongoing actions to Brazil, Guinea, and elsewhere. These are perspectives which only become clear, as I have tried to suggest, if we take a longer chronological and geographical framework for our study of early Newfoundland. They are nonetheless perspectives which allow us to see the northwest Atlantic as Europeans did in the early sixteenth century: a place of many possibilities, connected to a vast and expanding world.

NOTES

1 Bibliothèque national de France, Ms. Fr. 24269, "*Regyme pour congnoistre la latitude de la region et aussi la haulteur de la ligne equinotialle sur nostre orison.*" It was probably written in the mid-1540s, perhaps 1544, judging by the dates in the almanac. We do not know for sure who wrote this text, though several possibilities have been suggested. Names are written on the last page,

but we cannot be certain if these refer to the author. The text is likely to have been produced in Rouen, a city which we know was sending ships to New-foundland, Brazil, and Africa in the early sixteenth century. On the Norman context, see Bréard et al., *Documents relatifs à la marine normande*.

2 On the vocabularies see: Dalby and Hair, "'Le Langaige Du Bresil'"; Dalby and Hair, "'Le langaige de Guynee.'"

3 In this essay I use "Newfoundland" not to designate the island of Newfound-land or the modern Canadian province of Newfoundland and Labrador. In-stead, it is meant to signify the northwest Atlantic more generally, roughly the coasts and waters of what is today Atlantic Canada. This was often the way the term was used in the sixteenth century. Many alternative names were used in-stead of Newfoundland. Cartographers, especially in Iberia and the Mediter-ranean, preferred to call the region *Bacalao* or *Terra de Bacalao*, meaning "land of the cod." Mariners themselves preferred variations of *Terra Nova* – *Terra-nova*, *Terre Neufve*, *Tierra nueva*, *terra nuova*. I use Newfoundland for simplic-ity's sake but mean it to be understood in the same broad ways as *Terra Nova* or *Bacalao*. See Bouchard, "Towards Terra Nova," 71–115.

4 I follow Jennifer Lee Johnson in using the term "fishworker" to describe those who catch and process fish. The term stresses the labour involved with not merely catching but salting, drying, and packing fish, along with the labour of oceanic voyages. It avoids some of the vagueness of "fisherman" or "fisher," which has been applied to many different types and scales of maritime food production. Although European fishworkers at Newfoundland were all male, an issue which Peter Pope has explored, I prefer a gender-neutral term inas-much as we know that European women were involved with the fishery as investors, outfitters, and ship owners. See Johnson, "Eating and Existence"; Pope, "Fisher Men at Work."

5 On Newfoundland's place in this, see Pope *Fish into Wine*. See too, Davis, *The Rise of the Atlantic Economies*; McCusker and Morgan, *The Early Modern Atlantic Economy*; Armitage and Braddick, *The British Atlantic World*.

6 A multinational, seasonal fishing operation involving Breton, Portuguese, Norman, and English fishworkers was probably underway by 1505, and from the 1520s onward they were joined by Basque, Saintongeois, Galician, and As-turian mariners in a flotilla which eventually comprised several hundred ships a year. Although the post-1600 history of the fisheries continues to attract the bulk of scholarly attention, our understanding of the sixteenth century has

been greatly enhanced in the past couple of decades by the work of historians
and archaeologists such as Peter Pope, Brad Loewen, Laurier Turgeon, Michael
Barkham, Darlene Abreu-Fereira. On the early fishery at Newfoundland and
its origins see Bouchard, "Towards Terra Nova"; Turgeon, "French Fishers, Fur
Traders, and Amerindians"; Pope, "Transformation of the Maritime Cultural
Landscape"; Innis, *The Cod Fisheries*. In the past decade much of the work on
Newfoundland has been undertaken by archaeologists, who remain the most
active in expanding our knowledge of the early fisheries. See for instance the
excellent essays in Loewen and Chapdelaine, *Contact in the 16th Century*.

7 For some examples of Newfoundland as a starting point for fishing, see Bolster,
The Mortal Sea; Innis, *The Cod Fisheries*; La Morandière, *La pêche française*.
On whaling and the fur trade, see Jackson, *The British Whaling Trade*; Grenier,
et al., *The Underwater Archaeology of Red Bay*; Tuck and Grenier, *Red Bay,
Labrador*; Delâge, *Bitter Feast*; Allaire, "Le commerce des fourrures à Paris." On
empire, see Morison, *The European Discovery of America*; Biggar, *The Precursors
of Jacques Cartier*; White, *A Cold Welcome*; Gordon, "Heroes, History, and Two
Nationalisms"; Pope, *The Many Landfalls of John Cabot*.

8 Gimlette, *Theatre of Fish*, xvii.

9 On Atlantic history in general, see Thornton, *A Cultural History*; Greene and
Morgan, *Atlantic History*; Brown and Miller, *Princeton Companion to Atlantic
History*; Canny and Morgan, *Oxford Handbook of the Atlantic World*; Bolster,
"Putting the Ocean in Atlantic History"; Linebaugh and Rediker, *Many-
Headed Hydra*; Butel, *The Atlantic*.

10 Jeffrey Bolster attempted to make the northwest Atlantic fisheries part of a
bigger Atlantic story in his influential *The Mortal Sea*. In practice, however, his
approach reinforced the idea that Newfoundland was part of a distinctly
northern (read: Anglo-) Atlantic, a world of English and New England fishermen. More compellingly, Peter Pope has drawn our attention to the Atlantic
dimensions of the Newfoundland fishery and plantation at its height in the
seventeenth century. This nonetheless focuses on Newfoundland's place in a
post-1600 Atlantic which was already functioning as an integrated economic
and social system. Pope, "Outport Economics"; Pope, *Fish into Wine*.

11 Despite the long-acknowledged role played by Iberian, especially Basque,
mariners in the northwest Atlantic, there has been little attempt to connect experiences at Newfoundland to the Caribbean, Brazil, West Africa, and the At-

lantic islands. Even as Iberian historians have radically revised our understanding of the early Atlantic, especially through the "New Conquest History,"
historians of Newfoundland remain disconnected from these wider historiographical currents. Restall, "The New Conquest History." See also, de Avilez
Rocha, "The Pinzones and the Coup"; Stevens-Arroyo, "The Inter-
Atlantic Paradigm"; Wheat, *Atlantic Africa*; De Avilez Rocha, "Politics of
the Hinterland."

12 Historians have done little to systematically interrogate and explain an early
Atlantic, though some work has been done on a "medieval Atlantic." I take as a
starting point Felipe Fernandez-Armesto's crucial study of late medieval European activity in the Atlantic. This has recently been complemented by a useful
collection of essays on the "medieval" Atlantic, focusing on the Norse as well
as Iberia. Fernandez-Armesto, *Before Columbus*; Hudson, *Studies in the
Medieval Atlantic*.

13 On Ceuta and early Portuguese expansion see Disney, *A History of Portugal*;
Bethencourt and Curto, *Portuguese Oceanic Expansion*; Godinho, *Os Descobrimentos*; Marques, *A Expansão Quatrocentista*; Fernandez-Armesto, *Before
Columbus*. On the Canaries, see Abulafia, *The Discovery of Mankind*; Fernán-
dez-Armesto, *The Canary Islands after the Conquest*.

14 British Library, Cotton MS Nero B III No. 29, "A Privy Seal, for Orders to Pro-
hibit English Ships from Sailing towards Iceland. (Lat.) Nov. 28, 1415." (n.d.).
For some context, see the discussion of English fishing in Iceland in Prowse,
A History of Newfoundland, 24–9.

15 On the Iceland fishery see Gardiner, "The Character of Commercial Fishing,"
22; Gardiner and Mehler, "English and Hanseatic Trading"; Jones, "England's
Icelandic Fishery"; Power and Postan, *Studies in English Trade*.

16 On First Nations in Newfoundland, see Moussette, "A Universe Under Strain";
Laurier Turgeon, "French Fishers, Fur Traders, and Amerindians"; Loewen
and Chapdelaine, *Contact in the 16th Century*; Brad Loewen, "Sea Change,"
in this volume.

17 On the Norse, see: Pettigrew and Mancke, "European Expansion"; Fitzhugh
and Ward, *Viking*; Seaver, *The Frozen Echo*. For a recent take on the global
significance of the Norse voyages, see Hansen, *The Year 1000*. For a description
of the literary basis of the Vinland voyages and the long-term impact on European and American historical memory, see Kolodny, *In Search of First Contact*.

18 On Caboto and other early expeditions see Jones, "Alwyn Ruddock"; Allen, "From Cabot to Cartier"; Morison, *The European Discovery of America*; Condon and Jones, "William Weston."

19 For a discussion of Caboto and the problem of primary sources, see Pope, *The Many Landfalls of John Cabot*.

20 Biggar, *Precursors of Jacques Cartier*, Doc. XXXII, 102–11.

21 Ibid., 104.

22 On the early Castilian experience at Hispaniola see Deagan and Cruxent, *Columbus's Outpost Among the Taínos*; Abulafia, *The Discovery of Mankind*.

23 See: Biggar, *Precursors of Jacques Cartier*, Doc. XVI, "Letters Patent from King Emmanuel to John Fernandez. 28 Oct., 1499," 31–2; Doc. XXXIX, "Confirmation of the Letters Patent to Fagundes, March/May 1521," 127–31. Both documents are royal orders granting Corte Real and Fagundes rights to govern any islands or lands they discover "*com aquellas remdas, homrras, proveitos e imtaresses com que temos dadas as capitanyas das nossas Ilhas da Madeira e das outras*," and "*asy e pella maneira que teemos dadas as capitanias da nosa ilha da Madeira e das outras ilhas*," respectively.

24 Biggar, *Precursors of Jacques Cartier*, 31–2, Letters Patent from King Emmanuel to Joao Fernandez, 28 Oct. 1499. "*Sse queira trabalhar de hyr biscar e descobrir algumas ilhas de nossa conquista aa sua custa ... a nos praz e lhe prometemos por esta de lhe darmos como de fecto daremos a capitania de quallquer Ilha ou Ilhas, asy povoadas como despovoadas, que elle decobrill e achar novamente, e esto com aquellas remdas, homrras, proveitos e imtaresses com que temos dadas as capitanyas das nossas Ilhas da Madeira e das outras*."

25 "Islands and lands ... [but] this should not include the first land of Brazil, running from north to south, but instead towards the north (*ilhas e terras ... nem sse entendesse esta mercee da primeira terra do Brasill, da banda do norte des contra o sull, ssenam pera o norte*)." Biggar, *Precursors of Jacques Cartier*, Doc. XXXIX, 127–31, "Confirmation of the Letters patent to Fagundes."

26 Ibid. "*asy e pella maneira que teemos dadas as capitanias da nosa ilha da madeira e das outras ilhas*."

27 Biggar, *Precursors of Jacques Cartier*, Doc. VI–VII, 12–13.

28 Bouchard, "Shetland Sheep and Azorean Wheat."

29 Gillis, *Islands of the Mind*. See also, Duncan, *Atlantic Islands*; Phillips Jr, "Africa and the Atlantic Islands"; Royle, "A Human Geography of Islands." Kleinschmidt, *Ruling the Waves*.

30 Smith, "The Mid-Atlantic Islands," 27.

31 Stouraiti, "Talk, Script and Print."

32 Most notably the famous Cantino Planisphere, which shows the Caribbean as "Antilhas de Rey de Castilla" and Newfoundland as "Terra del Rey de Portugal." Biblioteca Estense, Modena. On "Terra Nova," see endnote 3 above.

33 On the Corte Real family see: Harisse, *Les Corte-Reals et leurs voyage*; Biggar, *Precursors of Jacques Cartier*; Morison, *European Discovery of America*; Hughes, "'German Discovery of America.'"

34 Biggar, *Precursors of Jacques Cartier*, 195–7.

35 Wintroub, *The Voyage of Thought*.

36 "*Et [les açores] sont en la moictie du chemin de Portugal et da la Terre Neufve.*" Fonteneau and Musset, *La cosmographie*, 134.

37 The outline of most of these voyages and efforts are covered in Morison, *European Discovery of America*. See too, the various documents in Quinn, et al, *New American World*, vol 1.

38 Biggar, *Precursors of Jacques Cartier*, 165–8; Biggar, *An English Expedition*.

39 Gange, *The Frayed Atlantic Edge*. See too, Barry Cunliffe's description of an Atlantic Europe in Cunliffe, *Facing the Ocean*.

40 Archives départmentales Cote d'Armor, H 69. A transcript can be found in Biggar, *Precursors of Jacques Cartier*, 118–23; Translation in Quinn, et al., *New American World*, 4: 87.

41 Camenisch et al., "The 1430s"; Ogurtsov, "The Spörer Minimum Was Deep." On climate in the fifteenth and sixteenth centuries in general, see: Campbell, *The Great Transition*; Holm, "Climate Change, Big Data"; White, *A Cold Welcome*; Behringer, *A Cultural History of Climate*.

42 *Pargos* likely refers to porgy. The letter is preserved in Ramusio's collection of texts. "*E partimmo di questo porto di Lisbona tre navi di conserva adí X di maggio 1501, e pigliammo nostro pareggio diritti all'isola della Gran Canaria, e passammo senza posare a vista di essa. E di qui fummo costeggiando la costa d'Africa per la parte occidentale, nella qual costa facemmo nostra pescaria, d'una sorte pesci che si chiamano pargos, dove ci tenemmo tre giorni.*" Ramusio, *Navigazioni et viaggi*, 1: 334.

43 The Rio do Ouo roughly corresponds with the site of present-day Dakhla, a major city in Moroccan-occupied Western Sahara.

44 Ramusio, *Navigazioni et viaggi*, 1: 301.

45 The Saharan African fisheries are unfortunately almost entirely unknown in

the English literature on the fifteenth and sixteenth century Atlantic. It is
more familiar to Lusophone and Spanish scholars, though even then there are
few who have studied the fishery thoroughly. See: de Armas, "Las Pesquerías
Españolas"; Pérez, "Las Pesquerías En Berbería"; Godinho, *Os descobrimentos*;
Mattoso, *História de Portugal*; Marques, *A expansão quatrocentista*.

46 "*In tutta questa costa si truova grandissima pescaria e senza fine di diversi e
    buonissimi pesci.*" Ramusio, *Navigazioni et viaggi*, 1: 261.

47 "Esta pesc grade pescaría." Bayerische Staatsbibliothek, Cod. Hisp. 27. Fol. 61.

48 "*Et toute ceste coste est terre basse, sableuse, et y a en elle grand pscherye de toutes
    sortes de poisons. Et icy viennent les navires d'Andélosie et de Portugal à la
    pescherie.*" Fonteneau and Musset, *La cosmographie par Georges Musset*, 327.

49 Alfonse, *Les voyages auantureux*, fol. 49v.

50 Hakluyt and Goldsmid, *The Principal Navigations*, vol XI: Africa. "The second
    voyage to Guinea set out by Sir George Barne, Sir Iohn Yorke, Thomas Lok,
    Anthonie Hickman and Edward Castelin, in the yere 1554. The Captaine
    whereof was M. Iohn Lok."

51 Sealing is mentioned in Godinho, *Os Descobrimentos e a economia mundial*;
    Marques, *A Expansão quatrocentista*; José Mattoso, *História de Portugal*, vol. I.

52 Fernandez de Navarrete, *Colección de los Viages*, No. LXXIV, 131–47.

53 The place of fishworkers in Columbus' voyage has recently been brought to
    our attention in de Avilez Rocha, "The Pinzones and the Coup."

54 On the historical context for early Portuguese activity at Rio do Ouro, see:
    Bennett, *African Kings and Black Slaves*.

55 On early voyages to Newfoundland and their mercantile purposes, see: Allen,
    "From Cabot to Cartier"; Jones, "The Matthew of Bristol"; Andrews, *Trade,
    Plunder, and Settlement*.

56 "*En Galice ya… ont des Carabelles et naviguent iusque au Cap Blanc en Afrique
    pescher des Chiens de mer & des Mulletz, et autres poissons qu'ilz salent et
    sechent au Soleil comme on faict la Morue aux Terres neufves*" Nicolas d'Ar-
    feville, "Extraict Des Observations de NICOLAY D'ARFEVILLE , Daulphinois,
    Premier Cosmographe Du Roy" (1582), Bibliothèque Nationale de France,
    Ms. Fr. 20008, fol. 10r.

57 Describing Cape Aguer in southern Morocco, Luis del Marmol-Caravajal
    wrote in the 1560s: "*El principio de la fundacion desta villa fue un castillo de
    madera que hizo a su costa en el seno de aquella punta un cavallero Portuges lla-
    mado Diego Lopez de Sequera por causa de la pesca de los bacallaos y de otros*

muchos pescados que muerne en aquella mar." Marmol-Caravajal, *Descripcion general de Affrica*, 18v.

58 Vieira, "A Comparative Approach to Historical Whaling Techniques."

59 For some general overviews and more specific case-studies of these fifteenth and sixteenth-century fisheries, see the various essays in: Barrett and Orton, *Cod and Herring*; Holm, *North Atlantic Fisheries*; Sicking and Abreu-Ferreira, *Beyond the Catch*.

60 Carew, *Calendar of the Carew Manuscripts*, 81.

61 Ibid. 422–3. As in the North Sea these were likely smaller vessels than those that went to Terra Nova.

62 This point has been made in Bernard, *Navires et gens de mer*; Huxley, "La industria pesquera."

63 Mitchell. "European Fisheries in Early Modern Europe," 5: 148.

64 For instance, on 2 June 1523, a letter between two English royal officials noted that "Hears that the Scots are going to set forth six or seven ships to the Islands, to intercept the Iceland fleet on their way home." Brewer, *Letters and Papers*, 3: 1287–1303, no. 3071, Surrey to Wolsey.

65 Brewer, *Letters and Papers*, vol. 4: no. 5101, "Shipping." As Wendy Childs has demonstrated, between 1436 and 1484 only 124 vessels are known to have traded at Iceland. This means that the yearly Icelandic fleet in the late 1520s outnumbered all the ships that had made the voyage the previous century. Childs, "England's Icelandic Trade."

66 This point has most clearly been made by Peter Pope in *Fish into Wine*, especially page 30. For more theoretical studies of how knowledge works in fishing communities, see: Acheson, "Anthropology of Fishing"; Berkes, *Sacred Ecology*.

67 References to "green cod" (i.e. *morue verte*) are common in English sources in the fifteenth century. Cf., Harvey, *Living and Dying in England*, 46–7, 226. On *morue verte* see: Turgeon, "Pour redécouvrir notre 16e siècle."

68 In general, recruitment seems to have looked a lot like that described in a later context in Vickers and Walsh, *Young Men and the Sea*. Recruitment in the seventeenth century was likely different from that of the sixteenth; see Bouchard, "Towards Terra Nova," 211–36, for a summary of the sixteenth-century evidence. See too, Turgeon, "French Fishers, Fur Traders, and Amerindians"; Huxley, "La industria pesquera"; Abreu-Ferreira, "Terra Nova Through the Iberian Looking Glass."

69 Barkham, "French Basque 'New Found Land'"; Barkham, "The Basque

Whaling Establishments"; Parks et al., *The Underwater Archaeology of Red Bay*; Tuck and Grenier, *Red Bay, Labrador*; Jong, *Geschiedenis*.

70 On knowledge and skill at the fishery see: Pope, *Fish into Wine*; Pope, "Modernization on Hold"; Mollat, *Histoire des pêches*; Echebarria, *Los Vascos en el Marco*. On knowledge and skill in fisheries in general, see: Acheson, "Anthropology of Fishing"; Charles, "Cognitive Maps of Time and Tide"; Berkes, *Sacred Ecology*.

71 Garcia, "Nuevos datos sobre bastimentos," 471.

72 Blake, ed., *Europeans in West Africa*, doc. 147, 2: 430–1.

73 This point has been made by other scholars of the fishery, most notably Turgeon, "Pour redécouvrir notre 16 siècle."

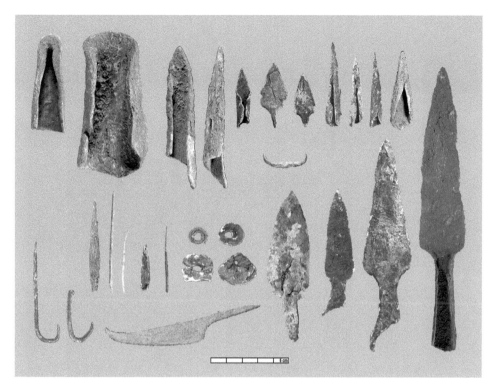

Figure 1.4
A small sample of copper artifacts recovered from the Île aux Allumettes Archaic site in the Ottawa River Valley showing the diversity of ornaments, tools, and weapons that were manufactured and exchanged.

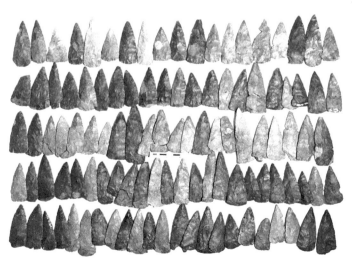

Figure 1.6
Onondaga chert bifacial cache blades recovered from the Early Woodland (Meadowood) period Lambert site in Saint Nicolas, Quebec, near Quebec City. The 109 blades shown here are part of a group of 180 blades that were intentionally burned as part of a burial ritual.

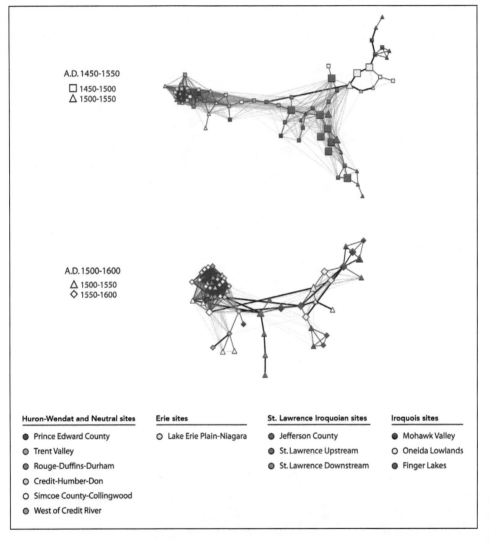

Figure 1.8

Visualization of a social network analysis (SNA) applied to Huron-Wendat, Haudenosaunee (Iroquois) and St Lawrence Iroquoian sites based on decorative attributes on ceramic vessels. The St Lawrence Iroquoians (indicated by red, blue, and orange squares and triangles) occupy a central position in the network (*top*), indicating their role as social brokers until their dispersal at the end of the sixteenth century (*bottom*). Note how the Huron-Wendat sites (*to the left*) seem to constitute a tight and dense network compared to the more diffuse networks of the Haudenosaunee (*to the right*) and St Lawrence Iroquoians.

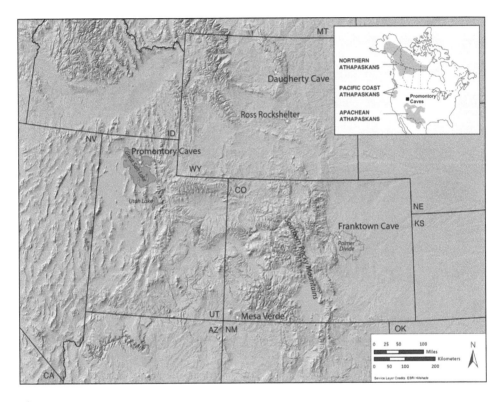

Figure 2.1

A map showing the distribution of sites mentioned in the text in interior western North America. The inset shows the three main geographic areas in which Dene or Athapaskan speakers lived in the nineteenth century.

Figure 2.2
Top, the view from Promontory Cave 1, with Cody Sharphead screening deposits; *bottom left*, Aileen Reilly recovering a bison limb from a multispecies bone bed at her feet in Cave 1; *bottom right*, Bruce Starlight, Tsuut'ina elder and ceremonialist, conferring with Ives over moccasins during one of his visits to Promontory Point.

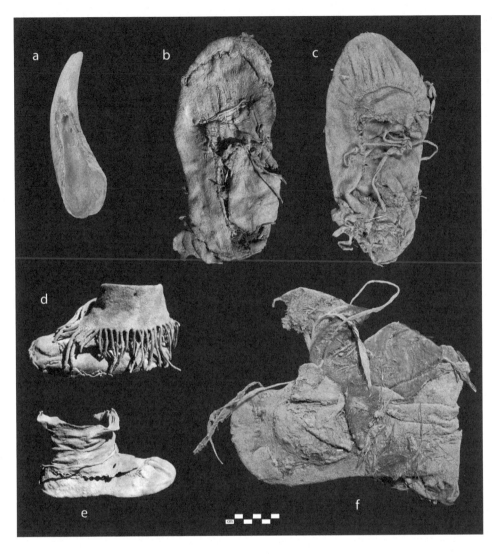

Figure 2.3

a) A bison horn spoon (UMNH 42B01 9501) from Steward's Promontory Cave 1 collections; b) a finely made, quill decorated BSM 2 (Bb) moccasin, UMNH 42B01:10241, radiocarbon dated to 784 ± 28 ¹⁴C yr B.P. (OxA-18162); c) a BSM 2 (Bb) moccasin, UMNH.A.2011.18 42B01:FS173, radiocarbon dated to 706 ± 25 (OxA-25183); d) a BSM 2 (Bb) child's moccasin with fringed ankle wrap, UMNH 42B01:10055, radiocarbon dated to 784 ± 28 ¹⁴C yr B.P.; e) a BSM 2 (Bb) child's moccasin, with higher ankle wrap, UMNH 42B01:10065 radiocarbon dated to 757 ± 23 ¹⁴C yr B.P. (OxA-23921); f) a Promontory Cave 1 moccasin (UMNH.A.8011.18, FS-42B01.801.1) with bison fur lining and ankle wrap.

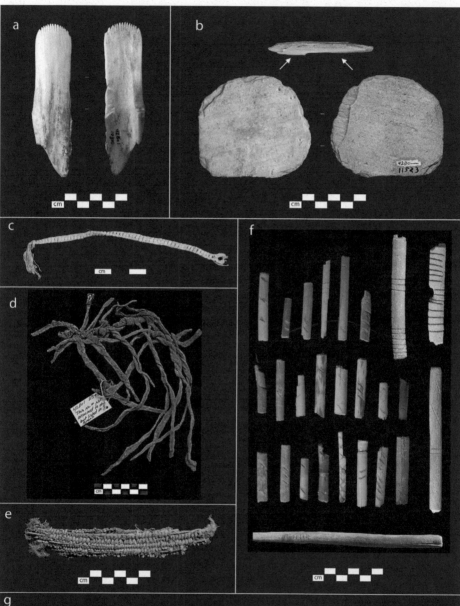

Figure 2.4

a) A finely made bone flesher from Promontory Cave 1 (UMNH 42Bo1 10306); b) a *chi-tho* or tabular biface (UMNH 42Bo5 11523) from Promontory Cave 5; c) UMNH 42Bo1 FS 210, a strand of intricate four-strand plat sinnet of a type known across the Canadian subarctic but unknown in the Great Basin apart from Promontory Cave 1 examples; d) UMNH 42BO1 11595, a lattice-like heavier leather construction, a probable dog travois basket fragment; e) a close-coiled, half rod, non-interlocking stitch, bundle stacked foundation basket fragment dating to 694 ± 24 ^{14}C yr BP (OxA-28441, UMNH 42Bo1 FS 1098, calibrated to AD 1275–1385 [2]) from our Promontory Cave 1 excavations; f) scored cane dice and decorated sticks, among the many Promontory gaming pieces; and g) the limb of a discarded Promontory Cave 1 juniper bow (UMNH 42Bo1 11602.2, perhaps scored to remove or affix a composite backing (b, d, and g).

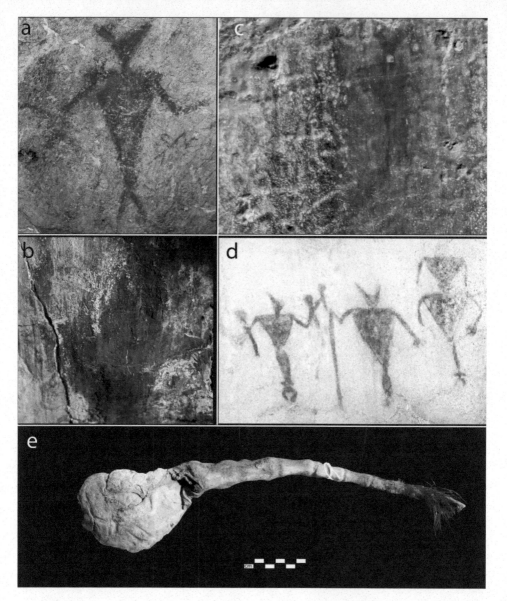

Figure 2.5
Ochre rock art figures from Promontory Cave 1 and Grotto Canyon, Alberta: a) One of the
pictographs from Promontory Cave 1; b) a second more elaborate Fremont rock art figure
from Promontory Cave 1; c) a pictograph figure from Grotto Canyon, near Canmore, Alberta;
d) a line of figures from Grotto Canyon, Alberta, with three likely rattles near the figure on
the left; e) UMNH 42B01 10233, a buffalo tail rattle from Promontory Cave 1.

4

Sea Change: Indigenous Navigation and Relations with Basques around the Gulf of Saint Lawrence, ca. 1500–1700

BRAD LOEWEN

Well before Europeans colonized their shores, Mi'kmaq, Inuit, and Iroquoian peoples around the Gulf of Saint Lawrence had enthusiastically adopted as their own a European device, the small, wooden sailing vessel known to Basques as the *txalupa* and to the French as the *chaloupe*, to trade, gain power, and expand their respective ranges significantly. *Txalupak* (the plural form in Basque) were all-purpose boats that could be rowed or sailed, and they greatly enhanced the seaborne mobility of First Nations around the gulf. These craft enabled Inuit to expand their habitat from Labrador to shores around the northeast arm of the Gulf of Saint Lawrence, known as Grand Bay. They also allowed Mi'kmaq in Acadia to cross Cabot Strait to Newfoundland and to mount raids against rivals across the Gulf of Maine. Not least, *txalupak* played a role in the maritime adaptation of eastern Saint Lawrence Iroquoians after the dispersal of their villages. Indigenous people throughout the Gulf of Saint Lawrence and adjacent Atlantic coasts acquired these boats from Basque mariners who came to these regions from northern Spain and southwest France, in pursuit of cod, whales, seals, and furs every summer from the early sixteenth century on. This chapter explores the changes to Indigenous societies enabled by the *txalupa*'s adoption and the Basque-Indigenous relationships built around this craft.

While Basques likely travelled inland in the sixteenth century and even gained a knowledge of Iroquoian peoples, they showed little interest in lands beyond the saltwater littoral, much less in founding year-round colonial settlements. Because most Basques came from Spain, they could not entertain colonial aspirations in territories claimed by France, a situation that allowed – or required – them to cultivate generally good, and often collaborative, relations with Indigenous peoples. In the absence of settlements, formal claims, royal proclamations, or other writs of Basque colonization, historians have tended to overlook this maritime form of Euro-Indigenous encounter; however, archaeologists have taken a keen interest in Basque-Indigenous relations. In this chapter, the Basques form the backdrop for a new look at three Indigenous groups around the gulf in the sixteenth and seventeenth centuries as they reshaped their maritime world, using new watercraft to adapt to changing circumstances and redraw the Indigenous cultural map.

THE *TXALUPA*

In 1983, Parks Canada archaeologists recovered a well-preserved example of a *txalupa* from the cold waters of Red Bay, Labrador, a major Basque whaling station on the Strait of Belle Isle. The craft seems to have been caught alongside a large whaler as it foundered and sank in 1565. The boat lay crushed beneath the ship's stern flank, and archaeologists were able to recover and reconstruct it (figures 4.1 and 4.2). It measures 8.03 metres in length, 2.01 metres in breadth, and its stem and stern rise in graceful arcs. The lower hull planks made of oak lie edge-to-edge in "carvel" fashion, while the upper planks, made of pine, have lapping edges in the "clinker" style. A mast for a square sail rose at the middle of the boat, and a foremast for a jib stood near the bow. Rigging ropes led through holes in the upper hull planks, so that one or two sailors could handle the craft. The boat also had thole pins for oars and thwarts for four rowers and a tiller at the stern. Used for fishing, whaling, and a host of other utilitarian functions, this versatile craft could accommodate up to eight people or a load of two tons.[1] Records describe voyages of hundreds of kilometres. In 2011, a replica sailed from Québec to Red Bay with a crew of five, reaching sustained speeds of fourteen knots under sail.[2]

These boats travelled across the Atlantic knocked down as kits. Once assembled on the shores of the gulf, they never returned to Europe.[3] Fishing and whaling crews stored them under water over the winter to keep their joints tight and to protect them from the weight of snow. Evidence for these practices

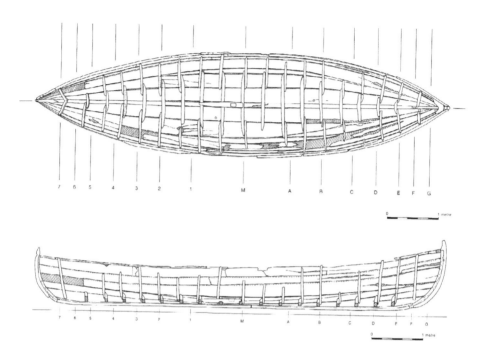

Figure 4.1
Reconstruction of the Red Bay *txalupa* by Parks Canada.

comes from deeds of sale in Europe by which captains and harpooners sold *txalupak* to one another during the winter off-season; the sale documents tell buyers where to find the boats and how to recognize them. At Trepassey, ten fishing *txalupak* marked with "two fishhooks and a bar on the side" found a new owner in 1606.[4] Other sales instructed the buyer to take the boats from Indigenous custodians. At Percé in 1608, two men named Rougefort and Jouanis – a Basque name – handed over two *txalupak* to a new owner.[5] As Nicolas Denys wrote, departing captains left their boats in the hands of Indigenous partners by various arrangements:

> The Natives of the coast use canoes only for rivers, and they all have *chaloupes* for the sea, which they sometimes buy from captains who are about to leave after completing their fishery; but most often, they take them from where the captains hide them on the coast or in ponds, so as

to use them on a later voyage. When the owners … recognize [the *chaloupes*], they make no more ceremony of taking them back than do the Natives in making use of them.[6]

We may estimate that European fisheries annually employed 500 to 1,000 *txalupak* around the Gulf of Saint Lawrence. Each year, captains replaced a third of this fleet, creating a steady supply of used craft that readily found Indigenous takers.[7] By the late sixteenth century, Inuit, Mi'kmaq, Abenaki, and Saint Lawrence Iroquoians had adopted the *txalupa* in numbers that would astound early European colonists.[8] These craft brought considerable prestige and power to their Indigenous owners. Some invested their boats with a totemic quality, as in a moose painted on the sail of a Mi'kmaw *txalupa* from Canso in 1608.[9] The Mi'kmaw chief Messamouët, at La Hève in peninsular

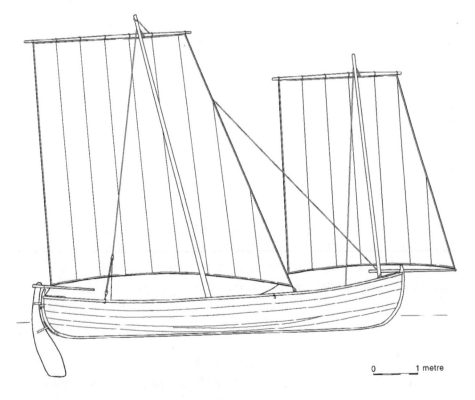

0 _____ 1 metre

Figure 4.2
Suggested rigging plan of the Red Bay *txalupa*.

Acadia, was himself a boat builder and each year sold his products to arriving Basque captains. Sometime before 1580, he passed a winter in Bayonne, where he stayed at the mayor's house.[10] Another chief, Membertou, assembled a fleet at Port Royal in 1607 to carry 400 warriors on a raid against a rival chief at Saco, on the opposite shore of the Gulf of Maine. This expedition across 350 kilometres of open sea, immortalized by an epic song, involved fifty to eighty Mi'kmaq boats mustered throughout Acadia.[11]

Some indicators allow us to estimate the extent to which the *txalupa* penetrated into Indigenous societies throughout the gulf. In the late seventeenth century, Louis Jolliet described four Inuit summer villages in southern Labrador, each having about ten lodges and five *txalupak*.[12] Each lodge belonged to a household that, according to historical studies of Indigenous demography, included about 3.6 persons.[13] Thus, a typical Inuit village numbered about thirty-six persons or about seven people for each *txalupa*. Figures recorded at Brador, at the western end of the Strait of Belle Isle, suggest a regional population of 300 to 400 Inuit living in about one hundred households and possessing fifty to sixty sailboats.[14] At these ratios, the Mi'kmaw community of Cape Breton Island, numbering about eighty-five households or 300 souls, may have possessed forty to forty-five *txalupak*.[15] Evidence cited earlier suggests that these vessels were equally common in most Mi'kmaq communities. To put their social impact in a modern perspective, we may compare these vehicles to the family car or the pickup truck of the twentieth century.

An examination of shifting Indigenous geography around the Gulf of Saint Lawrence helps to demonstrate the deep changes brought by the *txalupa*'s availability. Moreover, when we compare the maps of Indigenous cultural areas and Basque activity zones, we see that Indigenous cultural frontiers shifted in areas of intensive Basque presence, suggesting that Basque-Indigenous relations correlated with the *txalupa*'s availability and contributed to enhance Indigenous seaborne mobility, by setting people in motion across the gulf. After showing this overall geographic pattern, this chapter will look more closely at three sub-regions where narrower seas allowed intensive inter-coastal navigation in *txalupak*. In Grand Bay, Basque-Inuit partnerships built around the seal trade became a bulwark against French colonial expansion. In Cabot Strait, trade with Basques and access to *txalupak* led the Mi'kmaq in Cape Breton Island to enlarge their hunting territory to Newfoundland. Finally, in the

Saint Lawrence Estuary and Chaleur Bay, members of the Iroquoian diaspora from Stadacona parlayed their Basque trading and sealing partnerships into a strategic role in New France.

THE INDIGENOUS MAP OF THE GULF OF SAINT LAWRENCE, 1250–1700

Indigenous societies around the Gulf of Saint Lawrence were always mobile, but the degree and form of their mobility changed over time. As a general trend over several thousand years, we find progressively fewer indicators of long-distance exchange, travel, and migration. Unlike their highly mobile predecessors in Archaic times, Woodland-era (approx. 1000 BCE–1500 CE) peoples remained within their traditional territories. While bands moved about within their respective river valley territories, greater cultural areas remained stable. Most of the gulf's shorelines show an unbroken *in situ* evolution of material culture for as long as 1,500 years prior to European arrival, with an increasing self-sufficiency in local raw materials. As a result, the cultural boundaries around the Gulf of Saint Lawrence show little change for many centuries prior to European arrival.

Moving clockwise around the gulf, we may look briefly at the temporal depth of the four major cultural groups in place at the time of European arrival, about 1500 CE. Newfoundland peoples did not make pottery, a valuable archaeological tracer or *fossile directeur*, but their lithic material culture shows *in situ* evolution from 500 to 1850 CE. During these centuries, the characteristic Beaches complex of material culture evolved into the Little Passage complex and on to historic Beothuk culture, without any sign of incoming peoples.[16] Around the gulf's southern arc, from Cape Breton to Gaspé, new flows of material culture arrived from the lower Great Lakes and the Saint Lawrence valley during the Early Woodland period (1000–400 BCE). Most archaeologists see these flows as signs of long-distance exchange and cultural influence, and not substantial incoming population. Beginning in the Middle Woodland (400 BCE–1000 CE) and through the Late Woodland (1000–c.1550 CE), we find fewer indicators of such long-distance influences as material culture evolved *in situ* and the Mi'kma'ki cultural area consolidated.[17] We see a similar trend in the Saint Lawrence valley, where archaeology shows incoming waves of people during the Archaic period (9000–1000 BCE), the establishment of long-distance trade routes through the Early Woodland (1000–400 BCE), followed by the *in situ* development of Iroquoian-style occupation patterns and material culture from the Middle Woodland onward.[18] Out of this continuity came the highly recognizable Saint Lawrence Iroquoian pottery tradition, whose last and most distinctive stylistic phase began about 1350.[19]

The north shore of the gulf also shows *in situ* cultural evolution at least 500 to 1,000 years into historic Innu times, but this territory also saw the rise of cultural and demographic poles that attracted Iroquoian and early European trade. As in Newfoundland, the north shore peoples made no pottery of their own. However, their stone artifacts over time show a very ancient backdrop of raw material procurement throughout a vast hinterland in central Quebec and Labrador, out of which two areas of regional self-sufficiency emerged. Around Lac Saint-Jean, a preference for local chalcedony about 1000 CE signals the upwelling of a regional Kakouchak identity. This community became a magnet for long-distance trade along the continental divide of central Quebec. In a notable revival of ancient mobility patterns, copper and pottery flowed in from the Great Lakes, possibly transported in Cree and Algonquian canoes.[20] Farther east, on the middle north shore, the area near the Mingan archipelago began to rely on local chert about 500 CE.[21] This region's self-sufficiency metamorphosed into a pole that attracted small quantities of Iroquoian Owasco-like pottery by 1000–1300 CE and Saint Lawrence Iroquoian pottery subsequently.[22] Both of these poles on the north shore developed *in situ* without incoming migration.

Lastly, in the northeastern gulf, the boundary between north shore and Newfoundland peoples shifted slightly about 500 years before European contact. From about 500 BCE to 1000 CE, a group related to the north shore peoples, known as the Cow Head complex, interacted all along the coasts from Hamilton Inlet in Labrador to Gros Morne in western Newfoundland.[23] At the same time as the north shore poles consolidated, the seafaring Cow Head complex broke up. In its wake, ancestral Beothuk moved into northern Newfoundland and established a bridgehead at Blanc-Sablon about 1000–1550 CE, known as the Anse-Morel complex.[24] The Cow Head breakup also opened space for a group from central Labrador to expand southward. Archaeologists know this group as the Daniel Rattle complex (500–1000 CE) that evolved into the Point Revenge complex during its expansion phase (1000–1550 CE).[25]

While its cultural affiliation remains hypothetical, archaeologists tend to include it with the Algonquian peoples who became the Innu.[26] Following the
post-Cow Head reshuffle, cultural frontiers in the northeastern gulf remained
stable until the sixteenth century.

When we consider the full extent of the circa 1500 Innu cultural area along
the north shore, from Lac Saint-Jean to the Strait of Belle Isle, we see that its
outer boundaries were stable for at least 500 years before European arrival,
with no signs of incoming or outgoing populations. As in the rest of the Gulf
of Saint Lawrence, we see a general reduction of long-distance mobility and
inter-coastal travel since Middle Woodland times. In the century following
European arrival, we see a reversal of this long-term trend as indicators of Indigenous mobility increase substantially in maritime contexts around the gulf.
Archaeologists who trace the diffusion of lithic raw materials, used to make
stone tools, see evidence of reactivated sea routes during the early historical
period, linking areas as far distant as Anticosti, the Strait of Belle Isle, Cape
Breton, and Gaspésie.[27] In another throwback to earlier times, some populations moved into new territories, redrawing the cultural frontiers in three
areas of the Indigenous map of the gulf (figure 4.3).

First, Inuit advanced into the Strait of Belle Isle and Grand Bay, pushing
back resident Innu and Beothuk populations. Their southward expansion
began about 1500 CE when they crossed from Baffin Island to northern
Labrador. They reached the strait about 1550 and continued into the gulf as
far as Port-au-Choix and Gros-Mécatina.[28] Inuit expansion coincided with
Basque fisheries in this region. The regional pendulum swung back in the
eighteenth century, as the Innu returned to the coast below Gros-Mécatina,
coinciding with the eastward advance of French colonial seigneuries along
the north shore. Beginning at Tadoussac in 1635 and culminating with the creation of the Brador *commanderie* in 1703, the French seigneuries gradually
pushed out the Basques from Spain.

In the second change to the Indigenous map, Mi'kmaq crossed from Cape
Breton Island into southern and western Newfoundland in the seventeenth
century.[29] This seaborne expansion similarly coincided with the expansion of
Basque fisheries westward from Placentia Bay and with Beothuk contraction
northeast toward the Exploits River.

The third change is more complex. In the Saint Lawrence valley, Iroquoians
dispersed from their villages in the sixteenth century and melded with surrounding peoples, leaving the valley's cultural map in a state of flux. It is

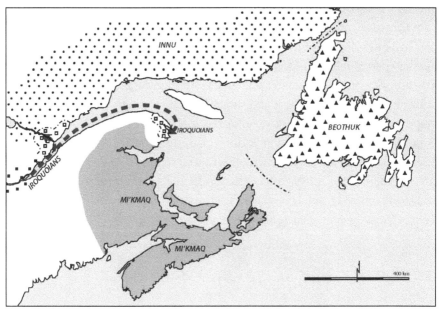

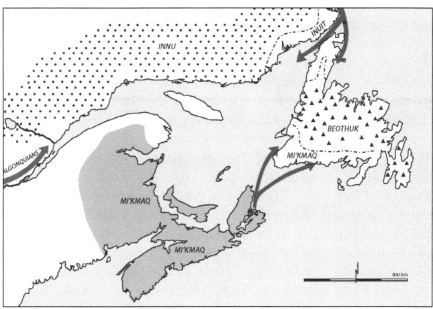

Figure 4.3
The Indigenous cultural map of the Gulf of Saint Lawrence, circa 1550 (*top*) and 1675 (*bottom*).

thought Iroquoians abandoned their villages in a wave beginning near Lake
Ontario soon after 1510, attaining the Hochelaga region (present-day Montreal) about 1565, and ending at Stadacona (present-day Quebec) about 1580.[30]
As the villages fell empty, Saint Lawrence Iroquoian material culture, horticulture, and personal names appeared in surrounding areas, supporting the
idea of population dispersal and integration into neighbouring groups and
regions.[31] The dispersal of Stadacona about 1580 coincides with the arrival of
Basque whalers and traders at Tadoussac and Gaspé, leading researchers to
look for correlations between the two watershed events. The ensuing flux
abated during the seventeenth century as French traders and colonists settled
in, and Algonquian navigators from the Ottawa valley came to dominate trade
routes from the Saint Lawrence Estuary to Lake Huron.

THE BASQUE MAP OVER TIME

Parallel to these changes to the Indigenous map, Basque presence in the Gulf
of Saint Lawrence also varied over time. Counting historical references and
archaeological sites, we know about 130 places where Basques fished, whaled,
sealed, or traded. Most places have associated dates, enabling us to trace the
evolution of regional Basque presence over time. Loewen and Delmas divided
Basque regional presence around the gulf into four distinct periods: before
1580, 1580–1630, 1630–1713, and 1713–60[32] (figures 4.4 and 4.5).

Before 1580, Basque ships and crews clustered at the gulf's Atlantic gateways.
This geographic focus likely had imperialistic reasons. Ships from Spain always
formed most of the Basque transatlantic fleet, a disparity that Spain used to
geopolitical advantage in its wars with France. Basque eyes and ears at the
straits gave pause to foreign rivals wishing to enter the gulf. This dynamic is
illustrated in 1543, when the deployment of large, armed whalers in the Strait
of Belle Isle outflanked the Cartier-Roberval colony near Quebec, forcing its
evacuation and halting French navigation into the gulf for thirty-six years.[33]

In 1579, following a surprise Anglo-Dutch embargo on oil imports from
Spain, Basque whalers were left with unsold oil on their hands and did not
return to the Strait of Belle Isle. Much as the deployment of heavy whalers
in 1543 halted navigation into the gulf, the 1579 embargo opened the flood-
gates of westward penetration into the gulf, and smaller Basque outfits from

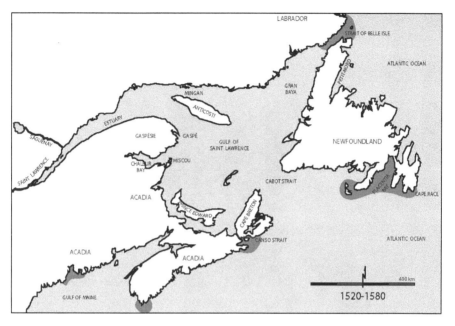

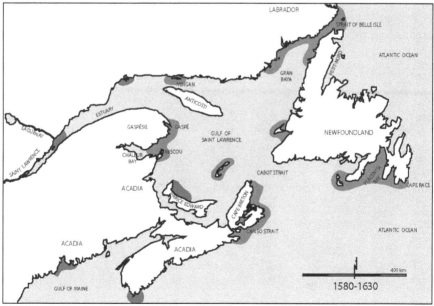

Figure 4.4
Areas of Basque presence circa 1520–80 (*top*) and 1580–1630 (*bottom*)

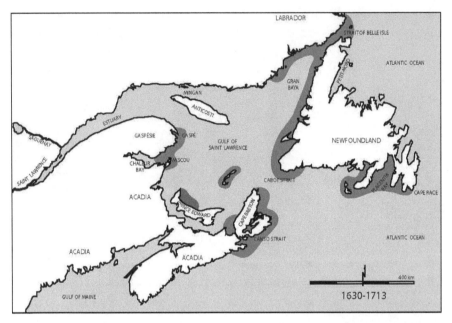

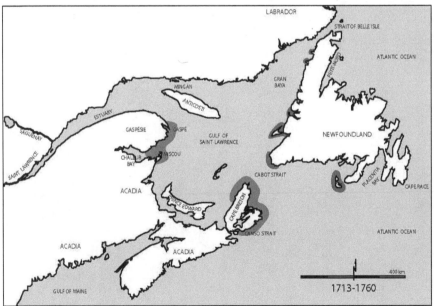

Figure 4.5
Areas of Basque presence circa 1630–1713 (*top*) and 1713–60 (*bottom*).

France were among the first to rush in. Whalers and sealers dispersed along the north shore as far as the Saguenay, while other captains pioneered the cod-fishing grounds of western Newfoundland and Chaleur Bay. However, heightened competition cut into profits, leading many captains to trade for animal skins on the side. The 1580–1630 period saw greatly intensified trade but also new conflicts as Basque and Inuit fought over access to prime sealing spots. Walrus hunters in the Magdalen Islands traded cannonballs with English corsairs in 1597, and Basque traders in several locations scuffled with agents tasked with enforcing the French fur trade monopoly. Gradually, France imposed its sway over the gulf, forcing Basque captains to devise more sustainable economic strategies.

The 1630–1713 period saw the highpoint of Basque cod fishing. At the same time, the fishery was increasingly restricted, as France obliged Basque ships from Spain to buy part of their outfit in French ports. Basque material culture, previously made in Spain, acquired a French character. The areas open to Basque crews also shrank. On the north shore, French authorities granted zones of exclusive access to colonial fishing entrepreneurs.[34] These "seigneuries" advanced eastward, eating into the enclave where Basques from Spain preserved their free access and where their relations with the Inuit obstructed the French advance. In 1703, the French founded Brador, gaining control of the Strait of Belle Isle and ending Basque fishing on the north shore.

Ten years later, France ceded Newfoundland to England, thus closing the island to Basque fisheries except for the "French Shore" on the northeast and west coasts. Between 1713 and 1763, some Basque captains moved to Cape Breton Island and Gaspésie; some took to buying cod from settler fishing communities, but many dropped out of the transatlantic fishery. The English conquest of New France during the Seven Years War ended the 250-year era of the Basque transatlantic fisheries.

BASQUE-INDIGENOUS RELATIONS: TRADING HUBS AND FISHERY PARTNERSHIPS

Basque-Indigenous relations around the Gulf of Saint Lawrence had two dimensions that enhanced the maritime mobility of Indigenous peoples and changed their cultural frontiers: trading hubs and fishery partnerships, both enabled by widespread adoption of the *txalupa*. The trade in furs and skins began as a sideline for Basque fishing captains and officers. It boomed after the gulf opened up in 1579 and many, if not all, captains took part. The golden age of Basque trading lasted about fifty years. In the early seventeenth century, the French trading monopoly attacked the Basque trade and succeeded in quashing it about 1635, except in Grand Bay where trade remained largely in Basque hands until 1703.

The trade took place as an adjunct to fishing. At the end of the season, having fulfilled their obligation to outfitters, captains moved to regular rendezvous to trade. Attracting up to five Basque ships and a dozen Indigenous *txalupak*, these trading hubs sprang up for a few short weeks each year. Captains and officers obtained small animal furs but mostly they acquired the hides of deer, moose, and seal that they resold to shoemakers and tailors back in the Basque Country, who transformed them into all-weather footwear and clothing for sailors.[35] In exchange, the captains offered used and surplus supplies stripped from the ship's outfit, such as biscuit, resin, staves, sea-clothing, hardware such as nails, fishhooks, axes, adzes, and utensils, and notably used boats, sails, and rigging.[36] The captain and officers kept the profits as part of their customary *droit de pacotille* – the right to petty trade accorded by outfitters – and shared them with the crew.[37]

These trading rendezvous had no buildings, inventories, or staff, functioning only as customary places where Indigenous traders arrived in sailboats with furs and hides collected from larger regions. Trading seems to have taken place without setting foot on land, with goods transiting directly from one ship or boat to the other. In this sense, it resembled early descriptions of Indigenous people handing items across gunwales or coming on board European ships to do business. This custom may have had origins in Native trade fairs; it also resembled European dockside trading.[38] Significantly, it left the distribution and collection apparatus entirely in Indigenous hands, while the features of waterborne rendezvous and over-the-gunwale transactions created a neutral trading space. As the *pacotille* trade intensified, it acquired a structure around regular hubs that we see as early as 1579 at Tadoussac,[39] 1586 at Gaspé,[40] and about 1590 in Grand Bay.[41] By 1626, it had taken a more fully articulated form with other meeting places at Miscou, Sept-Îles, Ingonish, and the island of Saint-Pierre, sometimes in direct competition with French trading posts.[42] Outfitters initially tolerated this sideline trade because it allowed them to negotiate lower salaries for the ship's officers and crew, but as the trade expanded, they increasingly asked for a part of profits and even equipped ships exclusively for trade. In this case, they offered textiles, cooking pots, axes, and personal objects such as beads, combs, mirrors, and clothing to obtain pelts of small fur bearing animals such as beaver, marten, and felines with higher value on the European consumer market.[43] It was this trade in items with higher mark-up values and not the petty trade in surplus nautical supplies for leather hides that attracted the ire of the Company of New France.

The second dimension of Basque-Indigenous relations consisted of partnerships serving the fisheries. These partnerships arose as captains sought local resources to reduce the cost of transatlantic fisheries. Fishing captains confided various tasks to Indigenous partners such as supplying foodstuffs, fuel, timber, and labour and ensuring the upkeep of shore facilities and small boats during the off-season. In this context, Indigenous partners learned various trades such as boatbuilding, charcoal burning, converting seal fat into oil, blacksmithing, rigging, and carpentry. Such understandings enabled Indigenous use of *txalupak* during the off-season and access to used and surplus construction materials such as staves, sails, nails, and timber.[44] In the southern gulf, as New France clamped down on trading, Basque-Indigenous trade partnerships mutated into fisheries partnerships. We get a glimpse of this sort of relationship in the record of a conflict that arose in the spring of 1663 between fishing crews at Caraquet, on Chaleur Bay. "Local people" (i.e., Mi'kmaq or métis) were readying a shore fishing room for the arrival of Joanis de Combes, a veteran Bayonne captain who was known in the area since the 1630s when he fished and traded at Miscou. When a ship from La Rochelle beat de Combes to Caraquet and tried to occupy the room, as it had the right to do according to the customary rules of the fishery, the "local people" refused to give up the spot. The La Rochelle crew ended up filing a complaint.[45] The incident illustrates the loyalty that could develop between Basque captains and their Indigenous partners.

In this general context of trade and fishery partnerships, we may look at specific ways in which the *txalupa* and Basque partnerships changed the Indigenous map of the Gulf of Saint Lawrence. These changes occurred in the three narrows where Indigenous navigators projected their cultures across ancient frontiers (figure 4.6).

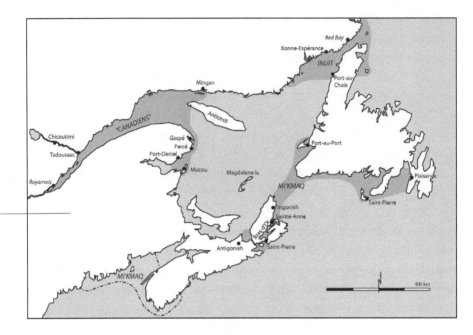

Figure 4.6
Areas of Indigenous intercoastal navigation associated with Basque trading hubs and
fisheries, 1580–1713.

GRAND BAY

Recent research has greatly improved our knowledge of Inuit expansion into
Grand Bay, the historic name for the northeast arm of the Gulf of Saint
Lawrence.[46] Inuit expansion coincided with Basque presence in this area in
the sixteenth and seventeenth centuries. Two commodities in particular linked
Inuit and Basques: the harp seal and the *txalupa*. The harp seal is a migratory
species that hunters captured at strategic sites along the coast in fall and
spring, a schedule requiring them to winter on the coast. It was fundamental
for Inuit subsistence and trade, and access to this resource defined their relations with other nations. Inuit hunters were happy to trade their surplus oil
and skins, but they quickly turned against competitors who sought to control
prime sealing spots in winter.

While the harp seal undergirded subsistence and trade, the *txalupa* enabled
Inuit to exploit widely distant areas in summer and winter and conduct long-

distance trade with Inuit further north.[47] Inuit arrival in the Strait of Belle
Isle coincided with their acquisition of *txalupak*. In 1543, raiders killed a party
of Basque carpenters working for a whaling operation and sailed away in their
boats.[48] However, as whaling boomed and *txalupak* proliferated, the Inuit
adopted peaceful means of procuring boats. In the 1570s, thirty Basque whalers
with 150 *txalupak* operated in the strait; each year, captains discarded and replaced a third of their boats.[49] For a regional Inuit population of about a hundred families, this steady influx of used sailboats was a boon that greatly
enhanced their seaborne mobility. Louis Jolliet, on his voyage to develop the
Labrador trade in 1694, diligently reported the pervasiveness of European material culture in Inuit society, and he took a special interest in their boats.[50]
Jolliet counted about one kayak per lodge and one *chaloupe biscaienne* for
every two lodges. He remarked the sailboats' good condition, their fresh paint,
recent repairs, and new rigging, as well as Inuit stores of pitch and nails in
casks bearing Spanish marks. As Jolliet moved north, the ratio of *txalupak* to
lodges decreased slightly, and he found the boats to be older and the rigging
more makeshift.

In the late 1620s, Basque-Inuit relations shifted from occasionally violent
competition for the seal resource to peaceful partnerships and trade.[51] Basque
sealers began wintering in the strait in 1603 and, the same year, Inuit confronted and killed Domingo de Alascoaga, captain of *La Marie* from the
Basque port of Ciboure.[52] In August 1626, Inuit slew Pedro de Echevarria, his
son, and other members of a San Sebastián outfit.[53] These incidents show
Basques edging toward the same kind of conflict that bedeviled Breton sealers
from 1588 to the eighteenth century in Newfoundland's Petit-Nord, where
their regular grievances portray Inuit with *txalupak* destroying sealing equipment, disabling ships, confronting captains, and killing isolated crewmen.[54]

Rather than digging in and escalating the conflict, however, Basque captains
chose to provide Inuit partners with sealing nets, show them how to use ovens
to make seal oil, and pay for their products in spring. The best-known sealing
captain, Antonio Iturribalzaga of Deba, never wintered in Grand Bay on his
voyages from 1624 to 1635, and he may have relied largely on Inuit suppliers.[55]
Seal oil had similar markets to whale oil, while sealskin had the quality of
being waterproof and Basque shoemakers used it to make sailors' footwear.
In 1620, another Deba captain invited an Inuit couple to the Basque Country.
The couple stayed at the residence of a tanner-shoemaker who transformed

sealskins into sailors' footwear. While the man returned to Labrador the following spring, the woman stayed with the tanner's family in Deba for many
years until her death. It is intriguing to think that the couple may have taught
Basque artisans how to process sealskin and sew watertight seams. As Basque-
Inuit conflicts ceased and entente blossomed, a French imperialist pamphle-
teer grumbled in 1690 that "the Biscayans fish as far as Grand Bay, where they
trade with the Natives we call Eskimos."[56]

Louis Jolliet's journal confirms that the Basque-Inuit trade primarily involved sealskins and oil in exchange for sailboats, rigging, nails, and nautical
supplies. Inuit "captains" brokered this trade. These men were mobile individuals who possessed *txalupak*, hunted, traded, led raids and expeditions,
but deferred to their village chiefs. They spoke European languages, affected
European sailors' styles and habits by introducing themselves as "captains"
and sporting "Spanish" moustaches, and their forwardness contrasted with
the more reserved manner of most Inuit. As middlemen, they relayed goods
from the Strait of Belle Isle to northern Inuit communities.[57] Inuit captains
also shuttled male crews between their home villages and the Strait of Belle
Isle.[58] These crews came from as far away as Zoar, 600 kilometres to the north,
and possibly worked on Basque stations.[59]

Some Basque captains traded directly with ordinary Inuit, who observed
the custom of boat-to-boat exchange as practiced since the sixteenth century
and still current at Port-au-Choix in 1714.[60]

> In the month of August, a great number of Natives come here to trade,
> giving their pelts for biscuit, alcohol, needles, thread, shoes, socks, shirts,
> jackets, pipes, tobacco, etc. ... The nature of the trade is to place the
> goods in a boat; either the Natives or the French [Basques] push the
> boats up against each other, choose the goods and state their value before
> pushing the boat away. The Natives come from the mainland in summer.
> They are from the nation of the Eskemoucks.[61]

In this description, the *txalupa* appears as an extension of Inuit territorial dominion that allowed navigators to approach European traders and conduct
business with them as equals. Boat-to-boat trading appears as a refusal to set
foot in the premises of European trading posts.

ARCHAEOLOGY IN GRAND BAY

Archaeology around Grand Bay deepens our understanding of Basque-Inuit relations. Beginning in the 1970s, archaeologists investigated the extensive remains of a Basque whaling station and associated shipwrecks at Red Bay.[62] Since then, their interest has widened to encompass thirty-nine Basque and Inuit sites that show a constant pattern of interactions (figure 4.7). In general, masonry ovens or abundant roofing tiles lead archaeologists to consider a site as Basque, while the presence of a semi-subterranean winter house or a summer tent ring leads them to consider a site as Inuit. These criteria identify fourteen Inuit sites around Grand Bay, of which nine include Basque materials, and twenty-five Basque sites, of which five include Inuit habitations.[63] Initially, archaeologists cautioned that Basque and Inuit features on the same site might result from separate occupations of a strategic location but work at Petit-Mécatina uncovered evidence of contemporaneous interactions. Other sites have since been re-evaluated and were found to have been shared by members of the two groups.

Petit-Mécatina has a long occupation sequence spanning the seventeenth century. The land site has two Basque structures, interpreted as a cookhouse and a smithy, as well as three Inuit winter houses. Inuit occupants produced charcoal fuel for the smithy. In the underwater portion of the site, stratified deposits show a sequence of clearing the land site of brush, squaring and notching wood for building a wharf or "stage" over water, and tossing codfish bones and some Basque items from the stage. Finally, tiles from a collapsed roof lie strewn across the underwater area. The combined land and submerged vestiges reveal three occupation phases, probably not continuous. The oldest consists of an Inuit house with barrel staves as flooring and traditional Inuit items. Next are the Basque cookhouse, smithy and stage with their abundant cod bones and material culture that is typical of pre-1630 Basque sites. A rockfall partially crushed these structures, perhaps resulting from an earthquake that devastated the north shore in 1663. In the last occupation phase, rebuilt Basque structures, Inuit winter houses and the charcoal pit are associated with French and Basque artifacts from about 1670–1730.[64]

Some Petit-Mécatina features have parallels at Red Bay, including an identical sequence of underwater deposits adjacent to a collapsed stage. Also at

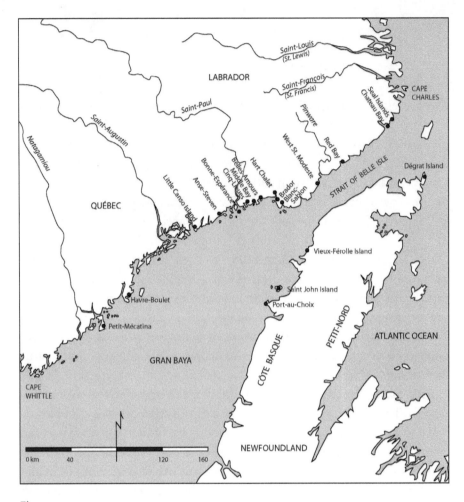

Figure 4.7
Major Basque and Inuit sites in Grand Bay and the Strait of Belle Isle.

Red Bay, an Inuit habitation with extensive organic remains recovered from an adjacent pond shows a late sixteenth-century occupation. In the seventeenth or eighteenth century, the occupants of an Inuit winter house operated a charcoal pit; about 1700–60, French and Innu sealers repaired and reused a Basque oven.[65]

A reassessment of sites with Basque-style ovens on the north shore of Grand Bay has shown that about half of these, notably small sites formerly interpreted as satellite whaling operations, likely relate to sealing. These ovens have one or two hearths and are located at tickles ideal for netting harp seals but with no place to moor a whaling ship. These sites lack other Basque structures but often have nearby Inuit winter houses that contain some Basque materials. These features point to the sites' winter occupation and suggest that Inuit sealers operated the Basque-style ovens. In all, six sites along the coast fit this profile (Dégrat Island, Seal Islands, West Saint-Modest, Capstan Island, Anse-Steven, Havre-Boulet). Only four sites indubitably show a Basque whaling industry (Chateau Bay, Red Bay, Middle Bay, Cinq-Lieues), while five sites in the strait lack sufficient data to classify them (Cape Charles, Pleasure Harbour, Rocketts Cove, Carroll Cove, Schooner Cove).[66] A recently discovered complex of two to four ovens and three winter houses at Bonne-Espérance Harbour fits the pattern of Basque-Inuit partnership around the harp seal fishery (figure 4.8).[67] These findings show a shift away from intensive Basque whaling toward a model of joint sealing ventures with the Inuit.[68]

The winter houses on the north shore show aspects of Inuit adaptation to the Grand Bay environment and their coexistence with Basques. Houses associated with Basque-style ovens are individual, indicating their occupation by small households as at Bonne-Espérance, Red Bay, Chateau Bay, and other locations on the Strait of Belle Isle. On sites without Basque-style ovens, clusters of two to four houses show the winter presence of a multi-household group (Petit-Mécatina, Little Canso Island, Hart Chalet). This contrast may mean that small detachments operated the sealing stations at exposed tickles, while the main community wintered in more sheltered spots. House builders excavated a space that defined the living area and provided sod for the base of the walls. They often used barrel staves as flooring. Archaeologists find this floor beneath the collapsed roof remains of wood, nails, and sod. Other typical features are an entrance tunnel and a midden. All these features could describe Inuit houses in Labrador; however, caribou bones predominate in Grand Bay middens, while mostly seal bones are found in Labrador, including in middens next to Basque-style ovens on the Strait of Belle Isle (Seal Islands, Dégrat Island).[69] The Grand Bay preference for a caribou diet is noteworthy in that it demonstrates that Inuit sealers practiced separate hunting strategies for subsistence and trade. These data show how Inuit households combined their traditional way of life with European trade opportunities in Grand Bay.

Finally, preliminary results from the Newfoundland shore of Grand Bay show the summer presence of Basque cod fishing crews and their interactions

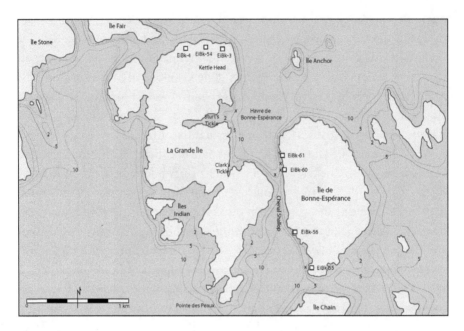

Figure 4.8
Inuit and Basque sites around Bonne-Espérance Harbour. Sites EiBk-3, 4 and 54 are
Inuit sites, EiBk-55, 56 and 61 are Basque sites, and EiBk-60 combines a Basque oven
with an Inuit house.

with Inuit. Testing at Port-au-Choix, Barbace Cove (EdBi-12) and Vieux-
Férolle Island has revealed French material culture from the eighteenth century, although only Basques are known to have fished and sealed here since
the 1630s. Port-au-Choix and Barbace Cove have vestiges of extensive Basque
cod fishing stations, while Vieux-Férolle is notable for a bakery oven and nine
summer tent rings showing the habitation of about thirty Inuit at this fishing
station. Nearby islands in the Saint John archipelago have five more sites with
tent rings, again indicating Inuit summer occupancy. These are the only tent
rings known in Newfoundland and they indicate that the coast from Vieux-
Férolle to Port-au-Choix was a theatre of Basque-Inuit interaction connected
to the cod fishery.[70] More research is needed to broaden our view of seasonal
complementarity between the Newfoundland and north shores of Grand Bay.

CABOT STRAIT

Cabot Strait was the theatre of another frontier change on the Indigenous cultural map, as Mi'kmaq mariners from Cape Breton Island extended their range of activities northward into Newfoundland. Ingonish, in northeastern Cape Breton, is a key to understanding Mi'kmaq navigation and migration to Newfoundland. This Basque fishing port was a hub for trade with Mi'kmaq who arrived in sailboats and offered deer, moose, beaver, and marten skins in exchange for surplus *txalupak*, sails, rigging, and biscuit.[71] In 1627, three captains from Saint-Jean-de-Luz fished and traded at Ingonish, while a fourth devoted his sojourn exclusively to trade.[72] *Txalupak* regularly connected Ingonish to Bay Sainte Anne and Aspy Bay.[73] Ingonish was the jumping-off point for Mi'kmaq from Bras-d'Or Lake who crossed to Newfoundland to harvest furs and skins.[74] By 1627, Mi'kmaq hunted as far east as Fortune Bay and funnelled their pelts and skins to Basque traders at Plaisance and Saint-Pierre-et-Miquelon.[75] Mi'kmaq sojourns in Newfoundland involved families who stayed for the winter hunting season and sometimes extended their residence for several years.[76] These extended stays evolved into permanent residence.

We gain a better understanding of the dynamics at Ingonish by following the Mi'kmaw community of Bras-d'Or Lake from 1630 to 1713, when the Cape Breton trade was in French hands. The Bras-d'Or Mi'kmaq delivered skins and furs to two French posts, located at Sainte-Anne in the north and Saint-Pierre in the south. This division may indicate the existence of two interrelated ancestral groups that shared Bras-d'Or Lake in winter and separated to the north and the south coasts of Cape Breton Island in summer. When winter resources were scarce around the lake, the groups stayed apart.[77] This occurred about 1660, when commercial hunting caused a shortage of moose for winter subsistence, and the two groups left Bras-d'Or in different directions.[78] Members of the northern group moved to Newfoundland, a territory they had used on a seasonal basis since the days of their trade with Basques at Ingonish. This move was a step in consolidating Mi'kmaw presence in Newfoundland. As for the southern group that traded at Saint-Pierre, it relocated to Antigonish on the Acadian mainland. Its members hunted seal and walrus in the Magdalene Islands, possibly with Basques, and discretely traded with Basque captains who sailed into the gulf via the Strait of Canso.[79] By the 1690s, game around

Bras-d'Or Lake had recovered and several families moved back from New-foundland. Most of the Antigonish group returned in 1713, thus reconstituting the ancestral Bras-d'Or community.[80] This history illustrates Mi'kmaw adaptations in the seventeenth century. While commercial hunting made subsistence around Bras-d'Or more precarious, the *txalupa* enabled the Mi'kmaq to expand their hunting grounds to Newfoundland, Antigonish, and the Magdalen Islands, transgressing ancient cultural frontiers.

By connecting ethnohistorical dots, we discern aspects of Mi'kmaw establishment around Fortune Bay, the ancestral coast of the Miaupukek community of Conne River. Mi'kmaq hunters offered skins and seal products to Basque captains fishing in Placentia Bay and sided with them against European competitors. In 1594, Indigenous individuals disrupted an English fishing venture on the west side of Placentia Bay:[81]

> came into the Bay of Placentia, and arrived in the Easterside thereof some ten leagues up within the Bay among the fishermen of Saint Iohn de Luz and of Sibiburo [Ciboure] and of Biskay, which were to the number of threescore and odde sayles, whereof eight shippes onely were Spaniardes, of whom we were very well used and they wished heartily for peace betweene them and us. There the men of Saint Iohn and Sibiburo men bestowed two pinnesses on us to make up our voyage with fish. Then wee departed over to the other side of the Bay, where we arrived in an harbour which is called Pesmarck,[82] and there made our stage and fished so long, that in the ende the Savages came, and in the night, when our men were at rest, cut both our pinnesse and our shippes boat away to our great hindrance of our voyage, yet it was our good fortune to finde out our pinesses and get them againe. Then for feare of a shrewder turne of the Savages, we departed for Cape Saint Marie, and having passed Cape Raz, we passed Northwarde foureteene leagues and arrived in Farrillon [Ferryland].

Early commentators supposed that the saboteurs were Beothuk,[83] but we now know Mi'kmaq in *txalupak* operated in this region. Abetting them may have been cagey Basque captains from Spain, who took pains to appear hospitable to the English master but doubtlessly realized he was spying and reporting on them.

Also fitting the pattern of Basque-Indigenous partnerships, in the seventeenth and eighteenth centuries, a seal fishery bloomed in Fortune Bay as far west as Great Jervis.[84] Sealing took place in winter when only Indigenous hunters were present, but we know Basques sailed to sealing spots on this coast thanks to archaeologist Iosu Etxezarraga's convincing analysis of the place-name Chapel Island.[85] Deriving from *txapel* (cap), this toponym fits a pattern of Basque place-naming in which sailor's pointed headgear such as a toque or a hood identifies conical mounts that pilots used as seamarks.[86] A red *txapel* appears in a sixteenth-century depiction of whalers in Labrador, and it was a nickname for Basque sailors in a rhyming salutation preserved in seventeenth-century Iceland, *Ongi etorri, Txapel Gorri* ("Welcome, Red-Cap").[87] It translates into French as *Chapeau-Rouge*, the historical name of Mount Soker that came to designate the entire Burin Peninsula. This pattern of ethnohistorical dots points to Fortune Bay as a destination for Mi'kmaq migrating from Cape Breton, drawn by trade with Basque captains they saw as allies, and travelling in all-purpose *txalupak*.

These historical elements encapsulate the sweeping effect of *txalupa* acquisition on Mi'kmaw mobility, trade, and cultural frontiers. We may infer that access to *txalupak* enabled the Bras-d'Or Mi'kmaq to collect furs on both shores of Cabot Strait and deliver them to Ingonish by sea. This was the first step in permanently occupying Newfoundland, where broader Basque partnerships came to fruition. The Bras-d'Or community thus took part in a larger pattern that transformed the different arms of the Gulf of Saint Lawrence from cultural barriers to cultural bridges.[88]

ARCHAEOLOGY IN CAPE BRETON AND NEWFOUNDLAND

The archaeology of Mi'kmaq on both shores of Cabot Strait during the contact period remains largely unstudied. On Cape Breton Island, the majority of known Indigenous sites are located on the west side of Bras-d'Or Lake, from Whycocomagh to Baddeck. Ron Nash has shown the continuous occupation of this rich biotope of bays, islands, river mouths and shallows over the last 3,000 years.[89] On sites CaCf-3 and CaCf-6 overlooking Cow Bay, near Wagmatcook, Nash found a local sequence of Woodland and seventeenth-century French pottery that link the Bras-d'Or Mi'kmaq to early transatlantic traders.

While the western reaches of Bras-d'Or Lake offered year round resources for subsistence and trade, during summer, some families moved to key locations on the saltwater littoral of Cape Breton that teemed with clams as well as bar, eel, and other fish that could be dried and stored for winter consumption. Nash reported Indigenous and European artifacts in such a coastal fishing location at Judique North, a barachois with a small river and marshy islands.[90] He also investigated a major coastal site, occupied from Archaic to historical times, on Delorey Island at the mouth of the Tracadie River in mainland Acadia.[91] This site provides an indirect view of the Bras-d'Or Mi'kmaq who moved to this area in the mid-seventeenth century, when hunting depleted game around Bras-d'Or Lake.[92] Trade relations also led some Cape Breton Mi'kmaq to hunt seal on the Magdalen Islands. At Fatima, Moira McCaffrey recovered Indigenous and French ceramics that may show these hunting parties.[93] Although the archaeology of Cape Breton Mi'kmaq during the contact period remains largely unstudied, this community's seaborne mobility appears at strategic sites beyond its western Bras-d'Or heartland.

Archaeological data for Indigenous sites from the seventeenth and eighteenth centuries in Newfoundland are similarly limited. However, a recent survey of Beothuk sites shows a clear geographic trend over time (figure 4.9). While ancestral Beothuk sites carpet all of Newfoundland, their distribution after the sixteenth century eloquently traces Beothuk retraction to the Exploits River basin. Beothuk notably vacated coastal areas where Basques fished.[94] We may also ask whether Beothuk retraction correlates with Mi'kmaw expansion, but on this question archaeological data remains imprecise, as known Mi'kmaq sites date from the nineteenth and early twentieth centuries. However, their presence along river systems draining toward the south coast is consistent with an arrival from Cape Breton Island and overland expansion.[95] Ingeborg Marshall and Ralph Pastore have studied historical and ethnographic data on relations between resident Beothuk and incoming Mi'kmaq; the two authors come to divergent conclusions as to the degree of competition for resources between the two Indigenous groups.[96] A review of seventeenth and eighteenth-century Indigenous sites may shed further light on Mi'kmaw expansion during this period, their relation to the early fur trade across Cabot Strait and to Basque fishing and sealing in Newfoundland.

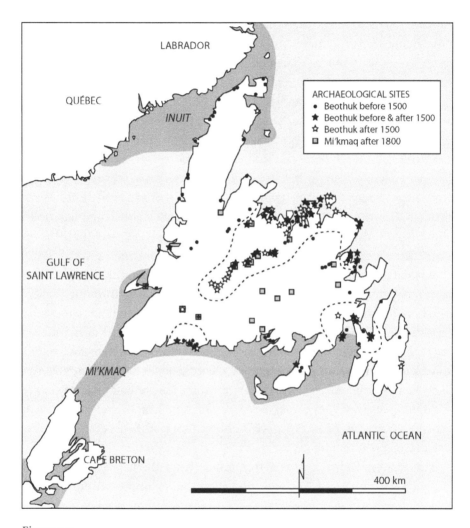

Figure 4.9
Ancestral Beothuk (dots), historical Beothuk (stars) and Mi'kmaq (circles)
archaeological sites in Newfoundland.

THE SAINT LAWRENCE ESTUARY

Like Grand Bay and Cabot Strait, the Saint Lawrence Estuary forms a narrowing sea that a *txalupa* sailing at five knots could traverse in three to fifteen hours, depending on the route. In the estuary, we find an abundance of archaeological and historical data that relates to changes on the Indigenous cultural map of the sixteenth and early seventeenth centuries. However, no previous synthesis has brought this data together into a common narrative, and we will attempt to do so. Along the Saint Lawrence valley, the abandonment of Iroquoian villages appears as a complex set of events cascading from west to east. Radiocarbon evidence indicates that the two or three villages of Jefferson County, New York, fell empty about 1510, while estimates place the Hochelaga exodus from Montreal Island around 1565–75. Historical sources confirm the evacuation of Stadacona, at present-day Quebec, no later than about 1580.[97] Although the exact circumstances of village abandonment remain unclear, many indicators point to security as the overriding reason. Early seventeenth-century French explorers ascribed the disappearance of the villages and language that Cartier had recorded in the previous century to "ordinary wars" among Iroquoians.[98] Archaeologists report the near absence of European material culture in Iroquoian settlements along the valley, indicating that the villagers vacated this inland route before European trade intensified along it.[99] Many indicators show a dispersal to several regions. Villagers likely had prior familiarity with the places where they rebuilt their way of life to differing degrees. They preserved aspects of their Saint Lawrence Iroquoian identity into the 1630s to 1650s, while the memory of their heritage persists in some places until today.[100]

The eastern Saint Lawrence Iroquoians lived in the area they called "Canada" (from Île aux Coudres to Quebec). They numbered upwards of 1,500 persons, including 500 to 800 in Stadacona and the remainder in surrounding hamlets.[101] Jacques Cartier extensively described Stadacona in 1534–42, but when his nephew Jacques Noël returned about 1583, he found the village empty and falling into ruin.[102] Archaeological knowledge of the eastern Saint Lawrence Iroquoians draws especially on excavations near the Saguenay mouth, which allowed Michel Plourde to reconstruct an annual cycle of "horizontal transhumance" in the fifteenth and sixteenth centuries.[103] In Stadacona and outlying hamlets, these people wintered on their reserves of corn, beans, squash, and dried or smoked meat. From mid-February to mid-April, hunters went to the Saguenay region to capture seals and replenish meat supplies. Come spring, once they had seeded fields and gardens in "Canada," many Stadaconans travelled to the Gaspé region to fish for mackerel and capelin, curing the surplus for winter consumption. The Gaspé convoy of 1534 numbered 200 people. Other Stadaconans remained behind to tend the crops and await the convoys that returned in time for the harvest. These Iroquoians thus appear as a sedentary people that sent large detachments on annual fisheries to the places they called *Honeda* (Saguenay) and *Honguedo* (Gaspé). Evidence of their long-distance trading extends as far as Mingan and the Strait of Belle Isle.

The discovery in the 1980s of seasonal occupation at the Saguenay mouth came as a surprise to archaeologists who had built an image of Iroquoians as sedentary villagers and agriculturalists. As the implications of this maritime projection sank in, Charles Martijn examined historical sources and argued that a "privileged partnership" blossomed in the 1530s between the Stadacona Iroquoians and Basques from Spain who fished in the Strait of Belle Isle.[104] He showed that some Stadaconans travelled to the strait and that Basque agents abetted their resistance to Sieur de Roberval's and Cartier's colony near Quebec in 1541–43. Martijn's perceptive reading of data available at the time paved the way for later studies showing that the Spanish spied on and pursued the colonists and that armed Basque whalers in the Strait of Belle Isle cut off the fledgling colony, forcing France to evacuate the settlers via the newly discovered Cabot Strait.[105]

In blaming Cartier for the souring of his Iroquoian relations, earlier historians overlooked the role of Basques from Spain who befriended the Stadaconans and took steps to isolate the French colony. Similarly, archaeologists may have underestimated the insecurity generated by Franco–Spanish rivalry in the Gulf of Saint Lawrence when assessing the reasons for Stadacona's dispersal. However, they based their dating of several key sixteenth-century artifact types on the near simultaneity of Stadacona's abandon, the founding of a Malouin-Basque trading post at Tadoussac in 1579–80, and the beginning of Basque whaling at the mouth of the Saguenay River no later than 1583.[106]

ARCHAEOLOGY IN THE SAINT LAWRENCE ESTUARY

In light of this scholarly consensus on the end of Iroquoian presence in the Saint Lawrence valley, archaeologists initially considered Iroquoian and Basque sites in the estuary to be separate in time, dating from, respectively, before and after 1580. However, recent reassessments appear to show interactions between Iroquoians and Europeans as late as 1635, potentially extending the timeline of Iroquoian presence in *Honeda* by half a century.[107] This reassessment sheds significant new light on Stadacona's dispersal and on post-1580 changes to the Indigenous cultural map in the estuary.

The Saint Lawrence Estuary and the lower Saguenay River have a large number of Iroquoian sites of which seventeen have components assigned to the sixteenth and seventeenth centuries. The region also has three Basque whaling sites assigned to 1580–1635 (figure 4.10). Our discussion focuses on two *"fossiles directeurs"* found on these sites: Iroquoian pottery and European glass trade beads, which guide our detection and understanding of Euro-Iroquoian interactions. The last phase of the eastern Saint Lawrence Iroquoian tradition, called the late Late Woodland, has distinctive pottery conventionally assigned to 1350–1580, with the *terminus ante quem*, or end date, of 1580 based on historical data for the abandonment of Stadacona.[108] As for European glass trade beads, their evolving styles undergird a widely used chrono-typology of "Glass Bead Periods" beginning with GBP1 (1580–1600), GBP2 (1600–30), etc. Of these periods, GBP2 is the clearest and best defined, as it is based on a limited and distinctive repertoire of beads diffused by French traders from 1599 to 1628.[109] The Glass Bead Periods correlate well with the timeline of trading posts at Tadoussac. Merchants from Saint-Malo set up a post in 1579, and Basque traders from Saint-Jean-de-Luz joined them following year. This arrangement coincides with GBP1. In 1599, the New France trade monopoly based in Normandy ran the post until the English occupation of the colony in 1629, corresponding to GBP2.

Reassessments of sites in the Saint Lawrence Estuary focus on the shared archaeological contexts of Iroquoian pottery assigned to 1350–1580 and European glass beads assigned to 1580–1630, in a bid to resolve their chrono-typological discordance. Michel Plourde has evaluated nine Iroquoian and three Basque sites at the mouth of the Saguenay.[110] The Iroquoian occupations begin in the late Middle Woodland (1000–1250 CE), and seven sites have ce-

Figure 4.10
Basque and Iroquoian sites in the Saint Lawrence Estuary and the
lower Saguenay River.

ramics assigned to the 1350–1580 stylistic phase. Of these, three show seal
hunting in late winter (Cap-de-Bon-Désir, Escoumins 1, Rioux) and two on
Île Verte show beluga hunting (Rioux, Turcotte-Lévesque). All but one (Cache)
of the late Iroquoian sites also have significant numbers of glass trade beads
assigned to 1580–1630. One site (Cap-de-Bon-Désir) also revealed an iron axe
and copper offcuts.[111]

The same area around Tadoussac has three Basque sites dated by historical
sources to 1580–1635.[112] They show single-hearth ovens for making oil from
sea mammals, buildings with Basque-style roofing tiles, and Iberian ceramics

similar to those at Red Bay. As a group, these Basque sites have few glass beads, Iroquoian pottery, or other indicators of Basque-Indigenous interaction. Hoyarsabal, on Île aux Basques, is the exception with its late Iroquoian pottery and three glass beads from 1580–1600. Geochemical analysis confirms the origin of the pottery clay in the Quebec area. Also on Île aux Basques, a late Iroquoian site (Cache) has Iroquoian pottery but no glass beads or Basque-related artifacts.[113]

Moving upstream along the Saguenay River, we find four sites showing a late Iroquoian presence.[114] A cluster of cave burials, investigated in the 1940s, shows iron nails and copper fragments associated with birchbark shrouds, stitched together in the manner of canoes. Two complex sites at Baie-Sainte-Marguerite and Anse-à-la-Croix include late Iroquoian pottery loosely associated with beads from 1590–1630. Finally, excavations at the Chicoutimi trading post, founded in 1676, unexpectedly revealed large quantities of glass beads from a much earlier period, circa 1590–1630.[115] These beads are associated with material culture of Saint Lawrence Iroquoians and Lac Saint-Jean Innu, identifying this site at the mouth of the Chicoutimi River as a counter for inter-Indigenous trade in the late sixteenth century.[116] Maps as early as 1569 identify this place as Yle Bordet, possibly referring to Robert Bourdet, a Bordeaux trader known in Acadia in 1564.[117]

As we travel upstream from Tadoussac along the Saint Lawrence, we encounter four late Iroquoian sites. Île-aux-Corneilles has no European artifacts, while a few Iroquoian pots appear on the 1541–43 French site of Cartier-Roberval, and on a seventeenth-century colonial farmstead at Rocher-de-la-Chapelle.[118] The most informative site is Royarnois, an Iroquoian hamlet near Cap-Tourmente with three longhouses, late Iroquoian pottery, glass beads from 1590–1630, and French earthenware related to types found in a 1626–28 level at Champlain's nearby Petite-Ferme.[119] The trade beads lay in sealed Iroquoian contexts. Claude Chapdelaine suggested that Iroquoians occupied Royarnois in summer, in a manner complementary to their winter sealing activities at the mouth of the Saguenay.[120]

We may draw two main conclusions from this body of evidence. First, the high frequency and late date of European materials (especially glass beads) on Iroquoian sites is entirely unlike Saint Lawrence Iroquoian villages farther west. Archaeologists who excavated the estuary sites initially cautioned that Algonquians without pottery might have left the beads after 1600. However, these sites show no other evidence of Algonquian presence. While we cannot exclude this possibility, the data as a whole tend to indicate an Iroquoian presence as late as 1600 and potentially 1630. If anything, Iroquoian activity in the estuary intensified after 1580.

Second, glass beads are absent or anecdotal on the three Basque sites. This finding is consistent with Basque sites in Grand Bay, indicating that Basque whalers, sealers, and fishing crews did not distribute glass beads.[121] Plourde suggested the beads on Iroquoian sites came from traders stationed at Tadoussac, where residents have found many GBP1 and GBP2 beads since the 1920s.[122] Thus, Basque traders established at Tadoussac mediated between Basque whalers who supplied their post in summer and Iroquoian sealers who operated in the area in late winter. Iroquoian summer activities included horticulture at Royarnois and trading with Innu from Lac Saint-Jean at Chicoutimi.

To recap the evidence relating to changes on the Indigenous cultural map in the Saint Lawrence Estuary, prior to 1580 some sedentary Iroquoians from "Canada" voyaged in large groups to the Saguenay, and farther downstream to Gaspé, to catch seal, beluga, mackerel, and capelin. This lifestyle apparently ended about 1580, when Iroquoians abandoned Stadacona and Basque traders and whalers set up at Tadoussac. Archaeological evidence in the estuary may indicate an Iroquoian shift toward a more mobile lifestyle in which sealing and trading played a significant role, in partnership with Basques at Tadoussac. The Iroquoian lifestyle in the 1580–1630 interval included a summer base at Royarnois, sealing and whaling near the Saguenay, and carrying the Tadoussac trade to Chicoutimi. According to this reassessment of the archaeological record, the *terminus ante quem* of the last stylistic phase of the Saint Lawrence Iroquoian ceramic tradition would coincide with the end of Glass Bead Period 2, about 1630.

SURVIVAL OF THE BASQUE-IROQUOIAN "PRIVILEGED PARTNERSHIP"

If we accept this archaeological reassessment, the estuary sites may show an Iroquoian presence after 1580 and bring the diaspora of the Stadacona Iroquoians into view. We may also associate these maritime Iroquoians with an enigmatic Indigenous people known from historical records in this region.

In his history of the word *Canadien*, Gervais Carpin drew attention to a large body of evidence associating this ethnonym with a specific Native people from 1600 to 1650, before it came to identify country-born French colonists.[123] Called *Canadiens* or *Canadaquois*, these people appear at Tadoussac, Gaspé, Percé, and Miscou. Champlain's 1612 map shows a village of *Canadiains* near Port-Daniel in Chaleur Bay. After 1650, French sources no longer mention the *Canadiens*, who seem to meld with the Mi'kmaq of Chaleur Bay.

French observers saw these *Canadiens* as relatively Europeanized. On a 1639 trip to Tadoussac, the Ursuline missionary Cécile de Sainte-Croix rejoiced in their "polite" ways and the Christian songs their children sang in their language.[124] French sources depict them as being specialized in distributing and collecting goods among the trading posts of the estuary and Chaleur Bay. Their use of a fleet of *chaloupes*, according to Carpin, distinguishes them in the historical record.[125] They ferried goods and furs between the French hub of Tadoussac and posts at Gaspé, Percé, and Miscou, run in the 1620s by the Basque captain Raymond de la Ralde (Larralde), an ally of Samuel de Champlain. The *Canadien* profile fits the men named Rougefort and Jouanis who, as we have seen, had custody of two *txalupak* for a French captain at Percé in 1608. It may also fit Armouchidès (although his name contains the Algonquian *elmu'ji*, dog), "one of the most knowledgeable and enterprising there are among the Natives," who collected pelts from Montagnais, Etchemin, and Algonquin in 1603 and hauled them to Tadoussac.[126]

Carpin draws attention to the Basque partnership with these people in Chaleur Bay, their alternative Basque name of *Canadaquois* ("People of Canada"), and the "Basque consonance" of their chief's name, Juanchou, that combines a common Spanish name with the Basque diminutive *–txu*.[127] Juanchou played a unique role in the history of New France after the English occupied Quebec in 1629, by arranging the repatriation of French settlers to Europe on Basque ships fishing at Miscou. After the war, the French rewarded his loyalty by inviting him to Paris where he met Louis XIII, who gave him gifts in the name of his people.

We suggest these *Canadiens* were descendant Stadaconans who moved from their villages in "Canada" to their sealing and fishing territories of *Honeda* and *Honguedo* and left traces of their activities on sites in the estuary. Having acquired *txalupak*, they intensified their hunt of marine mammals at the mouth of the Saguenay, possibly selling their surplus oil and seal skins to

Basque captains and traders, acting as suppliers and distributors for Basque trading hubs at Tadoussac, Gaspé, and Miscou. They continued this role after the French took over Tadoussac in 1599. Their Iroquoian identity as *Canadiens* survived to about 1650, after which they assimilated as Mi'kmaq and Innu to complete the Indigenous cultural boundary shift in the estuary.[128]

This survival of the "privileged partnership" between Basques and Stadaconans provides a suggestive context for interpreting an intriguing passage in Chrestien LeClercq's *Nouvelle relation de la Gaspésie*, published in 1691.[129] The Récollet missionary to Chaleur Bay described an oral tradition maintained by his "Gaspésiens" of epic raids they formerly prosecuted against "Petits Eskimaux" (by which LeClercq meant Innu) in the Mingan area, on the opposite side of the gulf. They conducted the raids as reprisals for Innu attacks on Basques. Other seventeenth-century sources confirm these seaborne forays.[130] Louis Nicolas ascribes them to "Acadiens" who attacked Innu west of Mingan, between the Saint-Jean River and Sept-Îles: "The *Acadiens* undertake the crossings of twenty or thirty leagues in small boats called Biscayennes, which are little skiffs that the Basques, who come each year to fish cod on the coasts of the *Acadiens*, abandon after using them for their fishery in Gaspé Bay or at Percé."[131]

Baffling as these raids in squadrons of *txalupak* may be at first sight, they fit into the system of seventeenth-century alliances that pitted Basques from Spain and their Indigenous allies against French and Innu, thus making the Innu the enemies of the Basques. French missionaries couched the Basque-Innu enmity in moral terms, claiming it stemmed from a grisly incident in which a Basque sailor or surgeon killed and mutilated an Innu chief's daughter, who was pregnant with his child.[132] While this story may be true, it does not explain why the faraway Chaleur Bay people would takes sides in the feud. We may hypothesize that the Chaleur Bay raiders were *Canadiens* bound by their ancestral "privileged partnership" with Basques.[133] Iroquoian ancestry could explain why LeClerq and Nicolas called them "Gaspésiens" and "Acadiens," rather than Souriquois (Mi'kmaq). Moreover, it would be consistent with the Mi'kmaw oral tradition in eastern New Brunswick of having Iroquois ancestors.[134] The presence of Iroquoians and Basques on the Innu coast north of Anticosti – an Iroquoian place-name – is confirmed by Saint Lawrence Iroquoian pottery recovered at Kégashka, and three Basque whaling ovens that operated on Île Nue de Mingan prior to 1679.[135] Such ties across

time and space bound generations of Basques and First Nations, and archaeology sheds light on how those ties were forged in the maritime context of
the Gulf of Saint Lawrence.

CONCLUSION

Of all the goods that Europeans brought to the Gulf of Saint Lawrence and
neighbouring Atlantic shores, the *txalupa* was possibly the most transforma-
tive for Indigenous societies. This watercraft greatly enhanced the seaborne
mobility and transport capacity of Indigenous societies and set them in
motion across the narrow arms of the gulf – Grand Bay, Cabot Strait, and the
Saint Lawrence Estuary to Chaleur Bay. These theatres stand out in 1580–1713
for their intensive Basque presence and for the changed boundaries on the
Indigenous cultural map, illustrating the thoroughgoing mutual effects of
Basque-Indigenous relations structured around the *txalupa*.

The *txalupa* grafted onto the subsistence schemes of Indigenous peoples
throughout the gulf, but in these sub-regions, it was also instrumental in integrating Indigenous and Basque commercial strategies and networks. *Txalupak* capacitated the Indigenous trade circuits structured around the trading
hubs where Native captains bargained over-the-gunwale with their Basque
counterparts. As the trade gained in value, shifting notably from leather for
surplus naval supplies to an emphasis on furs for manufactured consumer
goods, it gained a dedicated European infrastructure including warehouses
and staff, but its supply and distribution networks in the Gulf of Saint
Lawrence remained in the hands of Indigenous traders operating in *txalupak*.

While Basque fishing and whaling activities brought in a steady supply of
used *txalupak* that could be had for free, Indigenous navigators began to partner with Basque captains to obtain preferential access to good sailboats and
the materials needed to keep them in working order. For Indigenous navigators, *txalupa* ownership provided a means to prosecute gainful activities such
as collecting furs and hides from hunters in the gulf's vast hinterlands, producing oil from the fat of marine mammals. This system of Indigenous entrepreneurs who ran their own collection and distribution networks required
no other Basque input than furnishing the necessary equipment of boats, nets,
and ovens, reimbursing the furs, hides, and oil with tradable items, and even-

tually asking for specific goods and services that would improve the competitiveness of their transatlantic fishery. Enterprising Indigenous "captains" who partnered with Basques acquired a status second only to that of chiefs.

Basques played a previously underestimated role in structuring the lengthy precolonial period around most of the Gulf of Saint Lawrence. The Basque prism sheds significant new light on the Inuit expansion into Grand Bay, the Mi'kmaw migration to Newfoundland, and the diaspora of eastern Saint Lawrence Iroquoians. The workings of Basque-Indigenous relations were unique in each of these theatres, but they shared common themes. From a geographical perspective, we may note the recurring context of a narrow sea that allowed *txalupak* to knit its shores into a common cultural landscape, transforming the sea from a cultural barrier to a cultural bridge. In each theatre, we note the enthusiastic adoption of the *txalupa*, its use for Indigenous purposes, the construction of "privileged partnerships" around the Basque fisheries that ramified into broader economic and political realms, and the adoption of linguistic tools to facilitate these partnerships. Not least, we note the durability of these partnerships from generation to generation, without the influence of a state apparatus to enforce them.

In showing the relationships that Basques cultivated with Inuit, Iroquoian, and Mi'kmaq thanks to the introduction of the *txalupa*, this chapter allows us to reflect on the noncolonial Euro-Indigenous relations that the maritime context afforded. The maritime specificity of these relations has taken time to recognize, due in part to their lack of correlates in the binary precolonial–colonial structure of scholarly thought on this period. While Basques, who were mostly from Spain, sometimes acted as imperial agents in the sixteenth century, they lost their state support after 1580, and, by the seventeenth century, they were foreigners in a land increasingly under French dominion. Without state support, and as sailors, not settlers, they based their interactions with Indigenous partners on the framework provided by maritime customary law, built on pragmatic contracts negotiated for mutual gain, personal relationships and trust, and a seasonal presence in the land. These maritime interactions contrasted, on a structural level, with colonial Euro-Indigenous relations that rested on state law as promulgated, on treaties that institutionalized power relations, on bureaucratic relationships, and on permanent occupation of the land. The framework of maritime customary law helps us to conceptualize maritime Basque-Indigenous relations and compare them to colonial Euro-Indigenous relations framed by state law in the early modern era. For example, maritime customary law had a jurisprudence that governed the uses of the *txalupa* as an enabling tool that was vital for building partnerships and reaching complementary goals.[136] Many other aspects of maritime customary law undergirded the "privileged partnerships" that transformed the seasonal Basque occupation of individual fishing stations into a year-round influence throughout the gulf.[137] The historical legitimacy of maritime customary law, as well as its structural differences with state law, explain the impotence and unease felt by French colonial authorities with respect to the Basques, their liberties, and their Indigenous partnerships. Because of these noncolonial specificities, the Basque-Indigenous experience in the Gulf of Saint Lawrence stands as a reference point for understanding the broader history and archaeology of this period in North America.

ACKNOWLEDGMENTS

This paper being based on archaeological data generated over five decades, there are many people to recognize and thank, especially Réginald Auger, Saraí Barreiro Argüelles, Claude Chapdelaine, Katie Cottreau-Robins, Vincent Delmas, Sergio Escribano Ruiz, Iosu Etxezarraga, William Fitzhugh, Natalie Gaudreau, Mélanie Gervais, Robert Grenier, Latonia Hartery, Anja Herzog, Steve Hull, Dominique Lalande, Ihintza Marguirault, Charles Martijn, Moira McCaffrey, Alison McGain, Marcel Moussette, Pierre Nadon, Ron Nash, Françoise Niellon, Martin Perron, Erik Phaneuf, Jean-Yves Pintal, Michel Plourde, Peter Pope, Lisa Rankin, Justine Rioux, Marianne Stopp, Roland Tremblay, James Tuck, and Laurier Turgeon. The paper owes much to the timely comments of Katie Cottreau-Robins, Christian Gates St-Pierre, Steve Hull, Kevin Leonard, Moira McCaffrey, Greg Mitchell and Jean-Christophe Ouellet. My research has received support from the SSHRC and FRQSC funding bodies. A special thanks to Allan Greer for his always generous editorial suggestions and shepherding.

NOTES

1 Harris and Loewen, "A Basque Whaleboat."
2 Agote and Lopez, "Gure Itsasontziak," 47–9.
3 Loewen, "Saint Lawrence Iroquoians."
4 13 April 1606, Archivos Historicos de los Protocolos de Guipúzcoa (AHPG), Oñati, Spain. III, 2598, 3:50.

5 February 1608, Archives départementales de Seine-Maritime (ADSM), 2E (notarial records) Rouen, France. 28, 2E 70/119.

6 Denys, *Description geographique et historique*, 180.

7 Loewen, "Cultural Transmissions of the 'Biscayne Shallop.'"

8 Archer, "The Relation of Captain Gosnold's Voyage," 73; Burrage, *Early English and French Voyages*, 330; Whitehead, *The Old Man Told Us*, 21–2; Asher, *Henry Hudson the Navigator*, 60–1.

9 Lescarbot, *Nova Francia*, 577.

10 Whitehead, *The Old Man Told Us*, 28–9.

11 Whitehead, "Navigation des Micmacs," 227–32.

12 Delanglez, *Life and Voyages of Louis Jolliet*, 213–31.

13 Dubois and Morin, "La démographie amérindienne."

14 Fitzhugh, "Inuit Archaeology of the Quebec Lower North Shore"; Loewen, "The World of Capitena Ioannis."

15 Library and Archives of Canada, Ottawa (LAC), 1737. Dépôt des papiers publics des colonies; état civil et recensements: Série G 1: Recensements et documents divers: C-2574, Online source accessed 2021, https://heritage.cana diana.ca/view/oocihm.lac_reel_c2574/706?r=1&s=4; Dubois and Morin, "La démographie amérindienne en Nouvelle-France."

16 Stephen Hull, "Basques, Beothuk, and the Big Squeeze. Inside Newfoundland and Labrador Archaeology" (blog), 4 September 2020, Provincial Archaeology Office, St John's. Accessed 30 November 2021. https://nlarchaeology.word press.com/2020/09/04/basque-beothuk-and-the-big-squeeze/.

17 Leonard, "Mi'kmaq Culture," 34.

18 Gates St-Pierre, *Potières du Buisson*.

19 Tremblay, "Le site de l'anse à la Vache"; Tremblay, "Culture et ethnicité en archéologie."

20 Langevin, "Un fjord, une rivière, un lac et des ruisseaux," 352–8; Moreau et al., "Saint Lawrence Iroquoians."

21 Ouellet, "Préhistoire de la Moyenne-Côte-Nord," 144.

22 Ibid., 58, 65.

23 Hartery "The Cow Head Complex," 144–5; Stephen Hull, "Here, There and Everywhere: The Cow Head Complex. Inside Newfoundland and Labrador Archaeology" (blog), 12 April 2012. Provincial Archaeology Office, St John's, accessed 17 May 2022, https://nlarchaeology.wordpress.com/2012/04/06/here-there-and-everywhere-the-cow-head-complex/.

24 Pintal, *Aux frontières de la mer*, 169–257.

25 Stephen Hull, "Recent Period Tradition: Labrador. Inside Newfoundland and Labrador Archaeology," (blog), 23 March 2012. Provincial Archaeology Office, St John's, accessed 17 May 2022, https://nlarchaeology.wordpress.com/2012/03/23/recent-period-tradition-labrador/.

26 Ouellet, "Préhistoire de la Moyenne-Côte-Nord," 60.

27 Chalifoux, "Charactérisation des matières"; Gespe'gewa'gi, *Nta'tugwaquanminen*, 27–9.

28 Pintal, "La rencontre de deux mondes"; Fitzhugh, "After Red Bay"; Fitzhugh, "The Inuit Archaeology."

29 Martijn, "An Eastern Micmac Domain of Islands"; Marshall, "Beothuk and Micmac"; Pastore, "Collapse of the Beothuk World."

30 Abel et al., "Radiocarbon Dating the Iroquoian Occupation"; Tremblay, *Peuple du maïs*, 125; Chapdelaine, "Saint Lawrence Iroquoians," 165.

31 Ramsden, "Becoming Wendat"; Loewen, "Intertwined Enigmas."

32 Loewen and Delmas, "Basques in the Gulf of St Lawrence."

33 Ibid.

34 Loewen and Egaña Goya, "Un aperçu des Basques."

35 Castro, "The Basque Seal Trade."

36 ADPA, 3E-9751: 220–33, 1627.

37 Dieulefet and Loewen, "Sur la route des pêcheurs malouins."

38 Taché, *Structure and Regional Diversity*; Ward, *The World of the Medieval Shipmaster*.

39 Turgeon, "Basque-Amerindian Trade"; Turgeon, "Vers une chronologie des occupations basques"; Turgeon, "Pêches basques du Labourd."

40 Turgeon, *Une histoire de la Nouvelle-France*, 121.

41 Loewen, "The World of Capitena Ioannis."

42 Le Blant, "La Compagnie de la Nouvelle-France"; Allaire, *Pelleteries, manchons et chapeaux*, 79–80, 92.

43 Loewen et al., "S'adapter pour rester."

44 Fitzhugh, "After Red Bay"; Rankin and Crompton, "Meeting in the Straits."

45 LeBreton and Thériault, *À la découverte de l'île de Caraquet*, 41–3.

46 Fitzhugh, "After Red Bay"; Fitzhugh, "The Inuit Archaeology"; Pope, "Bretons, Basques and *Inuit*"; Rankin and Crompton, "Meeting in the Straits"; Loewen,

"The World of Capitena Ioannis"; Delmas, "Indigenous Traces on Basque Sites"; Rankin, "Labrador Inuit," this volume.

47 Loewen, "The World of Capitena Ioannis"; Rankin and Crompton, "Meeting in the Straits."

48 Biggar, *Documents Relating to Jacques Cartier*, 456.

49 Loewen, "Cultural Transmissions of the 'Biscayne Shallop.'"

50 Delanglez, *Life and Voyages of Louis Jolliet*, 213–31.

51 Loewen, "The World of Capitena Ioannis," 176–7.

52 Azpiazu, *La empresa vasca de Terranova*, 160.

53 Azpiazu, *Hielos y oceanos*, 194–5.

54 Pope, "Bretons, Basques and *Inuit*"; Crompton, "They Have Gone Back"; Rankin, "Labrador Inuit," this volume.

55 Castro, "The Basque Seal Trade."

56 Loewen, "The World of Capitena Ioannis"; Barkham, *Los vascos en el marco*, 178; Morandière, *Histoire de la pêche française*, 3:437.

57 Rankin and Crompton, "Meeting in the Straits."

58 Delanglez, *Life and Voyages of Louis Jolliet*, 1645–1700.

59 Rochemonteix, *Relation par lettres*, xxxiv–xxxv, lxii.

60 Barkham, *Los vascos en el marco*, 184.

61 National Archives (UK), CO 194/6, fol. 240–1, cited in Barkham, *Los vascos en el marco*, 182–3. "*En el mes de agosto gran número de salvajes vienen aquí para trocar dando sus pieles por pan, aguardiente, agujas, hilo, zapatos, calcectines, camisas, chaquetas, pipas, tobaco, etc. ... La naturaleza del commercio es poner los bienes en un bote; o los salvajes o los franceses empujan el bote desde uno a otro, sacan los bienes y ponen su valor antes de reempujar el bote al otro lado. Los salvajes vienen de tierra firme en verano. Son de la nación de los Eskemoucks.*"

62 Grenier et al., *Underwater Archaeology of Red Bay*.

63 Loewen and Delmas, "Basques in the Gulf of St Lawrence"; Fitzhugh, "After Red Bay"; Fitzhugh, "The Inuit Archaeology"; Delmas, "Indigenous Traces on Basque Sites"; Loewen et al., "S'adapter pour rester."

64 Fitzhugh, "After Red Bay"; Fitzhugh, "The Inuit Archaeology."

65 Delmas, "Indigenous Traces on Basque Sites"; Crompton, "They Have Gone Back."

66 Loewen, "The World of Capitena Ioannis."

67 Loewen et al., "S'adapter pour rester."

68 Fitzhugh, "After Red Bay"; Fitzhugh, "The Inuit Archaeology."

69 Ibid.; Auger, *Labrador Inuit and Europeans*; Gaudreau, "Stratégies de subsis-
    tance et identité culturelle."

70 Loewen et al., "S'adapter pour rester."

71 Archives départementales de Pyrénées-Atlantiques, 3E-9751: 220–33, 1627.

72 Ibid., 3E-9752: 282–5, 21 May 1628.

73 Archives départementales de Charente-Maritime, B-5665:1185–119v, 12 Novem-
    ber 1664; Jacques L'Hermitte, "Plan du havre d'Aspé," n.d. Bibliothèque na-
    tionale de France, Portefeuille 131, fonds du Service hydrographique de la
    Marine, Paris. https://gallica.bnf.fr/ark:/12148/btv1b59010748/f4.item; Pierre-
    Jérôme Boucher, "Plan de la Baye de Niganiche," 1737, Bibliothèque nationale
    de France, Portefeuille 131, fonds du Service hydrographique de la Marine.
    https://gallica.bnf.fr/ark:/12148/btv1b59010748/f6.item.

74 Donovan, "Precontact and Settlement."

75 Le Blant, "La Compagnie de la Nouvelle-France"; Allaire, *Pelleteries, manchons
    et chapeaux*, 79–80, 92.

76 Martijn, "An Eastern Micmac Domain of Islands."

77 Ibid.

78 Denys, *Description geographique et historique*, I:163.

79 Ibid., I: 137–42; Loewen et al., "S'adapter pour rester."

80 Martijn, "An Eastern Micmac Domain of Islands."

81 Hakluyt, *Principal Navigations*, 3:195.

82 Detcheverry's 1689 map shows Pesmarcq near Audierne (Oderin Island).
    [Carte de Terre-Neuve et Acadie] / Faict à Plesance par Pierre Detcheverry ;
    pour Monsieur Parat gouverneur de plesance en lisle de Terre Neuve, 1689.
    Bibliothèque nationale de France, département cartes et plans, CPL GE SH 18E
    PF 125 DIV 1 P 2/1 RES.

83 Harrisse, *Découverte et évolution cartographique*, lxii; Howley, *The Beothucks*,
    12–13; Bélanger, *Les Basques dans l'estuaire du Saint-Laurent*, 56.

84 Anonymous, "Côte Sud-Est de Terre-Neuve: baies du Désespoir et de la For-
    tune avec Saint-Pierre-et-Miquelon," 1773, Bibliothèque nationale de France,
    département cartes et plans, GE SH 18 PF 130 DIV 1 P 7/1.
    https://gallica.bnf.fr/ark:/12148/btv1b59704889.

85 Iosu Etxezarraga, personal communication, 2021.

86 Losier et al., "In the Midst of Diversity," 209.

87 Martijn et al., "Basques? Beothuk? Innu? Inuit?"; Deen, *Glossaria duo Vasco*, 100; cf. Miglio, "'Go Shag a Horse!'"

88 Martijn, "An Eastern Micmac Domain of Islands."

89 Nash, "Prehistory and Cultural Ecology."

90 Ibid.

91 Nash, " Mi'kmaq: Economics and Evolution."

92 Denys, *Description geographique et historique*, 1:163.

93 McCaffrey, "Inventaire des sites archéologiques préhistoriques."

94 Hull, "Basques, Beothuk, and the Big Squeeze."

95 Stephen Hull, "Newfoundland Mi'kmaq. Inside Newfoundland and Labrador Archaeology," (blog), 1 March 2013, Provincial Archaeology Office, St John's. Accessed 30 November 2021. https://nlarchaeology.wordpress.com/2013/03/01/newfoundland-mikmaq/.

96 Marshall, "Beothuk and Micmac"; Pastore, "The Collapse of the Beothuk World."

97 Abel et al., "Radiocarbon Dating the Iroquoian Occupation"; Loewen, "Intertwined Enigmas"; Plourde, *L'exploitation du phoque à l'embouchure*.

98 Trudel, "Un nouvel inventaire du Saint-Laurent."

99 Pendergast and Trigger, *Cartier's Hochelaga*; Moussette, "Un univers sous tension"; Birch et al., "Chronological Modeling."

100 Loewen, "Intertwined Enigmas"; Stephen Augustine, personal communication, 2017.

101 Clermont, "L'augmentation de la population"; Tremblay, *Peuple du maïs*, 35v.

102 Trudel, "Un nouvel inventaire du Saint-Laurent, 1603," 315.

103 Plourde, *L'exploitation du phoque à l'embouchure*.

104 Martijn, "The Iroquoian Presence in the Estuary."

105 Allaire, *La rumeur dorée*; Loewen and Delmas, "The Basques in the Gulf of St Lawrence."

106 Fitzgerald, "Chronology to Cultural Process."

107 Langevin, "Un fjord, une rivière, un lac et des ruisseaux"; Plourde, "Saint Lawrence Iroquoians, Algonquians, and Europeans"; Chapdelaine, "Saint Lawrence Iroquoians"; Delmas, "Indigenous Traces on Basque Sites."

108 Tremblay, "Le site de l'anse à la Vache"; Tremblay, "Culture et ethnicité," 3–8.

109 Kidd and Kidd, *A Classification System for Glass Beads*; Kenyon and Kenyon, "Seventeenth Century Glass Trade Beads"; Karklins, "Description and

Classification of Glass Beads"; Loewen, "Glass and Enamel Beadmaking in Normandy."

110 Plourde, "Saint Lawrence Iroquoians, Algonquians, and Europeans."

111 Ibid.; Loewen, "Cultural Transmissions of the 'Biscayne Shallop.'"

112 Turgeon, "Basque-Amerindian Trade in the Saint Lawrence"; Turgeon, "Vers une chronologie des occupations basques"; Turgeon, "Pêches basques du Labourd."

113 Delmas, "Indigenous Traces on Basque Sites"; Plourde, "Saint Lawrence Iroquoians, Algonquians, and Europeans."

114 Langevin, "Un fjord, une rivière, un lac et des ruisseaux," 163–72.

115 Chapdelaine, *Le site de Chicoutimi*; Moreau, "Des perles de la 'protohistoire' au Saguenay."

116 Langevin, "Un fjord, une rivière, un lac et des ruisseaux," 173–6, 222–30.

117 Ibid., 509–10; Turgeon, *Une histoire de la Nouvelle-France*, 103.

118 Moussette, *Prendre la mesure des ombres*; Chapdelaine, "Saint Lawrence Iroquoians."

119 Guimont, *La Petite Ferme du cap Tourmente*, 44, 139–41.

120 Chapdelaine, "Saint Lawrence Iroquoians."

121 Delmas, "Indigenous Traces on Basque Sites."

122 Plourde, "Saint Lawrence Iroquoians, Algonquians, and Europeans."

123 Carpin, *Histoire d'un mot*, 67–100.

124 Campeau, *Monumenta Novae Franciae*, 4:747.

125 Carpin, *Histoire d'un mot*, 77.

126 Laverdière, *Œuvres de Champlain*, 49.

127 Carpin, *Histoire d'un mot*, 77.

128 Loewen, "Intertwined Enigmas."

129 LeClercq, *Nouvelle relation de la Gaspésie*, 450–8.

130 Ouellet, *Chrestien Leclercq*, 507–25.

131 Nicolas, *Codex canadensis*, 120–1, cited in Ouellet, *Chrestien Leclercq*.

132 Ouellet, *Chrestien Leclercq*, 507–25.

133 Martijn, "The Iroquoian Presence"; Loewen, "Intertwined Enigmas."

134 Stephen Augustine, personal communication, 2017.

135 Ouellet, "Préhistoire de la Moyenne-Côte-Nord," 58, 65; Delmas, "Indigenous Traces on Basque Sites."

136 Loewen, "Cultural Transmissions of the 'Biscayne Shallop.'"

137 Martijn, "The Iroquoian Presence."

5

In the Round and on the Page: Canada in the English Geographical Imaginary, circa 1600

MARY C. FULLER

A GLOBE AND A BOOK

Between 1592 and 1603, the first English globe was produced by Emery Molyneux, Edward Wright, and Jodocus Hondius.[1] On the globe, the central and western regions of northern North America were delineated conjecturally or simply covered with some of the globe's extensive text. Regions to the east, however – present-day Newfoundland, Quebec, the Maritimes, and Eastern Nunavut – appeared at a level of detail that indicates some actual knowledge. The Molyneux globe, as it's known, stands as a visual summa of geographic information available to the English around the turn of the seventeenth century as it was configured by their particular interests and aspirations. In this essay, I explore what the globe and its most important textual analogue – the geographical compilations of Richard Hakluyt – can tell us about what is now Canada as it appeared in the English geographical imaginary, circa 1600.

An early modern globe's total representation of space belies an accumulation of differences and specificities that drew on a myriad of particular experiences and knowledge transactions.[2] In the case of the Molyneux globe, these would have included existing cartographic sources, such as recent atlases and world maps published by Abraham Ortelius and Nicholas Mercator.[3] The globe could also draw on an array of primary sources in various forms, a mix unique to this particular object: voyage narratives of varying

Figure 5.1
The interior of northern North America on the Molyneux globe is obscured
by a dedication to Queen Elizabeth.

intent and quality, logs with observations of coastlines and latitudes, interviews and depositions, correspondence, translation, archival and antiquarian research, borrowed or stolen sources, family records, Indigenous information. We can infer that this information was coloured and shaped by the varied individuals who recorded, transmitted, archived, and finally selected it to be represented in cartographic form.

The globe itself testifies to some of this infrastructure of activities and exchanges. Among the texts on its surface are the dedication to the queen (figure 5.1); a poem by the globe's patron, the merchant William Sanderson; and lists of prominent English navigators, some still famous, some now obscure, some closely involved with the production of the globe itself. Two of the globe's three makers had themselves sailed on voyages into the North Atlantic, and its patron William Sanderson was an important investor in numerous voyages of exploration, so an element of personal observation can be added to its sources.[4] (Molyneux wrote in a legend on the globe that he had corrected the distance from the tip of Cornwall to Cape Race, Nfld: "I

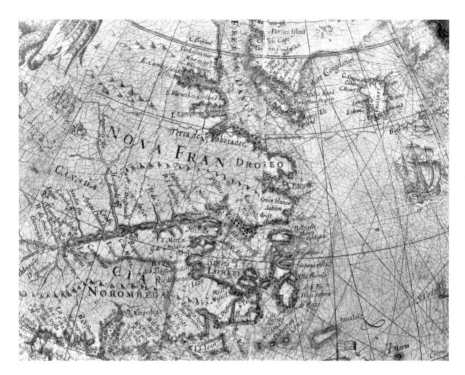

Figure 5.2
Eastern Canada appears on the Molyneux globe with considerable detail.

have been able to do this both in the first place from my own voyages and secondly from that successful expedition to the West Indies under the most illustrious Francis Drake."[5]) Knowing some of the globe's immediate sources provides context for the varied densities of information that its surface suggests: we know something about who these people were, what they planned, and where they went.

Looking at sources also begins to suggest not only the content but also the configurations of what the Englishmen behind the globe knew. We might suppose that just as not all spaces were equally known to the globe's makers and viewers, not all were equivalent in interest and value. Few, too, were conceptualized in ways that correspond to geographical identities in the present.[6] If central and western Canada were open for speculation or simply absent as represented space, parts of eastern Canada had several special interests for Elizabethan England. Early if poorly documented voyages under Henry VII

Martinus Frobißerus eques, Insulam Frislandiam & metam ìn cognitam, terram inter 60 et 63 gradum iacentem annis 1576.7. 78. notam orbi Christiano reddunt.
Noua Albion in gradu 45 latitudinis Septentriona. posita primùm a Francisco Draco patefacta est anno 1570. Item Austrem Iaua majoris, Insulę oram, notiorem quā erat antea nobis dedit. Littora & portus Noug Zemlę & mare ultra insulas Vaigatz Aquilonem versus per leucas plus minus 30 perscrutati sunt Arthur? Pette & Carolus Iackman Angli anno 1580.
Ioannes Dauis Anglus annis 1585. 86. 87 littora Americae Circium spectantia a quinquagesimo quinto gradu ad 73. sub polarem scutando perlegit.

Figure 5.3
A number of prominent English navigators are named on the surface of the globe, including Martin Frobisher and John Davis, both seekers of a Northwest Passage.

and Henry VIII provided willing minds with a foundation for claims to continental North America that antedated the discoveries of Columbus, arguments for the legal possibility and practical desirability of settling northern North America typically invoked the northern voyages of the Cabots and others.[7] The imperfectly known waters of Arctic Canada held open the possibility of a third route to the Pacific and the Indies once English navigators sought to the northeast and northwest of Europe alike. Finally, by 1600 English mariners had participated for more than a century in the Newfoundland cod fishery. The globe's representation of Newfoundland as a collection of islands – one of the common ways of representing it cartographically in the sixteenth century – testifies both to the familiarity of capes and harbours along the eastern edge of the island, and the massive lack of interest in knowledge of its outlines or interior. (As I've argued elsewhere, Newfoundland was also underrepresented in English narrative sources relative to the number, frequency, and duration of English contacts with the island.[8]) Mariners returning from the fishery were nonetheless a vector for geographic information. The midcentury cosmographer William Cuningham apparently knew little of the Americas apart from Peru and "the island of Brasil," associating the is-lands [*sic*] of "Yucatán, Cuba, Jamaica" with the Moluccas as part of Asia. Yet he was able to draw on vernacular knowledge of Newfoundland to inform readers that "in the place which shipmen call (Le Cap d'espoir en terre neuve) [the compass] declineth towarde the Weaste .33. degrees, and .45. minutes."[9]

For more insight into the underlying specificities of this globe's information and its implicit categories, a useful proxy can be found in the career of the English editor, geographer, and cleric Richard Hakluyt, both in his working life as a consultant, translator, and broker of geographical information and in three geographical compilations printed between 1582 and 1600: *Divers Voyages* (1582); *Principall Navigations* (1589); and *Principal Navigations* (3 vols, 1598–1600).[10] The great map historian Helen Wallis has described the two editions of *Principal Navigations* as a textual counterpart to Molyneux's globe: both were designed as records of "English enterprise and maritime discovery."[11] Published within years of each other, the globe and the two compilations drew their information from many of the same informants. In the preface to *Principall Navigations* (1589), Hakluyt heralded the forthcoming appearance of "the excellent newe Globe of M. Mullineux," and Molyneux's collaborator Edward Wright supplied Hakluyt with a new world map for PN 1600, with the globe as one of its sources.[12] Considering the globe and the book together allows us to confer cartographic with textual information and to consider what happens to the common project and the common fund of information as these are translated into two distinct media.

Each of these media objects – globe and codex compilation – has distinctive structural emphases that organize its geographical information. Unlike the continuous surface of the globe, which adjudicates and synthesizes its disparate sources, the form of the codex divides its materials: at the level of the document, assigning each a discrete title and (often) a named author, and then using paratextual groupings of progressively larger size to aggregate materials and identify groups as distinct from each other. Hakluyt's compilation followed a precedent set by the Venetian editor Giovanni-Battista Ramusio in *Navigationi et viaggi* (Venice, 1550–59), aligning geographical and paratextual categories. The one-volume first edition of *Principall Navigations* (1589) was divided into three sections, each devoted to a geographical region of English activity; in the longer second edition of PN, these sections became volumes, grouping materials under the broad headings of voyages to the South and Southeast; voyages to the North and Northeast; and voyages to the West and circumnavigations. Within the first two of these volumes, documents were generally organized in chronological sequence. In the third volume of PN 1600, however, materials on the Americas were divided under more finely grained regional headings, moving from the far Northeast of Greenland and Arctic Canada to the Straits of Magellan, and concluding with actual and attempted voyages into and through the Pacific. The categories thus created offer more than a convenient finding aid: they inform us on a conceptual architecture, organized in part by the varied and rarely overlapping projects that led English mariners into the waters of northern North America. They also afford us some idea of the editor's priorities, since in reality, voyage narratives – like voyages – crossed several geographical and thus paratextual boundaries but could only occupy one location in the book.[13] One example would be the voyage of Giovanni Verrazano. Verrazano sailed west under a commission from Francis I to roughly the latitude of the southern opening of the Gulf of St Lawrence, and his narrative could hypothetically thus be included in several of the third volume's categories on North America. Yet Hakluyt associated the Verrazano narrative not with materials on Canada, Norumbega, or even Virginia, but with the category of "Certaine voyages to Florida," largely materials on the ill-fated Huguenot colony at Cape May in the 1560s. (We'll return to this choice.)

Hakluyt's assemblage of sources, organized into volumes and under headings, drew lines across both the book and the imagined space of the world: between one author's work and another's, between one region and another, one project and another, one temporality and another, even what he chose to make public and what was collected but in reserve, in a text that may be aptly called an encyclopedia of borders.[14] The space we designate now as Canada was represented within *Principal Navigations* as the site of very disparate projects, itineraries that seemed to bear little connection with one another.

Hakluyt's weighty folio volumes have survived the years very well and in turn have ensured the survival of what would have otherwise been lost texts. Molyneux's globe has not been so fortunate: the globe Hakluyt would have known survives in only two copies, one in private hands.[15] The globe's world of information was compressed onto the engraved plates from which its gores were printed; this smaller physical compass made the globe's information, if not the actual, fragile spheres on which it was pasted, both more mobile, more easily reproduced, and thus more readily refashioned. After Molyneux's death in Amsterdam around 1586 or '87, his collaborator Jodocus Hondius would issue a Dutch edition of the globe dedicated to Maurice of Nassau, while the "English" globe continued to receive updates through 1597.[16] Although we have only a tiny fraction of what once existed, the "Molyneux globe" stands for multiple cartographic products, originally produced in different sizes, dedicated to different monarchs as part of different national programs, and (up to a point) subject to an ongoing process of revision in order to reflect new discoveries. Another cartographic product can be associated with Molyneux's globe, however, and provide additional perspective on a process of information-gathering, speculation, and synthesis that a singular object renders difficult to visualize: after Molyneux departed London for Amsterdam, his collaborator Edward Wright transferred the globe's information onto the planar map that accompanied the second volume of Hakluyt's collection.[17] Wright's map adopts a different approach than Molyneux's globe: areas the globe represents with wholly hypothetical lines are simply left blank on the map; in other areas, different outlines may reflect access to additional information or simply different hypotheses. One such divergence can be found for the interior of eastern Canada, in the representation of the St Lawrence River and the bodies of water connected to it. Hakluyt's text may provide us with a sense of what underlay these divergent representations and with an overview of the sources for imagining "Canada" and its regions, from England, in 1600.

GEOGRAPHIES, ITINERARIES, PARATEXT

Verrazano's voyage along the coasts of North America brings up a second significant point. Hakluyt's collection has often been thought of as if the title of his work thoroughly described its contents and project: the principal navigations (etc.) of the *English* nation. However, scholars have increasingly called attention to the fact that not all of Hakluyt's materials were *in* English, let alone by or about the English.[18] Sources by or about other European voyages and travels were especially prominent for the volume on the Americas, in which our materials are contained – the volume includes documents translated from (and sometimes printed in) Spanish, French, Latin, and Italian and concerns the activities of Spanish, French, Portuguese, and Italian travellers.

These translated materials call for particular attention in the context of a broadly nationalist project.[19]

Hakluyt accessed foreign sources through a variety of means. At one end were the relations of patronage and sociability by which he acquired materials from English libraries, texts, and informants, domestic sources whose interests were fully aligned with his; translators ranged from erudite Italian scholars at Oxford to Anglo-Spanish merchants, continental scholars, and of course the learned editor himself. At the other end of the spectrum, materials could be acquired through some degree of violence, from unwilling informants: narratives produced by captives or documents captured from foreign ships (like the treatise on China recovered from a Portuguese carrack taken by privateers).[20] While Hakluyt's Italian and Spanish sources largely clustered towards opposite ends of this spectrum of friendly exchange and antagonism, French sources exhibit a striking variety in their routes into the collection.

Some, like the voyage of Verrazano or the first two voyages of Jacques Cartier, were mediated through Ramusio's *Navigationi et Viaggi*. One narrative about the French settlement in northern Florida appeared *in* English before being published in France, its author Jean Ribaut having sought refuge and help in London.[21] Hakluyt would breach a friendship with the French cosmographer André Thevet by publishing another manuscript on Florida loaned to him by Thevet without securing the cosmographer's permission and against his wishes; in several places Hakluyt described the text as having been actively withheld from circulation and now liberated through publication, echoing language used to describe more literally stolen Spanish and Portuguese materials.[22] Yet another French source was actually seized from a French ship that had been taken as a prize on the way to the Azores.

Canada was one of the two regions most thickly documented in PN by French sources, the other being Florida.[23] French materials on North America had played a prominent and particular role in Hakluyt's career from the outset. The first publication in which we see his hand was *A shorte and briefe narration of the two navigations and discoveries to the northwest partes called Newe Fraunce* (London, 1580), a translation of Jacques Cartier's first two voyages by John Florio from Ramusio's Italian. In the preface to *Divers Voyages* (1582), a compilation linked to Sir Humphrey Gilbert's colonizing project of that year, Hakluyt wrote that he had "caused ... Cartiers two voyages ... to bee translated" and "annexed to this present" volume.[24] In the volume's preface, Florio wrote that if Ramusio's books could be translated in their entirety, "our Sea men of England, and others, studious of geography, should know many worthy secrets, which hitherto have been concealed."[25] Cartier's narratives *were* secret, more from inattention (or linguistic incompetence) than deliberate policy – by contrast with some of the more aggressive cases of Spanish and Portuguese materials seized on raids or in naval battles or translated by aggrieved former prisoners of the Inquisition like John Frampton and Thomas Nichols. The 1580 translation urged them gently into wider circulation.

Hakluyt's posting at the English embassy in Paris, 1583–88, allowed him more direct access to a wider spectrum of sources than those available to him through the volumes of Ramusio. On Hakluyt's account, it was in France that he conceived the idea that would become *Principal Navigations* because "I both heard in speech, and read in books other nations miraculously extolled for their discoveries and notable enterprises by sea, but the English of all others for their sluggish security, and continuall neglect of the like attempts especially in so long and happy a time of peace, either ignominiously reported, or exceedingly condemned."[26] In response to what he believed was a failure to disseminate the history of English maritime achievements, he determined to publish a record of that history inviting the "just commendation which our nation do indeed deserve." The work of assembling the first edition of *Principall Navigations* (1589) proceeded alongside an ongoing effort to collect and publish works on foreign travel both in English and in the original languages. These included an edition of Pietro Martire d'Anghiera's *De orbe novo* (Paris, 1587), an edition of Antonio de Espejo's *Viaje* (Paris, 1586), an English translation of René de Laudonnière's *L'histoire notable de la Floride* (London, 1587), the text borrowed from Thevet; French editions of Espejo (Paris, 1586) and Laudonnière (Paris, 1586) were also published by the editor's collaborator Martin Basanier, the latter at Hakluyt's expense.

Such print editions were only part of Hakluyt's research in Paris, however. In letters to Sir Francis Walsingham, the secretary of state, the editor described seeking geographical information from French informants and from manuscript sources in French collections. His position at the embassy, and the contemporaneous trade and colonization projects of his patrons during the 1580s, made such materials a target of interest as well as opportunity, and he played a more active, personal role in gathering French materials on North America than for any other region in his compilation.[27] Many of the fruits of Hakluyt's collecting efforts made their way into the compilation – but not all. For instance, Hakluyt generously cited Étienne Bellenger's account of a 1583 voyage to the Maritimes and his information on the fur trade but only in a manuscript treatise of advice to the government, "A Particuler Discourse" (1584), commonly known as "Discourse of Western Planting"; Bellenger's relation did not appear in PN. (According to David Quinn it *did* inform the representation of Cape Breton on the Molyneux globe and Edward Wright's map.[28]) Despite the accusations of secrecy and suppression that he levelled at Thevet and others, *publishing* information was not Hakluyt's only goal. In actuality, the materials Hakluyt collected might be published or withheld, included in the compilation or not, circulated in manuscript, sold overseas, made public only in cartographic form or (in the case of one important Mexican manuscript) simply buried in his library.[29] Publication was not simply a default choice; as we've seen in the case of Verrazano, a document's location within the compilation was also not always simply given by geography. These ideas can frame the more detailed look at Hakluyt's Canadian materials to which I'll now proceed.

In the "general Catalogue" (equivalent to a table of contents) that opens the third volume of *Principal Navigations*, Hakluyt organized its materials under fourteen regional headings, beginning with the Arctic and moving clockwise around the Americas to conclude with voyages of circumnavigation. Three of these regional headings relate to northern North America:

> voyages ... for the finding of a Northwest passage.
> voyages made to Newfoundland, to the isles of Ramea and the isle of Assumption, otherwise called Natiscotec, as also to the coasts of Cape Briton and Arambec.
>
> voyages made for the discovery of the gulfe of Saint Laurence ... and from thence up the river of Canada to Hochelaga, Saguenay, and other places.[30]

Materials included under these three headings describe several fundamentally different projects. In the first category, the Arctic voyages of Sir Martin Frobisher and John Davis were intended to search for a Northwest Passage to Asia in very high latitudes. Records consistently refer to both enterprises as "for"

China and the East Indies rather than *to* the Americas.[31] Davis's careful log indicates that he went as far south as Labrador but without reaching Newfoundland or the St Lawrence. The second category, "voyages to Newfoundland," is largely organized around Sir Humphrey Gilbert's 1578 patent for discovery. Though the patent was originally expansive enough to include the regions explored by Frobisher and Davis, by 1582, when he sailed west to explore sites for a colony, Gilbert had already sold rights to regions above 50°N to John Dee (one of the originators for Davis's project) and indeed had intended a more southerly destination before the need for provisions redirected his small fleet to St John's.[32] The adventitious land claim made there, and Gilbert's decision to return directly to England, made the voyage retrospectively "to" Newfoundland. The English whaling voyages in the Gulf of St Lawrence that join the Gilbert materials in this second category involved entirely different investors, planners, ships, and seamen and lack the elaborate theoretical and legal architecture of the Frobisher, Gilbert, and Davis voyages. Finally, Cartier's voyages into the St Lawrence in the 1530s and '40s occupy a category of their own, both in the paratext and in the arc of Hakluyt's career. At the origins of Hakluyt's geographical projects, they provide a particularly rich case study in how he acquired, assembled, interpreted, and disseminated geographical information from non-English sources. With this brief overview for orientation, I'll turn now to examine each of these three sections of the volume in turn.[33]

Voyages by Giovanni and Sebastian Cabot open the section of "Voyages … for the finding of a Northwest passage," the first of volume 3's geographical categories. Yet the *number* of sources on their voyages belies the very modest amount and quality of the information Hakluyt was able to gather, which amounted to letters patent, a map legend, some hearsay reports excerpted from continental sources, and the brief mention in an English chronicle of Indigenous people brought to London by the Cabots. A reader reliant solely on these sources would be persuaded that such voyages had happened, yet utterly uncertain about their details: who, when, and where. Hakluyt himself confused Sebastian Cabot's northern voyage ca. 1508 with voyages led by his father in the 1490s.[34] In 1501, more elaborate letters patent were granted to three Bristol merchants and their Portuguese associates to explore lands "unknown to all Christians," and other early westward voyages took place, but – apart from passing mention by another merchant, Robert Thorne, in a manuscript Hakluyt printed elsewhere in the compilation – these other voyages of northern exploration remained unknown until discovered, themselves, by the archival searches of modern scholars.[35]

While the paucity of documentation for the Cabot voyages reflects a general disinclination to create or preserve records of *any* English voyages before 1553, it is nonetheless striking given the importance these voyages would assume for English claims to the Americas. Unlike the case of Cartier, no Italian, French, or Spanish editor stepped in to preserve texts or facts; although Ramusio and Peter Martyr apparently knew and spoke with the younger Cabot, neither included more than vague and general information about his activities or those of his father. The English geographer and editor Richard Eden, active in the 1550s, had known Sebastian Cabot personally but did not obtain a narrative comparable to the accounts he compiled of English voyages to Africa in 1553 and '54, a region of far less interest to him that the northern waters explored by the Cabots.[36] In 1582, Hakluyt could still name the owner of Cabot's papers and expected them to be published shortly. "Shortly, God willing, shall come out in print all his owne mappes & discourses drawne and written by himselfe, which are in the custodie of the worshipfull Willia[m] Worthington one of her Majesties Pensioners, who (because so worthie monumentes shoulde not be buried in perpetuall oblivion) is very willing to suffer them to be overseene and published in as good order as may bee."[37] Nothing, however, appeared – or survived. Despite the evidence that Sebastian and Giovanni Cabot's multiple voyages to present-day Canada took place, the key knowledge transactions that would have preserved their details didn't quite happen.

The case was quite different for the Arctic voyages of Martin Frobisher in the 1570s and John Davis in the 1580s, which were copiously, even redundantly documented by Hakluyt, with multiple sources for each of six voyages filling out this category of the compilation. Hakluyt's sources were also of excellent quality. Participant accounts of the Frobisher voyages by George Best, Thomas Ellis, and Dionyse Settle had appeared in print – Settle's pamphlet had even appeared in French, German, and Latin editions on the continent – but Hakluyt also secured texts by Thomas Wiars and Christopher Hall (one of the ships' masters).[38] For the Davis voyages, which were *not* the subject of contemporary publications, he obtained journals, letters, and Davis' logbook for the voyage of 1587 and added a synthetic account excerpted from Davis's later treatise on the Northwest Passage, *Worldes Hydrographical Discription* (London, 1595). This careful treatment aligns with Hakluyt's celebration of voyages that participated in the search for northern sea routes to Asia, both in the northwest and northeast. Even though these fell far short of their aims to reach the court of China or to conduct trade with the East Indies, such materials – along with voyages into the White Sea and further east – were framed in PN as part of an ambitious program of exploration comparable to the maritime discoveries of Magellan and Vasco da Gama, which had opened direct trade routes to Asia for Spanish and Portuguese ships.[39] (Even after Hakluyt had begun to consult for the newly formed East India Company following the appearance of PN's second edition, he continued to collect materials on the Northeast and Northwest with "vigor and enthusiasm."[40]) The makers of the Molyneux globe, funded by Davis's major patron William Sanderson, accorded similarly prominent treatment to the Frobisher and Davis voyages (as well as to the Northeast Passage searches of the 1550s). English presence and observations are thickly layered onto the coasts on each side of what was now identified as the Davis Strait, so that toponyms record the personnel and patronage of Frobisher and Davis's voyages on the globe itself, and Frobisher and Davis are praised in a cartouche devoted to English navigators.[41]

Yet when Davis sailed down the coast of Baffin Island/Qikiqtaaluk in 1585, '86, and '87, none of the narratives of these voyages indicate that he was in fact exploring a coastline that had been partially described by Frobisher only a few years earlier. In 1595, Davis referred readers to the Molyneux globe for a visual summary of what he had found, "how far I proceeded and in what fourme this discovery lyeth, doth appeare upon the Globe which master *Sanderson* to his verye great charge hath published whose labouring indevour for the good of his countrie, deserveth great fauour and commendations. Made by master *Emery Mullineux* a man wel qualited of a good judgement and verye expert in many excellent practises." The globe indeed gives graphic expression to Davis's silence about his predecessor: the coasts and the presumed passage explored and mapped by Frobisher have been transferred to southern Greenland (see figure 5.4).[42]

Materials organized under the heading of "Voyages … for the finding of a Northwest passage" are all (in some sense) English voyages and sources, with one exception that is different in kind from the texts that adjoin it: Niccolò Zeno's narrative of voyages to the Arctic by two Venetian brothers in the late 1300s.[43] First published in Venice in the 1550s and reprinted by Ramusio, the

Figure 5.4
On the Molyneux globe the coastlines observed by Frobisher in what is now eastern
Nunavut are transferred east to southern Greenland.

narrative describes itself as the reconstruction of some family papers, which
the author had unwittingly torn and scattered when he was a child. Zeno's
ancestor sailed into the high Arctic and there encountered populous cities
with Latinate people, a monastery run on geothermal power and, in lands to
the west, gold, idolatry, and cannibalism. The narrative has been convincingly
shown to be a pastiche of works by Christopher Columbus, Amerigo Vespucci,
Francisco López de Gómara, and Benedetto Bordone, and the included map
(figure 5.5) drew from a number of identified sources. Zeno's work reflects
the role of Venice as a clearinghouse of geographical information and publication.[44] By the later decades of the 1500s, both document and map had
achieved credibility in learned circles, with Zenian place names and islands
making appearances in the work of Ortelius, Gerard Mercator, and others.[45]
Hakluyt contributed to this dissemination and authorization of the Zeno narrative, including it in *Divers Voyages* and again in PN 1600, citing Ortelius's
atlas "for the credit of the history."[46]

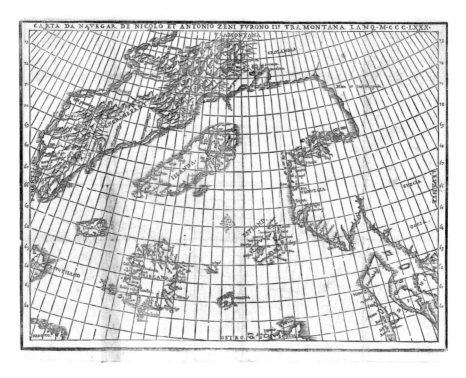

Figure 5.5
Niccolò Zeno's apocryphal map of the North Atlantic supplied a number of toponyms to early modern navigators and cartographers.

Not all was myth, however. Kirsten Seaver has surmised that in addition to its print and manuscript sources, Zeno's relation (like Cuningham's cosmography) drew on information from the northern codfish trade.[47] Indeed, as he described the hinterland of his fabulous monastery, Zeno wove in a detailed description of Inuit kayaks: "The fishers boates are made like unto a weavers shuttle: taking the skins of fishes, they fashion them with the bones of the same fishes, and sowing them together in many doubles they make them so sure and substanciall, that it is miraculous to see, howe in tempests they will shut themselves close within and let the sea and winde cary them they care not whether, without any feare either of breaking or drowning."[48] This information doubtless took a circuitous route to arrive in a Venetian book ca. 1558, but it was returned to its origins in 1576 when Frobisher sailed into the Arctic equipped with a Zenian geography of the region (cited by

George Best in his account of the three voyages).[49] There, perhaps the actual
kayaks observed by the Englishmen served to confirm the fantastic geography
in which they were embedded.

As we move south in Hakluyt's organizational schema, the next regional
category of materials is titled "Voyages ... to Newfoundland, to the isles of
Ramea and the isle of Assumption ... also to the coasts of Cape Briton." Yet
materials on the prolific fishery that had attracted English and other European mariners since the late fifteenth century are confined to an act regulating
the fishery under Edward VI and Anthony Parkhurst's description in a letter
to the editor's older cousin.[50] Documents included under this heading fall
loosely into two groups. The first group centres on the letters patent for discovery and settlement granted to Humphrey Gilbert in 1578. The rights of
discovery accorded to Gilbert had a vague and thus extremely broad scope
but in practice appear to have been directed at North America. As Gilbert's
project evolved over the years 1578 to '83, it came to focus on the mainland
south from Cape Breton and principally on what was later to be called New
England.[51] Eventually, and by a series of accidents, Gilbert's single voyage to
North America in 1583 made its brief and only landfall in Newfoundland at
the harbour that was already known as St John's; his ship was lost in a storm
on the voyage home.

Copious (and prominent) as these materials are, they included *little* first-
hand observation or experience of North America. As narrated by Edward
Hayes, the Gilbert expedition's presence in Newfoundland amounted to less
than three weeks and was confined to the Avalon Peninsula near St John's.
Otherwise, this group of materials draws primarily from the halo of theory,
celebration, projection, and planning around Gilbert's project and its aftermath, rich in ideas and anticipation but not in experience or empirical knowledge.[52] Among the Gilbert materials are a celebratory poem and later letter
by the Hungarian humanist Stephen Parmenius, who died at sea on the voyage, and a rare discussion of the legal rationale for claims of sovereignty over
American lands by Sir George Peckham. Peckham, a would-be colonist who
was also a Catholic, sought to reassure prospective settlers about the lawfulness
of English activities given Spain's prior assertions of rights. Although his geographical information was limited and vague Peckham's text has considerable interest for its thinking, as it drew on consultations with Hakluyt and
John Dee.[53]

A second group of documents under this heading is quite different in kind, concerned with voyage relations that appear to be of an entirely practical nature, written in what Hakluyt characterizes (in an unusual editorial comment) as "homely stile."[54] This group begins with an outlier, a rutter for the Magdalen Islands found in the *Bonaventure*, a French ship taken as prize by a Bristol merchantman; this is the captured document alluded to earlier. An accompanying letter by Thomas James informed the lord treasurer, William Cecil, that the *Bonaventure* had made "the discovery of an Island" with a rich walrus fishery, yielding tusks, hide, meat, and oil ("if it will make sope, the king of Spain may burne some of his Olive trees," James added combatively; he had taken the prize on his way to join Lord Thomas Howard, waiting off the Azores to intercept the Spanish treasure fleet).[55] The rutter inaugurated a series of English voyages aimed at exploiting the whale and walrus fisheries in the Gulf of St Lawrence and the Strait of Belle Isle. An unusual feature of this second group is Hakluyt's insertion of two notes by his own hand: a note about the walrus and a note concerning George Drake's voyage to the Magdelen Islands. While the first gives a lively picture of how walrus hides and tusks circulated in Elizabethan London – used as combs, knife handles, and antidotes to poison, compared to Moroccan leather shields in the Queen's armory – the second concerns a voyage that arrived too late in the season to take advantage of the walrus fishery and a narrative promised by the author that was not delivered in time to appear in the compilation. The editor typically confined his visible interventions to terse marginalia but evidently, despite its lack of success (or adequate documentation), this voyage was of considerable interest to Hakluyt as information on a "gainfull and profitable trade."[56]

The differences in *kinds* of documents from the earlier Gilbert project are evident: there are no Latin poems here. Hakluyt's framing sharpens the differences; although Charles Leigh's 1597 voyage to the Magdalen Islands is presented solely as an expedition in search of walrus, the voyage was in fact part of efforts to settle a colony of religious non-conformists there as well as to fish. This project echoed Peckham's earlier hope to establish a settlement for English Catholics in the regions under Gilbert's patent, but Leigh's narrative was not accompanied by surrounding documents comparable to those that communicated the official recognition and support attending Gilbert's voyage. Indeed, it is hard to discern from the text that four prospective settlers accompanied the voyage to survey potential sites for a colony. (One gave an

account of the voyage in a text published at Amsterdam some years later.[57])
Hakluyt's presentation treated Leigh's voyage as simply another attempt to
exploit the walrus fishery.

The details of Leigh's narrative indicate quite strongly that the *Bonaventure*'s voyage of 1591, which had informed the English of the region and its
resources, reflected ongoing activities rather than a "discovery."[58] English ships
entering these waters found a French and Basque fishery that was already well
established, and Leigh describes persistent and not always successful attempts
to distinguish the other European ships who had anticipated them at the
Magdalens that season into friends and foes. Ships from St Malo were regarded as friendly, informing Leigh's group that they supposed other ships
from the Basque country "to have bene of Spaine." Leigh and his colleagues
attempted to sequester the Basque ships' powder and shot until they could
ascertain their actual nationality, but it was in fact the Breton ships who attacked the English, setting up ordnance on shore; present also on shore were
three hundred Mi'kmaq "in readiness to assault us."[59] This episode provides
only a sample of the various conflicts Leigh described, which did eventually
include Anglo-Spanish battles, but it seems evident that prevailing conditions
of war and peace between governments in Europe did not adequately predict
relations and allegiances in the St Lawrence. Nor, in fact, was there common
purpose even within ships' companies. The Breton attack forestalled a mutiny
on Leigh's *Hopewell*, and the shipwrecked men of the *Chancewell* were treated
"in savage maner" by the crew of another French ship, even though its master
was friendly and well-disposed when Leigh found him.[60] The mutiny on
board the *Hopewell* would continue to simmer. After departing from the Magdalens, the *Hopewell*'s gunner and crew presented Leigh with a written request
to divert the voyage to prize-taking at the Azores or simply to return home,
refusing to pursue any further the fishing and whaling Leigh had intended.
(He also noted mistrust and "great enmity" between the *Hopewell* and the
segment of its company detailed to man a Spanish prize.[61]) Meanwhile, the
narrative by George Johnson, one of the would-be settlers, provides rich detail
of disputes among Leigh's passengers, who appear to take little notice of
events around them.

For the English, these were simply unfamiliar waters, as also evidenced by
the inability of the *Marigolde* to *find* the opening to the St Lawrence on another voyage four years earlier.[62] The region was an unfamiliar political en-

vironment of existing European and Indigenous presence, where English mariners navigated a complex landscape of rivalries, conflicts, and ambiguous allegiances. Hakluyt's praise of Leigh, Drake, and Wyatt as "the first ... of our owne Nation, that have conducted English ships so farre within this gulfe of S. Laurence" implicitly acknowledges belatedness with respect to the French, Bretons, and Basques who "do yerely returne from the sayd partes."[63] As the narratives suggest, not all mariners were eager or able to explore what was unknown to them.

The final of our three paratextual categories, "Voyages made for the discovery of the gulfe of Saint Laurence ... and from thence up the river of Canada," differs considerably from the preceding two. Hakluyt differentiated regions that arguably overlapped geographically (since Anticosti and the Magdalen islands are in the Gulf of St Lawrence) into the discrete paratextual categories, "Newfoundland and Anticosti" and "the St. Lawrence and inland." He also organized the contents of these contiguous categories so that while "Newfoundland and Anticosti" includes almost exclusively English materials, "the gulfe of Saint Laurence" contains only French sources. This linguistic sorting stands out given the complexity of encounters in these waters, as seen above.

Hakluyt was central to the transmission and dissemination of several key French travel narratives, and the materials on the voyages of Jacques Cartier found under this heading were perhaps the most important example.[64] As we've noted, the first publication associated with Hakluyt was an English translation of Cartier's voyages of 1534 and 1535, done by John Florio out of the Italian version presented in Ramusio's *Navigationi et viaggi*. Cartier's voyages had already attracted the attention of English geographers, as indicated by a reference to "the massively wealthy dominion of Saguenay" in a 1578 memorandum to the queen by John Dee; Dee's text aimed to advise the crown on the legal grounds supporting the patent for discovery granted to Sir Humphrey Gilbert in the same year, which as we've noted had a broad and vague geographical scope.[65]

Cartier's materials didn't appear in the 1589 first edition of *Principall Navigations*. In the second edition, however, Hakluyt joined to Florio's translations of the first and second voyages the only known account of Cartier's third voyage into the St Lawrence, with associated materials on the voyage of the Marquis de Roberval. The eventual disposition of the originals Hakluyt used is (typically) unknown; more unusually, so is their provenance – Hakluyt's is the only known version of the text. The complete acts and discoveries of an important French navigator were thus, if not rescued from oblivion, given additional visibility by the editor's diligence.

Yet just as all the materials on the St Lawrence are French, almost all of them are also firmly in the past. The sole contemporary materials in this category are two letters from Cartier's great-nephew Jacques Noël, one dated June 1587, both addressed to "John Growte," a student in Paris; they are contemporaneous with Hakluyt's time in Paris, and the second of the two may have accompanied the "aforesaid unperfite relation" of Cartier's third voyage.[66] In his first letter, Noël wrote that Growte's brother-in-law "Giles Walter" had that morning shown him "a Mappe printed at Paris, dedicated to M. Hakluyt an English Gentleman"; this was a map of the Americas (dated May 1587) accompanying Hakluyt's edition of Pietro Martire's De orbe novo (Paris, 1587). He wrote to request that Growte send him a copy of the map for himself. In a second letter, Noël apparently responded to an inquiry about surviving writings by Cartier. His letters testify not simply that he had been able to consult Cartier's own map but that he had personal knowledge of the Hochelaga region and of how the St Lawrence ran above the rapids there: "I have seene the sayd River beyond the sayd Saultes." They also register that Noël's sons were in the region of the St Lawrence at the time of writing: "my booke ... is made after the maner of a sea Chart, which I have delivered to my two sonnes Michael and John, which at this present are in Canada."[67] Apart from this passing mention in an undated letter, no narrative or other document appeared in either edition of PN to make clear the nature or extent of renewed or continued French presence in northern North America at the time of writing. Yet archival records (as well as the presence of European trade goods in the archaeological record) indicate that several decades before Hakluyt arrived in Paris, French ships making voyages to the Newfoundland fishery had already begun to diversify their activities by hunting for whales and seals in the Strait of Belle Isle and trading for furs at Cape Breton. By the 1580s, trade with "Canada" had resumed, along the banks of the St Lawrence.[68] Bellenger's 1583 voyage to Acadia, collected by Hakluyt for its evidence of the fur trade, was not an entirely new initiative; as we've seen, it also did not appear in PN.

One effect of segregating French materials on the St Lawrence was to frame them as having taken place primarily in the past, where they remained as a source of knowledge on which English planners could draw, rather than part of a continuum of activities extending into Hakluyt's own day. While the editor can be credited with ensuring the durable transmission of Cartier's final relation – the source of all later editions – he left its sequels largely in the shadows, where they persist as faintly visible traces.

ASSEMBLING A CONNECTED CONTINENT

Hakluyt's paratextual categories draw dividing lines around regions, itineraries, and projects; yet of course English thinkers also tried to put together and make sense of what they knew, and not always in ways we might expect. I'll close with three examples of the larger assemblies into which the English – not only Hakluyt but his associates and contemporaries – fitted what they knew about northern North America. The last of these will return us to the globe and map.

In 1577, the mathematician and magus John Dee wrote an important set of documents advising the crown on England's rights of discovery in the northern regions that were, at that moment, being explored and prospected by Martin Frobisher. (Readers familiar with his three voyages will recall that in 1577, after gold was apparently found in ore brought back by Frobisher in 1576, the enterprise was massively expanded in size and taken over by the crown.[69]) Frobisher's voyages were also the first time that England had significantly tested Spanish claims to the Americas, attracting close attention for that reason.[70] Dee was thus concerned with articulating a claim grounded in the principles of the law of nations. Unlike some of his contemporaries, Dee considered the papal grant to be legitimate but limited in scope to lands not "discovered" prior to the bull and located at or below the latitude of Spain and Portugal. While that construction of the bull opened the way for other claims, Dee's positive argument for an English claim in the North Atlantic rested on a reading of sources that claimed both an early conquest of regions in the North Atlantic by King Arthur and the persistence there of settlements descended from Arthurian colonists.[71] The apocryphal travels of the Zeno brothers to rich, populous, and urbanized territories lying to the northwest of Europe appeared to provide independent confirmation of a thriving Arctic civilization of European descent, whose libraries might supply additional evidence of Arthurian origins. The first document in Dee's portfolio of advice accordingly identified the Zenian island of Estotiland with Baffin Island/ Qiqiktaaluk and located it adjacent to the "massively wealthy dominion of Saguenaya." The thoroughly annotated surviving copy of Dee's Ramusio indicates that he read Ramusio's materials on the North – which would have included Cartier – as attentively as did Hakluyt. This set of connections between Arthurian legend, Venetian apocrypha, North Atlantic geography, and English claims of discovery can be traced through *Principal Navigations*, as Hakluyt reproduced sources that figured as key texts for Dee.[72] Such speculations were not only the province of theorists and editors, however. Dee transferred his Arctic interests to Adrian Gilbert and the navigator John Davis, who appears to have been his student, and Davis employed the Zenian toponyms in describing the region he explored. Davis was in turn a source for the Molyneux globe, and these toponyms can be observed both there and on Edward Wright's map.[73]

In the same years that Dee was composing his vision of a rich, Arthurian Arctic, one of the captains who sailed with Frobisher framed his narrative and descriptive account of the Arctic through a quite different lens. George Best began his account of the voyages with a short discourse "to prove all partes of the worlde habitable, thereby to confute the position of the five Zones."[74] Best engaged with an argument put forward in the influential treatise of John de Sacrobosco, *Tractatus de sphaera*, holding that only the temperate regions between the polar circles and the tropics would be viable for human habitation.[75] As early as the 1520s, Englishmen had seized on news of Spanish discoveries of fertile, rich, and populous regions in the torrid zone of equatorial America to argue that regions above the Arctic Circle might also defy the predictions of cosmographers that they would be uninhabitable and barren.[76] Best and others invoked a conceptual framework that organized the earth into zones defined by latitude, retaining the authority of its categories while reframing their predictive ability: his long discussion of the torrid zone in a text about the Arctic presumed that the two were analogous, zones of equally "extreme" climate. Unusually, however, Best drew immediately on his fellow mariners' *experience* of tropical West Africa. This experience would have been proximate: Frobisher himself had sailed to West Africa at least twice as a young man and was briefly taken captive on the trading voyage of John Lok in 1554. (Lok was the elder brother of Michael Lok, who became treasurer to the company that funded the Arctic voyages of the 1570s.[77])

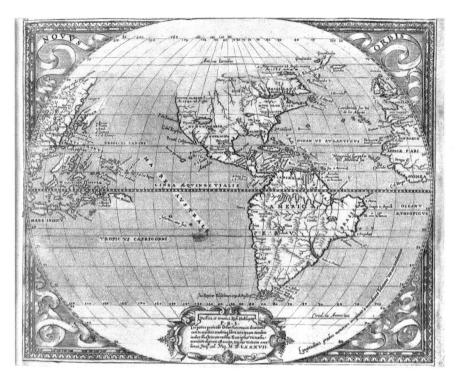

Figure 5.6
The map of the Americas included in Richard Hakluyt's edition of *De orbe novo* (1587) represented some of the latest information available from English voyages.

Frobisher's uncle, Sir John Yorke, was a major investor in voyages to Guinea for both trade and slaves; he did not survive to invest in his nephew's Arctic voyages, but at least a few Guinea investors – Sir Lionel Ducket, Sir William Winter – were among the adventurers.[78] Kim Hall has noted the foundational role of West African voyages in English seafaring, both in the skills acquired by seamen and the profits that nourished other enterprises.[79] In his reflections on the colour of Inuit people he encountered, Best also relied on his familiarity with Africans resident in England; their persisting presence there appears to date from the Hawkins voyages of the 1560s.[80] Best's connections between Guinea and the Arctic remind us that English mariners and merchants were not specialists and that ships, men, and money circulated between apparently unconnected regions at a considerable distance from one another.

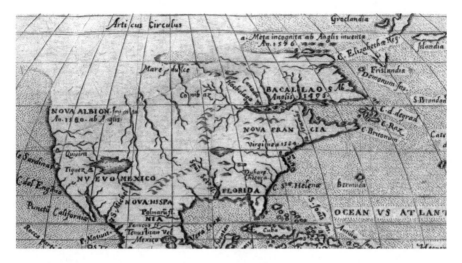

Figure 5.7
Jacques Cartier's nephew Jacques Noël suggested several corrections to the 1587 map's representation of the St Lawrence above Hochelaga.

The final story returns us to Cartier's relations for another connection across distance: this time across the American continent. Jacques Noël's first letter requested a copy of the map from Hakluyt's edition of *De orbe novo*, and this map was in some ways remarkable (see figure 5.6). "Based on a Spanish original," according to R.A. Skelton, the version that appeared in Hakluyt's edition of *De orbe novo* incorporated the most recent and sensitive English cartographic information: "data from Frobisher's Northwestern voyages, from Drake's circumnavigation and from Ralegh's colonial venture [that is, the colony at Roanoke Island, NC] ... which must've been supplied by Hakluyt."[81] Its appearance attracted new information of equally high quality. Noël drew on his own knowledge and that of his uncle, both recorded in their papers, to correct the map's representation of the upper St Lawrence: "I hold that the River of Canada ... in that Mappe is not marked as it is in my booke, which is agreeable to the book of Jaqes Cartier: and that the sayd Charte doth not marke or set down the great Lake, which is above the Saults, according as the Savages have advertised us, which dwell at the sayd Saults."[82] Noël's verbal corrections were assiduously highlighted by Hakluyt in the margins: "The Saults are in 44. deg. and easie to passe"; "But 5. leagues journey to passe the 3. Saults";

"Ten dayes journey from the Saults to this great Lake." All bear on a heading in the PN text that appears to indicate a map present in Cartier's lost original: "Here after followeth the figure of the three Saults."[83] Its absence in Hakluyt's version doesn't inform on whether a map was present in his source text: maps were invariably omitted from *Principal Navigations*.

Noël's second letter, apparently responding to an inquiry about his great-uncle's papers, added two notes that had been "written in the hand of Jaques Cartier" on a chart drawn by the navigator and in the possession of a master Cremeur. The first was affixed to the map beyond the place where the St Lawrence ("the River of Canada") divided: "By the people of Canada and Hochelaga it was said, That here is the land of Saguenay, which is rich and wealthy in precious stones. And about an hundred leagues under the same I found written these two lines following in the said Carde inclining toward the Southwest. *Here in this Countrey are Cinamon and Cloves, which they call in their language Canodeta*."[84] Hakluyt's contemporaneous manuscript treatise on colonization, "Particuler Discourse," made reference to the same information, suggesting that the St Lawrence above Hochelaga provided an easy route to lands where spices grew:

> in the ende of that seconde relation this postscript is added as a special pointe: To witt that they of Canada say that it is the space of a moone (that is to say a moneth) to saile to a lande where Cynamon and cloves are gathered, and in the frenche originall which I sawe in the kinges Library at Paris in the Abbay of Saint Martines yt is further put downe that Donnaconna the kinge of Canada in his barke had traveled to that Contrie where Cynamon and cloves are had, yea and the names whereby the Savages call those twoo spices in their owne langauge are there put downe in writinge.[85]

His own consultation of Cartier's "french originall," with the detail of Donnaconna's travels, did not appear in PN, present only in the manuscript treatise presented to Queen Elizabeth and a few of her counselors.[86] Did Hakluyt understand that North America, like the East Indies, might yield rich spices or simply hope that the Indies were (somehow) at no great distance? Other evidence suggests that the editor was constantly attentive to information that might suggest contiguity between Asia and North America. He wrote in the margins of a medieval mission to the Mongols that Mongol men wore clothes "like unto Frobisher's men," while women's dress resembled that of the women of Meta Incognita (Baffin Island/Qiqiktaaluk).[87]

Noël's letters make evident another imagined connection or proximity related to the St Lawrence. Along with his request for the map, he asked his correspondent to send him the "booke of the discovery of New Mexico." Antonio de Espejo's travels in New Mexico, *Histoire des terres nouvellement descouvertes* (Paris, 1586), had been translated by Hakluyt's collaborator Martin Basanier, after Hakluyt himself had published a Spanish edition of the text, *El viaje que hizo Antonio de Espejo* (Paris, 1586).[88] Espejo's narrative originally appeared earlier the same year, in the second edition of Juan González de Mendoza's *Historia ... Del gran reyno de la China ... Con un itinerario del Nuevo Mundo* (Madrid, 1586). Hakluyt's efforts to put this text expeditiously into circulation may be clarified by another detail. Anthony Payne suggests that the *De orbe novo* map referred to in Noël's first letter – "wherein all the West Indies, the kingdome of New Mexico, and the Countries of Canada, Hochelaga, and Saguenay are contained" – was originally prepared to accompany the Paris edition of Espejo, to which it is more relevant, but Hakluyt chose not to delay publication of the Espejo text until the map was ready.

Espejo had set out on an overland journey in 1582 to explore territories to the north of Mexico. As Ricardo Padrón has noted, Mendoza's account of the human geography of New Mexico "arranges the indigenous societies encountered by Espejo in ascending order of civility along a route of travel from south to north," concluding with news of a people just a little further on whose cities exceed Madrid in size; the presence of textiles and parasols resembling those found in China suggested that the peoples of New Mexico and beyond, in the temperate zones of North America, were trading with their equally civilized Chinese counterparts.[89] In the Spanish context, the Espejo expedition comported with hopes of connecting China with a larger, transpacific Spanish Indies, and contesting Portuguese claims to a sphere of influence that extended across all of Asia.[90] In the English (and French) context, its bearing was somewhat different.

Sharing with Dee the theoretical and pragmatic view that the north was either available or destined to become an English sphere of activity, Hakluyt emphasized that Espejo's journey towards ever more rich and well-governed regions kept "still the same NORTHERLY course" (emphasis in original).[91] Es-

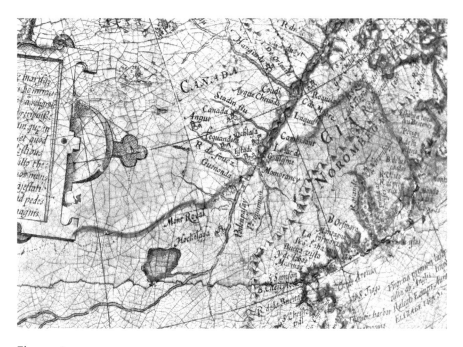

Figure 5.8
The Molyneux globe represents a different version of the St Lawrence above Hochelaga.

pejo's news of rivers and lakes trending towards the north appeared to dovetail with analogous reports from the east, both those related by Cartier and Noël's story of standing on a hill to look beyond the rapids and make sense of information that it was "ten dayes journey from the Saults" to a "great Lake, which is above the Saults, according as the Savages have advertised us." In the margins of Espejo's text, Hakluyt carefully noted not only "plenty of golde" but Indigenous reports of "a mighty lake" and of "a mighty River of eight leagues broad running towards the North sea."[92] As he wrote, "Perhaps this River may fall into the Chespiouk bay, or into the great lake at Tadoac." The adjacency of New Mexico and Hochelaga in Noël's description of the *Novo orbe* map, showing "the kingdome of Newe Mexico, and the Countreys of Canada, Hochelaga, and Saguenay," was not coincidental.[93] John Davis, too, cited Espejo's travels in support of a conjecture that "the distance is very small betweene the East parte of this discovered Sea and the passage wherein I have so painefully laboured."[94]

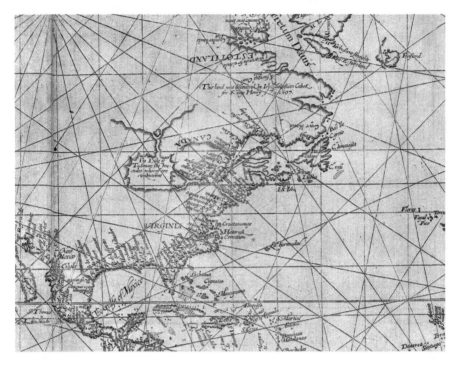

Figure 5.9
Edward Wright's world map, which appears in some copies of *Principal Navigations*, represents a third conjecture about the St Lawrence.

These varied conjectures and exchanges take visible form in Molyneux and Wright's cartographic work, but their differences suggest the processual nature of the understanding that underlay the maps. The Middle Temple globe shows a named Saguenay River flowing into the St Lawrence from the north at a point near the Ile d'Orléans (rather than in its actual location downstream from Quebec) and a tributary to the west of Hochelaga ending in a large lake; beyond it, the St Lawrence River continues across the continent and into the territories explored by Espejo. Edward Wright's map exhibits numerous differences from the globe; among them, it shows the St Lawrence debouching into a large body of water, open to the North, that resembles the lower part of Hudson Bay/Tasiujarjuaq, labelled "The Lake of Tadouac the boundes whereof are unknowne." Wright also located the Saguenay River correctly, downstream from Stadacona, with "Tadousen" – where it joined the St Lawrence – approximating Tadoussac, the site of a fur trade that drew traders from as far as Hudson Bay/Tasiujarjuaq, an impressively extensive "sea."[95] Indications of inland rivers and bodies of water were evidently matter for close attention and speculation, and we can (in turn) only conjecture about the exchanges, debates, and variant sources of information that led these collaborators to produce different representations so close together in time.[96]

By 1600, English mariners had coasted parts of northern North America for more than a century. The half-remembered landfall of John Cabot still lingered as the basis for claims to a landmass still rarely contacted, as the *De orbe* map recalls with the legend adjoining "Baccalaos," on the northern shore of the St Lawrence, "Anglis 1496." In practice, though, there was still no certain sense of how the land lay, who inhabited it, or what might bring English mariners there. Eastern Canada was at the edge of English geographical knowledge; not wholly unknown, like the West and North, or mundanely familiar, like the east coast of Newfoundland, it lay tantalizingly at the far end of multiply mediated chains of information. While Hakluyt's text provides some of the links in these chains, English cartographies indicate how provisional were the understandings of actual space they afforded.

NOTES

1   I am grateful to Lesley Whitelaw, librarian of the Middle Temple, for her generous assistance in using digital images of the Molyneux globe in close proximity to the globe itself and to Sylvia Sumira and Seohyung Kim for other globe-related assistance.

2   I borrow the term from Jardine and Sherman, "Pragmatic Readers." For a survey of the sources behind one map – the polar map attributed to Michael Lok in Hakluyt's *Divers Voyages* (1582) – see Quinn, *Richard Hakluyt, Editor*, 22–6.

3   Mercator's influential world map on the new projection (now lost) appeared in 1569, his atlas in 1595 (though with component maps circulating earlier); the atlas of Ortelius, *Theatrum Orbis Terrarum*, appeared in 1570.

4   See Wright, *Certaine Errors in Navigation*; McIntyre, "William Sanderson."

5   The legend is transcribed and translated from Latin by Wallis, "The First English Globe," 279. Translation *into* Latin was done by William Camden.

6   The very place name "Canada" presents a signal example: while in this essay I will use it as a synonym for northern North America, the Molyneux globe

identifies "Canada" as a subregion of "Nova Francia," on the north shore of the St Lawrence, *and* as the name of an Indigenous town along a tributary of the St Lawrence River. This usage ("Canada" as a territory located in the interior of the St Lawrence region) reflects the usage found in French sources, in turn borrowed from Indigenous usage: "Le mot 'Canada' fut emprunté aux Iroquoiens du Saint-Laurent qui l'utilisaient à l'origine pour identifier leur territoire situé le long du fleuve Saint-Laurent entre Gaspé et Québec" (Turgeon, *Une Histoire de La Nouvelle-France*, 91).

7 See Hakluyt, *Particuler Discourse*, chap. 18; Peckham, *A True Reporte*, chap. 3.

8 Fuller, *Remembering the Early Modern Voyage*, chap. 4. While several administrative documents relating to various fisheries were printed in Hakluyt's *Principal Navigations*, the sole quasi-narrative source devoted principally to the Newfoundland fishery was a letter to his elder cousin, who on John Dee's testimony was an expert advisor to government on the fishing trade (Parkhurst, "A Letter Written to M. Richard Hakluyt ... 1578," *PN*; Dee, *General and Rare Memorials*, 7). Documentary sources on the Newfoundland fishery in the period are reproduced in Quinn, *New American World*, vol. 4. A narrative treatment of English activities along with documentary and cartographic sources is provided in Cell, *English Enterprise*. Laurier Turgeon's recent history of New France provides perspective on the fishery from French sources (*Histoire de La Nouvelle-France*, chap. 1).

9 Cuningham, *Cosmographical Glasse*, 201–2, 199, 161. Cuningham should not be taken as an index of English geographical knowledge at midcentury; his contemporaries Richard Eden and Robert Recorde, who shared Cuningham's medical and mathematical interests, were consultants to the long-distance trading companies of their day, and both men's publications reflect much broader awareness of the new geographies of the preceding hundred years.

10 A compilation, to paraphrase a medievalist's definition, is "the assemblage of multiple discrete works into a larger structure whose formal interplay of textual and material parts" has the potential to produce a variety of literary (and I would add here, ideological) effects (Bahr, *Fragments and Assemblages*, 10). Unless otherwise noted, I have cited individual items from the second edition, *Principal Navigations* (1598–1600), indicated with "*PN*."

11 Wallis, "The First English Globe," 275.

12 Hakluyt, "To the Reader," *Principall Navigations*, sig. *4 verso; Wallis, "The First English Globe," 278.

13 That said, a few documents of particular interest to Hakluyt are duplicated, at least partially, in multiple parts of the compilation, but this strategy had obvious limits.

14 I am grateful to Sandro Mezzadra for this phrasing in his generous response to a talk delivered at the University of Bern Summer School in 2016.

15 Sumira, *The Art and History of Globes*, 65. Sylvia Sumira's presentation, at a 2010 London Rare Book School seminar led by Sarah Tyacke and Catherine Delano-Smith, provided valuable insights on the manufacture and conservation of early modern globes.

16 The only addition known to have been made after that date is the 1603 date of publication on the Middle Temple globe (Wallis, "Further Light on the Molyneux Globes"; Wallis, "Opera Mundi"). A copy of the Hondius globe is held at the Henry E. Huntington Library, but detailed examination for the purposes of this essay was not possible in 2020–21.

17 Barber, "Mapmaking in England," 1619.

18 Hakluyt's sources are given in Quinn and Quinn, "Contents and Sources of the Three Major Works." Joan-Pau Rubiés comments (on the earlier, 1589 edition of *PN*) that "Hakluyt conceived *The Principall Navigations* in parallel with a series of editions and translations of key texts … However … he also occasionally broke his own rules – that is, the separation of national and foreign narratives – in order to accommodate a number of particularly interesting texts within the collection … In that sense, the patriotic focus of *The Principall Navigations* coexisted in some tension with the practical needs of a wider proto-colonial project" (Rubiés, "The Rise of an Early Modern Genre," 32). Anthony Payne's discussion of Italian and French influences on Hakluyt provides useful context for his survey of the numerous translations the editor either published himself or encouraged others to publish (Payne, *Richard Hakluyt*, 23–8, 83–116).

19 I can only gesture here towards the very rich topic of translation in the early modern period. Michael Wyatt comments, in the context of Italy but with broader reference, that, "through the appropriation of other languages and their cultures, England tacitly acknowledged the scarcity of its own cultural capital but in so doing enabled the appropriating mechanisms that would provide one among the many diverse factors that came to advance its growing sense of a 'national' character and facilitate its global ambitions" (Wyatt, *The Italian Encounter*, 7). See also Sherman, "Bringing the World to England"; Fuchs, *The Poetics of Piracy*, chap. 1.

20 See "The Taking of the Madre de Dios," PN 2(ii):194–9. The book was Duarte
    Sande, *De missione legatorum Japonensium ad Romanam curiam* (Macao,
    1590); Hakluyt printed the text as de Sande, "An Excellent Description of the
    Kingdome of China," PN 2(ii):88–98.
21 Ribault, *The Whole and True Discoverye*.
22 Reprinted along with the text in PN, Hakluyt's dedication to Walter Ralegh
    described this account of a French colony as having been "concealed many
    yeeres" ("The Voiage of Captaine René Laudonniere," PN 3:301). The original
    publications were Laudonnière, *L'Histoire Notable*; Laudonnière, *A Notable
    Historie*. Hakluyt contributed a poem to the Paris edition, done by his collabo-
    rator Martin Basanier and noted in the dedication to PN vol. 2 that Basanier's
    edition was printed "at mine own charges ... which by the malice of some too
    much affectioned to the Spanish faction, had bene above twentie yeeres sup-
    pressed"; he translated the English edition himself (Hakluyt, "Epistle Dedica-
    torie," PN 2(i): sig. *3r; Payne, *Richard Hakluyt*, 87–92). Thevet's accusations
    are discussed in Lestringant, *Le Huguenot et le sauvage*, 255–8. On the use of
    Spanish sources and the idea of translation as aggression, see Fuchs, *The
    Poetics of Piracy*, chap. 1; Fuller, "Richard Hakluyt's Foreign Relations."
23 Hakluyt did not include Jean de Léry's important *Histoire d'un voyage*, a
    surprising omission; Hakluyt owned a copy of the book.
24 Hakluyt, "Epistle Dedicatorie," *Divers Voyages* (DV). Anthony Payne's census
    of surviving copies finds only one exemplar of DV that includes the Cartier
    translation, "with a contemporary binding instruction to include 'Florio ...
    iind'" (Payne, *Richard Hakluyt*, 83; Payne and Neville-Sington, "Interim
    Census"). Ramusio's account post-dated the anonymous *Bref récit* (Paris, 1545)
    on Cartier's second voyage; further accounts of Cartier's voyages would not
    appear in French until 1598.
25 Florio, "To the Reader," *A Shorte and Briefe Narration*. The authorship of this
    preface comes with a question mark. While it appears over John Florio's name
    signed the preface bears a detailed resemblance to passages from Hakluyt's
    "Particuler Discourse" (1584), and (as E.G.R. Taylor has noted) appears to
    draw on Anthony Parkhurst's letters to the elder Hakluyt. Frances Yates re-
    marked that its plain style differs sharply from all of Florio's other dedicatory
    epistles; style, too, aligns closely with Hakluyt's writing. At the very least, he
    must be viewed as an important, if invisible contributor (Taylor, *Original
    Writings*, 1:21–2; Yates, *John Florio*, 58–9).

26 Hakluyt, "Epistle Dedicatorie," PN. For a richly contextualized narrative account of Hakluyt's activities during the 1580s, as he travelled between Paris and London, see Peter Mancall, *Hakluyt's Promise*, ch. 6–8.

27 For Hakluyt's letters from Paris, see Taylor, *Original Writings*, 1:205–10, 2:343–5. Several dedications to Walter Ralegh during these years are also translated and reprinted by Taylor; Ralegh was at the time planning a settlement in the mid-Atlantic, with voyages of reconnaissance beginning in 1584. At the same time, Christopher Carleill, the stepson of Hakluyt's patron Sir Francis Walsingham, was pursuing a project of settlement in southern New England originally set forward by Sir Humphrey Gilbert. After the latter's death, however, the project apparently did not advance beyond the stage of proposals (see Carleill, "A Briefe and Summarie Discourse," PN). While Carleill's text proposed a settlement in 40°N, David Quinn believes that Carleill also planned a trading post at the mouth of the St Lawrence as an adjunct to his more southerly colony. Carleill's printed discourse and associated correspondence do not directly articulate such a plan, but in his treatise on American colonization Hakluyt *did* propose planting and fortifying at Cape Breton (Hakluyt, *Particuler Discourse*, 147, 67).

28 Bellenger's relation is British Library, Add. MS 14027, fo. 289–90v, printed in Quinn, *New American World*, 4:306–8. Hakluyt apparently visited Rouen and obtained the relation and (then or later) a map from Bellenger (Quinn, 4:306.) "Particuler Discourse" makes numerous references to information provided to him personally by "my frende Stephan Bellenger." Laurier Turgeon specifies that Bellenger's voyage was unusual in being financed not by private interests but by a figure in government aiming at establishing a coastal station and eventual mission. His discussion sets Bellenger's efforts in the context of comparable commercial voyages in previous decades. See Quinn, "The Voyage of Etienne Bellenger"; Turgeon, *Une Histoire de La Nouvelle-France*, 109–15.

29 The manuscript was the Codex Mendoza, purchased from Thevet, later published by Purchas, and now held at the Bodleian Library. For discussion of formal or informal censorship in relation to Hakluyt's materials in particular, see Hammer, "Myth-Making"; Payne, "Richard Hakluyt and the Earl of Essex"; Stout, "'The Strange and Wonderfull Discoverie of Russia': Hakluyt and Censorship."

30 For these headings, see PN 3: sig. A4 recto-A5 recto.

31 For records of cloth consigned to Davis for sale in China, see Cotton, *Eliza-*

bethan Guild, 82, 84. See also, the language of the letters patent authorizing Davis's voyages in search of a "Passage unto China and the Iles of the Moluccas" (Elizabeth I, "Letters Patents [...] Graunted to M. Adrian Gilbert," PN, 3:96). The syndicate backing Frobisher's voyages was referred to by its treasurer as "the Companye for discovrye of Cathai" (McDermott, *The Third Voyage of Martin Frobisher*, 55).

32 Quinn, *Voyages and Colonising Enterprises*, 1:52. For documents relating to the northern interests of Dee, Davis, and Adrian Gilbert, see Quinn, *Voyages and Colonising Enterprises*, 2:483–9. For Gilbert's early treatise on the Northwest Passage, see Gilbert, *Discourse of a Discoverie*. (The treatise is reprinted in PN vol. 3.) On the detour to Newfoundland, see Hayes, "Report of the Voyage," PN, 3:146–7. Expansively defined rights and limited understanding of the geography make Gilbert's target region hard to specify, but the documents indicate that it was considerably further south. Plans to continue Gilbert's colonizing project after his death at sea specified a location of 40°N for settlement, roughly the latitude of northern New Jersey. See Carleill, "A Briefe and Summarie Discourse" PN, 3:184.

33 Materials in these three categories are itemized in Fuller, *Lines Drawn Across the Globe*, Appendix 7, as well as in Quinn and Quinn, "Contents and Sources"; and detailed references are provided in the endnotes and bibliography for individual items discussed in this essay.

34 The evidence and its confusion in the sixteenth century – perhaps to be ascribed to Sebastian Cabot himself – are examined in Pope, *The Many Landfalls*, 43–68. John Day's roughly contemporaneous letter to Columbus on John Cabot's first voyage is printed in Quinn, *New American World*, 1:98–9. Further archival evidence on the early Cabot voyages and other early westward voyages can be found in that volume; more recent discoveries have been made by researchers at the University of Bristol (Jones and Condon, *Cabot and Bristol's Age of Discovery*; University of Bristol, "The Cabot Project," http://www.bristol.ac.uk/history/research/cabot/#research.) Useful context on Sebastian's connections and a later voyage to the Rio de la Plata can be found in Dalton, *Merchants*.

35 Jones and Condon, *Cabot and Bristol's Age of Discovery*, 57–61. Thorne wrote in 1527 that, "my father ... with another marchant of Bristow named Hugh Eliot, were the discoverers of the New found lands" (Thorne, "Discourse [...] to Doctour Leigh" PN, 1:219). Hakluyt printed his materials for the first time in 1582, as well in 1589 and 1600.

36 The two narratives composed by Eden at the request of interested friends (Eden, *Decades*, fo. 343 recto-40 verso) were reprinted by Hakluyt (Eden, "The Voyage of M. Thomas Windam [...] 1553," PN 2(ii): 9–14 Eden, "The Voyage of M. John Lok to Guinea, Anno 1554," PN 2(ii): 14–43).

37 Hakluyt, *Divers Voyages*, sig. A4 recto. (*Divers Voyages* and other unpaginated texts are cited by signature, leaf number, and recto or verso side.)

38 Best, *True Discourse* (1578); Ellis, *A True Report of the Third and Last Voyage*; Settle, *A True Reporte of the Laste Voyage ... by Capteine Frobisher* (1577). Editions of Settle's text were published in Latin and German at Nuremberg (1580) and Geneva (1578); Lorenzo d'Anania, *Lo scopremento*, relies on Settle's account of the 1577 voyage (Alden, *European Americana*, vol. 1).

39 For celebration of English efforts to search for a northern sea route to Asia see, for instance, Hakluyt's comments in the prefatory material to PN vol. 1.

40 Steele, "From Hakluyt to Purchas," 81.

41 The other voyages celebrated are Francis Drake's circumnavigations (1577–80) and a Northeast Passage search by Arthur Pet and Charles Jackman (1580).

42 Davis, "Worldes Hydrographical Discription," sig. B5 verso. I am grateful to Sarah Tyacke for calling my attention to Davis' silence. The "Greenland transfer," which endured into the eighteenth century, is discussed by Ruggles, "Cartographic Lure"; see also McDermott, *The Third Voyage of Martin Frobisher*, 51. Several maps predating Davis's voyages locate Frobisher's discoveries correctly, to the west of Greenland.

43 Zeno, *De i Commentarii [...] et dello Scoprimento [...] de due fratelli Zenii*; Zeno, "The Voyage of M. Nicolas Zeno," PN, 3:121–8.

44 See Horodowich, *Venetian Discovery of America*, chap. 5.

45 See maps of the northern regions in Ortelius, *Theatrum Orbis Terrarum*; Mercator, *Atlas*. Zeno's representation of Arctic geography as a whole was reproduced in a map of the North Atlantic added to Ruscelli, *La Geografia de Claudio Tolomeo* (1561). (Reproductions and discussion can be found in Burden, *The Mapping of North America*.) Later texts that cite, discuss, or reproduce elements of the Zenian geography (through 1898) are listed in Lucas, *The Voyages of the Brothers Zeni*, 212–24. A fuller picture of the relationship between Mercator, Ortelius, John Dee, and the Hakluyts, along with the use and discussion of the Zeno material, can be found in Sherman, *John Dee*; MacMillan, *Limits of the British Empire*; Taylor, "A Letter Dated 1577"; Taylor, *Original Writings*.

46 Ortelius, "A Testimony of Ortelius" *PN*, 3:128.

47 Seaver, "Common and Usuall Trade," 1.

48 Zeno, "The Voyage of M. Nicolas Zeno," *PN*, 3:123–4.

49 George Best conferred his observations of "Friseland," on 20 June 1578, with "a description set out by two brethren Venetians, Nicholaus and Antonius Zeni … they have in their Sea-cardes set out every part thereof" ("A true discourse of the three voyages of discoverie" *PN*, 3:62). Among the equipment for Frobisher's first voyage was "a great mappe universall of Mercator in printe," the (now lost) world map that "used much of the Zeno detail" (Waters, *Art of Navigation*, 530; Ruggles, "Cartographic Lure," 200–1).

50 Richard Hakluyt the elder (sometimes identified as the lawyer, to distinguish him from his cousin the editor and clergyman) was credited by Dee with a particular interest in fisheries (*General and Rare Memorials*, 7). On English writing about Newfoundland in the period more generally, see Fuller, *Remembering the Early Modern Voyage*, chap. 4.

51 Quinn, "Gilbert, Sir Humphrey." Documents and more detailed discussion can be found in Quinn, *Voyages and Colonising Enterprises*; Quinn, *New American World*, vols 3–4.

52 The central source on Gilbert's voyages, with documents and a detailed introduction, is Quinn, *Voyages and Colonising Enterprises*. For discussion of the writing associated with Humphrey Gilbert's project, see Fuller, *Voyages in Print*, chap. 1; Miller, *Invested with Meaning*, chap. 3; Quinn and Cheshire, *The New Found Land*.

53 Sir Francis Walsingham wrote to Hakluyt that he had learned from Peckham of the "great light" Hakluyt had provided regarding Western discoveries (Walsingham, "A Letter of [...] Sir Francis Walsingham [...] 1582," *PN*, 3:165–81. Peckham's consultation with Dee is recorded in Dee's diary for 3 July 1583 (Dee, *Diary*, 16.) These documents also appear in Quinn, *Voyages and Colonising Enterprises*, 2:280, 313, 346. On the broader picture of English thinking about the legal foundations of exploration and settlement in the period, with some discussion of Peckham, see Tomlins, *Freedom Bound*, chaps 3–4. A briefer discussion of Peckham appears in Fuller, "Missing terms."

54 Hakluyt, "The Voyage of M. George Drake of Apsham," *PN*, 3:193. Quinn's introduction to the documents provides context and information not present in Hakluyt (Quinn, *New American World*, 4:56–80).

55 James, "Letter to Cecil, 1591," *PN*, 3:191.

56 Hakluyt, "The Voyage of M. George Drake of Apsham," PN, 3:193. Some additional details are provided in the relation of the *Marigold*, a consort that lost sight of Drake's ship and did not succeed in finding the Magdalens (Fisher, "Voyage of the Marigolde," PN, 3:191–3).

57 Johnson, *A discourse of some trouble and excommunications in the banished English church at Amsterdam* (Amsterdam, 1603), excerpted in Quinn, *New American World*, 4:111–13.

58 Although narrative records are poor, archival and archaeological investigations led Selma Barkham to conclude that "there may well have been as many as two thousand men using harbours every year along the Strait of Belle Isle during the second half of the sixteenth century" (Barkham, "The Mentality of the Men," 110). See also Brad Loewen, "Sea Change," in this volume.

59 Leigh, "The Voyage of M. Charles Leigh [...] 1597," PN, 3:195–6.

60 Ibid., 3:196, 197–8.

61 Ibid., 3:197, 200.

62 Fisher, "Voyage of the Marigolde," PN, 3:192.

63 Hakluyt, "The Voyage of M. George Drake of Apsham," PN, 3:193.

64 Frank Lestringant's account of Hakluyt's mission in Paris provides historical context for the transfer of maritime information from France to England and the editor's success in organizing "la fuite des documents d'intérêt stratégique" (*Le Huguenot et le sauvage*, 325). Michel Bideaux's critical edition of Cartier, *Relations*, also attends to Hakluyt's role in transmission of materials about the Cartier voyages and provides a detailed and thorough examination of all surviving sources for the voyages.

65 Document 1, in MacMillan, *Limits of the British Empire*, 38.

66 Hakluyt's language might be understood to indicate that Noël was responsible for providing to him the account of Cartier's 1540 voyage to the "countreys of Canada, Hochelaga, and Saguenay" that directly precedes the latter in PN: "Underneath the aforesaide unperfite relation that which followeth is written in another letter sent to M. John Growte student in Paris from Jaques Noel of S. Malo, the grand nephew of Jaques Cartier" (Hakluyt, PN, 3:236). (A "Steven Noel" is named as Cartier's nephew in "The Third Voyage of Jaques Cartier ... 1540," PN, 3:324.) Scholars scrutinizing the materials closely have not reached consensus on the provenance of Hakluyt's text, however. Arthur Stabler proposes that Hakluyt obtained materials on the Cartier and Roberval voyages from André Thevet (cited in Lestringant, *Le Huguenot et le sauvage*, 329; see

also 333). Bideaux considers the question of provenance to remain open (Cartier, *Relations*).

67 Noël, "A Letter Written … by Jaques Noel" *PN*, 3:236. "Part of another letter written by Jaques Noel of Saint Malo," *PN*, 3:237.

68 Turgeon, *Une Histoire de la Nouvelle-France*, 107–12, 120–3. Renewal of French trade in the interior is mentioned briefly in a document under the "Newfoundland" heading in Christopher Carleill, "A Briefe and Summarie Discourse," *PN*, 3:187; Carleill is likely to have had this information from Hakluyt. See also Brad Loewen, "Sea Change," in this volume.

69 For details, see McDermott, "The Company of Cathay"; McDermott, *The Third Voyage*.

70 Allaire and Hogarth, "Martin Frobisher."

71 Quixotic to modern ears, this hypothesis derived from accounts of Arthur's conquests by the Anglo-Norman historian, Geoffrey of Monmouth. MacMillan's edition of Dee's policy recommendations to Queen Elizabeth and Sherman's study of his reading practices help to clarify the nature of his interest in King Arthur and its articulation with the Zenian geography of the Arctic (MacMillan, *Limits of the British Empire*; Sherman, *John Dee*). Dee's correspondence with Mercator on the evidence for Arthurian descendants in the Arctic was printed in the first volume of *Principal Navigations*; on Hakluyt's use of Arthurian materials, see also Fuller, "Arthur and Amazons."

72 On Saguenay, see MacMillan, *Limits of the British Empire*, 38. On Dee's Ramusio, now in the library of Trinity College, Dublin (shelf mark DD.dd.40–1), see Sherman, *Used Books*, 117–19. Hakluyt located a number of Arthurian materials in volume 1 of *PN*, devoted to the North, while the Zeno materials are adjacent to Frobisher's and Davis's voyages in volume 3.

73 In 1586, Davis wrote to his patron William Sanderson that one of his ships had "bene at Island, and from thence to Groenland, and so to Estotiland, from thence to Desolation, and to our *Marchants*" (Davis, "Letter to William Sanderson," *PN*, 3:108). Here, "Estotiland" probably signifies the coast of Labrador, where this ship had been dispatched to fish. It appears in that position on Edward Wright's 1599 world map.

74 Best, "True Discourse" *PN*, 3:48.

75 Sacrobosco's early thirteenth-century treatise remained a staple of English cosmography in the period; see Thorndike, *The Sphere of Sacrobosco*.

76 Thorne, "A Persuasion of Robert Thorne … to King Henry the Eight," *PN*,

1:212–14; Thorne, "Discourse ... to Doctour Leigh," *PN*, 1:214–20; Barlow, *A Brief Summe of Geographie*. For a thorough and important treatment of the science as it developed through the Middle Ages and into the context of European exploration, see Wey Gómez, *Tropics of Empire*.

77 Similarly, Anthony Parkhurst – *PN*'s sole informant on the Newfoundland fishery – was among the merchants present on Sir John Hawkins' slaving voyage to Sierra Leone in 1564. On Frobisher's captivity, see Eden, "The Voyage of M. John Lok to Guinea, Anno 1554," *PN* 2(ii): 17. On Frobisher and Africa, see McDermott, "'A Right Heroicall Heart,'" 55–60. On Michael Lok, see McDermott, "Michael Lok, Mercer and Merchant Adventurer." On Parkhurst, see Sparke, "The Second Voyage Made by John Hawkins 1564," *PN*, 3: 521.

78 McDermott, *The Third Voyage*, 56. On Yorke and Duckett, see Willan, *The Muscovy Merchants of 1555*, 131. One of Frobisher's captains was named Gilbert Yorke, but no relation is known to this author.

79 Hall, *Things of Darkness*, 19.

80 For a brief survey of the documents on African presence in sixteenth century London, see Habib, *Black Lives in the English Archives*.

81 Skelton, "Hakluyt's Maps," 65. Largely free of the Zenian cartography discussed above, the map locates Frobisher's discoveries correctly, placing "Meta Incognita" to the north of Labrador, separated from Greenland by a strait of water.

82 *PN*, 3:236. Noël's "booke ... agreeable to the book of Jaqes Cartier," presumably a private record, remains unknown.

83 Cartier, "The Third Voyage of Jaques Cartier," *PN*, 3:235.

84 Noël, "Part of Another Letter Written by Jaques Noel of Saint Malo," *PN*, 3:236–7.

85 "The Second Voyage of Jaques Cartier ... 1535," *PN*, 3:232; Hakluyt, *Particuler Discourse*, 83.

86 Hakluyt, *Particuler Discourse*, xv.

87 "Voyage of Friar John de Plano Carpini," *PN*, 1:54, 27.

88 Noël, "A Letter Written ... by Jaques Noel," *PN*, 3:236. I'm grateful to Anthony Payne for sharing unpublished work on Hakluyt and the Espejo text. For a treatment in print, see Payne, *Richard Hakluyt*, 87–9, and Payne, *Richard Hakluyt*, 91. Espejo's text was also included in *PN*, from which citations are taken. On Mendoza's *Historia*, see Padrón, *The Indies of the Setting Sun*, 183–200.

89 Espejo: "many mantles of cotton straked with blew and white, like those that
    are brought from China"; "certaine shadowes or canopies like unto those
    which are brought from China" (Padrón, *The Indies of the Setting Sun*, 196,
    199; Espejo, "The Voyage of Antonio de Espeio," PN, 3:392, 393).

90 On this larger ambition, and the conceptual imbrication of Mexico and
    China, see Padrón, *The Indies of the Setting Sun*.

91 Espejo, "The Voyage of Antonio de Espeio," PN, 3:394.

92 Ibid., 394–5.

93 Noël, "A Letter Written … by Jaques Noel."

94 Davis, "The Worldes Hydrographical Discription," sig. B7 recto.

95 Turgeon, *Une Histoire de la Nouvelle-France*, 132.

96 David Quinn suggests that perhaps Wright was able to draw on additional in-
    formation derived from Noël or another French informant to show an idea of
    Lake Ontario, "the great Lake, which is above the Saults." "Later [i.e., after the
    correspondence with Noel printed in PN], Hakluyt seems to have obtained a
    map through the Noël family, which showed the lake above the rapids, and it
    appeared in Edward Wright's map" (Quinn, *New American World*, 4:305). If
    Hakluyt did obtain such a map, we can wonder why it informed the 1599 map
    by Wright but not the globe to which Wright contributed during the 1590s.
    See also Skelton, "Hakluyt's Maps," 1:52.

6

Labrador Inuit at the Crossroads of Cultural Interaction

LISA K. RANKIN

INTRODUCTION

In the late-eighteenth century, Inuit occupying the central and southern coastline of Labrador inhabited cosmopolitan communities, located at a cultural crossroads where different populations of Indigenous and European people converged, intersected, and diverged in different seasons and on different scales from all points on the compass. Inuit villages did not house a global population per se but might be considered cosmopolitan in the sense that the Inuit who occupied them were aware of the world and of the peoples who existed beyond their territories, and they worked diligently to develop relationships (and economies) with those who came from different nations near and far. Furthermore, some Inuit had even travelled to Europe. Most of these had been abducted, but some were invited guests. Occasionally, some, like the Inuk woman Mikak, even returned to Labrador having forged new connections to Western society and with new ideas to share with their home communities.[1]

These relationships with Europeans, sometimes friendly and sometimes difficult, were desirable for Inuit for numerous reasons. Primarily they provided access, through trade, to materials manufactured in other parts of the world, goods such as metals, glass beads, and sail cloth that Inuit did not manufacture themselves. Inuit used these exotic items to make their daily lives easier, but the objects and the external connections they symbolized also

supported an internal system of economic and political leadership; the wear-
ing, use, and re-distribution of exotic goods signified wealth, status, and success. In this manner, trade items can be considered the physical manifestation
of the relationships and connections that Inuit forged with Europeans, and
prominently displaying exotic items on clothing and as jewelry demonstrated
the importance of the wearer. In southern and central Labrador this trade
permeated the lives of Inuit as they attempted to accommodate European
newcomers and the goods they provided into their cultural systems. It influenced day-to-day and seasonal tasks, the locations of settlements, the construction of houses, the formation of households, and relations between
communities. Inuit approached and engaged with Europeans in these cultural
exchanges on their own terms as active agents. However, there is little doubt
that these interactions influenced a cascade of social, economic, and political
realignments that we can identify archaeologically and that these changes intensified as Inuit became increasingly enmeshed in the global economy.

These encounters and the reactions they precipitated in Inuit communities
can only really be understood in the context of Inuit culture and history,
forged through centuries of tradition. European visitors, who authored the
documents that traditional historical analysis depends on, rarely situated Inuit
actors in the context of the long history of Labrador, nor could they understand that eventful history from an Inuit perspective.[2] However, archaeology
can offer us a glimpse of the Labrador Inuit world during that early modern
period of European contact. This paper incorporates the data recovered from
fifteen seasons of archaeological excavations at Inuit settlements on the
Labrador coast in hopes of infusing the historical record with Inuit actors
from their fifteenth-century arrival in Labrador to the advent of colonial settlers in the nineteenth century.

HOW ARCHAEOLOGISTS UNDERSTAND EARLY
MODERN INUIT HISTORY

With its focus on material culture and other physical remnants of past society,
archaeology can help to extend and enrich the early history of Labrador beyond the archival record. This is particularly important when the goal is to
infuse the historical record with the Inuit voices marginalized in written ac-

counts. When interpreting archaeological data, however, we must remain mindful that the record is often incomplete due to matters of preservation. Furthermore, we are speaking about a history which is not necessarily our own but which is filtered through a Western academic discipline. Importantly, in the early modern period where European texts, maps, and images are available, the archaeological record can be used alongside European documents to critique what little we know of Indigenous history from the European perspective to help counter polemics that present Indigenous communities in a negative manner or adopt tropes of Indigenous decline and obsolescence.[3]

Archaeologists begin from the premise that all cultures are dynamic and constantly in flux but responsive in culturally contingent frameworks to events and stimuli both internal and external to the community. This does not mean that we understand cultural histories as predictable but simply that culture change is most likely to occur in ways that can be understood within particular cultural contexts. Therefore, to understand Inuit participation in and reactions to the colonial encounters of the early modern period, archaeologists need to begin further back in time, to observe long-term cultural trends and understand what Inuit life was like before the encounters took place. By doing this we can observe changes in the archaeological record and interpret how and why those changes took place as part of a cultural continuum.

Archaeology also has a spatial component whereby artifacts, structures, communities, and even regional patterns of land-use must be understood both independently and in relation to one another. The placement of archaeological remains, observed at these different spatial scales is not random but represents specific decisions and actions of past people and reflects the relationships people have with material items, the land, non-human beings, and one another. Since we cannot observe people's action directly, we use the spatial distribution of archaeological remains to help us understand past behaviour and decision-making processes and the relationships those represent. Any changes to the spatial patterning of these past activities require explanation. Thus, archaeological interpretation is dependent on understanding the diachronic context of the data.

Finally, archaeologists also examine the archaeological record for long-term continuities in human behaviour over time and space. By identifying cultural elements which did not change we can better understand how change is incorporated into pre-existing cultural frameworks. We draw on this long-term context to help us interpret history as it might have been experienced, or lived, by past people.[4]

The incorporation of archaeological research into early modern history can be particularly fruitful, especially when the goal is to understand Indigenous agency and power in the early stages of the colonial project. There is a substantial archaeological record created by Indigenous agents that can be used in tandem with historical texts to develop a more robust and holistic presentation of early encounters between Europeans and Indigenous nations. Archaeology can help to provide the long-term historical contexts which demonstrate the significance of dynamic Indigenous histories long before they were subjected to the European gaze. Moreover, archaeological interpretation relies on the significance of place and the webs of relationships which underscore Indigenous world views and history-telling.[5]

SETTING THE SCENE: INUIT ORIGINS

Understanding ancient Inuit history is a prerequisite for interpreting Inuit actions and reactions to European encounters on the Labrador coast during the early modern era because it helps us to identify how these events were perceived by Inuit and how their reactions were informed by traditions developed over centuries. From this perspective there can be no prehistoric/historic dichotomy, and Inuit history does not become significant merely because they met Europeans. For Inuit, these encounters were simply new events within a long cultural and historical continuum.

Inuit history can be traced archaeologically to its origins on the shores of Siberia and Alaska around the Bering Strait early in the first millennium AD.[6] Here, ancestral Inuit developed and refined many of the traditions that would ultimately come to be key elements of Inuit culture including the hunting of walrus, whale, and seal (important to all aspects of survival in the north, from subsistence to housing to clothing); the use of watercraft and probably sled dogs for hunting and travel;[7] and a semi-subterranean house form capable of retaining heat.[8] From a North American perspective, this early maritime tradition developed into fully realized Inuit culture patterns in Alaska about AD 1000 when the ancestors of the Labrador Inuit intensified their economic pursuits[9] and perfected the technologies that assisted with daily life over the next several centuries. Marine mammal hunting, particularly of seals and bowhead whales, was complemented by caribou hunting, fishing, and the pursuit of smaller game and birds. To access these resources, it was often necessary to travel between distinct ecozones; moreover, a complex understanding of both animal behaviour and physical landscapes was required. Archaeological remains indicate that travel on the water, land, and sea ice was facilitated by kayaks (small, single person watercraft), umiaks (large, open, skin boats capable of carrying many people and goods), and komatiks (dog sleds).[10] The objects used in daily life (material culture) were made largely of locally-available resources, complemented through extensive trade networks that brought Asian metals and beads to northern Alaska, perhaps through middlemen, long before the arrival of Europeans.[11] Regionally available goods such as jade, chert, caribou skins, and ivory were traded between communities. Patterns of trade and exchange bring to light the significance of interactions between communities and probably with people from other cultures, many centuries ago.

Sod-walled, semi-subterranean houses, occupied during the winter months, were supported by driftwood and sea mammal bone and were entered through long, narrow entrance tunnels or passages which kept cold air from entering the main room. Wood or stone floors, and side benches positioned against exterior walls (used for sleeping and carrying out domestic chores) completed the domestic architecture. Light and heat were provided by hearths. Qargi, or non-residential workshops, were sometimes constructed for daily activities undertaken by men,[12] while women's activities were presumably centred within homes. Archaeologically, we see both an increasing number of settlements occupied over time as well as increases to the size of permanent settlements, suggesting that the Inuit population of Alaska was growing and that relationships between individuals and communities were increasingly complex and strained.[13]

By AD 1000, the ancestral Inuit of northern Alaska had developed all of the key cultural practices which persisted, albeit adapted to differing local circumstances, in Inuit lifeways of the early modern era. These include the mobility to traverse regions for significant resources and goods, interactions with communities near and far, and a pattern of domestic life that was sustainable in northern regions. Inuit daily life was shaped by relationships that were influenced by age, gender, and difference in individual status. These ancient origins provide a baseline for our understanding of Inuit history.

ACROSS THE ARCTIC AND TO LABRADOR

Around AD 1200 there was a sudden migration of Inuit from Alaska across the Arctic to northwest Greenland (figure 6.1). This epic 4,000 kilometre journey was undertaken across a landscape previously unknown to Inuit, and it proceeded with remarkable speed. Radiocarbon dates indicate that sites across the entire migration zone were relatively contemporaneous, suggesting that this journey may have taken as little as fifty years.[14] What led to this migration remains poorly understood, but several hypotheses have been put forward. The first involves possible population pressure and conflict in Alaska. Archaeologically, there is an increase in the size and number of villages in Alaska prior to the migration, suggesting some degree of over-population and resource strain. Additionally, slat armour recovered from ancestral Inuit sites may be indicative of increasing conflict.[15] As a result, some families may have decided to seek a more peaceful and sustainable life elsewhere.[16] A second hypothesis involves exploration of newly opened subsistence opportunities. The Medieval Warm Period, beginning around AD 950, opened Arctic waters, allowing for exploration by watercraft and also expanded the range of bowhead whales, a particularly significant resource. Friesen suggests that people would have seen significant populations of bowheads travelling east each spring and returning in the autumn, indicating that new, untapped whaling grounds would be available if they travelled east to find them.[17] Moreover, the opening of the Arctic waterways greatly expanded the range of the ringed seal, which was a main staple of the Inuit diet.[18] Finally, the desire to access both Norse and meteoric iron in Greenland has been proposed, particularly in light of evidence of local feuding, which may have disrupted access to other metal sources.[19] It is possible that Inuit were told about these iron sources by Dorset people, whose ancestors had migrated across the Canadian Arctic archipelago during an earlier era. Regardless, the migration brought Inuit into the vicinity of both the Cape York meteorites and Nordsetur district of Greenland frequented by Norse hunters, two potential sources of iron. In reality, all of these

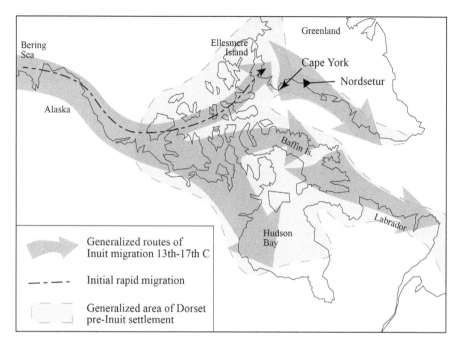

Figure 6.1
Map showing Inuit migration from Bering Strait region, with places mentioned in the text.

options may have played some part in the decision to undertake the journey across the Arctic.

Understanding demography in the distant past is often difficult for archaeology so we cannot be certain how many Inuit were involved in the initial migration, but it seems likely to have been undertaken by a small group. Friesen draws on ethnographic analogy to suggest that the journey was undertaken by a few extended family groups of fifteen to fifty people.[20] This estimate is similar to that recorded in the Inuit oral history of Qitdlarssuaq, a charismatic nineteenth-century *angakkuk* (shaman), who fled Baffin Island for Greenland with his family and followers after committing a murder.[21] Qitdlarssuaq followed shamanic visions, journeying to Greenland and back again over a thirty-year period. Several members of his group died throughout the journey. It is likely that early Inuit migrants would have been led by someone with similar skills to Qitdlarssuaq. If not an *angakkuk*, a skilled and trusted mariner who was held in some regard would have been needed to motivate and lead the group.

There are other hints from the ethnographic record that skilled leaders would have held considerable status and perhaps also wealth. Umiaks, kayaks, and komatiks were probably the primary means of transportation across the Arctic. An umiak is capable of transporting large numbers of people (generally women and children), as well as goods and dogs over long distances. Constructing an umiak would have been a considerable investment and historically was considered "the most valuable single piece of property that Inuit owned."[22] They were constructed from driftwood, covered in the skins of walrus or bearded seal, and required substantial maintenance.[23] Not everyone would have been able to acquire such a large boat and so an umiak owner would have been considered a wealthy man. Umiak owners were also regarded as prominent charismatic leaders, capable of forging alliances, organizing labour, and generating surplus commodities to support their followers.[24] In short, umiak owners took responsibility for the "material, ritual, and military well-being of the community."[25]

Umiaks were also used in resource gathering. Seal was an easily acquired and dependable food resource, and Inuit subsistence practices were predominantly based on hunting seal throughout their range.[26] Seal could be hunted in all seasons. In winter they were taken from breathing holes in the ice using thrusting harpoons; at other times, they were hunted either from the flow edge or in open water from umiaks and kayaks with throwing harpoons similar to those used for the whale hunting.[27] However, access to bowhead whale, important to the Inuit economy and social organization, seems to have had a central role in the Arctic migration, as early sites are concentrated at whaling grounds. Whales were harpooned in the open sea by crews using umiaks and fleets of sea-going kayaks.[28] This type of hunting required the considerable skills of a whaling captain, generally an umiak owner, to lead and choreograph the communal labour of the group. It was also dangerous and had a high risk of failure.[29] The difficulties of whaling are reflected in the ceremonies surrounding it and the prestige gained by those involved.[30]

Although a complete understanding of this Arctic migration is impossible due to the limited nature of the archaeological data, we can be certain that Inuit were accomplished long-distance travellers with the skills, technologies, and social organization needed to successfully inhabit the Arctic landscape.

Further, we can surmise that the complexities of this great migration, including the vision, the access to appropriate transportation technology, and even the hunting skills, were most likely to have been supplied or coordinated by influential charismatic leaders – quite possibly shamans. We can also be certain that this initial migration was not the last: other Inuit with material cultures we can trace to diverse regions in Alaska were quick to follow, establishing settlements supported by marine mammal hunting throughout the Canadian and Greenlandic Arctic within a century. These successive waves of migration would have been informed by earlier migrants and perhaps even Dorset populations. Once settled into different regions across the Arctic, Inuit adapted to local conditions, sometimes forming regional groups around wide territories, aggregating and dispersing into different sized kin or economic groups as the situation required.[31] In turn, these regional groups were linked through trade whereby valuable resources such as "iron, copper, ivory, sea mammal oil, caribou hides, wood and amber moved between adjacent groups … through down-the-line exchanges."[32] Norse iron from Greenland also seems to have made its way into this system, shown by numerous items recovered from Ellesmere Island.[33] This propensity for interaction, whether between Inuit groups or through encounters with outsiders such as Dorset or Norse populations, demonstrates that Inuit were never really alone on their Arctic journey, but also highlights another mainstay of Inuit culture – the management of interactions, and both indirect and direct trade – also forged in the deeper history of Inuit origins on the edges of the Bering Sea and no doubt requiring its own set of leadership skills.

When the Little Ice Age began to play havoc with Arctic sea ice conditions in the fifteenth century and access to bowhead whales became difficult, year-round settlement in the central and high Arctic was abandoned, and Inuit once again took to travel, ultimately to the shores of Labrador. Inuit venturing to Labrador would have encountered many familiar things, including the barren tundra-like landscapes of the northern and outer coastline, as well as the bowhead whales, seals, and herds of caribou that were the mainstay of their diet. But their experience in Labrador would also lead to new engagements – with the forested landscapes of the south and with new people. First Nations populations had made Labrador their home for millennia, and by the early sixteenth century Basque and Breton fishers and whalers were making seasonal visits to the southern reaches of the Labrador coast.

LABRADOR

It is generally accepted that Inuit had moved into Labrador by the latter half of the fifteenth century, probably migrating from Baffin Island[34] (figure 6.2). Sites associated with the initial Labrador migration are sparse, although Staffe Island 1 (JaDb-2) and Nunaingok 1 (JcDe-1), both located near the tip of mainland Labrador on the south side of the McLelan Strait, are likely candidates.[35] Both these sites contain tools made from fine-grained slates and nephrite which were exotic to Labrador, suggesting that they were brought by Inuit from the eastern Arctic. As well, harpoon technology and other implements found on early sites resemble those used by Inuit in more northerly regions.[36] A small scattering of early material culture has also been recovered from sites located between Killinek and Hebron, suggesting that a few other locales may also have been occupied quickly and that Inuit were migrating in a southerly direction.[37] Most sites indicate that Inuit rapidly integrated local lithic materials to make tools and in almost all cases we find items of European material culture, such as iron nails or the occasional glass bead. Access to these European items suggests that Inuit rapidly set about exploring the entire Labrador coastline, where they would have encountered Basque from French and Spanish provinces, as well as Breton and Norman fishers in the Strait of Belle Isle. Arriving Inuit would also have quickly noticed the First Nations populations who occupied inner islands along the central coast as they migrated south. Unfortunately, the archaeological record is unable to provide anything more than a superficial understanding of these potential encounters with First Nations neighbours. The earliest Inuit confined their settlement to the outer coast, so face-to-face contact may not have occurred immediately. But as Inuit expanded their settlement area to include the protected and resource-rich inner bays, their presence seems to have pushed First Nations populations towards the interior, the southerly reaches of the Labrador coast, and the Quebec north shore of the Gulf of St Lawrence.[38]

The speed with which European material was integrated into site assemblages following the Inuit arrival in Labrador is striking. For Inuit, the possibility of acquiring European metal and other goods may have been part of the lure to explore and settle the foreign, forested landscapes of the south. We know that trade was an important aspect of Inuit culture and that access to exotic goods and iron had been significant to Inuit for centuries. Locating a

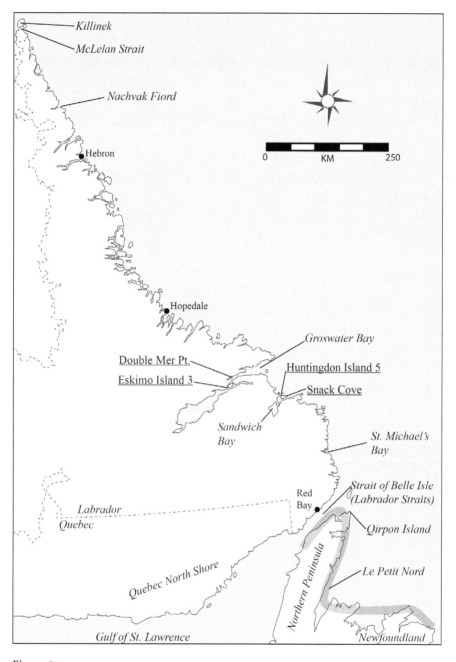

Figure 6.2

Map of Labrador showing places mentioned in the text. Modern settlements are represented by black dots; archaeological sites are underlined.

new source of iron and other interesting European goods would have been a significant matter for migrating Inuit, and many of these items were readily incorporated into Labrador Inuit lifeways.

The first documentary evidence that we have of Inuit presence in southern Labrador comes from a 1567 hand-coloured handbill printed in Augsberg, Bavaria, to advertise the display of an Inuit woman and child captured in Nova Terra, likely by French fishers in the Labrador Straits, in 1566.[39] Little more is known about the encounter which led to their capture, but archaeologically we know Inuit had undertaken some exploration of the southern Labrador coast before then. There is archaeological evidence of an Inuit winter occupation in Red Bay.[40] This site is undated but contains early Inuit tool-types generally abandoned by the sixteenth century. A second early Inuit sod-house site, recently examined by Stopp in St Michael's Bay, appears to have been occupied by AD 1500.[41] Little more has been gleaned to date from sixteenth-century documentation owing to the vague language used to describe the actors and places involved.[42] However, Barkham[43] and Martijn[44] describe friendly European–First Nation encounters in the sixteenth century, while suggesting that Basque-Inuit relationships were less than harmonious.[45] Once again archaeological data can be used to clarify matters.

In Sandwich Bay and Groswater Bay, located north of the Strait of Belle Isle, there is a relatively continuous record of Inuit occupation beginning in the late sixteenth century. Excavations undertaken at these sites by my students and me over the past fifteen years reflect the increasing participation of Inuit in the trans-Atlantic economy through time, shedding light on the ways that these interactions developed and the ways in which Inuit incorporated this new activity and the resultant goods into their daily lives, economies, socio-political strategies, and identities.

THE CHANGING LIVES OF SOUTHERN LABRADOR INUIT

At the very end of the sixteenth century, Inuit were residing at the site of Snack Cove, located on the outer coast of Sandwich Bay. This was a tundra-like environment, similar to locales favoured by Inuit during their initial migration to the Labrador coast, and it suggests that Inuit at Snack Cove were relatively new to the region and inhabiting the kind of landscape with which they were most familiar.[46] The site consists of four winter, semi-subterranean sod-houses and three summer tent rings, as well as numerous other archaeological features including burial cairns and kayak stands. The form of the three sod-houses we excavated at Snack Cove is also similar to Inuit houses occupied throughout central and northern Labrador during this era.[47] These were small nuclear-family houses, with a single room, rear sleeping platform, side alcoves to store belongings, and a slab stone floor fronted by a lengthy entrance passage facing the shoreline. It is not known whether the houses at Snack Cove were occupied simultaneously, but the radiocarbon dates taken from each house, which span the same late sixteenth to early seventeenth century period, suggest that this is a possibility.[48] The fauna recovered from Snack Cove are varied but dominated by ringed seal, caribou, sea birds, and fish.[49] For the most part, archaeological evidence indicates that this is a traditional Labrador Inuit settlement. However, artifacts recovered from each of the houses include both traditionally manufactured objects, such as slate endblades used for hunting, and a small number of Basque-, Norman- and Breton-derived objects including iron nails, Basque roof tiles, and a limited number of ceramics. All the European-manufactured material had been modified to suit Inuit purposes: such as roof tile used as oil lamps and iron hammered into ulu blades, the semi-lunar knife used by Inuit women. The site assemblage is devoid of formal trade items such as the beads, blankets, and folding knives that were eventually brought by Europeans to Labrador specifically to trade with Indigenous communities.[50] While it is possible that Inuit at Snack Cove received these goods from Inuit living even further south, we believe that the European items were more likely to have been scavenged by Inuit from seasonally abandoned European fishing and whaling stations located in the Labrador Straits, taking advantage of the European habit of caching supplies on shore at the end of their summer fishing and whaling ventures. Inuit also collected desirable objects such as iron nails from European middens and shore constructions.[51] Finally, each house contains caches of partially altered European nails and spikes, not yet fully formed into Inuit tools, which may have been prepared to trade with northern kin.[52]

We can only speculate on how this northern trade took place, but goods were probably handed between families in different regions in a down-the-line exchange similar to that which occurred in the Arctic.[53] By the late sixteenth century, significant Inuit settlement zones can be found along the length of the Labrador coast, generally clustering in places with access to abundant resources. These represent the places where Inuit might conceivably travel to meet one another and exchange goods. One of the closest settlement areas north of Sandwich Bay was located in the region of Hopedale, on the central Labrador coast. Here, forty-four Inuit houses at five distinct sites were located and excavated by Junius Bird during the summer of 1934.[54] Although the houses were poorly dated, Bird developed a relative chronology based on housing types. We now know that many of those houses (Bird's Type 1 series) probably date to the late sixteenth/early seventeenth century, including several houses at the site of Avertok (*Avigtuk*, the place of the bowhead whales), and that Inuit were probably drawn to the region by its rich marine resources, including bowheads, walrus, and various types of seal. Our understanding of the Arctic bowhead hunt (see above) suggests that this was a communal activity involving many hunters overseen by a whaling captain. Given that bowheads frequented the Hopedale region in the fall, Inuit from Sandwich Bay might well have expected to encounter numerous Inuit family groups in the Hopedale area at that time of year preparing for the hunt. Multi-community gatherings such as this would not only have supported a whale hunt and associated ceremony but allowed time to re-establish the connections between families from various regions through the exchange of goods, information, and spouses.

There is a further archaeological connection that we can draw between the Inuit settlements of Sandwich Bay and those examined in Hopedale, suggestive of interactions between the communities. This involves the construction of a very distinctive early seventeenth-century house form which has thus far only been encountered at Inuit sites near Hopedale, in Groswater Bay, and in Sandwich Bay. At the site of Karmakulluk, House 6 has a distinctly rectangular form with the shortest dimensions at right angles to the entrance passage.[55] The house had sleeping platforms located on the long walls, a paved floor, and a long entrance passage with cold trap (an interior step from the passage into the house which prevents cold air from entering the house).[56] House 2 at the site of Eskimo Island 3, located in Groswater Bay, is similarly described,[57, 58] and House 1 at the site of Huntingdon Island 5 in Sandwich Bay, which we excavated in 2009, is a nearly perfect match. All three houses date to the same era. What is fascinating about these houses is that they represent a sudden shift from the small, nuclear family, outer coast habitations, like those occupied at Snack Cove, to larger houses occupied by two or three families in inner bay settings.

Snack Cove was abandoned by the early seventeenth century, and Inuit settlement in Sandwich Bay shifted away from the open coasts of the outer islands to the sheltered, secluded inner bay site of Huntingdon Island 5. Over the course of several seasons, we excavated four of the five winter houses located there. House 1, the earliest of the sequentially occupied houses dating to approximately AD 1620, is a distinctly different household structure than those recorded at Snack Cove.[59] Like the early seventeenth-century houses recorded near Hopedale and Groswater Bay, House 1 was a large structure containing substantial side and rear sleeping platforms, as well as a cooking area to the left of the entrance passage, a lampstand, and a large rear hearth. This structure was capable of housing multiple families, perhaps accommodating as many people as had occupied all three houses at Snack Cove (perhaps fifteen to twenty-five people). Faunal remains from each of the three early seventeenth-century houses in the different regions indicate that the Inuit inhabitants followed a traditional subsistence pattern, and the material culture assemblages contain traditional artifacts as well as modified European-derived objects repurposed for Inuit use. In House 1 at Huntingdon Island 5, there are also European manufactured items which appear to be cached for trade,[60] but as with the artifact assemblages at Snack Cove, no formal trade artifacts were present, suggesting that direct trade with Europeans in the Strait of Belle Isle had not begun.

We do not know exactly why southern Inuit changed their residential pattern in the early seventeenth century. The movement to inner bays is not unique; it was happening throughout the Labrador coast as Inuit adapted to local ecosystems and took advantage of the broader range of subsistence resources available from these locations.[61] However, other criteria, such as safety and participation in the trade for European goods, may also have played a role. Inuit occupying Sandwich Bay lived on the margins of European activity. Occupying larger houses in more concealed locations might have offered them some measure of protection from European intrusion. Cohabitating families may also have worked together to both acquire and redistribute European manufactured goods.

While there is little detail about Inuit in the Basque documentary evidence, both Martijn[62] and Stopp[63] have found ample reference to the Inuit in sixteenth- and seventeenth-century French writings. According to Martijn,[64] the French regularly recorded Inuit thievery and noted that contact, when it did happen, was generally hostile. There are accounts of Inuit attacking French fishing boats in the water and stealing from French stations on shore.[65] The documentary references to hostility are so frequent that Martijn has suggested that Inuit were engaged in guerrilla warfare against the French.[66] Violent interactions were perhaps more likely to be recorded than encounters that ended peaceably, but there is increasing evidence to suggest that violence was the norm. Mitchell[67] has begun to tabulate the number of violent encounters and associated deaths of both French and Inuit during this volatile period, while Pope[68] has suggested that violent encounters with Inuit led the French to temporarily abandon their fishery on the Labrador coast in the early seventeenth century and retreat to the relative safety of the Petit Nord, although Inuit soon followed them there.

Thus, large Inuit houses which brought several families together may have appeared more intimidating to outsiders and offered more protection to occupants, especially if the occupants also travelled together for purposes of acquiring European material in potentially hostile situations. It also seems likely that these new multi-family households would have required a different kind of leadership than that needed to coordinate the activities of nuclear families. Inuit had relied on experienced, charismatic, and wealthy headmen to guide their hunting, trade, and travel for centuries. Travel over difficult seas into hostile encounters, as well as the establishment of new economic protocols to oversee trade with northern kin (which we might associate with the substantial caches of European-derived material found at Huntingdon Island), may well have resulted in the re-emergence of charismatic Inuit leaders, coordinating and perhaps controlling the activities of a larger household group. Hu[69] notes that changes to leadership style are more likely to happen on the margins or boundaries of a cultural system, where charismatic leaders are capable of seizing control of social, political, and economic systems if there is a demonstrable benefit from doing so. Southern Inuit were not only living on the edges of the Labrador settlement system, they were confronting new challenges, new people, and new resources. With this came the opportunity to establish new methods for achieving status and wealth through trade –

something we can recognize in the archaeological record by the mid-to late seventeenth century.

The archaeological assemblage recovered from House 2 at the Huntingdon Island 5 site (dated to approximately A D 1640), contains a selection of European-manufactured beads and may well be our first evidence of a more formal, direct trade between Inuit and Europeans. Beads, along with iron implements, blankets, and sail cloth were among the items that Europeans transported to Labrador specifically to trade with the Indigenous community.[70] Throughout the remaining decades of the seventeenth century, formal trade items became increasingly common in the Inuit settlements of Sandwich Bay,[71] and by the early eighteenth century direct trade was well established. Extended family households or communal houses became the norm for Inuit living in southern Labrador and throughout the Labrador coast. And charismatic traders or headmen, who controlled many aspects of Inuit social, political, and economic systems, are occasionally noted in European documents.[72]

While Basque fishers and sealers could still be found along the Strait of Belle Isle and the Quebec north shore through much of the seventeenth century,[73] it was the increasing presence of French and ultimately English that drew the Inuit into a deeper trade relationship in the eighteenth century. In an effort to end Inuit skirmishes with the French fishery, fishers were initially accompanied by armed escort vessels.[74] Eventually, fishers negotiated something of a truce with Inuit by agreeing to peaceful trade at Quirpon Island in the Strait of Belle Isle on specified occasions.[75] Following the Treaty of Utrecht in 1713, there was an expansion of French activity in southern Labrador. Census records indicate that between 1718 and 1743, an average of about 1,300 French fishers lived along the Strait of Belle Isle in the summertime.[76] As well, French colonial authorities began issuing land grants to Canadian concessionaires, typically merchants or civil and military officials, who believed they would be in a better position to establish peaceful relations with the Inuit.[77] These new residents of Labrador were permitted to use their concessions for sealing, hunting, fishing, and trade with Aboriginals.[78] However, overwintering concession crews probably never numbered more than 160 men.[79] Given the large number of French fishers compared with Canadian concession crews, Inuit were much more likely to have casual trade encounters with fishers, who were living along the Strait of Belle Isle in the summertime and the early autumn.[80] The character of the encounters between French fishers, concessionaires, and Inuit is often described in the eighteenth-century documentary record. Active, if unpredictable, trade is noted. So too are ongoing Inuit raids on fishing stations and concessions, whether they were actively manned or seasonally abandoned. Often raids ended in violence and sometimes loss of life.[81] Such encounters did not immediately change when Labrador was ceded to the English in 1763; instead, trade and violence remained common.

Throughout the eighteenth century, as participation in the European trade grew, the size of Inuit households also expanded. Small villages, sometimes containing two or three communal houses, could be found along the length of the Labrador coast and into Quebec's lower north shore.[82] Historical documents indicate that communal houses were occupied by distinguished headmen with multiple wives and extended families.[83] Households shared labour in subsistence activities and were capable of producing surplus goods such as baleen, furs, feathers, and sea mammal oils for trade. They also accumulated large quantities of European-manufactured goods. In archaeological excavations, these foreign-origin products carpet house floors and occur throughout the middens of the sites in Sandwich Bay (figure 6.3). European objects used in Inuit daily life at the time include pottery (English, French, and Basque), guns and gunflints, boats and boat parts, sailcloth, blankets, smoking pipes, various iron objects, beads and other items of adornment. They were acquired through interactions with fishers, sealers, Canadian concessionaires, religious men, explorers, and cartographers who were beginning to venture further into southern Labrador. To acquire these European goods, Inuit established a complex internal trade network spanning the Labrador coast. Items produced in northern communities were transported over long distances to European stations in the south. New forms of leadership, capable of organizing the communal labour of their households and distant kin emerged to direct this trade.

Our excavations at two eighteenth-century houses at the site of Huntingdon Island 5 and another at Pigeon Cove in Sandwich Bay, as well as a further three late eighteenth-century houses at Double Mer Point in Groswater Bay – all large semi-subterranean sod-walled winter houses – correspond to the European descriptions of Inuit communal house villages. These substantial houses maintained many of the traditional features common to Inuit domestic settings. All of these residences were constructed from locally available

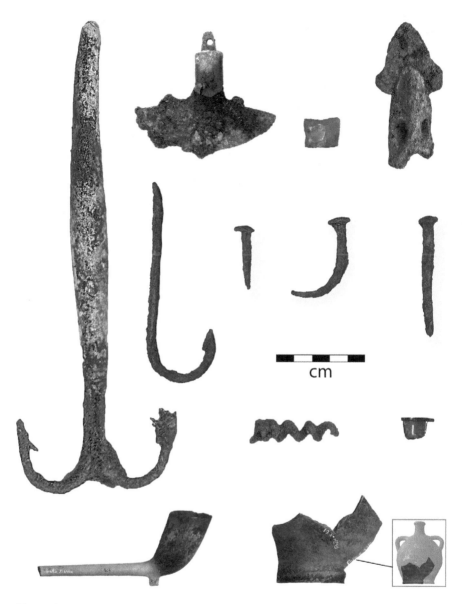

Figure 6.3
European utilitarian items from various early historic Inuit house sites, Labrador.
Top row: cod jigger, iron ulu with whalebone handle, European gun flint, iron-bladed whalebone harpoon head. *Second row*: iron fish hook, modified and unmodified iron nails. *Third row*: fragment of corkscrew, lip fragment of green glass bottle. *Bottom row*: kaolin pipe, fragment of Martincamp stoneware pottery.

materials, included multiple sleeping platforms to house as many as twenty to twenty-five occupants, as well as entrance tunnels with cold traps, and soapstone lamps for heat, light, and cooking. Furthermore, they all contained the remains of locally available wild foods, predominantly seal, used for food and clothing. Apart from the masses of European-manufactured items discarded in and around the dwellings, much about these houses is Indigenous. A closer look at the European goods reveals more about the manner in which they were incorporated into the lives of Labrador Inuit. For example, European goods did not replace all household items. Soapstone lamps were still used, and whale bone was used extensively to construct komatiks or to make handles for various other domestic tools. Still, at the Double Mer Point site, which dates to the final years of the eighteenth century, an astounding 97 per cent of the 5,000 artifacts recovered were created with material of European manufacture.[84] While most of these objects have origins in France and Britain, other objects, like an Ottoman pipe recovered at the Double Mer Point site, demonstrate the global reach of this trade in which Inuit participated. Equally astounding, however, is that 76 per cent of those items had been repurposed into recognizably Inuit objects that were never used in a European fashion.[85] The remaining 24 per cent of items were largely tobacco pipes – showing that sometimes Inuit adopted new activities that suited their way of life directly from the Europeans they encountered.[86]

The acquisition of European goods also transformed some elements of Inuit life. Iron implements, particularly, might have made daily tasks easier as they would not have required the same maintenance as slate or bone tools and were less likely to break while in use. Access to iron and other European materials may have allowed more Inuit to participate in the trade economy, as time, once spent in tool manufacture and maintenance, might be directed to producing a greater surplus for trade. There were also political changes: as more Inuit became involved in the European trade, signs of new forms of leadership appear in the archaeological record of southern Labrador.

In order to determine the long-term effects of the coastal trade network, Fay[87] compared the household artifact assemblages from nine of the best-excavated Inuit settlements occupied between the late sixteenth and late eighteenth centuries.[88] These sites spanned the Labrador coast from Sandwich Bay in the south to Nachvak Fjord in the north. She found that European trade occurred earliest on the southern coast of Labrador but that by the eighteenth-century Inuit households along the entire coast had accumulated similar amounts of European-derived objects. However, the assemblages in southern houses had the largest quantity of what we might describe as prestige items of European origin: objects like sword fragments, beads, coins, religious medallions, and cutlery (figure 6.4). Most of these objects exhibited perforations suggesting that they were worn on clothing and displayed to other Inuit and Europeans. They were not distributed into the trade network at the same rate as utilitarian goods but were kept in the homes of the southern Inuit. We believe that these objects were used to express the power and prosperity of the wearer. Kaplan and Woollett[89] suggest that such displays of material wealth were used to justify the huge economic effort that was required to operationalize the coastal trade network; since other Inuit did not get the benefit of this prestige directly, ideological intervention was required. This bodily decoration may also have been used to intimidate Europeans and amplify Inuit identity in the face of western encroachment.[90] But as most of the prestige items have been located in the south it seems likely that these objects served to elevate and justify the leadership of a small and particular group of southern Inuit in the eyes of other Inuit on the Labrador coast.

As Brad Loewen demonstrates in chapter 4, European fishing boats, or *chaloupes/txalupak*, were probably another signifier of this prestige. The most successful traders had access to these boats, often stolen from French or British owners, and use of these vessels to collect and redistribute trade goods provided an eloquent show of power to those around them.[91] While no whole chaloupes have been recovered from Inuit archaeological sites in southern Labrador, many boat parts have been found,[92] further supporting the importance of southern Inuit leadership in the European trade.

By the late eighteenth century, Labrador Inuit families throughout the coast resided in communal houses, supported by strong and respected household leaders who coordinated the daily activities of their extended families. The wealthiest, most powerful, and likely most charismatic, increased their status by leading their families on long-distance journeys to trade and coordinating complex whale hunts to feed their families and add sought-after baleen to the trade network.[93] The intensity with which southern Inuit pursued prestige suggests that this community also used their geographical access to the European trade to extend their influence beyond their own households and exert their power over other Inuit – perhaps in an attempt to control the coastal

Figure 6.4
Prestige, ritual, and decorative items of European origin, from various early historic
Inuit house sites, Labrador. *Top left*: coin perforated and strung to be worn as a pen-
dant. *Top right*: pair of eighteenth-century sword hilts. *Bottom left*: Shako plate from
British army helmet of early nineteenth century. *Inset* (with different scale): selection
of glass trade beads (*right*), cameo from religious signet ring (*left*).

trade network. Given that most significant leaders probably also acted as
shamans, their dominance would have been significant.

CONCLUSIONS

Inuit culture was forged early in the first millennium AD in Alaska and adjacent regions. While changes occurred throughout their epic Arctic migrations,
several characteristic attributes continued to define the Inuit way of life: the
skills, knowledge, and technology to thrive on the resources of a largely frozen

ocean and small patches of adjacent coast, a flexible social organization which enabled families and communities to gather for communal activities such as whaling and to disperse into smaller family groups for smaller tasks, a long tradition of marine travel and exploration, and an awareness of other cultures and of their potential to enhance Inuit lives through interaction and trade. All of these skills and customs developed under the guidance of strong, capable, and charismatic leaders who provided both organizational skills and spiritual guidance.

Inuit drew on these traditions to settle the coast of Labrador, initially establishing residences in the places that most resembled the Arctic world they had left behind but constantly exploring and travelling the entire coastline and adjusting their lifeway to take advantage of new resources they encountered – including those proffered by Basque, French, and English fishers and whalers who had begun to frequent the Strait of Belle Isle in the early sixteenth century. During the first 200 years that Inuit occupied Sandwich Bay and Groswater Bay, to the north of the strait, they redefined traditional practices, moving their settlements to protected inner islands to access locally abundant marine resources for subsistence and ultimately to produce products for direct exchange with Europeans during the summer months. As participation in this trade grew so did household size, offering potential for a new kind of leadership responsible for organizing the communal labour of their extended families and even distant kin in other regions as Inuit solidified a coastal trade network to access European manufactured goods. But all of these changes, including the acquisition and use of European goods drew on traditional Inuit skills, novel objects were incorporated in ways that continued to support a dynamic Inuit cultural system.

At the late eighteenth-century Double Mer Point village in Groswater Bay, where we continue to excavate, we recognize both change and continuity in Inuit lifeways. Inuit residents lived their lives on their own terms, participating in and perhaps even revelling in the benefits of the trans-Atlantic trade, but not becoming colonized by it. The sod-house, used for centuries, remained the primary style of winter dwelling, while tents stood near the three winter houses to be used in summer months. Food traditions continued to be based heavily on seal, supplemented by fish, sea birds, and terrestrial mammals. Many forms of traditional material culture, such as the soapstone oil lamps used to heat and light their homes, continued to be essential components of domestic activity. Even the abundant European goods entering this village were modified for uses determined by Inuit tradition rather than being used in European fashion: spikes and nails were turned into harpoons, knives, and other hunting tools; ceramics were often used as lamps; glass as cutting tools; and spoons, beads, and coins appended to clothing as decoration. The trade goods were therefore incorporated within Inuit ways of knowing and understanding the world.

This is not to say that Inuit lives did not change over time; nor did increased interaction with outsiders have no effect – on the contrary – but these changes occurred in a manner that was culturally consistent with traditions spanning centuries. The ways that Inuit chose to participate in the European trade demonstrates this. Inuit continued to recognize various kinds of internal authority and leadership that coordinated households, inter- and intra-group labour, long distance travel, and trade protocols, even as interactions and trade with Europeans developed. Within this context, those Inuit most successful at managing the intricacies of this trade were establishing themselves as powerful Inuit leaders.

While European documents are able to tell us that Inuit had become embedded in the trans-Atlantic trade of the pre-modern era, it is the archaeology of the preceding centuries that provides evidence of the long-term cultural context from which Inuit approached these encounters. What remains, perhaps, is to determine how Inuit perceived their role in their trade outside of the Labrador context. The tentacles of this trade would occasionally reach even more globally, and at Double Mer Point perhaps nothing demonstrates this better than the Ottoman pipe recovered from the house of a shaman and high-ranking trader. The journey of this single object, probably passed through the hands of many sailors, may well have taken it around the world before arriving at a small Inuit village in Labrador. Did Inuit perceive this vast outside world as something more than simple trade, and did they understand their role in shaping the early modern world? It is likely that at least some Inuit leaders did understand the complexities of the trade network and the world beyond their current settlements. We cannot forget that Inuit had always embraced and engaged with the outside world. The ancestors of the Labrador Inuit traded for iron and other exotics with the distant cultures of interior Asia and had traversed the top of the world. Perhaps we should end where we began, with the Inuk woman Mikak, captured on the Labrador coast, taken to England, wined and dined by the British elite, and returned once more to the shores of Labrador and provided with immense status by her kin for all that she had learned of the world beyond and the place of the Inuit within it.

ACKNOWLEDGMENTS

I am deeply indebted to the NunatuKavut community of Cartwright and the Nunatsi-avut community of Rigolet for inviting me to undertake this research and for the numerous supports they put in place so this work could continue over many years. I thank you for all of the boat drivers, places to stay, food drops, lab space, and mostly the friendship. The people of these communities are the descendants of Inuit discussed in the paper. Their pride in their heritage is inspiring.

NOTES

1 Fay, "Big Men, Big Women"; Taylor, "Two Worlds of Mikak, Part I"; Taylor, "Two Worlds of Mikak, Part II."

2 Martijn, "Inuit Presence in Northern Newfoundland"; Stopp, "Reconsidering Inuit Presence."

3 Ferris, *Native Lived Colonialism*; McNiven and Russell, *Appropriated Pasts*; Rankin, "Towards a Beothuk Archaeology."

4 Ferris, *Native Lived Colonialism*.

5 Moccasin, "Writings on Stone."

6 Mason, "The Context Between Ipiutak"; Mason, "Thule Origins."

7 Mason, "Thule Origins," 499.

8 In order to facilitate communication with non-specialists, I am eschewing the technical language archaeologists normally use to designate cultures and periods.

9 Friesen, "Pan-Arctic Population Movements."

10 Mason, "Thule Origins."

11 Jensen and Sheehan, "Late Western Thule," 517.

12 Mason, "Thule Origins."

13 Friesen, "Pan-Arctic Population Movements"; Mason, "Flight From Bering Strait"; Mason, "Thule Origins."

14 Friesen and Arnold, "Thule Migration"; Friesen, "Pan-Arctic Population Movements"; McGhee, "Population Size"; McGhee, "When and Why did the Inuit Move."

15 Jensen and Sheehan, "Late Western Thule," 528.

16 Friesen and Arnold, "Thule Migration"; McGhee, *Canadian Arctic Prehistory*; McGhee, "Thule Prehistory of Canada."

17 Friesen, "Pan-Arctic Population Movements," 683.

18 Stanford, *The Walakpa Site*.

19 McGhee, "The Peopling of Arctic Canada"; McGhee, "Radiocarbon Dating and the Timing"; McGhee, *The Last Imaginary Place*; McGhee, "Population Size," 181–91; McGhee, "When and Why did the Inuit Move."

20 Friesen, "Pan-Arctic Population Movements."

21 Mary-Rousselière, *Qitdlarssuaq*.

22 Spencer, *North Alaskan Eskimo*.

23 Whitridge, "The Construction of Social Difference."

24 Grier, "The Organization of Production"; Whitridge, "The Construction of Social Difference."

25 Whitridge, "The Construction of Social Difference," 101.

26 Ramsden and Rankin, "Thule Radiocarbon Chronology," 299.

27 Friesen, "Pan-Arctic Population Movements"; McCartney, *Thule Eskimo Prehistory*; McGhee *Canadian Arctic Prehistory*.

28 McGhee, "Thule Prehistory of Canada," 371.

29 Freeman, "A Critical Review of Thule Culture."

30 Grier, "The Organization of Production"; Sheehan, "Whaling Surplus"; Whitridge, "The Construction of Social Difference."

31 Savelle, *Collectors and Foragers*.

32 Whitridge, "Classic Thule," 831.

33 Schledermann, "Ellesmere," 250.

34 Schledermann, "The Thule Tradition"; Whitridge, "Reimagining the Iglu," 297.

35 Kaplan, "Economic and Social Change."

36 Kaplan, "European Goods," 50; Whitridge, "Reimagining the Iglu," 297.

37 Rankin and Crompton, "Meeting in the Straits," 13.

38 Armitage, *The Innu*; Loring, "Princes and Princesses."

39 Sturtevant, "The First Inuit Depiction by Europeans," 47.

40 Tuck, "Excavations at Red Bay."

41 Stopp, "Faceted Inuit–European contact."

42 Mailhot et al, "On est toujours l'Esquimeau"; Martijn, "La présence Inuit"; Rankin and Crompton, "Meeting in the Straits"; Stopp, "Reconsidering Inuit Presence."

43 Barkham, "A Note on the Strait of Belle Isle"; Barkham, "The Basque Whaling Establishments."

44 Martijn, "La présence Inuit."

45 See Loewen, "Sea Change," this volume, and Loewen, "The World of Capitena Ioannis," for evidence of friendlier relations between Basque and Inuit which may have occurred in some situations.

46 Rankin, "Inuit Settlement."

47 Brewster, *The Inuit in Southern Labrador*; Rankin, "Inuit Settlement"; Rankin, "Identity Markers."

48 Ramsden and Rankin, "Thule Radiocarbon Chronology."

49 Brewster, *The Inuit in Southern Labrador*.

50 Rankin and Crompton, "Meeting in the Straits."

51 Rankin, "Inuit Settlement"; Rankin, "Identity Markers"; Rankin and Crompton, "Meeting in the Straits"; Rankin and Crompton, "Kayaks and Chaloupes."

52 Rankin et al., "Southern Exposure"; Rankin, "Inuit Settlement"; Rankin, "Identity Markers."

53 Whitridge, "Classic Thule."

54 Bird, *Archaeology of the Hopedale Area*.

55 Ibid., 164.

56 Ibid., 165.

57 Ibid.

58 In 2019 we began new test excavation at Eskimo Island 3, House 2. Our work to date supports a rectangular house feature, but the longer walls may be at right angles to the entrance passage. Further work needs to be undertaken to better understand if this is the case.

59 Rankin, "Inuit Settlement"; Rankin, "Identity Markers."

60 Ibid.

61 Kaplan, "Labrador Inuit Ingenuity," 21–3.

62 Martijn, "Historic Inuit Presence."

63 Stopp, "Reconsidering Inuit Presence."

64 Martijn, "Historic Inuit Presence."

65 Ibid.; Stopp, "Reconsidering Inuit Presence."

66 Martijn, "La présence Inuit," 108.

67 Mitchell, "The Inuit of Southern Labrador," 322–3.

68 Pope, "Bretons, Basques and Inuit."

69 Hu, "Approaches to the Archaeology of Ethnogenesis."

70 Rankin and Crompton, "Meeting in the Straits," 21.

71 Rankin, "Inuit Settlement."

72 Kaplan, "European Goods."

73 Loewen and Delmas, "The Basques in the Gulf."

74 Martijn, "Historic Inuit Presence," 77–8.

75 Ibid.," 78.

76 Trudel, "The Inuit of Southern Labrador," Tableau III; Roy, *Inventaire de Pièces*.

77 Ibid., 99–120.

78 Ibid.

79 Niellon, "S'Établir sur la Terre de Caïn," 169.

80 Rankin and Crompton, "Meeting in the Straits," 22.

81 Trudel, "The Inuit of Southern Labrador"; Trudel, "Les relations."

82 Fitzhugh, "The Inuit Archaeology."

83 Jordan and Kaplan, "An Archaeological View."

84 Pouliot, "Étude de l'impact des interactions culturelles."

85 Ibid.

86 Ibid.

87 Fay, "Understanding Inuit–European Contact."

88 The sites are Snack Cove, Huntingdon Island 5, and Snooks Cove, excavated by my team, as well as Eskimo Island 1, 2, and 3, Oakes Bay, Black Island, and Kongu excavated by others.

89 Kaplan and Woollett, "Challenges and Choices."

90 Ibid.

91 Rankin and Crompton, "Kayaks and Chaloupes"; Taylor, "The Inuit Middleman"; Loewen, "Sea Change," this volume.

92 Rankin and Crompton, "Meeting in the Straits."

93 Taylor, "The Inuit Middleman."

7

Corridors of Jurisdiction: The Role of Aquatic Spaces in Sovereign Claims-Making in New France (1600s–1620s)

HELEN DEWAR

In the fall of 1619, in a well-appointed notary's office in Paris, representatives of the Prince de Condé, prince of the blood, and the admiral of France, Henri de Montmorency, his brother-in-law, signed a piece of paper by which the former ceded the viceroyalty of New France in exchange for 30,000 livres. Connected by marriage, these great nobles were shuffling assets – here the title of viceroy – the better to position both families. But the transaction also begs the question of why the admiral of France would be interested in what was a small habitation with little infrastructure and a handful of settlers on the shores of the Saint Lawrence River in a land under the control of Indigenous peoples. The response requires re-centring waterways in the story of the construction of authority and sovereignty in New France.

Scholars have emphasized the links between state formation in Europe and empire formation abroad. Whether in English, Dutch, or French cases, these processes proceeded through similar mechanisms, including cooption and clientele networks.[1] Subjects' ventures overseas led to an expanding state apparatus, notably a navy.[2] As scholars such as Julia Adams and Philip Stern have shown, state formation and empire formation were shaped by competing corporate groups, ranging from the state to innovative tools for trade and colonization like chartered companies. Such groups, each with their own delegated political powers, could at once facilitate and challenge both processes.[3]

Other scholars have demonstrated the importance of maritime space to the construction of imperial sovereignty in the early modern period. As Lauren Benton and others have demonstrated, territorial control was not the primary goal of European powers. They aimed, instead, to control trade, which meant claiming jurisdiction over particular oceanic routes.[4] European empires were "empires of access," at the heart of which were waterways leading to valuable resources. Consequently, European powers had to take into account the materiality of maritime spaces, adjusting to winds and currents.[5] The transoceanic circulation of subjects forced states to address just how far their control of, and responsibility for, subjects extended and led to the development of an international maritime legal regime.[6] It is perhaps for this reason that the discussion of the maritime dimensions of imperial space has thus far taken place almost exclusively in the context of international relations.

The case of Montmorency's acquisition of the viceroyalty of New France allows us to see the connections between state formation, empire formation, and jurisdiction over maritime space. Besides linking two phenomena that are typically studied separately, this chapter departs from previous work by examining the importance of maritime questions in intranational, rather than international, affairs. It begins with the role of New France in Montmorency's bid to increase the authority of the admiral, both in France and along oceanic routes. The second part examines New France's initial development as a maritime space and how French claims to control trade and navigation came to focus on the Saint Lawrence River. Finally, the third part explores circulation on, and the regulation of, inland waterways, which were subject to different rules as they passed through Indigenous homelands and hunting territories.

CONTROL OVER ATLANTIC TRADE ROUTES

Henri de Montmorency was keenly aware of the importance of maritime issues both for France's standing in Europe and for the power of the Montmorency clan inside the kingdom, power that was based on the acquisition of the highest maritime military offices. In his view, the admiralty could help France rival England and the Netherlands by developing the kingdom's naval forces and encouraging overseas colonizing and commercial enterprises.[7] New France fit into this vision by strengthening control over trade routes.

As admiral and then viceroy, Montmorency's efforts to increase his control over circulation and maritime space within the kingdom and overseas unfolded against the backdrop of vigorous debates among European powers over maritime sovereignty. European expansion into the Indian and Atlantic Oceans over the late fifteenth and sixteenth centuries had made maritime spaces strategically, politically, and commercially important and raised a number of questions about the exercise of sovereignty at sea.[8] Could a state or an individual claim legitimate ownership of the sea? Was it possible to own a particular maritime trade route? The series of papal bulls in the 1490s granting Spain and Portugal access to "undiscovered" lands made the issue of immediate concern, particularly to the two countries' European competitors. Pope Alexander VI authorized the Portuguese and Spanish to explore and claim lands to the east and west, respectively. By virtue of their territorial possessions, both powers could claim exclusive jurisdictional rights (*imperium*) over parts of the ocean but not territorial possession (*dominium*).[9] The ocean was thus divided into zones of influence. From the reign of François I, the French Crown had vociferously contested Iberian claims to police navigation in the Atlantic. Its contestations met with some success in 1559, when the rival powers agreed to "lines of amity," by which the area west of the Azores remained unaffected by the European peace they had agreed to. France was therefore not required to crack down on its corsairs in this area.[10]

The most famous and influential contribution to this debate over claims to oceanic space was undoubtedly Dutch jurist Hugo Grotius' *Mare Liberum*, or *The Free Sea*. Published in 1609 at the behest of the Dutch East India Company, the pamphlet was prompted by the controversy around the Dutch seizure of the Portuguese ship the *Santa Catarina* and its lucrative cargo in the Singapore Strait in 1603. More broadly, it appeared in the context of negotiations over the Twelve Years' Truce between Spain and the newly independent Dutch Republic.[11] Drawing on both Roman and natural law, Grotius argued that the sea could not be possessed, owing to its great extent and to the fact that its principal uses, fishing and navigation, could never be exhausted. States could, however, still claim jurisdiction in order to regulate and manage the ocean's resources as long as they maintained common use rights to fishing and navigation, which were open to all by natural law. For Grotius, therefore, the fundamental issue was access.[12] Given the implications of *The Free Sea* for maritime European countries, responses came from several quarters. English jurists, for example, argued for a distinction between territorial waters (subject to *dominium*) and the high seas (open to unrestricted navigation). The Portuguese, for their part, contended that the sea was common property that could be divided into zones of private-use rights, thereby allowing states exclusive use of particular trade routes.[13] If Grotius's work is at the foundation of modern international maritime law, European states hardly abided by his precepts at the time. Rather, they continued to claim exclusive jurisdiction over particular maritime regions through the seventeenth and into the eighteenth century.[14]

While the international dimensions of maritime sovereignty preoccupied the French Crown, control over maritime space was no less contested within the kingdom. Beginning in the late sixteenth century, the French Crown attempted to increase its control of maritime circulation through its officeholders, notably the admiral. The admiral of France's theoretically extensive jurisdiction was in practice limited by the competing claims of seigneurs, governors, and other regional admirals. Since 1582, the admiral of France had claimed control over ports, fortifications, ships, munitions, and maritime justice in Picardy, Normandy, Poitou, Saintonge, Guyenne, and Brittany, claims backed up by royal declarations in his favour. Provence, Languedoc, and several seigneuries, including Sables d'Olonne and Saint-Valéry, remained officially outside his jurisdiction. In reality, however, the admiral exercised effective authority in only Picardy and Normandy (and even there it was subject to challenge on occasion). In provinces like Brittany and Guyenne on the Atlantic coast, governors kept a tight hold on admiralty rights, justifying their claims with reference to traditional practices predating their attachment to the kingdom. Seigneurs, for their part, claimed rights to the shore and the waters off their seigneuries, demanding payment in specie or in kind from fishermen.[15]

As the admiral of France was theoretically responsible for the surveillance of all traffic entering and leaving French ports, one of his key prerogatives was the granting of *congés* or passports. A treatise on the admiralty published in 1584 lays out the conditions of travel. All ships' captains, whether they were commanding a ship for combat against France's enemies or for long-distance trade, needed a passport. For long-distance voyages, the latter typically specified the destination as well as the purpose of the voyage. Captains were also to have all documents registered with the clerk of the admiralty court and their merchandise inspected before leaving port. In time of war, no enemy ship could enter or be piloted into a French port without a passport. These requirements aimed to ensure both the security of French harbours and ports and the proper conduct of subjects towards allies of France. Closely tied as it was to the security of the kingdom, the power to grant passports, safe-conduct passes to enemy ships in wartime, and other security certificates was in theory reserved to the admiral, vice-admirals, and regional admirals such as the admiral of Guyenne (also known as the Général des Galères) in southern France. As was the case in other areas of the admiral's charge, however, provincial governors and lieutenants general continued to claim the power to regulate maritime movement.[16]

When Henri de Montmorency became admiral of France in 1612, he was following in a line of admirals who had made fitful progress in extending the admiralty's – and, by extension, the crown's – jurisdiction to the peripheries of France. With the king's encouragement, Montmorency, like his Uncle Charles whom he succeeded, used a combination of administrative and personal authority to strengthen his jurisdiction. To counter the claims of governors and regional admirals, he issued a decree asserting his prerogative as the sole legitimate provider of passports, called upon all captains to diligently register them, attempted to strengthen the local admiralty courts, and sent personal agents to ports to collect the duties owed him from these proceedings.[17] In 1622, he received direct support from the crown, when the king increased the authority of the admiralty courts, the admiral himself, and the royal council; four years later, the king named a secretary for each of the navies in the Ponant (Atlantic) and Levant (Mediterranean). Montmorency increased his personal authority by buying out rival claimants.[18] In 1613, for example, he purchased the office of admiral of Guyenne from Henri de Châtillon, Comte de Coligny, whose family was tied to the admiral's line through the latter's great-grandmother. This move expanded his and the crown's jurisdiction to the southwest. Montmorency henceforth became "Admiral of France, Brittany, and Guyenne." This title underscores the fragmented nature of admiral authority in France; it was his status as Coligny's successor, and not his capacity as admiral of France, that gave Montmorency legitimate power in that province.[19]

The purchase of the viceroyalty of New France was part of this consolidation of maritime authority. Like the acquisition of the admiralty of Guyenne, it served a dual purpose: dynastically, it realigned strategic interests among allied houses; institutionally, it strengthened the admiral's authority. Condé had spent the previous three years in prison for having led a rebellion against the queen regent. Upon his release, he had a change of heart and subsequently spent the 1620s leading royal armies on the king's behalf against Protestant dissidents. The viceregal commission was perhaps no longer of personal interest to him and fit better with his brother-in-law's position of admiral. Indeed, the two jurisdictions overlapped. As viceroy, Condé enjoyed the power to give passports to traders for travel to and trade in New France. When he became viceroy at the end of 1612, the prince granted portions of his trading privileges to merchants from several ports, including La Rochelle, Rouen, and Saint-Malo, for the coming season in exchange for a sum of 1,000 livres. In February 1613, the viceroy's lieutenant in New France, Samuel de Champlain, who was instructed to "associate and take with him such persons and for such amounts of money as he shall think proper," entered into an agreement with Rochelais and Rouennais traders for exclusive privileges in the Saint Lawrence River. He committed to provide the traders with passports for the four ships they planned to outfit for the voyage.[20] In fact, the entire agreement was conditional on the prince's commitment not to grant passports to other ships: "if it is found hereafter that My said Lord the prince, his lieutenant or others on his behalf or with his consent, gave or give hereafter other passports – for the present year 1613 to other ships – for the said four ships, the said merchants will not be required to pay the said twentieth [of trade profits] to My lord"; instead, Champlain would have to return the sum paid by the associates for the publication of the trading ban.[21] Other traders who had received part of Condé's privileges, notably those from Saint-Malo, protested, prompting negotiations for their entry into the company. Under the terms of a revised agreement in November 1613, the company was to be a partnership among the three ports.[22] The negotiations and protests over passports underscore their material and symbolic value for both granter and grantee.

Montmorency, for his part, continued to exercise his prerogative, granting passports to independent traders for travel to New France. Dissatisfied with the terms of the final agreement with Condé, the Rochelais traders withdrew from the company, which came to be known as the Company of Rouen and Saint-Malo (CRSM). The Rochelais's ability to engage in the fur trade in New France was not, however, conditional upon membership in the privileged company. Indeed, they could rely on the support of admiralty officials on both sides of the Atlantic. They enjoyed a special relationship with both Admiral Montmorency and his newly appointed vice-admiral of New France, Charles de Biencourt, seigneur of Port Royal in Acadia.[23] With passports and backing from these two sources, the Rochelais traded in the Saint Lawrence River from 1614 to 1622 in open defiance of the trading ban.[24] If these long-time traders to New France considered the company's exclusive privileges to impinge on their own rights, Montmorency viewed Condé's prerogative to give out passports to New France as a threat to his own at a time when he was attempting to consolidate his authority in France.

By becoming viceroy of New France in 1619, Montmorency extended his control over the circulation of subjects and goods across the Atlantic. Granting a passport was a powerful sovereign act. Not only did it dictate where a ship could go and what resources it could access, but it also implied a certain claim to control of oceanic space itself. Like other European states in the period, France attempted, through the admiral, to control what could be done in particular areas of the sea.[25] The ship, in turn, carried jurisdiction, making it a powerful instrument in constructing claims. Each voyage reaffirmed French control over the maritime route. As one of the highest-ranking military officers in the realm and now viceroy, Montmorency became a key figure in the extension of the king's sovereignty to the peripheries of France and along Atlantic trade routes to New France.[26]

The significance of the viceroyalty of New France for asserting and consolidating power over oceanic space is most visible in the manner in which Montmorency informed the CRSM of the change in viceroy. In the fall of 1620, the intendant of the admiralty of Normandy and the *procureur du roi* seized a cargo of furs from the company's ships upon their arrival in the port of Honfleur. They also forbade the crew from making further voyages to New France. The seizure, like other aggressive displays of personal authority within the French state apparatus, precipitated a protracted dispute over rights. After the company associates protested the action before the royal council, the parties agreed to a compromise among themselves: Montmorency's intendant of New France would release the furs provided that the company reimburse the admiralty of Normandy for the costs of the seizure and storage of the merchandise. More significantly, the CRSM associates promised to "desist ... from all pretentions that these associates could have and claim to continue in the future the said voyages and trade to the said country of New France, under the guise of power by treaties made formerly ... with the preceding governors of the said countries for the king, without license, confirmation and consent from the said seigneur de Montmorency viceroy," while reserving the right to demand payment for any merchandise belonging to them still in New France.[27] However, they later decided to renege on the agreement. Before the courts once more, the ensuing dispute focused on whether the trading privileges to the colony remained in the hands of the company as per their eleven-year contract with Condé or whether the revocation of all previous commissions allowed Montmorency to enter into new agreements with other parties. It expanded to involve several third parties, including the new company to which Montmorency had given trading privileges, and was not resolved for more than two years.[28]

Given the growing importance of maritime trade routes in the competition for standing among and within European polities in the seventeenth century, the seizure of a ship had particular material and symbolic importance. It deprived the captain and owners of access to resources and the accompanying profits from trade. More significantly, the ship lost its status as a vector for spreading jurisdiction. As the company with (supposedly) exclusive trading privileges in the Saint Lawrence River, the CRSM's ships projected French claims to sovereignty over the spaces of New France and the ocean leading to them. For Montmorency, the seizure was a means to assert his prerogative to limit access to the Saint Lawrence River, along with the right to choose with whom to associate for the trade of the colony.

This show of force underscores the maritime significance of New France for Montmorency. Indeed, the admiral was not interested in New France as a settlement or a territory with particular resources. Control of the colony, instead, reinforced his claim to exclusively police travel along one of the main Atlantic trade routes used by French subjects.[29] From this perspective, territorial possession was secondary. Controlling access to the Saint Lawrence via the viceroyalty and the measures to increase the admiral's authority in France were part of the same program to strengthen royal control over the most valuable resource for European powers: circulation.[30]

THE SAINT LAWRENCE AS A CONDUIT FOR FRENCH
COMMERCIAL AND POLITICAL POWER

New France initially took form as a maritime space. From the early sixteenth century French fishermen made annual voyages to fish off the coasts of Newfoundland and Acadia. This activity later shaped the geography and nature of royal regulation of commerce and navigation. While the French Crown claimed the Saint Lawrence as a space for French shipping and commercial regulation, its representatives struggled to establish effective control.

Documentary and cartographic evidence illustrates New France's status as a maritime space. On early modern maps, rivers were avenues for increasing knowledge of new lands and peoples and extending sovereignty. Royal commissions to viceroys, and later governors, also privileged aquatic features, such as coasts, harbours, and islands, to define jurisdictions.[31] In the case of early seventeenth-century letters patent, including those granted Condé and acquired, following his purchase of the viceregal title, by Montmorency, political and commercial jurisdictions were articulated differently. Condé's commission delineates the viceroy's/lieutenant general's governmental jurisdiction, which encompassed the Saint Lawrence Valley and Acadia, with reference to land.[32] The preamble to Condé's commission refers to the "countries, lands and confines of New France," while the king calls on the prince to "represent our person throughout this country of New France."[33] If the limits of "New France" are fluid in these passages, the viceroy's political jurisdiction is nevertheless bounded in space.

The geography of commercial power is, by contrast, aquatic.[34] In Condé's commission, waterways are designated as particular types of commercial zones. For example, the king extended the prince's privileged trading area below Quebec in 1613: "our cousin and those who will have power from him to trade and traffic with the Natives of the said country and to establish there our authority and the habitations of our subjects, from the place of Quebec and above it, alone shall have the same power, for their greater security, to trade *from the said river of Matane* [in the Gaspé] *up to the said Quebec and in all the ports, harbours, roadsteads and rivers being between those of Matane and Quebec on either shore* and to build such forts and strongholds as they may find the most useful."[35] The Saint Lawrence River and its tributaries thus constituted a privileged fur trading area, enjoyed by the viceroy and the company to whom he subsequently delegated these privileges. The non-privileged trading space below Matane is similarly described according to maritime features: "reserving nevertheless to all our said subjects the liberty to trade *the length of the other coasts, ports and harbours* of the said New France, except as stated above the said place of Quebec and above as far as one can extend."[36] The waters off Acadia were thereby left open to all subjects to trade and fish. Only certain subjects – those tied to the privileged trading company – could travel up the Saint Lawrence for particular purposes – in this case, fur trading. The royal commissions granted to Condé and later Montmorency thus regulated access to and use of resources and the waterways leading to them.

The long-standing close association between the fishery and the fur trade shaped the use of aquatic features to delineate privileged and open fur trading zones.[37] From the early 1500s, thousands of fishermen from Basque, Breton, and Norman ports crossed the Atlantic each year to the Banks of Newfoundland and the coasts of present-day Labrador, Quebec, and Nova Scotia to engage in fishing, whaling, and, later, fur trading. Although traders began making voyages primarily for the fur trade from the 1580s, the link between the two activities remained and shaped the latter's development.[38] The term *traite* (as in *traite des fourrures*) had maritime origins and denoted trade between a ship and people living on the coast. In the same vein, the practice of granting fur trade licences for travel into the *Pays d'en haut* from the mid-seventeenth century was modelled on the passport system for maritime travel.[39] The maritime origins of New France thus had lasting impact.

Powerful fishing interests shaped the spatial configuration of privileges in New France. In the sixteenth century, European fishermen had developed a system of self-regulation for the designation of fishing grounds, the repartition of shore stations, and the resolution of disputes. When the French Crown began regularly granting governmental authority and exclusive trading privileges to noblemen in the late sixteenth century, this tradition of the fishing commons came under threat.[40] French fishermen considered their annual transatlantic voyages to fish and trade for furs as a customary right and, consequently, protested vociferously against viceregal commissions and exclusive grants to trading companies. The crown was thus forced to make concessions. While Pierre du Gua, sieur de Monts' commission of lieutenant general in

1603 designated the entire region of Acadia as a privileged trading area, Condé's letters patent ten years later limited the privileged zone to the Saint Lawrence River. Later, grants to chartered companies, notably that of the Compagnie de la Nouvelle-France in 1627, insisted that the fishery would remain open.[41] It was, then, only resources on land that lent themselves to exclusive privileges. The intertwined histories of the fishery and fur trade and the strength of fishing interests, however, made enforcement of privileged trading zones, even for land resources, difficult.[42]

The French claimed the Saint Lawrence River as a space for the regulation of commerce and navigation. Believed to be a route to Asia, it, along with its tributaries, were at the centre of French explorations following the foundation of Quebec in 1608. Outlining a project for the colonization of New France for which he was seeking royal financial support in 1618, Champlain committed "to discover the South Sea passage to China and to the East Indies by way of the river St. Lawrence, which traverses the lands of the said New France, and which river issues from a lake about three hundred leagues in length, from which lake flows a river that empties into the said South Sea." He went on to say that the king would profit greatly from the customs duties collected, as "all the merchants of Christendom would pass through the passage sought by the Sieur de Champlain, *if it please the King to grant them leave to do so."*[43] For Champlain, the Saint Lawrence was the means by which the French could control the most sought after maritime commercial route. European access to and circulation on the river could be more easily supervised than along the winding coastlines of Acadia where policing of trade was all but impossible. A more defensible site than previous settlements in Acadia, the habitation of Quebec facilitated this control. The French thus originally conceived of the Saint Lawrence River as a navigable waterway, a transoceanic passage; it only gradually transformed into the interior waterway so prominently featured in Canadian historiography.[44] The thousand-mile estuary stretching to Quebec was a continuation of oceanic space and subject to the same assertions of control.

The Saint Lawrence played a significant role in French political and commercial claims in North America. Like Montmorency's granting of passports for travel across the Atlantic, the action of designating the Saint Lawrence River as a privileged trading zone implied a claim to jurisdiction over the river itself. During the four years prior to the granting of Condé's commission as viceroy, unrestricted traffic in the Saint Lawrence had led to increasing numbers of French traders visiting annually between Tadoussac and Quebec. Indeed, Champlain complained bitterly about the independent traders who, in his eyes, took advantage of the toil, expense, and risks borne by himself, de Monts, and the latter's company: "Had they been willing to share our explorations, use their resources, and risk their persons, they would have shown that they possessed honour and a love of renown; but, on the contrary, they clearly show that they are driven by pure malice to seek to enjoy equally with us the fruits of our labours."[45] Champlain's frustration aside, the passage highlights the scale of commercial activity each summer. Located at the mouth of the Saguenay, Tadoussac had become the main trading hub by 1600 in part because it was where several Indigenous trade routes converged. The Innu, on whose territory this trade took place and who had granted permission for the French to establish a post there, controlled who could trade directly with the French. They thus protected their role as intermediaries in trade networks that extended as far north as James Bay and as far west as southern Ontario.[46] The increased competition among French traders from 1609–13 was consequently beneficial to them, as it decreased prices for European goods. When the French unilaterally changed the trade terms with the establishment of the privileged trading zone in 1613, the Innu interpreted this move as an attempt to dictate who they could trade with and, by extension, limit their autonomy. Reserving navigation in the Saint Lawrence River to the privileged company under Condé and later under Montmorency was not simply an assertion of French commercial power. As with claims to specific oceanic routes, the establishment of rules governing access to the river was a political act. While the target of these restrictions was European and French competitors, they were also a challenge to the Innus' control over their territory and the waterways at its heart.[47]

The Saint Lawrence River was subject to multiple claims to political, commercial, and military power at different times. It was an important "transportation corridor" for trade, war parties, and seasonal migrations. Conflict between the Innu, Algonquins and Wendats to the north of the river, and the Haudenosaunee (or Iroquois Confederacy) to the south made it a site of attacks in the early seventeenth century, leading those who came down river to trade at Tadoussac to take alternative routes.[48] As the Saint Lawrence was the main waterway running through their territory, the Innu along with their Algonquin allies had ambitions to control navigation along it. The river was, however, one of the spaces where they exerted the least control, in contrast to the Saguenay. According to Alain Beaulieu, geographic, demographic, and technological factors combined to prevent the Innu from regulating access to the Saint Lawrence. Their options were, therefore, limited in the face of French claims from 1613 onward. The French travelled freely along the Saint Lawrence, without need of Indigenous guides, in stark contrast to their travels into the interior.[49] A typical trading season saw frequent travel between Tadoussac, Québec, Trois Rivières, and Gaspé by agents of the privileged company, viceregal representatives like Champlain, and missionaries. Unable to fully challenge French claims to control navigation in the river, the Innu registered their protest by trading with interlopers.[50] For their part, the French had ambitions to make the Saint Lawrence a primary trade corridor. This objective factored into Champlain's decision to enter into military alliances with the Innu, Algonquins, and Wendats against the Haudenosaunee, beginning in 1609. Champlain, de Monts and company aimed to eliminate Haudenosaunee attacks along the Saint Lawrence in order to expand trade with Indigenous groups living in the Ottawa, Batiscan, and Saint Maurice valleys.[51] Trade and military alliances facilitated exploration, which in turn fostered relationships with Indigenous groups in the interior with the ultimate aim of bringing them and their lands under French control. Regulating navigation in the Saint Lawrence represented, then, a first step in constructing sovereignty in North America.[52]

Control over circulation along the Saint Lawrence was, however, a subject of contestation among the French themselves, beginning with those who had been delegated powers and privileges from the viceroy. In the spring of 1621, Champlain and the other overwinterers at the Quebec habitation received word that Montmorency had decided to replace the Compagnie de Rouen et Saint-Malo with a new company under the leadership of Guillaume de Caën, a captain in the king's navy, and his uncle, Ézéchiel de Caën, a merchant from Rouen and member of the Compagnie des Indes orientales. The new Compagnie de Montmorency would enjoy exclusive fur trading rights in the privileged zone in exchange for contributing to the colony's administration costs and transporting a fixed number of settlers. Champlain received letters instructing him to seize the goods of the CRSM and informing him that Guillaume de Caën would arrive shortly with two armed ships and written confirmation of his authority. Without a decree from the king authorizing a seizure and outnumbered by the employees of the CRSM, Champlain opted to allow the latter to continue trading until the arrival of de Caën, "who had all proper authority, bearing with him a decree in his favour."[53] After all, the lawsuit before the royal council between the CRSM and Montmorency, which now also included the new company, had not yet fully settled the matter in either enterprise's favour.[54] This situation set the stage for assertions of and contestations over political and commercial authority along the Saint Lawrence River over the course of the summer.

At the beginning of June, a CRSM vessel carrying company agent François Gravé Du Pont and three clerks was sighted in the river near Quebec. Uncertain of their intentions, Champlain took the precaution of arming a group of men in the half-completed fort at Quebec and raising the drawbridge, before joining the rest of the residents inside the habitation. Two men met the company's clerks at the river to discover the nature of their business.[55] Gravé Du Pont's ship had set sail with no more than the company's permission, having left before the council made its decision and in spite of the admiralty's refusal to grant it a passport. With none of the customary papers, the CRSM's associates and agents "had determined to fall back on simple obedience to the King." While Champlain rebuked them for their actions, the clerks in turn questioned his authority to put a man in charge of the fort "without instructions from the King."[56] This jockeying continued until the arrival of de Caën with a decree from the royal council, which allowed both companies to trade for the 1621 season while the royal council considered whether the two companies should be merged or a new company formed. Despite the decree's injunction against "causing the other any hindrance or violence on pain of death," de Caën announced his intention to seize Gravé Du Pont's vessel, which he planned to use to pursue interlopers in the river. This led Gravé Du Pont, the CRSM, de Caën, and his men to make various appeals to Champlain during the following month.[57] While Champlain exhorted de Caën "not to slacken in the service of his Majesty nor in the observance of his decrees," the latter referred to "his appointment, and ... the special commands received from the King and my said Lord [Montmorency]," to justify his position. With no sign of a resolution, Champlain went to Tadoussac to "take the Sieur du Pont's vessel under my protection, wishing to preserve it in order to uphold the King's authority and the honour of my said Lord, before all his crew: afterwards he [de Caën] could do as he liked, as he had force on his side; but in order to preserve the form of legality, I had to take up that position." The lieutenant then left the site and de Caën seized the vessel, refusing to recognize "any jurisdiction in that locality."[58] In the end, de Caën returned the ship to Gravé Du Pont, claiming it was insufficiently armed. One suspects that the show was far more important than the outcome.

This episode highlights Champlain's struggle as the viceroy's representative to establish effective authority over circulation in the Saint Lawrence River. Gravé Du Pont's ship crossed the Atlantic and made it all the way up the estuary to Quebec before it was spotted. De Caën, for his part, claimed for himself the powers of commercial regulation and policing in the river as the head of the privileged company under Montmorency. If the seizure of the CRSM's ship sent a message to the company and its agents, it was also a direct challenge to Champlain and his claimed political and legal jurisdiction in the river and the trading posts along it. The lieutenant's actions, ranging from sending emissaries to negotiate with de Caën to protecting Gravé Du Pont's ship, were linked to the campaign to establish effective maritime jurisdiction in France and overseas. That Champlain could not prevent the seizure, however, exposed the absence of effective authority over the maritime spaces of New France.

This situation was reinforced by the frequent presence of illegal traders, their Indigenous trading partners, and foreign rivals in the river. Rochelais traders traded with the Innu near Tadoussac in open defiance of the ban. In his accounts, Champlain noted their presence throughout the first half of the 1620s. The Rochelais usually escaped any patrols by the trading company due to their small, fast, and well-armed ships.[59] (Champlain failed to recognize the significance of the Innu's actions: a deliberate protest over French claims.) In 1622, reports of a "Spanish" (probably Basque) vessel engaged in whaling and spying near Tadoussac met with no response for "lack of sailors and men capable of a bold stroke."[60] Company and lieutenant alike lacked the material power to uphold their theoretical commercial and political jurisdiction, making the Saint Lawrence a contested corridor of control not only among the French but also with Indigenous Peoples and European rivals.

INLAND WATERWAYS, INDIGENOUS TERRITORIALITY,
AND FRENCH CLAIMS TO SOVEREIGNTY

When the French turned to the interior of North America, they entered a different type of aquatic space from a European perspective: inland waterways. These spaces were also configured differently in Indigenous political geography. Both European and Indigenous approaches distinguished the sea and the Saint Lawrence Estuary from inland waterways. This distinction shaped French penetration inland and assertions of imperial sovereignty.

In France, maritime and riverine spaces were subject to different jurisdictions. The admiral of France exercised authority over maritime spaces, encompassing (in theory) the sea, all coastal waters, coasts, estuaries, and ports.[61] Inland waterways did not fall under his jurisdiction. In the Middle Ages and for much of the early modern period, control of interior navigation was fragmented. Rivers were subject to multiple claimants, including the king, cities, ecclesiastical institutions, and seigneurs, who variously levied tolls for travel or duties for fishing. In some cases, the king ceded his rights and the surveillance of river circulation to corporations of merchants.[62] The crown attempted to take back control of inland navigation in the fourteenth and fifteenth centuries, but fragmented regulation continued even beyond reforms instituted by Jean-Baptiste Colbert in the late 1660s. While competing claims were a challenge to the consolidation of maritime authority as well, the latter was prioritized over inland navigation in the seventeenth century given the close association between control of the sea and state power and prosperity.[63] Thus, upon becoming viceroy, Montmorency incorporated New France into the primary agency of maritime jurisdiction in France, the admiralty. When Champlain turned to inland exploration, he was already familiar with the distinct regulation of this zone.

Indigenous peoples also seemed, in effect, to distinguish between the ocean and inland waterways. Rivers, streams, and lakes formed the spine of Wendat, Innu, and Algonquin homelands and hunting territories. Facilitating seasonal migrations, they were integral to Indigenous approaches to the use and management of resources. Social groupings increased or decreased in size, as did the spaces occupied, according to season. Generally speaking, small family bands fanned out across the group's territory to hunt in winter, while they assembled in larger numbers at river mouths leading to a lake or the sea in summer to harvest marine resources. Summer was also an important period of travel for trade, diplomacy, and war.[64] The Jesuit Paul Le Jeune described the winter he spent with an Innu band in 1633–34. In mid-October, they went down the Saint Lawrence, spending a month hunting wildfowl. They then headed into the interior, choosing their winter location based first on where other groups had gone before changing direction in response to reports on the availability of game. It was not until the following April that they returned to the place on the Saint Lawrence where they had left their canoes.[65] As this account suggests, mobility on water was at the heart of Innu and other Indigenous groups' relationship to the land.

While the ocean and Saint Lawrence Estuary were open to navigation, Indigenous groups regulated movement along the inland waterways that defined their homelands. Again, Le Jeune's description is instructive: "These Natives have a fairly remarkable custom when other nations arrive in their country, they do not dare pass through without the permission of the Captain of the place, otherwise their canoes are smashed. This permission to pass requires presents in hand: if the Captain does not accept their presents, not desiring to let them pass, he tells them that he blocked the way and that they shall not pass."[66] Access to and regulation of resources was closely tied to kinship networks and alliances. Nipissing and Algonquin bands, for example, had permission from the Wendats to spend the winter in their territory, while bands along the Ottawa River wintered among the Tionontati (Petun to the French).[67] As we have seen, the Innu oversaw trade at Tadoussac and protected their role as intermediaries. The principal chief at Tadoussac in 1603, Anadabijou, granted permission to the Kichesipirini, an Anishinaabe group in the Ottawa Valley, to trade directly with the French, having secured their aid in a raid against the Mohawk. Five years later, a Petite Nation chief, Iroquet, who was to participate in the planned 1609 war party against the Haudenosaunee for which the French had given their support, invited his Wendat trading partner, Ochasteguin, to join them. The latter thus became the first Wendat to enter into direct relations with the French. As this constituted a new trade route for the Wendats, Ochasteguin and his family could control who would have access to it. In order to prevent bad feelings within their tribe and the confederacy as a whole, they extended the trade to both groupings. The Kichesipirini, for their part, required the Wendats to pay a toll in order to pass through their territory along the Ottawa River. Conversely, conflict between

Wendats and Algonquins and other Indigenous groups beyond Lake Huron meant that the former had limited knowledge of lands and waters much further west.[68] Such arrangements controlled riverine access and circulation.

Champlain's travels into the interior in 1613 illustrate the different set of regulations to which the French had to conform along inland waterways. Champlain wished to venture into Algonquin–Anishinabe territory with the goal of encouraging bands to come downriver to trade and of reaching the "northern sea" by way of the Ottawa River. Such a journey depended on Indigenous guidance. Having requested three canoes and three guides from a group of Algonquins, he obtained "with much difficulty" two canoes and one guide "by means of presents." Champlain and his men were discouraged at several points along their journey by parties of Algonquins they met along the route, who "declar[ed] that the way was bad."[69] Reaching Lower Allumette Lake, Champlain met with the chiefs of the region at the camp of Kichesipirini Chief Tessouat. Once again, the explorer asked for canoes and guides, to which the chiefs only reluctantly agreed, "on account of the toils I should undergo" and the unfriendliness of the peoples on Lake Nipissing. They subsequently withdrew this offer of support, however, forcing Champlain to end his expedition prematurely. Two years later, the Wendats succeeded in convincing the Algonquins to permit Champlain to travel through their territory to Wendake where he met the chiefs and spent the winter. Both the Algonquins and the Wendats prevented him, however, from venturing further west to visit the Neutrals. As these two expeditions demonstrate, the two groups were reluctant to have the French establish trade and diplomatic relations with groups to the north and west for whom the former were intermediaries. They consequently asserted their cultural and political power to control with whom the French established relations as well as French knowledge of interior waterways, lands, and peoples.[70]

Access to and security along riverine routes were part of the reciprocal relations at the heart of the French–Indigenous alliance. When Champlain met a party of Algonquins during his 1613 journey, he reaffirmed his commitment to support the latter against the Haudenosaunee before requesting aid in his explorations, which was then granted.[71] The French were in turn called upon to facilitate Indigenous travel downriver. At the beginning of Champlain's 1615 voyage, Wendats and Algonquins who were at the Lachine Rapids asked for manpower "to help them in their wars against their enemies, representing to

us that only with difficulty could they come to us if we did not help them, because the Iroquois, their ancient foes, were continually along the route and
prevented them from passing."[72] This situation also prompted the Algonquin
chief Darontal, with whom Champlain spent the winter of 1615, to request
that the French establish a post at the Lachine Rapids, which Champlain
promised to do.[73] While such a post was not created, company agents who
wintered among the Wendats accompanied the latter as well as Algonquin
and Nipissing trading parties down the Ottawa River each summer to help
protect them. They, like Wendat traders, were allowed to trade with nearby
Indigenous groups; they were not, however, permitted to travel further inland
to contact other groups.[74] During the 1610s, the French entered alliances with
several Indigenous groups and penetrated inland via riverine routes, due
partly to such mutual commitments, partly to the relative power and influence
of different groups among themselves.

For the French, access to and exploration of inland waterways were a
means to expand imperial space. The objective of extending sovereignty over
Indigenous peoples and lands, on the one hand, and the real limits to French
power and authority, on the other, is illustrated by an agreement that Champlain reached with an Innu ally, Miristou, son of Anadabijou, in 1622. Champlain agreed to convince the fellow members of Miristou's band to elect him
as chief. In return, Miristou promised to bring his thirty "companions" to
settle and cultivate the land near the Quebec habitation. While the exchange
brought Miristou greater status among his fellow band members, Champlain
aimed to increase imperial power within Indigenous spaces. He hoped that
his intervention in this election of a chief would become a precedent, by
which "we should begin to assume a certain control over them." The Indigenous settlement near Quebec would bring them into "perfect friendship" and
present an opportunity for conversion and assimilation.[75] Unsurprisingly, in
Champlain's account, it is the French who wield political and cultural authority. For all the imperial bravado, however, the main goal of these overtures
was to be "assured that, if we take them anywhere with us to make discoveries,
they will not abandon us on the way … Without their help it would be impossible for us to make discoveries … nor could we make use of natives of
other tribes, for … the moment anything vexed them, they would leave us in
the middle of an expedition."[76] This passage exposes the fear, vulnerability,
and powerlessness of Champlain and the other French inhabitants beyond

the Saint Lawrence Estuary and trading posts. While explorers, traders, and other agents of empire carried jurisdiction with them in the latter spaces, they found themselves in Indigenous spaces of power along the inland waterways and dependent on allies for guidance. Mobility over water, then, at once promised to spread various forms of power and laid bare the fiction of imperial spaces.

Maritime jurisdiction, empire formation, and state formation were intimately intertwined. Montmorency's acquisition of the viceroyalty in 1619–20 was a natural extension of his efforts to increase his surveillance of maritime navigation and commerce in French coastal waters and at sea. His order for admiralty officials to seize the CRSM's ships points to the maritime significance of the colony for the admiral. By exercising exclusive jurisdiction over the granting of passports and trading privileges as viceroy and admiral, Montmorency could control the circulation of French subjects and goods along one of the most used Atlantic trade routes. Land was, for admiral and king alike, an afterthought.

Whereas Montmorency sought to assert his authority over French commercial shipping between France and the Saint Lawrence River, powerful fishing interests in Atlantic ports succeeded in resisting royal regulation. They thereby shaped the configuration of maritime spaces in New France. The coasts and waters of Acadia remained open to all to trade and fish while the Saint Lawrence River was designated a privileged trading zone. As navigable water that only gradually became an internal waterway, the Saint Lawrence Estuary was claimed as a space for French shipping and commercial regulation. Effective control, however, remained elusive, due to the competing claims of rival trading companies and viceregal representatives, as well as French and foreign interlopers and their Indigenous trading partners. Champlain's efforts to consolidate authority in the face of these challenges were linked to those of Montmorency in France.

Inland waterways were configured differently from both European and Indigenous perspectives. In France, they fell outside the admiral's jurisdiction. If the king made periodic efforts to reduce the claims to various tolls and duties, authority remained fragmented and contested. In Indigenous political geography, inland waterways defined homelands and hunting grounds.

Conditions of access, ranging from invitations to the payment of tolls to refusals to travel, depended on kinship and alliance networks. While the French navigated freely on the Saint Lawrence, when they turned to its tributaries they entered Indigenous spaces of cultural and political power. Champlain relied on Indigenous guides on his expeditions into the interior and could only venture as far as the Algonquins and Wendats permitted. These bands thus regulated French access to and knowledge of inland resources, peoples, and territories.

As the chapter's focus on three spaces – the Atlantic Ocean, the Saint Lawrence River, and inland waterways – has shown, French assertions of imperial jurisdiction, construction of colonial sovereignty, and state formation all proceeded through aquatic channels. This was especially true in early seventeenth-century New France.

NOTES

1 Mancke and Reid, "Elites, States, and the Imperial Contest for Acadia"; Braddick, *State Formation in Early Modern England*, ch. 9; Heijmans, *The Agency of Empire*, 2, 6; Roper and van Ruymbeke, "Introduction," 2; Ruggiu, "Colonies, Monarchy, Empire and the French *Ancien Regime*," 201–3.

2 Mancke, "Empire and State," 196, 200; Braddick, *State Formation in Early Modern England*, 411. On the different path to state formation that the Dutch took, see Brandon, *War, Capital and the Dutch State*, 1–12, 19–20.

3 Stern, *The Company-State*, 6, 14; Adams, *The Familial State*, 17–22, 58, 107; Brandon, *War, Capital and the Dutch State*, 11–13, 26, 34.

4 Benton, *A Search for Sovereignty*, 37, 105–6; Steinberg, *Social Construction of the Ocean*, 71–2.

5 Desbarats and Greer, "Où est la Nouvelle-France?" 43; Marsters, "Approaches to Empire," 4–5, 7–8.

6 Mancke, "Empire and State," 200.

7 Dessert, *Les Montmorency*, ch. 7, esp. 163–4.

8 Desbarats and Greer, "Où est la Nouvelle-France," 43; Mancke, "Early Modern Expansion and the Politicization of Oceanic Space," 229; Mollat du Jourdin, *Europe and the Sea*, 114–15.

9 Steinberg, *Social Construction of the Ocean*, 77–84; idem, "Lines of Division, Lines of Connection," 256–7.

10 Mancke, "Empire and State," 199.

11 Armitage, "Introduction to Hugo Grotius," xi–xiii.

12 Ibid., xv–xvii; Steinberg, *Social Construction of the Ocean*, 91–4, 97; Benton, *A Search for Sovereignty*, 135.

13 Steinberg, "Lines of Division, Lines of Connection," 259–60; Steinberg, *Social Construction of the Ocean*, 95–8; Armitage, "Introduction to Grotius," xvii–xviii.

14 Steinberg, *Social Construction of the Ocean*, 98.

15 Valin, *Nouveau commentaire sur l'ordonnance de la marine*, 38–40; Hocquet, "Pêcheurs, hôtes et seigneurs," 107.

16 Du Voisin de La Popelinière, *L'Amiral de France*, folio 51v–52, 54v–55, 66. The origin of regional admirals was on account of the distance between what were considered the separate seas surrounding France. See ibid., 64–5.

17 James, *The Navy and Government*, 58; also 24, 40, 50, 62, 76. The strengthening of the French admiral's authority appears to have been the reverse of the trend in England at the beginning of the seventeenth century. There, the admiralty's jurisdiction was in decline amid competition from the common law courts. See Baker, *Introduction to English Legal History*, 106–8; Sanborn, *Origins of Early English Maritime Law*, 303; Carter, *History of English Legal Institutions*, 172, 173–4; De Luca, "Beyond the Sea," chaps 4, 5.

18 By the time he was finished, Provence was the only province officially outside his jurisdiction. See Valin, *Nouveau commentaire sur l'ordonnance de la marine*, 38.

19 In Brittany's case, admirals of France were given separate letters patent for this position, a practice that continued in the late seventeenth century. See ibid., 37.

20 Le Blant and Baudry, *Nouveaux documents sur Champlain*, 256–7. All translations from this collection are my own.

21 Ibid., 259.

22 Ibid., 310–21; Biggar, *Works of Samuel de Champlain*, 4: 214; Biggar, *Collection of Documents*, 36–7; Gosselin, *Nouvelles Glanes historiques normandes*, 34; Trudel, *Histoire de la Nouvelle-France*, 2:191–2. On Champlain's preference for one large company, see Biggar, *Early Trading Companies*, 85.

23 The Rochelais had an agent at Biencourt's seigneury of Port Royal from 1615 to 1621. See Parker, *La Rochelle and the French Monarchy*, 72.

24 For the congés they were granted, see 25 June 1633, Arrêt de Parlement de Rouen, 1B 981, Archives Départementales de Seine Maritime.

25 Steinberg, *Social Construction of the Ocean*, 98.

26 On the coastal geography of the French state's mercantilist policy, see Lespagnol, "État mercantiliste et littoral dans la France des XVIIe–XVIIIe siècles."

27 Le Blant and Baudry, *Nouveaux documents sur Champlain*, 406.

28 For the two sides' positions, see ibid., 417–19.

29 On the importance of the scale of activity in the North Atlantic compared to in the South, see Turgeon, "Pêches basques du Labourd," 169.

30 Steinberg, *Social Construction of the Ocean*, 72–3, 98.

31 Desbarats and Greer, "Où est la Nouvelle-France," 42, 46–7.

32 Montmorency's letters patent are no longer extant. Since a template was established with the Sieur de Monts' commission in 1603, there are grounds for thinking that they closely resembled Condé's, conferring governmental authority over the Saint Lawrence valley and Acadia, and exclusive trading privileges from Matane to Quebec and beyond. For the emphasis on landmarks in de Monts' commission, see Lescarbot, *Nova Francia*, 2.

33 Le Blant and Baudry, *Nouveaux documents sur Champlain*, 233, 234.

34 On the concept of spaces of power, see Mancke, "Spaces of Power in the Early Modern Northeast," 32–49, esp. 32–4.

35 Le Blant and Baudry, *Nouveaux documents sur Champlain*, 308 (emphasis added).

36 Ibid., 235 (emphasis added).

37 For a different explanation, see Mancke, "Spaces of Power in the Early Modern Northeast," 38.

38 Turgeon, *Une histoire de la Nouvelle-France*, 101–4.

39 Havard, *Histoire des coureurs de bois*, 23, 42–4.

40 Greer, "La pêche, les communs maritimes et l'empire," 175–9.

41 "Monopole de la traite avec les Indiens accordé par le roi à Pierre Du Gua de Monts et ses associés," 18 December 1603, fol. 49v–50, C11D, Library and Archives Canada [hereafter LAC]; "Acte pour l'établissement de la Compagnie des Cent Associés pour le commerce du Canada, contenant les articles accordés à la dite Compagnie par M. le Cardinal de Richelieu, le 29 avril, 1627," in *Édits, ordonnances royaux, déclarations*, 5–11; Greer, "La pêche, les communs maritimes et l'empire," 179. Before de Monts' commission, another titleholder,

Pierre Chauvin, sieur de Tonnetuit, had his privileges limited to the Saint
Lawrence River in 1600 after protest from a competing titleholder, the Sieur de
la Roche, lieutenant general of "Canada, Labrador, Sable Island and Norumbega." See Thierry, "La Paix de Vervins," 385.

42 Innis, *Cod Fisheries*, 84–5, 93.

43 Biggar, *Works of Samuel de Champlain*, 2:331; emphasis added.

44 See, among others, Creighton, *Empire of the St Lawrence*; Innis, *Fur Trade*;
Harris, "The Saint Lawrence," 171–9. For an historiographical review and
proposed new interpretive framework, see Marsters, "Approaches to Empire,"
341–8.

45 Biggar, *Works of Samuel de Champlain*, 2:218.

46 Trigger, *Natives and Newcomers*, 141, 172–3; Beaulieu, "'L'on n'a point d'ennemis plus grands que ces sauvages,'" 370.

47 Ibid., 375–6.

48 Mancke, "Spaces of Power in the Early Modern Northeast," 37; Trigger, *Natives
and Newcomers*, 174.

49 Navigation of the Saint Lawrence was not, however, without its perils. On later
state-directed efforts to master its hydrography, see Marsters, "Approaches to
Empire," 121–5; Pritchard, "Hydrography in New France," 10–21; Furst, "Suivre
la voie fluviale."

50 Beaulieu, "'L'on n'a point d'ennemis,'" 379–80 and n.60.

51 Trigger, *Natives and Newcomers*, 173, 175.

52 Beaulieu, "'L'on n'a point d'ennemis,'" 380.

53 Biggar, *Works of Samuel de Champlain*, 5:14–17, quotation at 17.

54 Ibid., 5:18, 22–3. De Caën and his associates intervened in the suit sometime
after assigning a *procureur* to represent them in April 1621. See "Procuration en
blanc par Guillaume de Caen pour intervenir au procès pendant entre le duc
de Montmorency et le Sieur Legendre et ses associés," 1 April 1621, no. 48,
étude XVI, Minutier Central, LAC.

55 Biggar, *Works of Samuel de Champlain*, 5:25–31.

56 Ibid., 5:28, 30–1 (quotations in order of appearance); see also 35.

57 LeBlant and Baudry, *Nouveaux documents sur Champlain et son époque*, 435.
On these representations, see Trudel, *Histoire de la Nouvelle-France*, 2:279–80.

58 Biggar, *Works of Samuel de Champlain*, 5:35–47, quotations (in order of
appearance) at 43, 46, 46–7.

59 Ibid., 5:3, 50–1, 178. For examples of other French interlopers, see ibid, 5:101, 208.

60 Ibid., 5:90.

61 Du Voisin de La Popelinière, *L'Amiral de France*, 52, 84. On the admiralty's jurisdiction in England, see De Luca, "Beyond the Sea," 286.

62 Bautier, *Sur l'histoire économique,* 20-2; Szulman, *La Navigation intérieure,* 35–6.

63 That said, the greatest advancements of state control occurred during the same period for both, the 1660s–1720s. See Lespagnol, "État mercantiliste et littoral," 349–50, 354–5; Szulman, *La Navigation intérieure,*" ch. 1, esp. 25–43.

64 Bohaker, "*Nindoodemag,*" 39–40; Greer, *Property and Dispossession,* 43–8; Morin, "Propriétés et territoires autochtones," 131; Lozier, *Flesh Reborn,* 28–31.

65 Greer, *Property and Dispossession,* 45–6.

66 Quoted in Savoie and Tanguay, "Le nœud de l'ancienne amitié," 31. My translation.

67 Lozier, *Flesh Reborn,* 32; Bohaker, "*Nindoodemag,*" 42–3; Trigger, *Natives and Newcomers,* 205.

68 Trigger, *Natives and Newcomers,* 174–5, 178; Bohaker, "*Nindoodemag,*" 39, 42; Biggar, *Works of Samuel de Champlain,* 3:118–19.

69 Biggar, *Works of Samuel de Champlain,* 2:255, 264–5.

70 Ibid., 2:chap. 2, 3, 4; 3:chap. 1, esp. 100–5; Trigger, *Natives and Newcomers,* 177–81, 197.

71 Biggar, *Works of Samuel de Champlain,* 2:264–5.

72 Ibid., 3:31.

73 Ibid., 3:172; see also 2:281.

74 Trigger, *Natives and Newcomers,* 194–207.

75 Biggar, *Works of Samuel de Champlain,* 5:62, 70 (quotations in order of appearance).

76 Ibid., 5:70–1. For examples of how Champlain did, nevertheless, begin to exercise a certain influence over Indigenous groups and their political and diplomatic affairs in the 1620s, see Beaulieu, "'L'on n'a point d'ennemis plus grands que ces sauvages,'" 384–7.

8

Saved from the Waters: The Drowning World of Paul Lejeune

KATHERINE IBBETT

There has been much discussion in recent years about the precise location and extension of New France. As Catherine Desbarats and Allan Greer have shown, the term New France is "fundamentally imprecise": the space of New France as a project was always piecemeal, provisional, projected, and ever shifting.[1] Yet wherever else it was, New France took place on the water, clinging to the river as both infrastructure and organizing principle, as Helen Dewar's chapter in this volume makes clear.[2] Even the frontispieces of what since the nineteenth century have been called the Jesuit Relations, those missionary reports sent to the metropole and forming one of the richest sources of narrative from New France, announce they will tell us what happened "en la Nouvelle France *sur le grand Fleuve de S. Laurens*" [emphasis mine], *on* the great Saint Lawrence River. It is that prepositional space – on and sometimes in – which I describe here. *In*, because the river ceaselessly and cruelly revealed human vulnerability to the elements.[3] Even the toponymy of the new territory marked this painful history, with Portage du Fort, a particularly difficult rapid, named for a *voyageur* who had drowned there, and the Sault au Recollet, similarly, named for the Recollet brother Nicolas Viel who had drowned at that point in spring 1625.[4]

In what follows I describe how this threatening waterworld shaped the metaphors with which French writers "before Canada" sought to make sense of New France and ask how we might read that history in different ways. Writing of colonial authors' observation of New France, the historian Christopher

Parsons has noted "the immersive perspective of early authors such as Champlain, Sagard, and Le Jeune."[5] Here, I take that language of immersion seriously: what happened when colonial authors got wet? What happens to our sense of this period if we take that immersion seriously?

In drawing on this language of the wet and the dry, I want to nod to the rich work of literary scholar Steve Mentz, whose account of what he calls "shipwreck modernity" puts the narrative of the maritime disaster, what he calls "wet catastrophes," at the heart of early modern travel writing and who notes that via a narrative "progression of shock, immersion, and salvage" such stories often "contain a dry counter-movement that attempts to make sense and meaning out of disaster."[6] Mentz writes chiefly about oceans, and I will be moving down a very different waterway, "le grand Fleuve de S. Laurens." I want to hold on, though, to Mentz's image of the post-disaster as a way to think about the waterworld of "before Canada," in order to acknowledge the disastrous effects of European settlement and eventual nation-building in that world. In following downstream behind colonial writers as I do in this chapter, I mean not to look to their work as a model but rather to ask how we might as scholars and readers today acknowledge the disaster left in their wake.

That move from writing the ocean to writing the river is significant. The great eddies of sea studies, from Paul Gilroy's *Black Atlantic* to Bernard Bailyn's *Atlantic History* and on, have substantially reshaped the way we think about the early modern world; this oceanic turn means that today many scholars might more readily identify their discipline via an ocean than via a landmass.[7] In recent years Atlanticists have attended, too, to the curious liminal zones that are neither land nor ocean. Andrew Lipman's *The Saltwater Frontier*, for instance, follows the New England coast to trace a "borderland that was not entirely based on land," looking to what he calls an "amphibious genre of 'surf and turf' histories."[8] And a wave of recent writerly accounts of the Atlantic take the ocean as both material ground and metaphor for the history of slavery: Jessica Marie Johnson's *Wicked Flesh* (2020), which begins its history of women in the Atlantic world with the figure of "the woman in the water," Tiffany Lethabo King's *The Black Shoals* (2019), which imagines the shoal, a formation that is neither sea nor land, in relation to the encounter of Black and Native studies, and Christina Sharpe's *In the Wake* (2016), to whose painful play on the term "wake" I return at the end of this chapter.[9] If these bodies of water have produced distinctive contours of the imaginary and new scholarly

cartographies, the river moves us in another direction again. It signified a particular promise for the colonial writer, and in turn it allows us to see something
particular in their work.

When the French returned to the Saint Lawrence valley in the seventeenth
century, with an eye on Jacques Cartier's writings of the century before, it
was with a revived confidence that the extraordinary internal river system
and its links to the Great Lakes might provide an easy transit system across
the Americas to the riches of China and other lands. In a 1630 letter to the
king requesting the continuation of his pension (that is, with an eye on his
own interest as well as that of France), Samuel de Champlain extolled this
new France for "la communication des grandes rivieres et lacs, qui sont
comme des mers traversant les contrées, et qui rendent une grande facilité
à toutes les découvertes, dans le profond des terres, d'où on pourroit aller
aux mers de l'occident, de l'orient, du septentrion, et s'étendre au midi."[10]
That wet dream was to animate many French colonial projects, dominating
reflections on New France throughout the century; the beguiling frontispiece
to Louis Hennepin's *Nouvelle découverte d'un très grand pays dans l'Amérique*
(1697), featuring a lazy river (the Mississippi) slipping invitingly round before
the viewer, shows that Champlain's confidence in the model of riverine com-
municative penetration still held sway at the end of the century, in a very different political context and on a very different river.[11] If we slip down this
idealized waterway from Champlain to Hennepin, perhaps a few bends
down the river we might bob up against Donald Creighton's fabled Laurentian thesis, which read a history of Canada issuing forth from the St Lawrence
drawing the country together on an east–west axis: just as French colonial
writers, before Canada, saw the river as the key to global treasures, so in 1937
Creighton imagined Canadian history shaped by a river which "invited jour-
neyings; it promised immense expanses, unfolding, flowing away into re-
mote and changing horizons ... The river was not only a great actuality: it
was the central truth of a religion."[12]

All of these rivercentric accounts – Champlain to Creighton, Hennepin to
Frye – make the river into a precondition for what we might call Canada, for
the petition to settle a state or the attempt to make a history out of it; they
make a teleology from a water course. And yet we know that rivers do not always enable smooth and unruffled travel in one direction, metaphorically or
otherwise. The historian of early modern empire Lauren Benton has argued

that riverine regions "often militated against political stability," giving rise to "a potent connection between riverine expeditions and the legal politics of treason."[13] (Benton's examples are mostly drawn from English and Spanish sources, but she also takes up the moment of Jean Duval's plot against Champlain in 1609; a still better New French example would be the endless disorder of La Salle's Mississippi excursions, recorded with spiteful verve by that river rover Louis Hennepin.) Europeans had already discovered how tricky navigation could be on river waters, and Benton shows that as a political project, too, the river could turn out to be less of an invitation and something more like a threat.

In recent years, early modern scholars have figured the capabilities, knowledge, and *techne* of ocean-going mariners as a way of thinking through certain forms of narrative. For Margaret Cohen, maritime texts give us a model of embodied intelligence as "a capacity: a distinctively modern form of practical reason," and her surprising and illuminating history of the novel traces this embodied intelligence from Samuel de Champlain's *Traité de la Marine et du devoir d'un bon marinier* (1632), read as a foundational text for this integration of varied forms of knowledge, to Joseph Conrad, Herman Melville, and Jules Verne.[14] (In Cohen's reading Champlain certainly launches a teleology, but perhaps not the one he had imagined in his letter to Richelieu.) Michael Wintroub, similarly, traces a microhistory of the forms of knowledge vehicled by a ship out of Dieppe deterministically named *La Pensée*, showing navigators who were not merely intelligent but also collectors of intelligence.[15] More broadly, critical attention to the genres of colonial writing has remained focused on this question of skill, even if only the skill of self-presentation. Michael Witgen argues that French writers as disparate as Pierre-Esprit Radisson, Samuel de Champlain, and Paul Lejeune all forge a distinct literary genre, that of the narrative of discovery.[16] The telling of these stories, Witgen argues, presents the writer as explorer–entrepreneur, addressing himself to European readership in order to usher in future colonial investment.

Yet in river waters, the French were not always skilled navigators but sometimes more hapless and uncomfortable travellers. Even the canoe, long central to Canadian national mythology, tells a different story before Canada, when its colonial usage and navigation on internal waters often betokened not dexterity or direction but rather a clumsy precarity, dependent on but sometimes loathe to credit Indigenous skill and labour.[17] In what follows I attend not to the Champlain–Creighton axis, the smooth and skilled navigation of mighty rivers, but rather to the distinct modes of writing that emerge from failed encounters with water, as the European moves not *along* the river but rather down – and sometimes up again – in it. What can this movement offer us as a model for reading before Canada?

I take as my case study the Jesuit Paul Lejeune, whose reports from the Saint Lawrence float between physical and figurative waters and who persistently sets out a journey from surface to depth and back again. Lejeune had arrived in New France in 1632, was Superior of the Jesuit missions until 1639 and wrote at least ten of the annual volumes sent back to France. A convert from Protestantism who had studied rhetoric at the Jesuit Collège de La Flèche, he crafted his writings with the rhetorical flair of that erudite tradition. His writing is also punctuated by a series of flounderings in deep water. In tracing Lejeune's watery movements, I mean not to make missionary work a model for thinking about before Canada but rather to look beneath his rhetorically crafted surfaces to glimpse something left behind by his writing and to imagine how we might bring that to the surface of our attention today.

Even from Lejeune's earliest text, we see something of how the journey to New France shifts the set of watery topoi available to writers. Lejeune's first piece from New France was the *Briève relation du voyage de la Nouvelle France* of 1632, which formed a prototype for the subsequent letters home. The *Briève relation* begins at sea, where Lejeune learns that being afloat is somewhat different from watching from the shore: "J'avois quelquefois veu la mer en cholere des fenestres de nostre petite maison de Dieppe: mais c'est bien autre chose de sentir dessous soy la furie de l'Ocean, que de la contempler du rivage … on laissoit aller le vaisseau au gré des vagues et des ondes, qui le portoient par fois sur des montagnes d'eau, puis tout à coup dans des abysmes."[18] From the outset, Lejeune signals that to travel to New France will be to leave behind a set of philosophical commonplaces. Instead of contemplating the choleric sea, Lejeune feels the ocean "under" him. The allusion to the contemplation of the ocean from the shore is drawn from the *proemium* to Book II of the Roman poet Lucretius's epic philosophical poem *De rerum natura*, which turns around an image that would become dear to early modern writers. There Lucretius draws a comparison between the philosopher's pleasure in his withdrawal from the world and the experience of someone who stands on the shore and witnesses a storm at sea.[19] The Lucretian shoreline becomes what Jennifer Oliver calls "the site of warning against taking to the seas."[20] In asserting the difference between seeing ("veu") and feeling ("sentir"), Lejeune of course participates fully in the textual tradition, common to much European travel writing, that announces the abandon of textual topoi for lived experience. But his taking to experience, shaped by an up and down of water from waves to the abyss neatly reworked in his sentence's parallelisms (par fois ... tout à coup), is also proleptic in its argument for a knowledge brought about through the water's depths. This will not be the only time that experiencing the water's ups and downs allows Lejeune to arrive at a surprising form of philosophical reflection.

Lejeune's initial descriptions of New France, like those of many European writers in the Americas, stays close to similitude: the Saguenay fjord is "as beautiful as the Seine, and almost as swift as the Rhone."[21] His writing is richly attentive to the natural world, since the missionizing plan was from the outset imagined in ecological terms: if Indigenous populations could be sedentarised and made to cultivate the land, Lejeune reasoned, their wildness would then give way to Christian flourishing.[22] But the hopefulness of this relation to the land's settlement does not extend to the precarious waters, whose dangers are carefully noted. In January 1633 he watches Indigenous men trying to cross the Saint Lawrence in canoes, dodging the ice floes, and notes that although they were very skilled ("habiles"), some were drowned nonetheless.[23] (His accounts run from drowning to smaller hazards: a Frenchman so thirsty that he licked the snow off his shovel has his tongue frozen onto the metal.[24]) Lejeune makes clear he can see some room for joy in this winter landscape; that same year he reports rolling down snowy hills "without any other trouble other than my black habit becoming a white one, all that to my great amusement," and in a particularly lyrical passage some years later he marvels at his first ice storm, which turns the woods into a crystal forest.[25] But he also learns a new wariness of icy depths: one cannot roll across the ice in spring, he notes, "because of the danger of finding an opening that would have you sink down below."[26] In many of these remarks, the water's surface functions as a sifting mechanism, distinguishing between who sinks and who survives: Lejeune notes carefully a drunk man, who eventually gets out of the water "after having splashed around a great deal," "bien barboté"[27]; in May 1637, the body of an

Indigenous man who had died in April along with another when their canoe was smashed by ice is found "floating on the river," but his companion's body is lost forever; the same year, another Indigenous man is found floating in the lake.[28] In 1639, he writes that he saw "something [je ne sçay quoy] floating on the river"; at first it looks like a log, then he sees it is a stag swimming across; they shoot it.[29] And in one curious formulation of his early years in New France, Lejeune describes the ships from France bringing families to settle as "floating households," "maisons flotantes."[30] Lejeune's joy at the arrival of the floating house puts floating as figure for settler survival, for the attempt to stay afloat and make a home in these new waters. Yet as we parse who survives and who sinks in his record, a grimmer history emerges.

Lejeune's narratives of vulnerability on water share much with other early modern European narratives of shipwreck which, writes the literary scholar Steve Mentz, were often seen through the lens of Providentialism. In such accounts, Mentz shows how "events in the world appear contingent, to mortal eyes, but really are Providential, in terms of God's plan."[31] Lejeune's Providentialism is inflected with an occasional reflection on the specifically colonial contingency of Indigenous labour. In the 1634 volume of the *Relations* (one that, in Canadian literary history, has sometimes been separated out for its "literary" qualities) Lejeune recounts a perilous journey with Pierre-Antoine Pastedechouan, an Innu converted in childhood who has subsequently renounced his faith and is often named by Lejeune as the Apostate.[32] Lejeune, who has been wintering with the Innu, is ill, lending a certain vulnerability to the tale, and his travel account swiftly turns into a parable as they move along towards Kebec in a partly frozen river. As they are perched in their fragile birchbark canoe (named by Lejeune, analogically, as a gondola), the ice makes a zeugmatically splashy opening "qui donna à l'eau dans nostre canot et à la crainte dans nostre cœur," [bringing water into our canoe and fear into our heart]: the structural equivalence of canoe and heart points to the strange affective charge of vulnerable watercraft in these scenes. In Lejeune's telling of this story, the Indigenous men who guide the boat to the safety of an island appear as ministers of a river religion, mending broken birchbark canoes with "une espece d'encens" [a kind of incense], i.e. a resin that runs out of pine trees. These navigators manage to find a little gap in the ice and slip away again, knowing that they sail down such a narrow crevice that if the winds were to start up they would be crushed "comme le grain entre deux pierres de moulin" [like grain between two millstones]. Lejeune's language here briefly returns us from the waterworld and lands on the shore of his interest in cultivation; his desire to grow and mill grain in the Saint Lawrence valley, in order to enable sedentarisation and thus conversion, emerges in the earthy simile. Fortunately, Lejeune writes, his guides "are very skilled" ("habiles") and it is also true, he notes, that God, whose goodness is everywhere, "se trouve aussi bien dessus les eaux et parmy les glaces que dessus la terre" [is found upon the waters, and among the ice, as well as upon the land], certainly recalling the God of Genesis who moves "super aquas," on the face or surface of the waters. In this story, if God is everywhere, the Indigenous guides seem sometimes to be his intermediaries.[33]

Lejeune's reflections certainly place human fragility in a providential perspective, but they also inflect it with an eye to Indigenous interventions, sharing out the labour of rescue between God and Lejeune's Indigenous companions and making some reference, however brief, to his companions' skills on the water.[34] Lejeune concludes the story by turning away from that rescue, writing "In truth, whoever dwells among these people can say with the Prophet King, *anima mea in manibus meis semper*," quoting Psalm 118's "my soul is always in my hands." But the question of quite whose hands operate salvation on the waters is ambiguous throughout Lejeune's river scenes: God's salvation frequently works through the manual labour of the unconverted or apostate.[35]

Lejeune's aquatic passages are of course in part a meditation on baptism, a theatrical extension of the sacrament the Jesuit hoped to bring to this waterworld. Throughout his work, stories of drowning are clustered in proximity to references to baptism; we might say that both drowning and baptism are ways of making distinctions through water, both mechanisms to differentiate between those who survive, those who are saved, and those who are lost. In 1636, Lejeune describes a recently baptized man who tries to get across the Montmorency falls and drowns.[36] Lejeune describes the Jesuit distress at this event but also reports on an anxiety that it will be misunderstood: what if the event is misinterpreted by Indigenous onlookers, who might understand baptism as in fact a precursor to drowning? Since it was so often a rite performed by the Jesuits in extremis, just as a person was dying, the Wendat suspected that it in fact marked the individual for death.[37] The story seems to revisit the Lucretian topos of the spectator on the shore, but here only the theologically correct onlooker can reflect upon the incident in the proper way.

In a number of pairings of baptism and near-drownings, Lejeune crafts his stories carefully to establish the importance of a profession of faith and a transmission of good news. In a set of accounts of "successful" or salvatory failures on water, Lejeune displays the swift translation of accident into address. In 1638, he tells the story of two Indigenous men stranded on an ice floe, conscious that if the ice were to shift, "ils couleroient à fond."[38] After a lengthy account of the adventure, Lejeune reports that they came back to shore, to share their news, and were swiftly baptized. The emphasis on speech emerging from the waters is important: Lejeune as narrator is able to listen into the dialogue, presumably because the men in turn "publierent" the story of what happened on their floe. Rescues are there to be reported: first to the Jesuit, second to the readers in France.

A similar story takes place in the *Relation* of 1640 and 1641. In this story, embedded in an account of the new Christians, the convert Noel Negabamat reports getting stuck on an ice floe. "After having prayed out loud, I said to my people: let us fear nothing, let us die bravely; we are baptised: *courage*, we will go to Heaven."[39] In Lejeune's telling, Negabamat places the vast and threatening waters of the river in narrative proximity to the baptismal waters that give the converts the certainty they will survive drowning: a droplet against the deluge, to counter the Indigenous fear of baptism.

Lejeune's use of the *Relation* texts to account for successful baptisms is extended rhetorically by these scenes of survival via the waters. Yet his rhetorically adroit overturning of the drowning-baptism fear is perhaps somewhat confusing in scale. Jesuit practice of baptism of course did not draw on the resources of the river for a rite of immersion, in the way that Protestant reformers might have done by plunging a body in; instead, the Jesuits splashed water on the forehead in accordance with sacramental practice in France.[40] This technical misscale functions as a form of *copia* carefully drafted for his French audience: so much, so very much water here in New France, and so much potential for salvation.

This relation between immersion and transmission is reworked extensively in a set of lengthy and seemingly connected stories of surfaces and surfacing which punctuate Lejeune's work, appearing in 1632, 1633, 1634, and 1638. Although Jesuit accounts frequently feature notes on who drowned where, at these moments Lejeune drafts another kind of story about someone falling down into the waters but managing to come up again to tell the tale. In these stories, Lejeune turns this movement into a narrative rhythm, giving us a heavily metaphorical journey. We are far here, messily far, from the figure of the spectator on shore or the traveller on a ship; these accounts share instead an uncanniness that seem to set them closer to something like a tale from the underworld, and in their reaching for a different vocabulary they seem to deliberately recognize the mythological potential of this journey to the bottom of the river. What can we see of before Canada from that muddy place? I'll set out the stories one by one.

1632: LEJEUNE SAUVÉ DES EAUX

Lejeune's narrative movement down into the waters certainly owes something to his own accident. In his first account from Canada, the *Briève Relation* of 1632, Lejeune gives an extraordinary description of his own almost-drowning, a passage whose terms illuminate the structural distinctions and lyrical feel of the later stories, in which a lengthy narrative serves to set out a way of thinking. (I set them out in French here to give a better sense of their narrative rhythm and shared vocabularies.) One August day, he recounts:

> je pensay estre noyé avec deux François qui estoient avec moy dans un petit canot de Sauvage, dont nous nous servons. La marée estoit violente, celuy qui estoit derriere dans ce canot le voulant détascher du navire la marée le fit tourner, & le canot & nous aussi, nous voyla tous trois emportez par la furie de l'eau, au milieu de cette grande riviere de sainct Laurens. Ceux du navire crie sauve, sauve, au secours, mais il n'y avoit point là de chalouppe, nous attrapons le canot, comme je vy qu'il tournoit si fort que l'eau me passoit de beaucoup par dessus la teste, & que j'estouffois, je quittay ce canot pour me mettre à nager, je n'ay jamais bien sceu ce mestier, & il y avoit plus de 24. ans que je ne l'avois exercé: à peine avoy-je avancé de trois brasses, que ma soutane, m'enveloppant la teste & les bras, je m'en allois à fond, j'avois dejia donné ma vie à nostre Seigneur, sans luy demander qu'il me retirast de ce danger, croyant qu'il

valloit mieux le laisser faire, j'acceptois la mort de bon cœur; bref j'éstois
dejia à demy estouffé, quand une chaloupe qui estoit sur le bord de la
riviere, & deux Sauvages accoururent dans leur canot, il ne paroissoit
plus qu'un petit bout de ma soutane, on me retira par là, & si on eût
encor tardé un *Pater*, j'estois mort, j'avois perdu tout sentiment, pour ce
que l'eau m'estouffoit, ce n'estoit point d'apprehension, je m'estois resolu
à mourir dans les eaux, dés le premier jour que je mis le pied dans le
vaisseau, et j'avois prou exercé cette resignation dans les tempestes que
nous avons passé sur la mer, le jugement me dura tant que j'eu des forces,
et me semble que je me voyois mourir, je croiois qu'il y eut plu de mal
à estre noyé qu'il y en a: bref nous fumes tou trois sauvés.[41]

Lejeune's breathily swirling account sets out a number of the topoi of river
writing: the precarity of the canoe, the affective force of the waters' fury, with,
here, a cheerful acknowledgment of his lack of skill; indeed, to be able to
swim was a rare capability among Europeans in this period, even for sailors.
Meanwhile the rescue, less than a *Pater* later, floats once again somewhere between the will of God and the skill of the Indigenous canoeists who rescue
the French. This account is, in Lejeune's writing of water, unique in its first-
personness and in its calm note about seeing himself dying; if Lejeune lacks
a capacity to read or navigate the waters, he is nonetheless brought to see
something via his lack of knowledge. In this vision he sees that he sees nothing, and in that, vaults to salvation, the description leaping from choking to
saving, in brief, *bref*.

Lejeune's swift movement, from lengthy narrative of suffering to salvation,
all hinges on that "bref." And it is worth saying that elsewhere, Lejeune can
be very brief indeed: in the year after this near-death experience, he tells us
almost mockingly of a young Huguenot boy who drowned before he was sent
home, it being illegal to be other than Catholic in New France: "strange effect
of the providence and predestination of God! *Unus assumetur, alter relinque-
tur, the one shall be taken, the other left.*"[42] (The tag is from Luke 17, with reference to the destruction of Sodom, coming just after a passage on the flood.)
In such a way does salvation function on the waters: for the Jesuit, (someone
else's) good work of the speedily rescuing canoe, for the Huguenot boy the
narrative ellipsis of predestination, which does not afford him his own story
of surfacing from the depths. The gesture to the Huguenot boy comes just

after Lejeune has told a story of Brébeuf fetching water from the river to baptize a child: the one shall be taken, the other left.[43] In brief, *bref*: I suggest that to look at "before Canada" from the bottom of the river must mean that we look to see those whom are taken and those whom are left, to think about just who survives and who sinks – or is made to sink – in these narratives.

1633: TO DREAM OF RESTORING THE WORLD

In 1633, as Lejeune is beginning to try to understand Indigenous belief systems, he recounts another story of drowning. This time the story is at a much larger scale: not the drowning of a man, but the drowning of the whole world. Here is what he says the Innu tell of the history of the world:

> Ils disent qu'un nommé Messou repara le monde perdu dans les eaux; Vous voyez qu'ils ont quelque tradition du deluge, quoy que meslée de fables, car voicy comme le monde se perdit, à ce qu'ils disent.
>
> Ce Messou allant à la chasse avec des loups cerviers, au lieu de chiens, on l'advertit qu'il faisoit dangereux pour ses loups (qu'il appelloit ses freres) dans un certain lac aupres duquel il estoit. Un jour qu'il poursuivoit un eslan, ses loups luy donnerent la chasse jusques dedans ce lac: arrivez qu'ils furent au milieu, ils furent abymez en un instant. Luy survenant là dessus, et cherchant les freres de tous costez, un oiseau luy dit qu'il les voyoit au fond du lac, et que certaines bestes ou monstres les tenoient là dedans: il entre dans l'eau pour les secourir, mais aussi-tost ce lac se deborda, et s'aggrandit si furieusement, qu'il inonda et noya toute la terre.
>
> Le Messou bien estonné, quitte la pensée de ses loups, pour songer à restablir le monde. Il envoye un corbeau chercher un peu de terre, pour avec ce morceau en restablir un autre. Le corbeau n'en peut trouver tout estant couvert d'eau. Il fait plonger une loutre, mais la profondeur des eaux l'empescha de venir jusques à terre. En fin un rat musqué descendit, et en rapporta: Avec ce morceau de la terre il remit tout en estat, il refit des troncs d'arbres, et tirant des flêches à l'encontre, elles se changeoient en branches. Ce seroit une longue fable de raconter comme il repara tout: comme il se vangea des monstres qui avoient pris ses chasseurs, se

transformant en mille sorte d'animaux pour les surprendre: bref ce beau
Reparateur estant marié à une soury musquée, eut des enfans qui ont
repeuplé le monde.[44]

Lejeune's telling of the myth takes up some features of his account of his
own drowning, and especially the narrative temporality between the "longue
fable," which he tells us is too long to recount, and the conclusion, once again,
"bref." If "bref" marks a compression of the longer narrative, it also here allows for an extraordinary perspective on a future repeopling of the world;
this, much like Champlain's 1630 vision, is a story of the "before" of a later
fruitfulness. Lejeune's account is also, of course, interested in the relation of
this Innu story to Christian belief. He both pushes away the Indigenous account (the distancing repetition of "ils disent" and its labelling as fable) and
draws it close to his own world, underlining its proximity to stories of the
flood as told in Genesis. Lejeune's story tracks in particular the bond between
human and nonhuman – the lynxes known as brothers, Messou's transformation into animals, his union with the muskrat – but it also draws out the
similar bonds in the Hebrew Bible's account of the flood, and the bird, a crea-
ture from a different element, who is sent forth to imagine life *after* the waters.
Along the way, we might say his reading makes a more creaturely account of
Genesis possible.

It is not clear, notes Micah True, that Lejeune's mastery of the Innu language
was sufficient at this date for him to fully understand the story told to him;
True follows Lucien Campeau's suggestion that this version of the story might
be as much Lejeune's invention as anything.[45] The story certainly seems to
track closely the story of Lejeune's own near-drowning and salvation and,
where Messou is, compared to Noah, unclear about what is happening, his
amazement tracks more closely the clear-eyed confusion – seeing that one
does not see – which Lejeune sets out in his own account. The multivalence
of the repairer figure can be seen, too, in a curious moment later in the same
Relation when the structure of the world's swamping appears again in the reported speech of an Innu man, who says that when the English controlled
Québec "la terre n'estoit plus terre, la riviere n'estoit plus riviere, le ciel n'estoit
plus ciel," but that since the return of Champlain all has been restored.[46] In
this cosmology as first understood by and then told by Lejeune, the repairer
of the world is its colonial master.

For seventeenth-century European theologians and philosophers, a reflection on the flood commonly marked an inquiry into the nature of historical transmission. Jonathan Sheehan describes how antiquarians across Europe seized on American accounts of rising waters as "the key to the recovery of the unique origins of mankind," writing that "we can understand the Flood as a seventeenth-century meditation on the *durability* of memory across time and space."[47] And if missionary investigations into the flood's vestigial presence in American collective memory insisted on the need for these stories to be recuperated by the narrative whole of the Christian Bible, European scholars more generally insisted on the fragmentary and rudimentary status of such orally transmitted stories without the salvatory European model of writing. The story of the flood makes for an urgent reflection on the possibilities of transmission across place and time, something of grave importance to colonial writers like Lejeune.

In an elegant reading of this passage placed in the context of European scholarly debates about the origins of Amerindian peoples, Micah True argues that Lejeune tells this story with an eye on the distant shore of his French readership. Drawing on the editorial work of Lucien Campeau, True suggests that by the time Lejeune retells this story in 1634 he is aware for the first time that his letter home has been published and circulated, and is more careful to frame the story as a corrupted version of the flood. The 1634 *Relation* marks the point at which Lejeune first knows his writing is reaching an audience outside his order; it is written still partly for an internal audience, but also with that wider readership in mind.

True's deft reading of Lejeune's intertextuality shows that later, when drawing on a distinction between writing and orality common to European accounts of the Americas, the Jesuit returns to this early reported account. In the 1637 *Relation* Lejeune mentions the story of Messou as part of a reflection upon the importance of writing in transmission of religious knowledge: Christians know their stories because they write them down, whereas Lejeune considers the Innu to have only an imperfect knowledge of the flood because they rely on oral transmission.[48] Of course, Lejeune means Biblical texts – but his *Relations*, too, seek to build a textual tradition for the church of New France. In this way Lejeune's text, too, is a vessel that reaches across waters to a secure future; it becomes a technology not just of recording but also of transmission, of survival of the Christian community.

1638: LIFTED TO THE SURFACE

In 1638, with an eye now securely on this wider readership, Lejeune tells still
another story of drowning and resurfacing. This time, ringing the narrato-
logical changes, it is not his own story, nor the story of Messou, but a third-
person account of an Algonquin and a Wendat seminarist named (after
Cardinal Richelieu) Armand, making their way to Wendat country at the moment that the snow melt was causing the river to run fast.[49] When their canoe
overturns, Lejeune recounts that the Algonquin

> qui n'avoit rien que son corps dans le canot, ne pensa qu'à se sauver; il
> fut bien-tost à bord hors du danger: mais Armand voulant sauver une
> Chapelle que le Pere portoit pour dire la saincte Messe, & quantité de
> pourcelaine, & autre baggage renfemé dans une caisse, s'engagea si avant
> qu'on le perdit de veuë: voila la caisse et le calice, & l'aube, & la chasuble,
> & tout son equipage abysmé d'un costé, & luy de l'autre. [...] Ce pauvre
> jeune Chrestien aiant combattu contre la mort jusques à avoir les mains
> toutes écorchées, & le corps tout brisé, se trouve assis au fond de l'eau
> sur une roche: il en fait une Chapelle plus favourable que celle qu'il venoit
> de perdre: je veux dire qu'il s'adresse à Dieu du fond des abysmes, non
> de la bouche qu'il tenoit bien fermée, mais du cœur, qu'il respandit de-
> vant sa bonté.
>
> Vous estes le Maistre de la vie, luy disoit-il, la mienne n'est plus à moy,
> car je ne sçaurois conserver, vous pouvés tout, laissez-moy mourir, faites-
> moi revivre, vous estes mon Dieu. A peine son ame avoit-elle poussé ces
> affections, que son corps se vit eslevé sur l'eau, où il rencontre des bros-
> sailles qu'il attrappe en telle sorte, qu'il trouva toujiours dequoy se tirer
> jusques au bord du torrent malgré sa rapidité: ses compagnons l'aiant
> veu disparoistre, regardoient si les ondes ne jetteroient point un corps
> mort; quand ils en virent un vivant, ils s'escrierent de joye, le P. accourt
> pour voir son pauvre nourrisson ressuscité.[50]

Lejeune's passage, clutching at the chapel, carries with it many narrative
forms: epic, with the visit to the underworld that can only be recounted by
those who miraculously return, and, with the description of Armand's re-

nunciation of agency to the divine crisscrossed by the careful parsing out of his grasping of branches, somehow mingling apologetics with an adventure story. The account of the elevation of the soul and the sinking of the material goods makes for a striking echo of early modern images of the Last Judgement, with on one side the sinners cast down and on the other the saved, safe in their elevation, *ressuscité* in the two senses of the French word, resuscitated and resurrected. (It is also a detail backed by archaeological records: we know from such work that losses of goods were particularly common at rapids and that where bales of fur might float for a time, other trade goods sank immediately.[51])

This story, with the clumsy seminarian clutching the portable chapel, recalls nothing as much as Peter Carey's 1988 novel *Oscar and Lucinda* and its magnificently bizarre image of a glass church floated down an Australian river, a figure Carey has described as "a box of Christian stories travelling through a landscape filled with Aboriginal stories."[52] Carey's formulation might often be a useful way to describe the Jesuit texts themselves, here building their church upon a rather surprising rock, except that here our Armand is both Wendat and Christian; as Lejeune inches through his stories of dips into the river this figure of conversion, who brings together two identities, becomes the missionary's ideal navigator. Where Indigenous intervention is what keeps Europeans afloat in many of these accounts, here Lejeune seems to figure conversion – the French intervention – as a different order of flotation device.

Throughout the passage, the narratorial (or *navigatorial*, I might say) perspective is particularly strange, allowing Lejeune to swoop underwater to hear the first-person prayer of the boy and then come on back up to tell it to his readers. In its successful accounting for this underwater learning experience, its successful conversion, this passage speaks to the failure of other watery moments in the Jesuit archive: it is clearly a baptism narrative, a story about coming closer to God through water, but it manages to tell that story, whereas many accounts of actual adult baptisms in these texts, those of potential converts who don't make it as far as Armand, are marked by linguistic failure; throughout the *Relations*, candidates for baptism are turned away from the saving waters for their inability to correctly learn their catechism, and few of them get to tell their own tale. Here, in contrast, for the Wendat man to use what Lejeune sees as the right words, addressing himself to the right place, brings about a miraculous buoyancy. Armand's elevation to the surface is one of the strangest passages in the *Relations*, and in it the question of an Indigenous voice speaking through the waters laps away at the reflections on transmission and address that trickle through all Lejeune's stories from the bottom of the river.

Taken together, Lejeune's repeated wet-to-dry narratives insist on the importance of textual transmission across time and place, of "publishing" what happens under the water, even as they underline the contingency of such address. In this, they dramatize at some length a set of tropes familiar in colonial writing. Even the texts that are eventually transmitted to early modern European readers were sometimes materially marked by water or at least by the trope that they had been: André Thevet addresses his 1558 *Les singularitez de la France antarctique* to the reader as though the volume in European hands were itself a miraculous survivor of the waters: "Ce pendant si vous plait agreablement recevoir ce mien escript tumultuairement comprins et labouré par les tempestes, et autre incommoditez d'eau et de terre" ["Please kindly receive this, my book, tumultuously tossed by storms and other incommodities on water and land"].[53] A similar adventure story is told about the survival of the manuscript of the Portuguese epic *Os Lusíadas*, supposedly rescued from a shipwreck in the mouth of its author Luis de Camões.[54] We know, of course, that the "incommoditez" of water destroyed still other texts completely: in the upper country, the *coureur de bois* Radisson and his brother-in-law Des Groseillers lost the journal of their travels when they went over one particularly tough set of rapids: "My brother lost his booke of annotations of the last yeare, of our being in these foraigne nations. We lost never a castor, but, may be, some better thing."[55] Still more hauntingly wet is a map made by Louis Joliet, stemming from the 1673 Marquette journey through the Great Lakes and down the Mississippi. Getting down as far as the Arkansas river, the expedition then returned to Montreal, but fifteen minutes from landing Joliet's canoe was overturned in the Lachine rapids, and his logbook and preliminary maps (along with three of his companions) were lost in the waters. Joliet's version was roughed out on the return to Montreal, and it served as the basis for many later maps of north America.[56] A great deal of what we know about New France, then, emerges from the water, and Lejeune's dramatizations of almost-drowning participate in this staging of American difficulty for the benefit of a rapt European audience.

But if we tell those stories only in that way, we too fall, I think, into the riverine seduction of the before Canada narrative, reading these as glimpses from the before-time, flotsam from the past; we are brought then to imagine these sodden survivors' tales chiefly as the *start* of something. I want to suggest that Lejeune's disasters also allow us to read another way, certainly against the way he might have intended but perhaps in a way that allows us to read against the tide of the European concept of nation.[57] For Lejeune's stories, and more broadly colonial writing's interest in the watery disaster, also bear reluctant witness to those who did *not* survive: to the man floating in the water after the massacre, to the men who drowned despite their skills. The account of the Indigenous body renamed for the French cardinal and lifted to the surface asks us, I think, to remember other unsaved bodies, who are (metaphorically, at least) sunk, unsaved in two ways. These stories, with the surface as dividing line between life and death, allow us to think of this period before Canada as a time marked also by an *after*, the aftermath of destruction.

"In the wake."[58] The words are those of Christina Sharpe (Canada Research Chair in Black Studies at York University), from the title of her extraordinary and important book on representations of Black life in the wake of Black death, a book that draws on and challenges the metaphors common to Atlantic history. Sharpe's rereading of the ocean entwines the multiple significations of wake – amongst others, the path of a ship, the attending to the dead, consciousness – in a reading of what she calls "the conceptual frame of and for living blackness in the diaspora in the still unfolding aftermath of Atlantic chattel slavery."

In an account of the personal weight of these readings, Sharpe writes of how "the sense and awareness of precarity … texture my reading practices." In moving from the ocean to the river in my reading of aquatic disaster, I want to suggest that what Sharpe calls her "wake-work" has rich potential for a reading of before Canada, a riverine concept to be understood in ebb and flow with the violent oceanic history Sharpe reads through her variously scaled vignettes. Lejeune's drive to textual transmission asks us insistently to look to salvation, to look to what survives, to what comes after the before. But if, following Sharpe, we allow instead an "awareness of precarity to texture [our] reading practices," then we can read "before Canada" for the loss of Indigenous life that it represents: looking not to those who made it out of the waters, but mourning those unnamed, drifting bodies who did not.

NOTES

1　Desbarats and Greer, "Où est la Nouvelle France?" 62.

2　Dewar, "Corridors of Jurisdiction," in this volume.

3　Québec parish registers from the seventeenth and eighteenth centuries show that, in the circumstances where death was recorded by a priest, over a quarter of recorded deaths in the parishes along the banks of rivers were by drowning. Greer, *People of New France*, 24.

4　On that death and its retellings see Skinner, *Sinews of Empire*, 255; Trigger, *Children of Aataentsic*, 395.

5　Parsons, *A Not-So-New World*, 57.

6　Mentz, *Shipwreck Modernity*, 1, 11.

7　Gilroy, *Black Atlantic*; Bailyn, *Atlantic History*.

8　Lipman, *The Saltwater Frontier*, 5, 11.

9　Johnson, *Wicked Flesh*; King, *The Black Shoals*; Sharpe, *In the Wake*.

10　Champlain, *Œuvres complètes de Champlain*, 2:626.

11　Louis Hennepin's *Nouvelle découverte d'un très grand pays dans l'Amérique* (1697) was published fourteen years after he had dedicated his very similar *Découverte de la Louisiane* to Louis XIV; failing to receive the honours he sought from the French king, in the second publication Hennepin took his (largely plagiarised) Mississippi journey across the Rhine with a dedication to William of Orange. For the frontispiece in question, see this link to the German edition of 1699: https://jcb.lunaimaging.com/luna/servlet/detail/JCB~1~1~3168~5020004:-Native-American-holds-a-peace-pipe?sort=image_date%2Csubject_groups&qvq=w4s:/who%2FHennepin%25252C%2BLouis%25252C%2B17th%2Bcent.;q:hennepin;sort:image_date%2Csubject_groups;lc:JCB~1~1&mi=8&trs=10.

12　Creighton, *Empire of the St Lawrence*, 6–7. On the significance of the Laurentian thesis for understanding Anglophone Canadian literary writing, see Bennett, "The Waters of Life and Death," 77–84.

13　Benton, *A Search for Sovereignty*, 58–9.

14　Cohen, *The Novel and the Sea*, 2.

15　Wintroub, *Voyage of Thought*.

16　Witgen, *An Infinity of Nations*, 36–8.

17　On early French admiration for Indigenous skills on and in the water, in their first journeys in the Saint Lawrence valley, see Greer, *Property and Disposses-*

sion, 40. On the canoe in nationalist myth-making, see Havard, *Histoire des coureurs de bois*, 761.

18 *Brieve relation du voyage de la Nouvelle France*, 5. On the status of this report, see Trigger, *Children of Aataentsic*, 32.

19 "Suave, mari magno turbantibus aequora ventis, /e terra magnum alterius spectare laborem; / non quia vexari quemquamst iucunda voluptas, /sed quibus ipse malis careas quia cernere suave est." [Pleasant it is, when on the great sea the winds trouble the waters, to gaze from shore upon another's great tribulation: not because any man's troubles are a delectable joy, but because to perceive what ills you are free from yourself is pleasant.] Lucretius, *De rerum natura* Book 2, lines 1–4, 95.

20 Oliver, *Shipwreck in French Renaissance Writing*, 5. Where Hans Blumenberg's famous 1985 study of this motif, *Shipwreck with Spectator*, distinguishes between aesthetic and moral reactions to the shipwreck, Oliver argues that there is no opposition between these two in early modern writing.

21 On this practice of colonial analogy see Benton, *A Search for Sovereignty*, 19; Parsons, *A Not-So-New World*, 34, 65.

22 On Lejeune's ecology of salvation, see ibid., chapter 3, 69–96.

23 "quoy qu'ils soeint tres-habiles, il ne laisse pas de s'en noyer quelques-uns," Lejeune, *Relation de 1633*, 63.

24 Lejeune, *Relation de 1633*, 70.

25 Lejeune, *Relation de 1636*, 203.

26 Lejeune, *Relation de 1633*, 73.

27 Lejeune, *Relation de 1634*, 214.

28 Lejeune, *Relation de 1637*, 256, 301.

29 Lejeune, *Relation de 1639*, 120.

30 Lejeune, *Relation de 1636*, 7.

31 Mentz, *Shipwreck Modernity*, 5–6.

32 Lejeune, *Relation de 1634*. On Pastedechouan, see Anderson, *Betrayal of Faith*; on his difficult relationship with Lejeune, for whom he had served as a language teacher, see Anderson, *Betrayal of Faith*, 136–8. On the framing of Lejeune's 1634 *Relation* as literary, see Melançon, "La Nouvelle-France et la littérature," 42; on the editorial status of that volume, see also Anderson, *Betrayal of Faith*, 237.

33 Lejeune, *Relation de 1634*, 313, 314.

34 Lejeune's nod to Indigenous navigational skill distinguishes him from other
    colonial writers, who often, as Christopher Parsons writes, "marginalized
    complex technologies and skills as unlearned and unrefined reactions of
    sauvage cultures." (Parsons, *A Not-So-New World*, 39). See, for example, the
    dehumanising dismissal of Buade de Frontenac, the governor of New France,
    who wrote to Colbert that "Les gens du pays ... naissent tous canoteurs et sont
    endurcis à l'eau comme des poissons" ("The people from here are all born
    canoeists, like fish in the water"). Letter of 13 November 1673, quoted Havard,
    Histoire des coureurs de bois, 283.
35 In an ontologically pithy twist on a zeugma, the voyageur Pierre-Esprit
    Radisson could be more direct in his parsing of the labour of salvation; in his
    fourth *Relation*, he writes that he is cured of an injury, perhaps a hernia, by
    means "that God and my brother did use." Radisson, *Collected Writings*, 1:284.
36 Lejeune, *Relation de 1636*, 210.
37 On the Indigenous fear that baptism was dangerous, see Lejeune, *Relation
    de 1636*, 29. On Jesuit baptismal practice, see Anderson, "Blood, fire, and
    'baptism,'" 145–7.
38 Lejeune, *Relation de 1638*, 54.
39 Vimont, Lalemant and Le Jeune, *Relation de 1640 et 1641*, 43–4. (Although
    Vimont's name appears on the title page as author, this relation is thought
    to have been written by Le Jeune, who signed its letter of transmittal.)
40 In the 1634 *Relation*, an Indigenous man asks for a bit of water to be thrown
    over him (Lejeune, *Relation de 1634*, 9). For an account of Jesuit baptism, see
    also Trigger, *Children of Aataentsic*, 505–6, who also notes (p. 764) that the
    Jesuits Lalemant and Brébeuf had boiling water thrown over them by the
    Iroquois in a parody of baptism.
41 *Brieve relation du voyage de la Nouvelle France*, 63–5.
42 Lejeune, *Relation de 1633*, 257 [*sic*: for 157].
43 Ibid., 254.
44 Ibid., 77–8.
45 True, *Masters and Students*, 123. True demonstrates that, nonetheless and prob-
    lematically, Lejeune's account has come to stand as a standard version of Innu
    belief in subsequent European scholarship.
46 Lejeune, *Relation de 1633*, 177 [*sic*: for 277].
47 Sheehan, "Time Elapsed, Time Regained," 325, 327.

48 True, *Masters and Students*, 127–8; see also Campeau, *Monumenta Novae Franciae*, 2:403.

49 On the Wendat convert and seminarian Armand-Jean Andehoua, see Jackson, "Silent Diplomacy."

50 Lejeune, *Relation de 1638*, 62–5.

51 Skinner, *Sinews of Empire*, 212.

52 Peter Carey, interview at the Hay Festival, Hay-on-Wye, UK, May 2016.

53 Thevet, *Les singularitez de la France antarctique*, 163.

54 See Mentz, *Shipwreck Modernity*, 2.

55 Radisson, *Collected Writings*, 1:238.

56 For the map, see Louis Joliet, *Nouvelle Decouverte de plusieurs Nations Dans la Nouvelle France en l'année 1673 et 1674*. Hand-coloured manuscript, 1674, 67 cm x 88.5 cm., John Carter Brown Library Map Collection, https://jcb.lunaimag ing.com/luna/servlet/s/tq1aa8. This map figures also in Palomino, *La mesure d'un continent*.

57 On reading Lejeune differently, see Anderson, *The Betrayal of Faith*, who describes encountering evidence of what the missionary "tried to ignore, deny, or suppress"; in an image that speaks to this dynamic, Anderson imagines the Jesuit "determined to squeeze the young Innu's ungainly and reluctant foot into the glass slipper of his opportunistic providentialism," 238–9.

58 Sharpe, *In the Wake*. I also want to acknowledge the richly productive linguistic play of the Algonquin Anishinaabe performance studies scholar Lindsay Lachance, which has helped me think through this work; I heard Lachance speak of what she calls "landing" practices in Anishnabeg thought and collaborative practice and was brought to read Lejeune differently as a result. Lindsay Lachance, "Manifesting Constellations of Love in Relational Indigenous Dramaturgies," keynote address, "Emotions in Conflict," biannual conference of the Society for the History of Emotions (Ottawa, October 2019).

9

Debt, Liquor, and Violence in the Fur Trade

ALLAN GREER AND SAMUEL DERKSEN

INTRODUCTION

"Before Canada" the emergent capitalist global economy met Indigenous North America mainly through the fur trade and, from the sixteenth century to the nineteenth, this growing commercial system had a profound impact, extending its reach right across the continent, far from the enclaves of colonial settlement and well beyond the reach of European jurisdiction and sovereignty. Exchanges took place, for the most part, in Indigenous-controlled territories; the whole enterprise depended on the knowledge and skilled labour of Indigenous men and women to kill beaver and other animals and to clean and process their pelts. Traders (we use that term to designate the European and Euro-Canadian actors who came seeking furs) had to adapt to Indigenous ways and insert themselves into Indigenous networks, not only to make their enterprise profitable but also simply to survive. They were not carriers of settler colonialism as they had no interest in eliminating the Indigenous presence. Nor were they modernizing capitalists busily transforming "traditional" societies into industrial wage-workers; instead, like many corporate enterprises operating in the contemporary Global South, they looked for ways to extract profit from non-capitalist societies without remaking the latter in their own image.[1]

In the tradition of historical writing initiated by Harold Innis's magisterial *Fur Trade in Canada* (1929), the fur trade is portrayed as a vast and expanding process of economic development led by heroic white men who laid the foundations for a transcontinental nation.[2] Inspired by Innis, but also determined to overcome the colonialist bias of his approach, scholars have made great efforts since the 1970s to bring out Indigenous dimensions of the trade. Initially, the influence of world systems theory brought the question of "dependency" to the fore, leading to a preoccupation with the degree to which imported goods may have become vital necessities for Indigenous peoples.[3] More recently, the emphasis has been on the social and cultural dimensions of an emergent "fur trade society" in western Canada. A rich literature has accumulated focusing on precisely the peoples and processes that were overlooked by the staple-trade approach of the Innis School: the Indigenous people who hunted the fur-bearing animals and prepared the pelts, as well as the French Canadian voyageurs who moved merchandise over vast distances,[4] the Métis who emerged from the meeting of peoples,[5] and the women who played a crucial role in shaping and sustaining fur trade society.[6] The accent has been on cultural hybridity, shifting identities, and the forms and conventions surrounding the fur trade. Invaluable though this work has been in counteracting the colonialist simplifications of an earlier generation of scholarship, it has tended to look away from the fur economy itself, ceding that terrain to scholars trained in the discipline of economics. Meanwhile, the economic historiography of the fur trade has moved on from Innis's political economy to a more quantitative approach based mainly on analysis of the plentiful business records of the Hudson's Bay Company.[7] Firmly convinced that "the economy" exists as a universal reality that can be abstracted from other aspects of human existence, some historical economists feel their figures can provide a measure of standard of living, industriousness, and responsiveness to price stimuli, enough to allow a comparison between the situations of Cree people of the Hudson Bay watershed and English peasants of the eighteenth century.[8] The problem is that data on prices and the volume of trade tell us little about the nature of the actual exchanges and the circumstances in which products changed hands. Moreover, this particular approach to the fur trade has tended to ignore the hugely consequential Montreal-based trade, rich in qualitative sources but poor in numerical data.

Whereas the persistent tendency of fur trade historiography, both economic and cultural, has been to emphasize cultural compromises and a certain convergence of interests connecting Indigenous hunters and Euro-Canadian traders, we would like to suggest that the demands of capital accumulation produced tensions and conflict and that these frequently revolved around the European concept of debt. Debt, we suggest, was more than a simple expedient to facilitate transactions. As the point where the cultural compromises of fur trade society ended, debt relations were of central importance throughout the history of the fur trade, though more so in some phases than others. The precisely quantified debt, derived from European laws and accounting practices and recorded in traders' account books, was frequently at odds with Indigenous customs of obligation. Accordingly, imposing such a strange practice on Indigenous peoples and in an environment lacking courts, laws, and currency was a central challenge for traders. Though they generally valued the products traders provided, Indigenous people were often resistant to the demands of monetized debt. Faced with this resistance and in the absence of coercive legal institutions, traders were only able to impose their version of debt obligations partially and only with the help of alcohol and violence.

In a pioneering study on the James Bay Cree and the Hudson's Bay Company "debt system," Toby Morantz argued that "credit was an integral part of the fur trade and, surprisingly, has received little attention in fur trade studies."[9] Even more surprisingly, the subject has still not received much attention more than three decades since she penned these words. Historians frequently note the presence of debt relations but none has followed up on Morantz's early foray to assess its implications.[10] Yet credit and debt were arguably a central aspect of the fur trade, especially where the Montreal-based trade is concerned. The Hudson's Bay Company (HBC) was generally more restrained in its use of both credit and alcohol, which means that economic historians' heavy reliance on HBC records may have contributed to an under-appreciation of this phenomenon in the economic history of the fur trade. Our aim in what follows is to survey the evidence from a wide range of periods and circumstances in order to demonstrate that debt relations were of crucial importance throughout.

Let's first back up and consider trade before the advent of monetized debt. Goods travelled over long distances and connected disparate peoples for millennia before Europeans brought their economic practices to these shores, as Adrian Burke and Christian Gates St-Pierre remind us in their contribution to this volume; they show further that objects such as stone points were often produced specifically for trade. In the absence of money, however, products were acquired for use and distribution rather than for the sake of accumulating wealth. Moreover, all indications are that exchanges were surrounded by ceremonies and rituals that highlighted the human relationships expressed in and reinforced by the presentation of valued objects. Distant peoples who might otherwise be enemies could perhaps be won over through gifts of pottery or wild rice or carved pipe bowls and, through that means, brought into networks of alliance and extended kin. Such allies could be expected to offer gifts in return, objects that would be valued for their beauty or utility but also as the embodiment of human connections. Tentative trade alliances might lead to intermarriage or assistance in war if the parties involved were able to cultivate good relations and iron over any tensions and misunderstandings that might arise over time.[11]

Since at least the time of Marcel Mauss, anthropologists have been fascinated by the role of material exchanges in socio-political relations, characterizing non-capitalist societies as resting on a "gift economy" marked by an ethic that Marshall Sahlins calls "reciprocity."[12] Mauss felt that the obligations of reciprocity were compatible with, or were even a version of, debt. Yet there is no evidence of numerical accounts being kept in pre-colonial North America. People might feel an obligation to help out their friends, to feed them when they are hungry, defend them when they are attacked, give them presents in return for their gifts; they might well have a general sense that reciprocal gifts and gestures were either appropriate or inadequate. However, this reciprocity unfolded over time and under shifting circumstances that made strict commensurability impossible: there was no table of equivalence to translate the value of a bear skin into so many argillite pipes or so much assistance in war. In other words, the ethic of mutual support did not lend itself to mathematical accounting. Following David Graeber, we argue that capitalist credit and debt were something quite distinct from the sense of reciprocity and mutual support that organized exchanges before the advent of the fur trade.[13] Indigenous ethics of obligation were not necessarily at odds with capitalist calculation – in many circumstances, hunters willingly discharged their debts to the traders' satisfaction – but they were different, and this divergence frequently led to frustration and ill will on both sides.

As fur traders extended their reach across the continent, following pre-existing Indigenous trade corridors as they went, they had to find ways to insert themselves into Indigenous cultures of alliance and exchange and then bend these to the purposes of accumulation. Though they came bearing iron blades, copper pots, wool blankets, guns, beads, and other appealing goods from abroad, making them welcome visitors and desirable allies in most cases, they still needed to actively cultivate close relations if they were to secure their "returns" of fur on an ongoing basis. Mostly the trade took place on Indigenous terrain, and as scholars in the field have demonstrated repeatedly, traders had to adjust to that reality, learning the languages and customs of their clients and providing the proper assortment of goods at a standard of quality that met their customers' exacting standards.[14] Commercial relations were sustained through adherence to a series of social and diplomatic protocols developed through negotiation and exchange between European traders and Indigenous hunters.[15] And yet, no matter how deeply immersed the trader might become in the cultural milieu of his Indigenous hosts, he remained firmly attached to the global capitalist economy and answerable to employers (HBC) or suppliers (Montreal-based trade) who needed to make money both to discharge debts to their suppliers and to realize a profit. The fur trade was rooted at one end in a world of law and money, one where unpaid bills could provoke legal action, court-ordered seizure of goods, and even imprisonment. At the other end, deep in Indigenous country where currency and courts were essentially unknown,[16] traders had to contrive devices to extract value from this non-capitalist environment. Chief among these was the concept of debt. It was a matter of selecting some of the goods and services that passed between traders and Indigenous neighbours, designating them as merchandise and then reckoning an obligation to repay as though it was legal and monetized. In the midst of unquantified practices of mutuality and reciprocity, traders unilaterally introduced a capitalist version of debt frequently at odds with Indigenous understandings of what and how people owed one another. They faced the difficult challenge of both adapting to Indigenous economic cultures and at the same time subverting them, which naturally provoked resistance.[17] In his global survey of the history of debt, Graeber discerns a consistent association linking quantification and violence in the extended campaign "to turn morality into a matter of impersonal arithmetic."[18] In the case of the Canadian fur trade, we find that alcohol also played a crucial role.

There are, of course, exceptions to this generalization: debt and liquor seem to have been largely absent during the very earliest stages of the long history of the fur trade. The Atlantic coastal trade of the late sixteenth century remained basically alcohol-free for the simple reason that distilled liquor was not widely available at the time. (French traders and colonists brought wine as part of their ships' provisions but the Mi'kmaq they encountered found it disgusting to drink a liquid that looked so much like blood.[19]) From the late Middle Ages through the sixteenth century, alcohol was a medicine, distilled in small quantities by apothecaries as a health enhancing elixir known as the "water of life" (*aqua vitae* or *eau de vie*). It was only over the course of the seventeenth century, which is to say at the time the fur trade moved inland and became established as a colonial enterprise, that distilled drinks came to be produced in industrial quantities and marketed as a beverage. The French distilled grape wine for this purpose and brandy (*eau de vie*) came to be appreciated throughout Europe and its overseas colonies; until the nineteenth century, French brandy represented the standard of quality to which other liquors aspired. The main producing regions were the hinterlands of Bordeaux and La Rochelle, ports that happened to be active in the North American trade.[20] Meanwhile, the Dutch and English made do with fermented cereal grains while Caribbean plantation colonies distilled rum from the by-products of sugar refining. Distilled spirits emerged in the early modern period, alongside tobacco, coffee, tea, and chocolate, as a mind-altering and habit-forming substance that could be used – as opium would later be used by the British forcing their way into the China trade – to blow open societies that resisted the intrusion of global capitalism. Moreover, as a concentrated product that, unlike wine at this time, lasted indefinitely, liquor lent itself to trans-oceanic commerce. It played a central part in the African slave trade and was integrated into many other elements of Europe's overseas expansion.[21] The "Age of Exploration and Empire" which framed the Canadian fur trade could also be called the "Age of Alcohol."

Monetized debt had a much deeper history in Europe and Asia, but it only became an organizing factor in the fur trade towards the middle of the seventeenth century when the establishment of colonies and trading posts made ongoing commercial relations possible. Credit and debt, allied with newly available brandy, were part of that connection almost from the beginning, notably in seventeenth-century New France.

NEW FRANCE

The French colony on the St Lawrence had taken root under the auspices of the Compagnie de la Nouvelle-France. The latter enjoyed a monopoly over the fur trade, which it exercised only at the level of exports from the colony; resident colonists were free to trade with Indigenous peoples as long as they sold the furs they acquired to the company at a set price.[22] In the mid-seventeenth century, the fur trade consisted mostly of micro-exchanges between a multitude of resident colonists and Indigenous traders who brought pelts down to the St Lawrence settlements every summer. The scenes that unfolded at and around Quebec, Trois-Rivières, and Montreal annually were festive and chaotic. Since the trade was effectively unregulated and not yet dominated by any large concern, ordinary settlers and townsfolk competed to secure a piece of the action. The price they received for furs from the monopoly company was set by law and so they competed, not in pricing, but in vying to establish personal ties, however temporary, with Indigenous visitors. Hence the use of alcohol, newly introduced into Atlantic commercial circuits and already part of a French culture of camaraderie and hospitality, to dissolve reticence and nurture ties. Both colonists and Indigenous drank, often to excess, giving rise to the scenes of debauchery and fighting that alarmed church authorities. In addition to brandy-fuelled good cheer, these petty traders also offered credit, advancing goods on the understanding that they would be recompensed with furs the next year. It was a way of providing Indigenous hunters with the knives, blankets, pots, and ammunition they needed for a productive winter hunt, while individual French traders secured themselves a share of future fur harvests. In this way, debt performed its function of establishing economic connections and of maintaining them over time.

However, these personal connections proved fragile as a result of the fragmented and intensely competitive atmosphere of the seventeenth-century fur trade. No sooner was a debt relationship established than some third party would attempt to waylay the Indigenous debtor and buy up his pelts with good merchandise, leaving the creditor in the lurch. Habitant-traders thus faced a double challenge: first they had to attract Indigenous customers and then they had to induce those customers to pay what they considered was owed them rather than using their furs to purchase new supplies from someone else. In transactions between colonists, creditors had legal recourse to recover outstanding debts. Here, as in Europe, people went to great lengths to avoid litigation, but all parties knew that the courts stood ready to enforce obligations if called upon and that awareness acted to discipline debtors. However, Indigenous peoples refused to accept French jurisdiction, even in the heart of the Lawrentian settlements, and so a regime of legal pluralism developed that effectively exempted them from both criminal and civil law. In a thorough review of Quebec court records, Denys Delâge and Étienne Gilbert found no cases of Indigenous people being sued for unpaid debt.[23] This would remain a crucial and enduring condition of the Canadian fur trade: it took place in the absence of legal institutions for enforcing obligations. In monetary as well as in legal terms, Indigenous space was differentiated from French colonial space: an intendant's ordinance of 1685 forbade the carrying of coins and bills of exchange in the upcountry fur trade.[24] Consequently, beginning with the habitants of New France, traders had to find other ways to recover advances given to Indigenous partners. It could be an aggressive business, comparable in some respects to the illicit drug trade of recent times.

In the 1660s and 1670s, Atikamekw hunters carrying the produce of their winter hunt down the St Maurice River to Trois-Rivières every summer had to portage past a set of rapids known as La Gabelle,[25] twenty kilometres above the small colonial town. There, as soon as they had put in their canoes, they would find themselves assailed by a crowd of settlers who had ascended the river expressly to intercept them. Boisterous, friendly, but also a bit menacing, it seems, the colonists were determined to get their hands on the beaver pelts and moose skins the Atikamekw were carrying; to that end, they offered conviviality fuelled by brandy and good imported tobacco. Bacchanalia ensued. Appalled by reports of this disorderly behaviour at the edge of the colony, the sovereign council of New France took steps to suppress it, largely out of concern for the way that it diverted habitants of the region from the cultivation of the land and other productive activities. As the council saw it, these colonists abandoned their farms to rush up the St Maurice because, "having made large loans to the Indians, were compelled every year to go ahead of them to secure as many of their pelts as possible to deduct from their debts." If it had effective jurisdiction over the Atikamekw, the council might have ordered them to come straight to the town and pay their debts or face legal action. That solution was out of the question, however, so it instead ordered the traders to elect two representatives who would travel to La Gabelle with a list of everyone's debts and then return with furs to be distributed to creditors on a pro rata basis. That device failed miserably, given the lack of trust in this highly competitive environment where traders seemed desperate, not only to collect what they felt they were owed, but also to capture some of the furs owed to others. And so, the annual stampede up the St Maurice continued.[26]

Indigenous hunters/traders approaching Montreal and Quebec had to run a similar gauntlet of colonists playing the combined roles of bartender, friend, merchant, and debt collector. Governor Louis de Buade de Frontenac issued an ordinance in 1674 condemning the "violences" committed against Indigenous people by settlers at Lachine and other places on or near the island of Montreal to enforce payment for brandy, tobacco, and other supplies.[27] Much of the text of this ordinance is couched in terms of regulating alcohol, ever since Bishop Laval's 1660 condemnation of the brandy trade,[28] as authorities in New France had become accustomed to attributing all the ills of colonialism to the poisonous effects of liquor on Indigenous people. However, it seems clear that the real problem lay in the aggressive way petty traders were imposing debt obligations on Indigenous people and then enforcing payment by hook or by crook. The central thrust of Frontenac's ordinance (however ineffective it may have been) was to enjoin colonists "to commit no violence against the Indians under the pretext of making them pay."[29] Complaints about similar behaviour had arisen ten years earlier, at a meeting at Quebec where colonial authorities and Jesuits met with Algonquin and Innu leaders to discuss questions of jurisdiction in the wake of a series of violent incidents. In 1664, war was raging with the Five Nations and these Indigenous allies of the French could not safely venture into the woods to hunt; nevertheless, colonists were harassing them to repay previous advances of merchandise. This was the main grievance of the Innu and Algonquin and they complained bitterly that "French creditors" were "pillaging and abusing them if they could not pay."[30] The common theme across these incidents is the use of debt, alcohol, and force to extract payment in the form of pelts: at the time, in the amount, and under the circumstances specified by the French. We suggest that such a way of framing obligations constituted the essential violence of an emergent debt regime.

It was in this context of credit relations and the impulse to head off Indigenous traders on the approaches to urban markets that young Frenchmen began travelling all the way to the sources of fur production and overwintering with hunters, especially in the region of the upper Great Lakes. Occasional expeditions had been mounted earlier, but it was only in the late 1660s, when peace had been established with the Five Nations, that the *pays d'en haut* emerged as a major centre of French–Indigenous exchange. One important motive for this *course des bois* was to ensure that advances of merchandise made in the fall would be repaid at the end of the winter by eliminating any opportunity for competing traders to waylay furs on their way to Montreal. Present at or near winter hunting camps, *coureurs de bois* established relationships with their Indigenous hosts that were deeper and more lasting than the brief liaisons that took place at La Gabelle and Lachine. First Nations of the upper country were generally keen to bring these outsiders with their useful objects into their networks of kin and alliance and the successful *coureurs de bois* were those able to adapt to Indigenous cultural expectations in a pattern of mutual adjustments that Richard White famously named the "Middle Ground."[31] Navigating the Middle Ground entailed all sorts of sharing, gifting, favours, participation in ceremonies, and, in many cases, marrying.

As Gilles Havard points out, the fur trade hinged on a conjunction of Indigenous customs of reciprocity with a European capitalist notion of debt. "The European system of credit," he writes, "accorded with the principle of gift and counter-gift."[32] No doubt the principle of credit and debt *coexisted* with the principle of gift reciprocity in the fur trade, but were these two principles really in harmony? Cultural compromises were demanded of both sides for the trade relationship to persist, but the traders' insistence, at the end of the day, on construing complex obligations as quantifiable debts constituted an imposition, ultimately at odds with the spirit of gift exchange. What if hunters who had received supplies of ammunition or blankets could not produce many pelts in a given winter because weather conditions were unfavourable or because, to ward off starvation, they needed to concentrate on hunting deer or moose or because a death in the family required them to suspend hunting as a mourning gesture or because they were coping with the effects of an epidemic or because going to the best beaver hunting grounds would expose them to enemy attack? According to the dictates of mutual support, the ability to pay crucially affected obligations, for this was a human, not a mathematical, relationship, but to the capitalist logic of debt, such considerations were irrelevant; *coureurs de bois* would therefore press for what they were owed according to that logic, and their methods were not always gentle. An early Jesuit missionary on Lake Michigan reported being sum-moned to the land of the Potawatomies, "that I might curb some young Frenchmen, who, being among them for the purpose of trading, were threat-ening and maltreating them."[33] One might wonder how a handful of French traders could get away with this kind of bullying among populous nations well able to defend themselves. The answer may have to do with the fact that hunting-gathering peoples tend to disperse in the winter and so a small group of well-armed traders could sometimes enjoy a localized and temporary pre-dominance of power. On the other hand, when the balance of power tipped in the other direction obnoxious *coureurs de bois* might find themselves stripped of their merchandise ("pillaged") or dead.[34] The traders and their capitalist calculations did not always prevail, but it does seem clear that debt was where the compromises of the Middle Ground ended.

In the western interior, as in the St Lawrence valley, *eau de vie* functioned as an essential device for countering competition and cultivating close rela-tions with Indigenous suppliers. During his 1754–55 inland reconnaissance mission from Hudson Bay, Anthony Henday reported on French traders on the Saskatchewan River serving watered-down brandy to Assiniboine hunters who came to their post.[35] Henday makes it clear that the alcohol was offered not as a commodity for sale but as a gesture of hospitality prior to trade. The Hudson's Bay man wrote with envy of the French ability to win Indigenous goodwill through performances of generosity. For Indigenous peoples of the west, drinking was still a rare event in the 1750s, a special occasion to enjoy an altered mental state in the company of friends and allies. There was still no question of becoming truly addicted simply because supplies would have been too limited.

It is hard to get a precise reading on how much liquor flowed through the arteries of New France's inland commerce, but all indications are that amounts were far less than the fulminations of the clergy would suggest.[36] A major factor limiting supplies was the comparatively high price of French brandy. Colonial authorities worried that competing traders from New York and New England were gaining advantage over Canada's traders by deploying large quantities of low-priced rum, most of it manufactured in the North American colonies using molasses smuggled in from the French West Indies.[37] Distilling was not well developed in the French Caribbean thanks to mercan-tilist policies designed to protect France's domestic grape-based industry.

Shut out of the metropolitan market, producers in the French islands were allowed to export to Canada, but rum prices, while cheaper than those for *eau de vie*, remained fairly high because of the small scale of the colonial distilling industry and because import duties were charged. This situation, in which price limited the flow of alcohol, would change dramatically at the time of the British Conquest.

RUM AND THE BRITISH CONQUEST

An alcohol revolution was one of the earliest effects of the British conquest of Canada. Even before the fighting ended at Montreal, merchants were converging on Quebec, bringing British and colonial merchandise to supply the troops and to take advantage of the shortages the war had occasioned throughout the colony. The *New Hampshire Gazette* reported from Quebec on 29 August 1760, "That provisions of all kinds was in the greatest plenty, and Rum in particular, cheaper than in Boston."[38] Rum was consumed by British soldiers and French Canadian habitants and it almost immediately displaced brandy as the liquor of choice in the fur trade. With kegs of cheap rum weighing down the canoe fleets mounting the Ottawa River from the 1760s on,[39] the fur trade became more addicted to alcohol than ever before, now without the clerical denunciations and excommunications that, along with high prices, had placed a limit on the use of spirits under the French regime. The history of the fur trade and the transition to British rule is usually recounted as a marriage joining French Canadian expertise, Scottish entrepreneurialism, and British capital, but liquor may be an equally important key to understanding the transformation of the trade in the 1760s.

Anglophone traders quickly adopted the techniques developed in New France, including the strategy of combining debt and alcohol. A young Peter Pond was introduced to the trade by French and Indigenous veterans gathered at Prairie du Chien (now Wisconsin) in the fall of 1773; they were there, he wrote, to make "thare arangements for the InSewing winter ... Like wise Giveing Creadets to the Indans who ware all to Rondaveuse thare in Spring."[40] In 1765, Alexander Henry (the Elder) claimed to have distributed 3,000 "plus" (ie., the value of a prime beaver skin) to Indigenous hunters in the Upper Great Lakes.[41] Although the system of seasonal credits had been established in the seventeenth century, it is mentioned more frequently in the record after 1760, partly because the new generation of anglophone traders had political reasons to emphasize the risks associated with granting credit beyond the reach of colonial jurisdictions. In a petition asking for release from restrictions that had been placed on the trade by military authorities at the time of Pontiac's War, merchants insisted that they needed to travel into the western interior specifically in order to secure their debts. "Without the Indians Have Credit given them, 'tis impossible to carry on a Trade to advantage. And when we are on the Spot to winter with them, we have always an Opportunity of knowing their Dispositions, pressing them to exert their Diligence, and are ready in the Spring to receive what is due." The Council of Quebec noted the riskiness of advancing credit beyond the reach of the law, acknowledging, "the great difficulty, under which the Traders at present labour, the means of recovering and securing their Property in the upper country, as well as of apprehending fugitive Debtors."[42] By 1786, representatives of the Montreal merchant community were claiming to hold debts worth a total of 300,000 pounds from the Indigenous peoples in territories south of the Great Lakes that they feared would be surrendered to the United States.[43] Traders highlighted the risks they ran in advancing goods to Indigenous suppliers, but their profits were still substantial, thanks to the practice of charging extraordinarily high prices for their merchandise to make up for all the "bad debts" that accumulated when Indigenous people deliberately or inadvertently neglected to play the part assigned them in the credit system.

THE NORTH WEST COMPANY

In 1779, a group of powerful Montreal traders formalized the ad hoc non-competition agreements that had defined trade in the northwest, entering into a partnership they called the North West Company (NWC), which became the dominant Montreal firm in the northwest trade over the next four decades.[44] The NWC's flexible business organization helped them to suppress competition and *voyageur* wages while expanding their trade ever further to the north and the west. Every stage of the North West Company's operations, from transatlantic shipping to the acquisition of furs at distant outposts, rested on lines of credit; moreover, the immensely extended lines of transportation meant that suppliers had to wait two to three years for a return on their advances.[45] The lines of credit and debt stretched across an ocean and up the broad St Lawrence before snaking their way along the narrow waterways of Canadian Shield as far as Lake Athabasca and beyond and where they made contact with the non-capitalist hunting-gathering societies that sustained them, these lines ended like a harpoon with a sharp point and a hook. A summary of North West Company debt practices can be found in an 1816 pamphlet published by Lord Selkirk, principal shareholder in the rival Hudson's Bay Company.

> It is the established custom of the fur traders to supply the Indians with goods on credit, exacting from them a promise to deliver, in return, a stipulated number of beaver skins, or an equivalent in other furs. From the improvident character of the Indians, there are few of them, who, on the approach of winter, are not in want of supplies, without which they cannot proceed to their hunting grounds: – and, not having the means of making immediate payment, the produce of their winter hunt is anticipated, and pledged to the traders. It may well be imagined that the traders incur a very great risk of bad debts; and this, no doubt, is one cause of the excessive disproportion between the intrinsic value of the goods which are sold to the Indians, and of the furs which are obtained in exchange. The facility, however, with which the Indians obtain this sort of credit is very pernicious … The traders of the North-West Company, have the superiority of direct force, find it for their interest to keep up the practice, as tending to rivet the subjection in which they hold the Indians. These traders, acknowledging no submission to any magistrate, ask for no other authority than superior strength to take the property of their debtor, and think themselves entitled to add personal correction, if the Indians should hesitate to comply with the demand. The oppression which arises from this summary mode of proceeding is chiefly felt where there is a competition among different traders.[46]

This passage from Selkirk's polemic is not without exaggeration; the author simplifies complex and shifting power relations when he implies that the NWC traders always enjoyed "the superiority of direct force" and kept Indigenous people in "subjection." Moreover, in line with Malthus-era views of the British labouring classes, he characterizes hunters as "improvident." In fact, both Natives and traders used credit relations as a device to ensure the continuance of the trade. And yet, in its essentials, the indictment rings true and accords with what NWC traders reveal in their own writings.

The remarkably detailed journals of Alexander Henry the Younger, a North West Company employee who was eventually elevated to partner in the firm, are filled with allusions to debt and alcohol.[47] His text begins in the summer of 1800 in the midst of a voyage from the head of Lake Superior to the "Forks of the Assiniboine" (the site of Winnipeg). There he effected a junction with a group of forty Saulteaux (aka Western Ojibwe), Anishinaabe people who were then in the process of relocating from the vicinity of Sault Ste Marie, where fur-bearing animals had become scarce.[48] With them, Henry's crew proceeded south, up the Red River, into the prime beaver grounds of what is now Minnesota. His canoes were carrying a case of guns, two kegs of gunpowder, and a supply of lead shot, items needed both for hunting and military security. There was also a "bale of kettles," some wool blankets and other unspecified "merchandise" that probably included twine for fishing nets as well as beads, silver, and other decorative items. These were the durable products Henry referred to as "dry goods" to distinguish them from the consumables that formed a large part of his cargo: kegs of rum and "high wines" (a molasses-based distillate that had not been refined or aged, essentially low-quality rum), as well as coiled ropes of the Brazilian tobacco his customers prized. Dry goods and liquor were deployed and accounted for in very different ways. Henry's account books have not survived, but his journal contains numerous entries like the following from 23 August 1800: "This morning the Indians paid me a visit very early, to demand Dry Goods on credit in expectation of getting Liquor which is customary on their taking debt. We generally give them some Liquor to encourage them to hunt and pay us."[49]

As a savvy and experienced trader, Alexander Henry embedded his commerce within Saulteaux ceremonial practices. He mastered the rudiments of the Anishinaabeg language, he inserted himself into Saulteaux kin networks by taking as wife the daughter of a prominent chief, he donated ammunition to Saulteaux war parties, and he provided gifts for funeral ceremonies. Even so, there was only so far he could bend in his efforts to adapt to Indigenous customs, for, in another context, far from the Red River Valley, Alexander Henry was a debtor, dependent on the colonial and trans-Atlantic networks of credit that financed North West Company operations. In Lower Canada, debts were reckoned in the pounds, shillings, and pence of Halifax currency, and in Britain they were in sterling; these obligations were enforceable in law. Henry was at all times subject to the discipline of this monetized, legally sanctioned system of circulating credit, even as he operated in an environment with no courts or currency. Like other fur traders, this led him to introduce a simulacrum of capitalist credit arrangements into a relationship that was otherwise dominated by non-capitalist Indigenous ways.

Following well-established fur trade practice, Henry would outfit hunters in the fall with the tools they needed for a productive winter hunt; of one family, he notes on 15 September, "I … gave out to the Indians their necessaries for debt, to the amount of twenty skins each man, and an assortment of small articles gratis."[50] Ideally, the Saulteaux would return to the post with furs to pay off their debts at some time in the course of the winter or else the following spring. Their arrival would be the occasion for further gifts of rum and tobacco. If they did not have enough to fully discharge the amount owing, the balance would be rolled over to the following year; if they had more than enough furs to pay off what was owed, the surplus could be used to buy luxuries such as beads or silver decorative items. When fall came around again, even hunters who had been highly successful the previous year would have to take on more debt in order to procure the ammunition and other supplies needed to prosecute the next winter's hunt. Fur and provisions flowed into the trading post while liquor and dry goods flowed out, but Alexander Henry orchestrated the trade so as to ensure that most Saulteaux could be categorized as debtors. These arrangements resembled the "truck system" that kept the fishers of Newfoundland perpetually impoverished and attached to their local merchants.[51] And, as with the economic organization of the fishery, fur trade debt seemed designed to empower the trader and perpetuate relations of production.

Alexander Henry spoke of debts as amounting to so many "skins," invoking a flexible unit of account which, like the Hudson's Bay Company's "Made Beaver," represented a prime beaver pelt or, more commonly, a certain number of lower-grade furs judged equivalent to that value. In the absence of coinage, the "skin"/Made Beaver filled some of the functions of currency in the fur trade, except that it represented a rather imprecise and flexible measure of value, one that the trader could manipulate in response to market conditions.

When a Saulteaux hunter delivered a variety of animal pelts to the post, it was Henry who determined how many "skins" they represented. (Though of course he would face pushback if the Saulteaux felt the evaluation was unfair, it was still the trader who set the initial terms for any haggling.) Henry also reserved to himself the power to decide which of the objects he turned over to the Saulteaux were "gratis" and which constituted merchandise supplied on credit. There is no indication that the Saulteaux understood their obligations in the same way. And even if they tried to give the trader what he demanded, hunters might still fall short in any given year due to the vagaries of nature, warfare or even theft by rival fur traders. Henry was not indifferent to these constraints, but he did not see them as affecting the debt owed. Those who brought in their twenty skins he considered "good Indians"; those who failed, for whatever reason, would be branded "idle" or "dishonest" or "scoundrels." The harsh moral indictments suggest that we are far from the realms of "le doux commerce" that, according to Enlightenment thinkers, brought amity between the nations of the world: an undercurrent of mutual antagonism ran through Alexander Henry's trade with the Saulteaux.

Alcohol in this context was a necessary lubricant. Henry sometimes passed out "drams" to compensate individuals for rendering services, such as canoe repair, and he occasionally sold it to Indigenous people as a commodity. More typically, his rum was presented as a gift, usually to mark the giving or discharging of credit.[52] With an appreciation for the way gifted objects could reinforce the effect of words, Henry would sometimes issue exhortations, as he did in the spring of 1801 when a party of Saulteaux arrived with beaver and bear skins. "I assembled them all together and gave them five Kegs of mixed Rum gratis and two Chiefs Clothings ... with a long speech how they must conduct themselves in future and of my determination of building a fort this summer at the Panbian [Pembina] River."[53] The rum he presented was heavily watered down but still plentiful enough to allow his customers to get fully intoxicated. Sometimes, according to Henry, long-suppressed hostilities were released and violent episodes ensued: he reported, "terrible fighting among themselves" and multiple instances of men stabbing and beating women. "If there is a murder committed among the Saulteaux it is always in a drinking match," observed the man who supplied the liquor he himself described as "the mother of all evil."[54]

Henry and his crew of voyageurs also drank heavily, occasionally indulging in all-night benders that he described as "making merry." A drunken New Year's Day party prompted him to remark that his own people were "more troublesome than double their number of Saulteaux."[55] His journal entry for 6 May 1804, records another alcohol-fuelled brawl: "Engaged my men, settled their accounts, and gave them a treat of High wines &c. They were soon merry, then quarrelled and fought. I saw five battles at the same moment in the Fort, and soon after nothing was to be seen, but bloody noses, Bruised faces, Black Eyes, and torn Jackets and Shirts."[56] The Indigenous wives of voyageurs were sometimes beaten by their intoxicated mates; more than one despaired to the point of suicide.[57] For French Canadian employees of the North West Company, as well as for Indigenous customers, debt, alcohol, and violence combined in an explosive mix. However, the trader deployed his supply of liquor differently for these two categories of people: the Saulteaux received drinks occasionally and mostly for free, whereas the voyageurs enjoyed a more continuous flow of rum but found that it was usually charged to their tab. In settling accounts with his men every year, Henry would take the annual salary each voyageur was owed by the terms of his contract (*engagement*) and subtract the value of supplies – mostly liquor – he had received over the course of the year. The supplies were of course charged at inflated prices, ensuring that salaries rarely had to be paid. With no prospect of taking any cash home to Lower Canada – many indeed accumulated growing debts to their employer – voyageurs often elected to sign on for another three-year term. Accounts from the NWC's English River district indicate that every single voyageur was indebted to the company beyond the value of their salary.[58] It was the objective of a good bourgeois to retain his workforce while minimizing labour costs and liquor served to offset wages while helping to ensure that the men took out their frustrations on one another. In Alexander Henry's North West Company, alcohol was the key to personnel management.

In dealing with his (largely illiterate) voyageurs, as well as with the Saulteaux hunters, Henry enjoyed the immense advantage of exclusive control over the account books. He determined which supplies were considered gifts and which were recorded as merchandise entailing a monetary or quasi-monetary obligation. He alone retained the power to say what his employees and his customers owed him and he alone could supply the drug that enticed them into debt and, on crucial occasions, kept them distracted. Of course, the Indigenous peoples he dealt with were by no means powerless, and Henry's ability to impose his version of accounting varied with the circumstances, including the numerical strength and military organization of his counterparts. When he moved to posts in the vicinity of present-day Edmonton, Henry was quite intimidated by the mounted Blackfoot and Cree who would come to trade and then steal his horses when departing. Indigenous power and ambient circumstances determined how effectively he could enforce debts as he defined them, but the authority of the ledger remained central to Henry's fur trade.

THE ATHABASCA COUNTRY

In the North West Company's northernmost trade region, administered from Fort Chipewyan on Lake Athabasca, but including the Peace River, Great Slave Lake, and the Mackenzie River, the Nor'Westers encountered rich beaver grounds and a comparatively small and scattered population of Dene hunters who lacked the horses and rich supplies of bison that empowered peoples of the plains.[59] A smallpox epidemic in 1780–81 devastated these northerners and left them all the more vulnerable to the bullying ways of Montreal traders who were frequently able to concentrate a large enough force of voyageurs to physically dominate the vicinity of their posts.[60] Further undermining Indigenous power were the upheavals and conflicts occasioned by the advent of the fur trade; as people flocked to the prime beaver hunting grounds, strife broke out among different Dene groups, conflict made all the more deadly by the uneven distribution of imported firearms. Denesuline (Chipewyan) from the east used guns procured from the HBC's Fort Prince of Wales (Churchill) to raid T'astsaot'ine (Yellowknife), Tlicho (Dogrib), Dehcho, Deh Gáh Got'ie Kue, and Sahtú (Slavey) peoples of the Mackenzie River drainage basin and steal their furs.[61] Following the establishment of a permanent North West Company presence in the Athabasca region during the 1780s, many Denesuline migrated to the vicinity of Lake Athabasca, attracted by the presence of company posts which obviated the need to undertake the arduous and dangerous trek to Hudson Bay.[62] The North West Company took full advantage of the combination of plentiful furs and comparatively small Indigenous populations that characterized the Athabasca country.

Although the Dene clearly desired the products the nwc had to offer, they could not always satisfy the traders' demand for a steady supply of fur because, in the north even more than in other regions, the commercial imperatives of the fur hunt were frequently at odds with the survival imperative of the food hunt. The Denesuline were particularly torn. They had long depended on the great caribou herds of the "Barren Lands" that stretch northwestwardly from Hudson Bay, but participating fully in the beaver hunt required a geographical shift that could imperil their subsistence.[63] Consequently, many Denesuline were understandably ambivalent about the fur trade.[64] Other Dene peoples, perfectly at home in the Athabasca–Great Slave–Mackenzie region, still faced dilemmas, especially in winters of cyclical scarcity of game animals such as the Arctic hare, in balancing the demands of fur production and subsistence. Making matters worse is the fact that beaver hunting in the far north was a labour-intensive affair as hunters had to spend long, wearying hours in frigid temperatures smashing through thick layers of ice with iron chisels to gain access to beaver lodges.[65] It was exacting work, especially for men who might, in periods of local game shortage, be undernourished.[66] Between Indigenous people, who had to balance the need to sustain trade relations against the need to hunt for subsistence, and nwc traders who insisted Dene hunters bring in furs and acquit their debts regardless of the circumstances, conflict was inevitable. The traders regarded those who failed to supply the requisite number of furs as a "lying, lazy, rascally set of vagabonds,"[67] and they did not hesitate to seize moments when the balance of power was in their favour to impose their demands by force. Since initially the demand for alcoholic beverages was limited amongst certain Dene communities, most notably the Denesuline, traders were all the more inclined to rely on physical force, not only to drive Dene people to the fur hunt but also to prevent them trading with competitors.

The nwc faced periodic competition in the Athabasca Country from the XY Company, an operation founded by dissident Nor'Westers, and the hbc.[68] hbc representatives consistently complained of the nwc's violent conduct and bullying tactics.[69] Peter Fidler, in command of the hbc's Nottingham House, complained frequently of the nwc's use of ruthless tactics to keep

Dene hunters away from the post: "They [the Denesuline] are very much intimidated by the Old Co [NWC] & if they are known...] if they are known to give a skin elsewhere, they are sure to receive a good drubbing."[70] When the HBC returned to the Athabasca region after a decade's absence, Governor George Simpson reported from Fort Wedderburn that "While the North West Compy. were in full possession of the Country, the Chipewyans [Denesuline] were reduced to the most servile and abject state; absolate [sic] despotism was perhaps never carried to such lengths as over these poor creatures."[71] Simpson may have exaggerated the "abject state" of the Dene but not the ruthlessness of the Nor'Westers. When two indebted Dene showed up empty handed at Fort St John on the Peace River, the NWC clerk, "threatened them of abandoning the Fort in the Spring as well as beating, and using them like dogs if they did not work better for the future."[72]

When frustrated in their attempts to impose capitalist discipline, some traders indulged in genocidal fantasies. At Rocky Mountain Portage Fort on the Peace River, NWC clerk Archibald McGillivray reacted to the failure of Dene in the vicinity to pay their debts with this proposal: "I think the best method would be to have hang some of the greatest rascals as an example to the others, & if that would have no effect on them to destroy their whole race, for what are they good for they make little or no packs."[73] In reality, the Nor'Westers would detain delinquent debtors and put them to work supplying the post with food.[74] Post journals also speak routinely of slapping, kicking, and pulling the ears of hunters who failed to deliver enough furs.[75] On the other hand, the journals also tell of Indigenous resistance. In another incident at Fort St John, the NWC clerk began by verbally chastising a Dane-zaa (Beaver) leader known as L'Homme Seul for his "scandalous hunt," but when he attempted to pull L'Homme Seul's ears, the Dane-zaa leader, "rising suddenly took hold of one of my hands whilst his son and several others surrounding me held the other without however attempting to do me any harm or injury." After being checked by L'Homme Seul, the clerk continued to berate and threaten, but he acknowledged the seemingly remarkable fact that "none of them were beaten."[76]

Most shocking in this context is the North West Company's recourse to trafficking women. "The method by which they get most of the Che-pa-wy-an [Denesuline] Women," wrote HBC surveyor Philip Turnor in 1791, "is by the Masters seizin them for their Husbands or Fathers debts and then selling them to their men from five hundred to two thousand Livres and if the Father or Husband or any of them resist the only satisfaction they get is a beating and they are frequently not satisfied with taking the Woman but their Gun and Tent likewise."[77] This report cannot be dismissed as the fabrication of a hostile rival. The Nor'Westers spoke frankly about trafficking women in their own journals. The kidnapping of women was intended both to discipline male hunters and, like internal sales of alcohol, to offset employees' salaries. In April 1800, NWC commander at Fort Chipewyan, James McKenzie, agreed to sell the Denesuline wife of a NWC engagé to the highest bidder to help the voyageur repay his outstanding debt to the company.[78] Later in his journal McKenzie reported a confrontation with a party of Dene over this very subject. "They desired that we would trade no more in women on any account. Told them that we would do as we thought proper for it was not … their business to prescribe rules to us."[79]

The Northern Dene were by no means passive in the face of this coercion. Outside fortified posts like Fort Chipewyan, the NWC's stronghold in the Athabasca country,[80] the balance of power was more favourable to Indigenous communities. When company employees hunted for game, travelled between posts, or sought out Dene producers at their hunting grounds, they were sometimes attacked by embittered hunters.[81] The HBC's George Simpson observed that, beyond their fortified positions, the Nor'Westers dared not "venture to introduce the force necessary to carry on their usual system of violence and outrage."[82] Astute traders were aware of the limited and contingent nature of their power and calibrated their violence accordingly.[83]

HUDSON'S BAY COMPANY

The HBC tended to be much more restrained in its use of both debt and alcohol than the aggressive and extravagant Canadian traders. Among chartered overseas trading corporations, it was one of the most conservative, avoiding the rapid expansion and excessive borrowing for which the East India Company and the Royal Africa Company were notorious while maintaining solid financial stability through most of its long history.[84] Its accounting practices were always far more rigorous than those of its fur trade competitors and its executives generally took a dim view of the practice of providing drinks and credit to Indigenous suppliers.[85] And yet, at the posts on the edge of Hudson Bay, such practices were never absent. We get a glimpse of a typical conversation at the Prince of Wales Fort trading wicket in a Cree phrasebook published by chief factor James Isham in 1743.

E ope'n yr. Bundles of beavr.	opohaw aurtiwitt
B I have gott no Beaver	Nemattau aurtiuc
E what was you a doing in the winter	
B I was starv'd in the winter was the Reason I Killd. no Beaver	
E Where is my Debt	Donnonna enmisinnahiggan[86]

The English trader, "E" in this stock dialogue, insists on repayment of advances made the previous year, unmoved by the Cree hunter's ("B") explanation that the need to procure food prevented him from acquiring beaver fur. This passage nicely illustrates an enduring theme in fur trade history, the tension between subsistence hunting and fur production; it also demonstrates that the HBC operated on a credit basis, even at a time when its monopoly was scarcely challenged by competitors. Historians of the company find that, during its first century of operations, the HBC offered merchandise on credit but sparingly.[87]

Something similar might be said of the company's use of alcohol, at least up until it moved inland in the late eighteenth century. Visiting Indigenous parties were regaled with alcohol, mostly a concoction known as "British brandy," a grain liquor coloured to look like French *eau de vie*. After 1760, the company turned increasingly to rum. Some liquor was gifted and some traded; indeed, the fact that it could be watered down made alcohol a significant source of profit.[88] However, because drinking occurred only at the trading post and because Indigenous suppliers from the hinterland could only make the long trek once a year, not much was consumed in aggregate. Ray and Freeman give total figures for all HBC forts that range between eleven and 2,348 gallons per year for an average of 960 gallons annually between 1700 and 1763, a small fraction of the 50,000 gallons of rum the North West Company admitted to distributing in the early nineteenth century.[89] Carlos and Lewis show that, in most years, liquor was a less important consumable than Brazilian tobacco at York Factory; they argue that the amounts dispensed at bayside posts fell far short of the volumes supplied by English fur traders in other parts of North America.[90] Liquor and tobacco were nevertheless essential gifts that enabled Indigenous travellers to celebrate their safe arrival at the post, even as it served to reaffirm good relations with company traders. As the HBC expanded its operations inland in response to the incursions of Montreal-based competitors, they had to fight fire with fire and, accordingly, credit and alcohol flowed more freely.

Even in areas that were comparatively sheltered from competition, such as the eastern James Bay region studied by Toby Morantz, the "debt system" remained a fixture for two hundred years, notwithstanding occasional attempts by HBC executives to curtail or abolish it.[91] Morantz notes that traders actively perpetuated debt by refusing to allow hunters who had a particularly good year to carry credit for surplus furs over to the following year; at the same time, heavily indebted hunters would be encouraged with premiums and partial write-offs. Even if a post suffered some losses through bad debts, the consistent objective was to keep people attached to the trading post and to divert their efforts towards the commercial fur hunt (as well as occasional labour to supply and maintain the post). Morantz argues that the James Bay Cree were never really in thrall to the company, but it does seem clear that the latter's credit practices were manipulative in their intent. And they were consequential: the author points out that when the HBC abruptly terminated credits for a few years in the 1930s, "many Cree starved to death."[92]

When the HBC began going head-to-head with the North West Company, first along the Saskatchewan River in the late 1770s and then in the Athabasca region in the 1790s, it had to set aside its cautious approach to alcohol and debt. An early venturer into the interior, Philip Turnor, commented in 1778, "The Honourable Hudson's Bay Company may think it imprudent to give the Indians Liquor but without it, it is impossible to get them to doe any thing."[93] We have not been able to locate aggregate statistics on alcohol imports through Hudson Bay for this competitive period, but inland post journals make it apparent that Indigenous visits were much more frequent than at the tidewater forts, that rum was now the beverage of choice, and that it was routinely distributed to visitors coming to take credit, to pay debts, and to trade. As for credit, a clerk at Cumberland House spelled out the need for profusion in a climate of intense competition, explaining that he had, "fitted the Indians out with a part of every article of trading goods in the Company's warehouse as presents and as much debt as they would take ... such is the pass at present ... the Canadians [NWC] is the Cause of it."[94] In 1820, at the height of the conflict between the rival companies, the factor in charge of Fort Wedderburn reported total "Indian debts" of 7,070.5 skins, worth £950, though these were listed in the accounts at half that value because collection was uncertain.[95]

Competition ended with the merger of 1821, through which the HBC effectively absorbed the North West Company. With its monopoly re-established, the company launched a campaign of reform and retrenchment aimed at cutting costs and rationalizing operations. In this connection, a top priority for Governor George Simpson was to reduce the use of alcohol and to eliminate the "debt system" entirely; "credits," he insisted, "tend to make the Indians dishonest and indolent."[96] To post commanders around the Northern District, Simpson suggested various measures to liquidate existing debts, by employing Indigenous debtors as transport workers or by writing down some debts.[97] However, he was unable to replace the "debt system" with what he called the "ready barter system" due to resistance from both Indigenous hunters and company traders on the ground.[98] John Stuart expressed a widespread objection: "There is not one much conversant with Indians who dos not Know that the Indian Trade never was and never can be carried on to advantage where no Debts are given. They are naturally improvident, and it is only the supplies given in the fall on debt that enables them to hunt in Winter."[99] Talk of Indigenous "improvidence" conveniently diverted attention both from the way the trade had been structured from the beginning to ensure that hunters became indebted and from the determination of company agents like Stuart to preserve the coercive powers that the debt system afforded them.

Alexander Stewart, in charge of HBC operations at Fort Chipewyan explained to Simpson why alcohol was as important to the trade as credit. He reported that Indigenous orators had subjected him to long, eloquent speeches complaining of the company's newly instituted measures, "but most particularly now the depriving them of Rum, which to abandon entirely they think impossible and rather than submit they would have no traders ... they will retire to their Lands where they can be very independent, a sufficiency to make them *enjoy the presence of each other when assembled here* Spring and Fall would be all they would want."[100] This passage is of special interest for the light it seems to shed on fur trade drinking patterns. Stewart makes it clear that the Dene people he dealt with drank not because of individual addiction (through most of the year, they would not have touched a drop) and not simply to nurture their alliance with the HBC men but rather as a bonding experience among themselves. Hunting peoples of the northern boreal forests lived most of the year in small, scattered bands; getting together in larger numbers would have made for a potentially exciting but perhaps also a slightly awkward occasion. Getting intoxicated together helped transform these occasional gatherings into significant social, and perhaps even spiritual, events.

CONCLUSION

For us as much as for Harold Innis, the spatial extent of the fur trade still seems quite amazing. Beginning at the Atlantic shores of the Maritimes in the sixteenth century, it penetrated further and further inland until, by the end of the eighteenth century, it had reached as far as the Arctic and the Pacific. As of about 1820, at a time when colonial settlements occupied only a small fraction of the northern half of the continent, the trade had pervaded almost every corner of the land, such that few Indigenous people were untouched by its effects. Most of this vast territory was free of any significant imperial sovereignty, government, or jurisdiction. It remained an Indigenous-controlled country, unconquered by any invading armies. And yet capitalism was everywhere, doing its best to impose its rules and extract its tribute. The Canadian fur trade should be seen as one instance among many around the world where global capitalism extended its reach well beyond the formal conquests of European imperialism.[101]

Of course, the hunting peoples who participated in the fur trade were not passive victims, as research in the field has amply demonstrated. Euro-Canadian traders were commonly sought out as allies and as suppliers of highly valued products as well as weapons that might otherwise flow to enemies and potential enemies. Indigenous peoples drew traders into their respective worlds, helping to orient them to the land, sometimes providing them with intimate partners and assuring their very survival. Those traders had no choice but to adapt to the customs in which their hosts wrapped material exchanges, while doing their best to supply goods that met the latters' exacting specifications. Adaptation was mutual and out of these encounters came the hybrid ways of western fur trade society. All this notwithstanding, we miss something essential about the nature of the fur trade when we focus exclusively on styles and customs and lose sight of its capitalist underpinnings. No matter how deeply they inserted themselves into the Indigenous milieu, traders were still tethered to European centres by a very long leash of monetized debt; moreover, their economic survival required that they find ways to attach Indigenous hunters to that same restraining cord. Customs of reciprocity helped to ensure fur returns but only to a degree, for a non-capitalist ethic of obligation is not the same as a regime of impersonal and precisely enumerated debt.

Making their way in Indigenous space, traders needed to cultivate good relations even as they followed mathematical accounting practices that often seemed alien, and even frankly offensive, to their hosts. The latters' very different approach to obligations was a source of perpetual frustration, which is why expressions of anger and contempt come up again and again in the journals and correspondence of the fur trade. These same sources provide plentiful indications that the bad feelings were mutual. Attempting to force Indigenous debtors into compliance with their definition of what hunters owed in the absence of formal legal institutions and consistently discontented with the performance of Indigenous debtors, traders had frequent recourse to alcohol and violence. Coercive and manipulative tactics had to be adjusted to shifting circumstances and power balances and they were never fully effective, but as our survey of two and a half centuries of fur trade history has shown, these measures were pervasive and recurrent devices used to enforce European conceptions of debt and credit. Their prevalence over the long run challenges engrained narratives that present fur trade exchanges as harmonious and mutually beneficial. We argue instead that violence and manipulation formed a basic feature of an intercultural exchange founded on debt.

ACKNOWLEDGMENTS
The authors are truly grateful to Catherine Desbarats, Toby Morantz, and Carolyn Podruchny for their comments and suggestions on an early version of this chapter. Thanks also to Manuel Covo and Bruce White for help with sources.

NOTES

1 See works associated with the new history of capitalism, such as, Kocka, *Capitalism*; Beckert, *Empire of Cotton*; Edwards, Hill and Neves-Sarrie, "Capitalism in Global History."

2 Innis, *Fur Trade in Canada*; Creighton, *Empire of the St Lawrence*; Rich, *The Fur Trade and the Northwest to 1857*.

3 See, for example, Ray, *Indians in the Fur Trade*, 137–65; Bishop, *The Northern Ojibwa and the Fur Trade*.

4 See, for example, Podruchny, *Making the Voyageur World*; Peers and Podruchny, *Gathering Places*; Havard, *Histoire des coureurs de bois*.

5 For example, Brown, *Strangers in Blood*; Devine, *The People Who Own Themselves*.

6 For example, Van Kirk, *Many Tender Ties*; Sleeper-Smith, *Indian Women and French Men*.

7 Ray and Freeman, *Give Us Good Measure*; Carlos and Lewis, *Commerce by a Frozen Sea*.

8 Ibid., 167–83.

9 Morantz, "'Gift-Offerings to their Own Importance and Superiority,'" 136. Morantz expanded on this topic in a later article: "'So Evil a Practice." See also, Francis and Morantz, *Partners in Furs*, 51–3; Giroux, "Dette et colonisation."

10 Other works that have commented perceptively on debt relations include, Krech, "The Trade of the Slavey and Dogrib"; Yerbury, *The Subarctic Indians*; Whelan, "Dakota Indian Economics," 256; White, "The Trade Assortment"; McCormack, *Fort Chipewyan and the Shaping of Canadian History*," 36–8; Colpitts, *North America's Indian Trade*; Brophy, "Reciprocity as Dispossession"; Brophy, *A Legacy of Exploitation*.

11 In addition to Burke and Gates St-Pierre, "After Beringia," in this volume, see Wright, "Before European Contact," 21–38; Earle, "Migration"; Curtis and Desrosiers, *Ramah Chert*.

12 Mauss, *The Gift*; Gregory, *Gifts and Commodities*; Sahlins, *Stone Age Economics*.

13 Graeber, *Debt*.

14 See, especially, Ray, "Indians as Consumers"; Ray, *Indians in the Fur Trade*; White, *Middle Ground*, 94–141.

15 Promislow, "'Thou Wilt Not Die of Hunger.'"

16 This claim requires qualification. The Hudson's Bay Company's charter conferred significant judicial powers and the company did use makeshift tribunals to discipline its own workers. However, there was no serious attempt before the establishment of the Red River Colony to exercise territorial jurisdiction or to subject Indigenous people to English private law. See Smandych and Linden, "Administering Justice without the State." We should note also that the Indigenous societies involved all had their own sense of the relative value of objects and their own practices for regulating disputes, even if coinage, account books, and formal tribunals removed from the rest of society were not part of their respective repertoires.

17 In this brief overview of almost four centuries of fur trade history, we will be preoccupied mainly with European traders' attempts to impose debt obligations, but we are keenly aware that their Indigenous counterparts were anything but helpless victims.

18 Graeber, *Debt*, 14.

19 Ferland, *Bacchus en Canada*, 229–30.

20 Dion, *Histoire de la vigne et du vin*, 425–48; Braudel, *Civilization and Capitalism*, 241–9; Cullen, *The Brandy Trade*.

21 Ambler, "Alcohol and the Slave Trade"; Green, *A Fistful of Shells*, 406–7. On the larger context, see Matthee, "Exotic Substances"; McCusker, "The Business of Distilling"; Bradburd and Jankowiak, "Drugs, Desire, and European Economic Expansion."

22 Innis, *Fur Trade*, 39; Dechêne, *Habitants and Merchants*, 74. A succession of different régimes governed the fur trade over the course of the history of New France, but there was always room for a multiplicity of colonial merchants to compete for Indigenous pelts. Note the contrast between the fragmented and competitive trade under the French régime and the quasi-monopolies enjoyed by the British Hudson's Bay Company and North West Company in their respective heydays.

23 Delâge and Gilbert, "Les Amérindiens face à la justice coloniale," 38–9. The authors cite (37) the revealing case of a man prosecuted for illegal trade who argued that as an Indigenous person of Chickasaw origin (and therefore probably an ex-slave) he was exempted from trade regulations. On criminal law, see Grabowski, "French Criminal Justice and Indians." On legal pluralism, see Benton and Ross, *Legal Pluralism and Empires*.

24 De Meulles ordinance, 5 March 1685, in Shortt, Smith and Lower, *Documents relatifs à la monnaie*, 66–7. (Reference provided by Catherine Desbarats.) Brian Gettler describes a continuing colonialist reluctance to allow northern Indigenous peoples to gain access to currency in modern times. Gettler, *Colonialism's Currency*.

25 The name refers to the salt tax that was assessed in some provinces of *ancien régime* France. The *gabelle* divided the kingdom into distinct economic zones with barriers interrupting road and river traffic along the boundaries. Colonists seem to have semi-facetiously applied the term to the point of division between French and Indigenous politico-economic spaces.

26 Bibliothèque et archives nationales du Québec [hereafter BANQ], TP1, S28, P1841, arrêt du conseil souverain, 26 April 1677 (our translation); "Nomination des sieurs Lemoine et Bauje pour retirer des sauvages," ibid., 26 April 1677. On a similar episode at Trois-Rivières in 1668, see Wien, "Le Pérou éphémère," 174. On the very extensive, small-scale commerce, conducted in and around Trois-Rivières in the 1660s and involving Indigenous people and settlers of all ranks, see Grabowski, "Le 'petit commerce.'"

27 BANQ, R1, P23, Ordonnance de Frontenac, 14 août 1674. Governor Frontenac was heavily invested in the fur trade on his own account and so the pious sentiments expressed in his edict can be seen as a cover for what was really an attempt to suppress competition. (See Robichaud, "Habitants, autorités et délits," 207–26.) Similar orders were issued a generation later, prohibiting any trade at the approaches to New France's cities, "même pour prêts fait aux sauvages." BANQ, E1, S1, P225, ordonnance de Jacques Raudot, 23 May 1707.

28 See Vachon de Belmont, *Histoire de l'eau-de-Vie*; Mancall, *Deadly Medicine*, 137–54; Ferland, *Bacchus en Canada*, 248–67.

29 A decade later, Governor Denonville reported that a band of Abenakis established at Chambly had fled the colony and moved to New England because of "les persecutions des creanciers" relating to "les grandes deptes causées par l'eau de vie." Archives nationales d'outre-mer [hereafter ANOM], Colonies, C11A, 10: 72-73v, Denonville au ministre, 10 August 1688 (our translation).

30 BANQ, TP1, S28, P100, Arrêt du conseil souverain, 21 April 1664. "Il fut fait défenses aux Français créanciers desdits Sauvages de les piller et excéder faute de payement d'autant que pendant ce temps de guerre il est impossible aux Sauvages de satisfaire entièrement ne pouvant faire leur chasse qu'à demi."

31 White, *Middle Ground*.

32 Havard, *Empire et métissages*, 380. Our translation.

33 Thwaites, *Jesuit Relations*, 54:195, See also, Havard, *Empire et métissages*, 380–1.

34 White, *Middle Ground*, 75–82; White, "The Fear of Pillaging."

35 Henday, *A Year Inland*, 186, 188. On brandy in the French trade to the Hudson Bay watershed, see also Matthew Cocking's account in Warkentin, *Canadian Exploration Literature*, 151–2; Peyser, *Jacques Legardeur de Saint-Pierre*, 155.

36 Dechêne, *Habitants and Merchants*, 82–3; Dale Miquelon, *New France, 1701–1744*, 151–3; Denys Delâge, "La traite des pelletries aux XVIIe et XVIIIe siècles," 383. These studies, based on merchant accounts, note that much of the liquor shipped to the western interior was destined to slake the thirst of soldiers garrisoning French forts in the region and the voyageurs who transported the goods, leaving only modest quantities for Indigenous fur suppliers.

37 "Mémoire sur les affaires du Canada, avril 1689," in "Lettres et mémoires de François-Madeleine-Fortuné Ruette d'Auteuil, procureur général du conseil souverain de la Nouvelle-France," in *Rapport de l'archiviste*, 1922–3, 7.

38 *New Hampshire Gazette*, 29 August 1760; Greer, *Peasant, Lord, and Merchant*, 158.

39 Charles Grant estimated the contents of the average canoe headed inland in 1780 at 300 pounds of dry goods and 200 gallons of rum and "wine." Wallace, *Documents Relating to the North West Company*, 64–5.

40 Gates, *Five Fur Traders*, 38–42 (quotation pg. 42).

41 Masson, *Les Bourgeois de la Compagnie du Nord-Ouest*, 1:7–8.

42 Quoted in Innis, *Fur Trade*, 174, 175. On British policy surrounding the fur trade in the 1760s, see Colpitts, *North America's Indian Trade*, 226–7.

43 "Report of the Merchants of Montreal by their committee to the Honorable Committee of Council on Commercial Affairs and Police," [undated but context suggests 1786] *Michigan Historical Collections* 11 (1887): 473.

44 During the North West Company's operation between 1779 and 1821, nine different corporate agreements were signed to perpetuate the company's operations. McQuarrie, "Running the Rivers," 29–30.

45 Pannekoek, *The Fur Trade and Western Canadian Society*, 8.

46 Selkirk, *A Sketch of the British Fur Trade*, 44–5. For a rejoinder, in which NWC spokesmen claim that annual shipments of liquor had been reduced from 50,000 to 10,000 gallons, see Wilcocke, Ellice, and McGillivray, *A Narrative of Occurrences*, ix. An earlier estimate by William McGillivray cited figures ranging from 9,600 to 16,299 gallons annually around the turn of the nineteenth

century. Library and Archives Canada [hereafter LAC], "Sketch of the Fur Trade, 1809: some account of the trade of the North West Company," MG19-B4, vol. 1:7.

47 Henry, *Journal of Alexander Henry the Younger*. For perceptive analyses of the fur trade that draw on this document, see White, "A Skilled Game of Exchange"; Peers, *The Ojibwa of Western Canada*.

48 Peers, *The Ojibwa of Western Canada*, 27–61.

49 Henry, *Journal of Alexander Henry the Younger*, 1:29. See also, ibid., 1:3–4, 27, 41, 53, 69, 83, 128, 136, 156, 167, 177, 178, 2:350, 404, 406, 407, 418, 420, 424, 427, 437, 441, 468; Cameron, "A Sketch of the Nipigon Country with extracts from His Journal, 1804," McGill University Libraries Rare Books and Special Collections [hereafter ROAAr], Masson Collection, MSG 472-1, no. 25, pg. 48.

50 Henry, *Journal of Alexander Henry the Younger*, 1:53.

51 Ommer, *Merchant Credit and Labour Strategies*; Cadigan, *Hope and Deception*, 100–20.

52 Henry, *Journal of Alexander Henry the Younger*, 1:128–9, 136.

53 Ibid., 117.

54 Ibid., 139. See also, 121, 126–7, 136, 138, 140, 142, 158.

55 Ibid., 125. See also, 140, 142; Cormier, *Jean-Baptiste Perrault*, 48–50; Nelson, *My First Years in the Fur Trade*, 43.

56 Henry, *Journal of Alexander Henry the Younger*, 1:159. See also, 137, 140.

57 Ibid., 165, 352. On women's suicide as vengeance, see Peers, *The Ojibwa of Western Canada*, 57.

58 Hudson's Bay Company Archives [hereafter, HBCA], "North West Company English River District Journal and Account Book, 1785–1787," F.2/1, fol. 15-57. See also, Podruchny, "Unfair Masters and Rascally Servants?," 64–5; Podruchny, *Making the Voyageur World*, 44–7. Note that not all the North West Company's workforce was fleeced in this way. Whereas voyageurs on extended service typically lost their salaries to debt and liquor, short-haul canoe men ("pork-eaters") working the route from Montreal to the upper lakes often earned enough to finance the purchase of land. Humphries, "Working the Short-Haul Fur Trade."

59 Sloan, "The Native Response to the Extension of the European Traders"; Krech, "The Trade of the Slavey and Dogrib"; Yerbury, *Subarctic Indians*; Abel, *Drum Songs*, 17–42, 65–87.

60 On the smallpox epidemic in the subarctic, see Sloan, "The Native Response,"

282–3; Abel, *Drum Songs*, 71–5; Binnema, *Common and Contested Ground*, 119–28; Fenn, *Pox Americana*, 167–95; Daschuck, *Clearing the Plains*, 38–43.

61 Yerbury, *Subarctic Indians*, 55; Abel, *Drum Songs*, 56–64, 68–70, 76–7; Ray, *Life by the Frozen Sea*, 48–9. Wherever possible we have attempted to use the names that contemporary descendants of these historic communities use, rather than terminology that European traders used to describe these groups. It is important to note that most Dene peoples arriving at fur trade posts did not consider themselves part of the broad cultural groups European traders identified, but rather these terms gained prominence as European and Indigenous outsiders attempted to identify and categorize Dene communities. In the case of the historic communities that European writers referred to as the Slavey, we have included three different names that contemporary communities use to identify their respective Dene cultural groups.

62 On Denesuline migration in response to NWC arrival in the Athabasca region, see McCormack, *Fort Chipewyan*, 18–20; Smith, "Chipewyan," 273–4.

63 Smith, "Chipewyan," 272–6; Abel, *Drum Songs*, 24–39, 78; Sloan, "The Native Response," 282–4.

64 Abel, *Drum Songs*, 78; Smith, "Chipewyan," 280.

65 Jérémie, *Twenty Years of York Factory*, 42.

66 Ibid.

67 LAC, Selkirk fonds, MG19-E1, vol. 31:9316–17.

68 Keith, *North of Athabasca*, 27–31; Pendergast, "The XY Company," 29–69; Innis, *Fur Trade*, 198–203, 256–61.

69 Keith, *North of Athabasca*, 30; Allen, "Fidler, Peter."

70 HBCA, "Fort Chipewyan Journal, 1802-1803," B.39/A/1, fol. 9. For additional HBC references to NWC violence and intimidation in the Athabasca region, see: HBCA, B.39/A/1, fol. 2; HBCA, "Fort Chipewyan Journal, 1803-1804," B.39/A/3, fol. 5, 6; HBCA, "Fort Chipewyan Journal, 1804-1805," B.39/A/4, fol. 11; HBCA, "Fort Chipewyan – Post Journal, 1805-1806," B.39/A/5a, fol. 2-3, 17-18.

71 Rich, *Journal of Occurrences*, 356.

72 LAC, Selkirk fonds, vol. 31:9375.

73 LAC, Selkirk fonds, vol. 31:9317–18.

74 James McKenzie, "Journal, 1799–1800," ROAAr, Masson Collection, MSG 472-1, no. 16; Alexander McKenzie, "Journal of Great Bear Lake 1805–1806," ibid., no. 6:8–10.

75 For two examples, see: LAC, Selkirk fonds, vol. 31:9258; ibid., 9272–3.

76 LAC, Selkirk fonds, vol. 31:9384–5.

77 Tyrrell, *Journals of Samuel Hearne and Philip Turnor*, 449.

78 James McKenzie, "Journal, 1799–1800," 36.

79 Ibid., 39.

80 Parker, *Emporium of the North*, 86–8.

81 For examples of Indigenous violence in the Athabasca Department, see: HBCA, "Fort Chipewyan Journal, 1804–1805," B.39/A/4, fol. 11; LAC, Masson Collection, MG19-C1, vol. 7: 31–7; ibid., vol. 6:69–70; McGillivray, *Journal of Duncan M'gillivray*, 13–17, 62–5; James McKenzie, "Journal, 1799–1800," 38–9; Keith, *North of Athabasca*, 20–1, 121 n92.

82 Rich, *Journal of Occurrences*, 394.

83 See, for example, the calculated mixture of threats, violence, and cajoling practiced by James McKenzie, in charge of Fort Chipewyan on Lake Athabasca. "This Indian certainly deserved to be reproved for his misbehaviour on his last Voyage in search of his relations but I thought it would be more in favour of the Companys [*sic*] Interest to try to please him. Any Insults or Menaces bestowed on these fellows this year they will perhaps have it next year in their power to retaliate." James McKenzie, "Journal, 1799–1800," 29–30.

84 Wagner, "Asleep by a Frozen Sea or a Financial Innovator?"; Phillips and Sharman, *Outsourcing Empire*, 69, 94–102.

85 Colpitts, "Accounting for Environmental Degradation"; Spraakman, *Management Accounting*.

86 Isham, *James Isham's Observations, 1743*, 49–50.

87 Ray, *Indians in the Fur Trade*, 137–8.

88 Ray and Freeman, *Give us Good Measure*, 128–43.

89 Figures from ibid., 132–4, table 17. Comparative figures for the North West Company cited above, fn 54.

90 Carlos and Lewis, *Commerce by a Frozen Sea*, 89–95.

91 Morantz, "So Evil a Practice." See also Ray and Freeman, *Give us Good Measure*, 54–9.

92 Ibid., 219.

93 Tyrrell, *Journals of Samuel Hearne and Philip Turnor*, 208. At Cumberland House in 1775, Indigenous people refused to trade when no alcohol was available. Ray, *Indians in the Fur Trade*, 142–3.

94 Quoted in Colpitts, "Accounting for Environmental Degradation," 29n45.

95 Rich, *Colin Robertson's Correspondence Book*, 114.

 96 Rich, *Journal of Occurrences*, 389.

 97 Fleming and Rich, *Minutes of Council, Northern Department*, 60.

 98 Bishop, *Northern Ojibwa and the Fur Trade*, 118–24; Hanks, "Swampy Cree,"
     107–9, 114; Ray, *The Canadian Fur Trade in the Industrial Age*, 84–5.

 99 Yerbury, *Subarctic Indians*, 118.

100 Fleming and Rich, *Minutes of Council*, 168 fn 2. Emphasis added. Cf., Davies,
     Northern Quebec and Labrador Journal, 214. On collective drinking as an
     important social bonding practice in cultures around the world, see Dietler,
     "Alcohol: Anthropological/Archaeological Perspectives."

101 For other such instances, see Beckert, *Empire of Cotton*; Green, *A Fistful of
     Shells*.

10

Maple, Beaver, and New Roots for a Global Early Canada

CHRISTOPHER M. PARSONS

Canadians live in a spectacularly beautiful country, and they are proud of it. Recent conversations surrounding the 150th anniversary of Confederation revealed the extent to which Canadians root their national identity in an almost metaphysical relationship with the nation's unique geography and natural spaces. The Canadian government announced that "discovering Canada's natural beauty and strengthening environmental awareness" would be a major facet of the year's celebrations.[1] In a poll commissioned by Global News that same year, 39 per cent of Canadians said that "the country's nature and landscape is the best thing about Canada."[2] Looking in from abroad at the state of national identity during the sesquicentennial, the BBC reported that "Canadians are immensely proud of what has been carved out of wilderness and a harsh climate, but they wear their identity lightly."[3] However, they're often led to believe that this nature is something pristine and eternal.

Over the course of the twentieth century, artists, authors, and cultural critics working in a variety of media sought the roots of a uniquely Canadian identity in a uniquely impressive Canadian nature. Whether evoked in the popular histories of the Canadian frontier, the experience of the Calgary Stampede, or artistic work such as that of the Group of Seven, the founding myth of Canada locates itself in close contact and frequent conflict with an unpeopled wilderness that, far from being entirely conquered, remains an important touchstone for Canadian identity to this day. To travel to national parks, to canoe through the Canadian Shield, or to experience the strangeness of the

northern lights is therefore presented as a sort of time travel and an opportunity to experience the agency of these spaces for ourselves as though they
exist outside of time and history.

Even as we recognize the extent to which this is the enduring trick of a settler colonial nation that rhetorically erases millennia of Indigenous histories
and makes possible the continued dispossession of aboriginal peoples, these
mythologies persist, troubling programs to expand access and encourage new
visitors to natural spaces in Canada. Even more troubling is the extent to
which these myths have been embraced and amplified by a newly resurgent
white supremacism. As now defunct white nationalist group Northern Dawn
explained, "[Nature] is an inextricable part of our identity; a strange but not
unjustified remnant from the early days of this country, when the pioneer
spirit still held strong. It harkens back to the predominantly European settlers
who were left to their own devices to tame the vast wilderness that was the
least hospitable part of the Americas."[4] Even Alberta separatists staunchly in
favour of industrial oil extraction proudly claim to be "a people who forged
a strong connection to the land in order to survive," adding later that "[w]e
inherently care about the land we occupy because it is who we are."[5]

Both environmental historians and policy makers have sought, in recent
decades, to make Canada's natural heritage more accessible and inclusive.
Historians, for example, have successfully shown how the creation of the nation's national parks was often predicated upon the forced removal of Indigenous people and the continued exclusion of socially and economically
marginalized communities.[6] As Meg Stanley and Tina Loo have recently written about Banff National Park, the invisibility of non-white visitors, "particularly after the 1940s, may mean that people of colour stopped trying to get
into hot water at Banff, at least in ways that left an archival trace."[7] Parks managers at both the provincial and national levels, on the other hand, have
sought to attract immigrants and new citizens through programs such as Alberta's Nature as a Second Language Program and the national collaboration
with Mountain Equipment Co-op named Learn to Camp. In Alberta, for example, courses that led recently arrived refugees and immigrants on guided
two-night camping experiences in conjunction with a local charitable organization aimed to help attendees form community and bonds in their new
homes and increase future visits to the park system.[8] Where their predecessors
might have sought to create an exclusive playground, twenty-first century

parks managers recognized a need "to connect more tangibly with the country's diverse constituencies."[9]

This chapter suggests that we revisit early histories of environmental encounter as part of this broader effort to make Canadian nature more inclusive.[10] Revisiting narratives that pitted hardy explorers and pioneers against impersonal and immobile environments, we might instead highlight those elements of these places that early colonists themselves frequently noted: plants and animals that, by nature of their mobility, connect the story of Canadian places to broader global movement and migration. In the first section of this chapter, I will analyze how and why the image of an essentially fixed environment first took root. Buffeted by and between imperial and hemispheric identities throughout the twentieth century, academics, authors, and artists frequently sought out an unmoving nature in which to moor an ever-threatened Canadian identity. The result was popular and academic works that oriented their audiences towards the physical geography of these places: soil, stone, and river systems. After that, the chapter turns to two quintessentially Canadian features of the country's environment history, the beaver and the sugar maple, to see what the story of these supposedly "national" organisms reveals about deep global connections.

The Europeans who settled in New France followed patterns of movement across the northern hemisphere that were carved out by millions of years of geological, climatological, and evolutionary history; first the French followed the cod, and then they settled among maples before continuing west to chase beavers. Looked at from a wider perspective, the French and other Europeans who traversed the Atlantic belonged to one species among the many who circulated in a global northern hemisphere. Recognizing this intercontinental mobility allows us to better understand how the flora and fauna of early Canada facilitated contact and conversation and reflected the ancient origins of Canada's links with Europe and Asia.

Throughout the twentieth century, the present and future of what it meant to be Canadian frequently remained an open question. Buffeted by both domestic and international events, artists, scholars, and authors looked to Canadian nature for a fixity that Canadian identity seemed to lack. This produced a richly developed vocabulary and visual culture that rooted an at times nascent, threatened, and resurgent nationalism in Euro-American encounters into an idealized wilderness. When the nation itself seemed in flux as rela-

tionships with Britain and America waxed and waned, novels, academic studies, and artistic work focused popular attention on those most stable elements
of Canadian nature: geological structures, forests, and hydrological networks.
The genres and forms through which these questions were pursued were rich
and varied; as Claire Campbell has recently written, "Wilderness is a form of
imaginative rhizome that sprouts in different forms – in politics, culture, identity, and other forums of Canadian public life."[11] In this section, we trace the
evolution of these representations and investigate how a focus on fixed environments both discursively dispossessed Indigenous peoples and overlooked
global connections. The result was that natural spaces became predominantly
white spaces, marginalizing alternative stories and limiting access to other
types of Canadians.[12]

In his justly famous *Fur Trade in Canada*, Harold Innis narrated the unfolding of Canadian history as the "effects of a vast new land on European
civilization."[13] This focus meant that he brought serious attention to even
the beaver, about which he wrote, "The history of Canada has been profoundly influenced by the habits of an animal which very fittingly occupies
a prominent place on her coat of arms." He continued in this materialist vein
when he argued that "It is impossible to understand the characteristic developments ... of Canadian history without some knowledge of its life and
habits."[14] This is a startling statement that would not be out of place in a recent issue of the journal *Environmental History*. As much as he seems to direct our attention to *Castor canadensis*, however, it is on the animal's habitat
that Innis primarily focuses, and it was the Saint Lawrence River and the
waterways of the Canadian Shield and Great Lakes watershed that provided
so much of their inspiration. Innis' work was profoundly continental and
investigated how human societies lived with and adapted to the ecological
adaptation of beaver to very specific physical environments. While his *Fur
Trade* told a story of the continent's hydrology, his *Cod Fisheries* told that of
the "submerged areas" of the continental shelf.[15] While both Indigenous and
colonial peoples moved across the continent as they organized a staples trade
out of fish and fur, the paths they took and the societies that they grew
mapped onto far deeper geological histories.

If we can see the willfully Eurocentric exaggeration in the artist Arthur Lismer's claim that Canada was "unwritten, unpainted, [and] unsung" before
the nationalism of the 1910s and 1920s, the work of the Group of Seven and

similarly inspired artists and authors from coast to coast made bold claims to a deep relationship between Anglo-Canadian identity and the nation's landscape.[16] Although this was a particularly Anglo-Canadian (and Ontarian) project, French Canadian artists also looked to Quebec's landscapes to foster a national mythology.[17] Anglo-Canadian artists actively sought out unpeopled landscapes to celebrate direct experience of an untrammeled natural world and went so far as to effectively erase the presence of Indigenous peoples and histories to further their goal.[18] Québécois artists similarly focused on the rural landscapes of their province, foregrounding the deep roots of settlement along the Saint Lawrence.[19] Whether in Marc-Aurèle Fortin's lushly painted rural landscapes or Lismer's evocative representations of the Canadian Shield, geology and hydrology stood omnipresent in the nation(s)'s past and present.

Scholars of Canadian history actively contributed to a nineteenth-century project that looked to geography and geology to support "the idea of a transcontinental nation."[20] Collectively, these authors looked to what they considered the earliest periods of Canadian history (by which they invariably meant the arrival of European explorers and settlers) for the clearest evocation of the natural world's influence on the arc of Canadian history. A few years before Innis argued in his *Fur Trade* that Canadian history had "emerged not in spite of geography but because of it," Marion Newbigin's *Canada, the Great River, the Lands, and the Men* (1926) similarly highlighted the importance of geography and, in particular, the centrality of the Saint Lawrence in the nation's history. She wrote that she sought her answer to the question of "[h]ow it is that Canada to-day is an entity distinct from the United States" solely in the "French period," explaining that it was in these early years that a unique culture had emerged along the St Lawrence in the "Indian-haunted wilderness."[21]

This scholarship celebrated a stadial narrative that, even as it foregrounded the environment, actively effaced the presence of Indigenous peoples. Innis's *Fur Trade* explained, for example, that "Fundamentally the civilization of North America is the civilization of Europe."[22] Andrew Hill Clark's geographies of Maritime Canada – while less explicitly racist – consigned aboriginal peoples to silence as his studies effectively recapitulated a familiar narrative of colonial resettlement and displacement.[23] In this, they followed the historian W.F. Ganong, himself a botanist and geographer as well as a historian, who had written early in the twentieth century that the history of New

Brunswick (I suspect he would have felt the same about Canada more generally) could be neatly retold as a transition between "the roving Indian, the
hurrying explorer seeking a passage to the west, the picturesque French fur
trader, the colonizing Englishman, the independent New Englander, the exiled
Loyalist, and the sturdy immigrant from Europe."[24] The story of Canada then
was one of conflict and eventual victory over a natural world that, even as it
left its imprint, was consigned, like aboriginal cultures, to a romantic and
mythologized past.

Donald Creighton drew inspiration from this approach as he articulated
what came to be known as the Laurentian School, an interpretation in which
the natural geography and, particularly, the hydrology of the Saint Lawrence
region exerted a powerful influence on Canada's culture, economy, and politics.[25] In Creighton's telling, the imperial conflicts of the seventeenth and
eighteenth centuries were, in fact, a duel of rivers. As he explained in *A History
of Canada, Dominion of the North*,

> Champlain did not create the rivalry between those who lived in the val-
> leys of the St. Lawrence and the Ottawa and those who lived in the valley
> of the Hudson. It arose long before he arrived in North America and it
> has lasted centuries after his death. It grew naturally and inevitably out
> of the rival ambitions which these two great regions inspired in the
> minds of those who lived in them. It had its roots in the very divisions
> of the geography of North America itself.[26]

In his *Commercial Empire of the St. Lawrence*, Creighton explained more suc-
cinctly that, in Canada, "geography directed the activities of men with a blunt
sternness."

In each case, early Canadian histories celebrated the unique geography of
northern North America as a constitutive element in the nation's making. In
the alchemy of a national myth, northern environments transmuted European
history into Canadian. Nature's agency was a localizing force and Creighton,
A.R.M Lower, W.L. Morton, Innis, and others flirted regularly with environmental determinism.[27] Creighton, for example, suggested that the influence
of the environment on early Canada was "an invitation which was at least half
a command."[28] This was therefore a force that awaited European arrival, taking
explorers and settlers alike into the sinews of the nation's waterways and

moulding them into Canadians. By their very form, these epic stories had little room for Indigenous histories or knowledge. Indeed, there was little room left for the latter in narratives that unfolded as an encounter between Europeans and the North American wilds.

At Canada's centenary, even as Canada sought to position itself as a modern nation, it looked to these colonial and pre-Confederation encounters with a formidable natural world to explain its unique character.[29] In the same decade that a maple leaf was chosen to grace a new flag, Northrop Frye's investigation of Canadian literary history nonetheless located a "deep terror in regard to nature" at the root of Canadian writing.[30] Other authors such as Margaret Atwood and critics such as Margot Northey highlighted the supernatural presence of wilderness in many of the nation's foundational texts.[31] Atwood, in particular, continued to position the environment as a fundamentally localizing force that drew would-be settlers in, disrupting their connections to the outside world and who they might have been before they arrived. She imagines the nineteenth-century would-be settler Susanna Moodie, for example, leaving "cities rotting with cholera" only to find that:

My brain gropes nervous
tentacles in the night, sends out
fears hairy as bears,
demands lamps; or waiting

for my shadowy husband, hears
malice in the trees' whispers[32]

As she later added, "Canadian authors as a whole do not trust Nature, they are always expecting some dirty trick."[33]

The geographer Graeme Wynn has recently written that public conversations about the nature of Canadian identity at the centenary similarly inspired those historical geographers who, as the Laurentian School of Donald Creighton waned in importance among historians, became the leading voices in the study of New France and early Canada in English Canada. Cole Harris, Wynn wrote, felt that Canadian literary and intellectual traditions "had made geography a virtual protagonist in accounts of the country that emphasized the importance of the St Lawrence axis and built interpretations around natural endowments (fish, beavers, trees) that became staple resources driving economic and social development."[34] Historical geography, Harris felt, and the evidence of decades of scholarship has proven him right, was particularly well suited to focus attention on historical landscapes as an object of study.

For the study of what we could call early Canada, historical geographers continued to lead the field in the decades after the centenary. Harris, Wynn, Conrad Heidenreich, John Warkentin, Serge Courville, Louis-Edmond Hamelin, and many others working both in French and English came to the field with a sensibility that anticipated many of the innovations that environmental history would claim, but decades before the latter emerged as a field. As Harris explained in his and Warkentin's 1974 *Canada Before Confederation*, "Geographers seek to understand the actual settled land (the landscape, some geographers would say), the differing character of the earth's surface (regional variety), and the complex, interlacing relationships between man and land."[35] And yet, from our perspective, its focus is startlingly Eurocentric. In the same volume, Harris, for example, explained that he and his co-author were "concerned with the European rather than the Indigenous inhabitants of Canada, partly because of our incompetence to comment on the geography of Indian or Eskimo life, but also because, for better or worse, the developments in this period that transformed the geography of Canada were triggered by Europeans."[36] In this he seems to echo those scholars – Harold Innis and the geographer Andrew Hill Clark – who Harris identified as the two "geographical poles around which" the first volume of their atlas of Canadian history was "built."[37]

The chronology of these studies also emphasized national rather than global environmental histories. In focusing on landscape and the material world, the temporal scale considered by historical geographers frequently dwarfs their historian counterparts. Graeme Wynn's *Canada and Arctic North America: An Environmental History* and Serge Courville's *Le Québec: Genèses et mutations du territoire* both begin with the last ice age and the arrival of the ancestors of Canada's Indigenous peoples.[38] The narrative that ensues in such studies is thus the unfolding drama of a hybrid human and non-human landscape situated firmly within a continental frame. Logically, such an approach could serve to decentre Canada's history from such axes as Confederation, the conquest of Quebec, or the arrival of Jacques Cartier, but, in practice, these texts instead provide chapters on the early eras (often tellingly called "prehistory") to set the stage for the arrival of Europeans and the commencement of what is implicitly presented as "real" history. This does great disservice to the complexity and extraordinary duration of aboriginal history and experience, and, from a natural historical perspective, it continues the early-twentieth-century tendency to treat geography and nature as a static background against which colonialism happened.

In focusing so intently on geography and an abstract sense of a wilderness landscape, Canadians have overlooked opportunities to explore the global dimensions of our environmental history. Where geography (and, in particular, geology and hydrology) has been a primary determinant in narratives about how Europeans became Canadians, we can instead look to more mobile elements of our environments to tell more mobile histories. As an example of how this might be done, in this next section I will trace out the longer histories of those two most Canadian of species – the sugar maple and the beaver – to sketch out a more truly global history of early Canada.

Most of those European traders, settlers, and explorers who first came to what is now Canada in the sixteenth and seventeenth centuries did so along routes traced out by fish, flora, and fur-bearing animals that had traversed oceans and land bridges over millions of years. Part of a far larger "world hunt," French, English, Basque, and Portuguese travellers sought out new sources of animal-based commodities.[39] As Jeffrey Bolster explains of the European fishermen who came to the stretch of waters between Newfoundland and Cape Cod, "they encountered a familiar marine ecosystem that was 'new' only in the sense that it had not been systematically harvested for centuries by fishermen using sophisticated technologies to catch, preserve, and market sea fish."[40] As these same fishermen began to trade furs with the Indigenous peoples and move onshore to gain access to more and better furs, they similarly encountered terrestrial ecosystems composed of numerous species of flora and fauna with close relatives in Europe. New France was new, then, in that its founders promised that colonialism could renew and improve French and Indigenous cultures, but there was little about it that would have seemed unknown or unknowable.

To tell fuller stories of fish and fur-bearing animals, we need to move back in time to a period long before they became caught up in the trade in staples. To do so requires starting from a much earlier moment in world history, before North America had separated from Europe and Asia and before a single northern forest ecosystem had fractured and become differentiated because of tectonic movements.[41] In the case of maple and beaver, scientists continue to debate the precise geographical origins of these genera – by this I mean the broader groupings of maples and beaver rather than the individual species found in the Americas and Eurasia – but the emergence of these individual species can be localized both chronologically and geographically with a higher degree of certainty through archaeological and genetic analyses. In effect, as they crossed the Atlantic in the sixteenth and seventeenth centuries, the French who came to North America recreated distinctive biological linkages that had existed in the distant past before the Atlantic and Pacific oceans became insurmountable barriers for terrestrial species but, through island chains and land bridges, had been thoroughfares for the movement of plants and animals.

Maple and beaver were both global before they were North American. Land bridges connected North America to both Europe and Asia. In the west, the Bering Strait disappeared as water levels dropped, leaving a passage to traverse continents; to the east, volcanic activity created island chains that sped flora and fauna across the Atlantic. Of the two, the genus castor is significantly younger than that of maples. Beavers arrived in North America approximately 7.6 to 8 million years ago via the Beringian land bridge.[42] Maples, for their part, might have originated in North America, although recent genetic analyses suggest an Asian origin. The species we know in the northeast, however, likely emerged along with other recognizable species around the world by the end of the Eocene epoch, around 34 million years ago.[43] Maple likely arrived from a North Atlantic land bridge through which much of the forest complex of North America – pine, oak, and other similar trees, for example – travelled.[44] These species moved as part of a broader and broadly extensive northern hemisphere ecology, setting roots and – over the ensuing time as they became separated and localized – evolving to become new species in parts of North America, Asia, and Europe, though they remained largely absent from southern continents and tropical environments.[45] To be sure, glaciation and other major climatic shifts pushed and pulled these species across the continent, but they remained part of a relatively continuous northern hemisphere forest even as they began to evolve in distinctive directions.[46] When looked at from a sufficiently long temporal perspective, it is apparent that the Europeans who crossed the Atlantic in the Early Modern period followed in the ancient footsteps of these and other species.[47]

The plants and animal populations that met early French observers in Canada had, in a geological sense, only recently settled in the region. Continually changing climates and the waxing and waning of ice ages has been a primary driver of distribution and evolutionary histories of North American life.[48] Regular periods of global cooling that produce glaciation and glacial ages follow predictable "variations in the Earth's orbit."[49] Millions of years ago, these variations resolved into delineable hundred-thousand-year cycles, during which the earth might be covered in kilometre-thick ice, 60 to 90 per cent of the time.[50] Across millennia, ice ages began as sheets accreted slowly as winter snows failed to melt, gradually blanketing entire regions in snow and ice. Smaller oscillations (there were twenty-four "interstadials" during the last ice age) altered these patterns, producing local histories of freeze and thaw throughout North America.[51] Correspondingly, the climatic bands in which flora and fauna thrive have changed repeatedly, at times contracting or plunging south and, at others, expanding quickly as colonizing species grew rapidly in soils only recently thawed out.

Almost twenty-thousand years ago, during the most recent glacial maximum (the period during which the ice reached its greatest extent), much of what is now Canada was covered by the Laurentide and Cordilleran ice sheets that, together, stretched "unbroken from the Arctic islands to the latitudes south of the present Great Lakes, and from the eastern shores of Newfoundland to the Queen Charlotte Islands."[52] This was part of the broader Wisconsonian Glacial Episode that lasted nearly sixty thousand years and only really ended almost ten thousand years ago. During the glacial maximum, plants and animals that are now common in Canada and the northern United States thrived far to the south, even as they may have remained present relatively close to the ice sheets and their current range.[53] The contribution of geography and the resiliency of individual species produced complex histories of movement and adaptation unique to individual regions.[54] Some species, such as the sugar maple, remained protected in isolated pockets known to scholars of paleobotany and climate history as glacial refugia. The fingerprints of these refugia remain visible in the genetics of modern-day descendants of the sugar maple populations that burst north as climates recovered and ice sheets melted. Canada's maples today, for example, demonstrate a more distant relationship with relatives found in Central America that remained isolated behind mountain ranges and volcanic activity than those that had survived in what is now the United States.[55] On the other hand, other plants such as species of hickory, were likely widely distributed across the ice-free south in conifer-dominated forests.[56] Some animals, such as freshwater fish, were less able to move and more likely to succumb to rapidly changing climates.[57]

As the ices melted, temperate flora and fauna rapidly recolonized the open lands and flora and fauna that we now identify as Canadian formed part of a broader return to northern latitudes in the wake of deglaciation. Populations of temperate-climate trees, for example, could gain from one hundred to a thousand metres each year. Small plants that had taken root in the permafrost just south of the ice sheets pushed north first, but they were soon joined by broader biological communities as the ice receded. Methods of dispersal – wind or plant pollinated, for example – could have dramatic effects on the speed with which this process took place, and even relatively adaptable species such as beavers depended on the emergence, expansion, and connection of riverine networks and ecosystems in which they lived. Beavers follow in the wake of specific trees such as birch, spruce, poplar, and aspen and had pushed north during several millennia-long warming periods, altering landscapes and returning nutrients to regions as they created ponds and slowed rivers.[58] Other species suffered in the transition, however. The giant beaver *Castoroides*, whose fossils have been found from Florida to the Yukon, likely succumbed to warming climates that dried the swamps and shallow lakes in which it had thrived, becoming extinct around 10,000 years ago, before moist conditions once again returned.[59]

In addition to climate change, Indigenous populations powerfully shaped the landscape as they too resettled land that had only recent been buried under tonnes of ice. As active cultivators and breeders of plants, they brought food crops with them and slowly coaxed plants such as corn, beans, squash, and tobacco north to support agricultural communities. Recent research suggests, for example, that Indigenous communities intentionally cultivated nut and fruit-bearing trees and encouraged their spread before the arrival of Euro-peans.[60] The effects of these choices remain visible to this day.[61] Additionally, the ancestors of contemporary Indigenous peoples of North America cleared land and purposefully used fire to influence plant distribution and ecosystem composition.[62] Pressures from human hunting and climate change similarly influenced the population of animals.[63] These practices were regularly ob-served in early colonial records. Robert Morrissey, for example, has described how proto-Illinois communities set fire to prairie landscapes to aid in driving bison to large-scale hunts as climate change drove bison and human populations into close contact.[64]

These forces – orbital variations and climate change acting at the scale of millennia and Indigenous populations selectively supporting the spread of preferred plants and animals – together created the ecosystems that Europeans encountered when they first crossed the Atlantic. Far from simply an inert natural backdrop to the human history of colonization and conquest that was to unfold, the forests and landscapes of early Canada composed an archive of a rich environmental history.[65] And of course, they remain a dynamic force as flora and fauna push northward in response to human-induced climate change. Sugar maple, for example, will likely become even more Canadian as, in northern states near the Canada–US border such as Vermont, trees suffer in wetter and warmer climates.[66] Conservation scientists, on the other hand, are actively suggesting that beaver be reintroduced into their ancestral territories to combat the effects of climate change on threatened watersheds.[67] The history of these species remain, therefore, monuments to movement and adaptation even as they remain closely identified with national culture and identity.

Early modern observers were, it seems, more attuned to this movement than many in our own moment. If today the maple is one of the most recognized symbols of Canadian nationalism, for seventeenth- and eighteenth-century authors who recognized that maple grew in both French and North American forests, these trees instead provoked consideration about the nature of the relationship between the Old World and the New. Maple was among the most celebrated of botanical finds in the first decades of French colonialism. French authors who had close contact with Indigenous peoples recounted the pleasant taste and convenience of the maple tree's sap almost immediately upon arrival. Although the production of maple syrup and sugar by boiling down the sap does not appear in French texts until the latter part of the century, missionaries such as Gabriel Sagard and settlers such as Nicolas Denys regularly noted the production of a sweet drink that could also possess medicinal properties. Little ink was spilled describing the tree, but that is likely because most of these authors correctly identified the tree from which the sap was collected as a maple and, therefore, neither new nor particularly botanically interesting.

As French familiarity with the taste and pleasure of maple syrup and sugar increased, however, it furnished an opportunity to explore how it was that maple trees in Canada differed from those in France, where the sweet sap was nowhere to be found. The botanical study of Canadian maples in the eighteenth century highlighted the morphological characteristics that made them novel species. The work of Jean-François Gaultier, royal physician and corresponding member of the Académie royale des sciences, for example, focused on the unique shape and coloring of the tree's leaves to distinguish the several species of maple found in New France. Gaultier and his predecessor Michel Sarrazin took pains to send specimens of the plant and the seeds necessary to grow them in France. Once across the ocean, they were gathered together with other European species that were native to Europe and compared and classified.[68]

Understandably, most of the written accounts that testify to French experience with Canadian maples focused on the syrup and sugar that could be produced. The presence of the tree's sugary sap provoked considerable wonder and curiosity about what it was that made maples in Canada produce sugar whereas European species could not. Michel Sarrazin, royal physician, colonial official, and a talented naturalist, explained that it owed much to climate. A summary of his work sent to the Académie royale des sciences explained that:

> This sap, in order to be sweet, requires a singular circumstance that nobody would ever guess and that Mr. Sarrazin has acquired from experience: 1. At the time that one draws the sap, it is necessary that the foot of the tree be covered by snow. 2. This snow must be melted by the sun and not by a warm air. 3. It must freeze the night before. This type of manipulation, through which nature makes the maple sugar, closely resembles the delicate operations of chemistry.[69]

Several French sources attest to experiments either realized or planned that attempted to test this hypothesis in France.[70] Well before Buffon's famous theorization that American inferiority was attributable to climatic difference, the study of maple made clear that Canadian winters were a major reason for biological differences between Europe and North America.[71]

It seems equally likely that French interest in the tree affected indigenous use and processing of maple syrup. The question of whether maple syrup and sugar are indigenous inventions or French seems an archival dead end and irrelevant if our interest is in how environments facilitated communication rather than establishing precedence. Certainly, knowledge of the sweet sap was indigenous and seems to have belonged to all of the nations and cultures with whom the French interacted. Over the course of the seventeenth century, however, conflicting accounts of the processing of this sap into syrup and sugar attributed the invention to both French and aboriginal peoples.[72] Joseph-François Lafitau, for example, recounted the production of maple syrup and sugar by Haudenosaunee women in his 1724 *Moeurs des sauvages américains*, but his text incidentally highlighted the circulation of knowledge and the tools used to process the trees' sap. He related that "The French work them better than indigenous women [les sauvagesses], from whom they have learned how to make it," both making clear his cultural chauvinism and arguing that Indigenous peoples developed the process for turning sap to sugar before Europeans.[73] In an accompanying image, however, he also demonstrated that the introduction of French metal pots was now an important part of the process for Indigenous communities who harvested and processed the syrup. In this way, maple trees can show us how the global distribution of maple facilitated cultural dialogue, pointing us towards environmental histories that invited local and global exchange rather than determining conflict.

Like the maple, the American beaver has long been an emblem of Canadian identity and nationalism, gracing both officially designated symbols such as the nation's coat of arms and, unofficially, "Canadian" brands such as Roots and Molson.[74] We owe the most detailed study of *Castor canadensis* during the colonial era to Michel Sarrazin. His focus on the beaver and other fur-bearing mammals might not be surprising. Beaver, of course, continued to be crucial to the colonial economy into the eighteenth (I would say nineteenth) century. Yet French naturalists and administrators continually reminded correspondents such as Sarrazin that it was novel plants and animals that they sought. In 1726, for example, naval minister Jean-Fréderic Phélypeaux, comte de Maurepas advised the intendant Michel Bégon not to send specimens of "bears, beavers, or turkeys" and instead to focus on "exotic" specimens.[75] Yet, in 1704 and again in 1730, it was Sarrazin's work on, respectively, beavers and

American maples that members of the Académie read and discussed at their bimonthly meetings.

The Canadian beaver was studied closely on both sides of the Atlantic. In each instance, Sarrazin turned his considerable talents and minute focus to discerning the identity of American flora and fauna. Using the linguistic tools of scientific taxonomy and anatomical tools provided by his Parisian patron René-Antoine Ferchault de Réaumur, he lavished attention on what made each species unique and different from those in Europe.[76] Beavers were also transported across the Atlantic for study in Paris. In the seventeenth century, for example, the publication of the l'Académie royale des sciences described the dissection of a beaver that "was taken from Canada, in the environs of the Saint Lawrence River" at the royal library.[77] There is no indication to suggest that this animal had made the trip across the Atlantic alive, and many fish, animal, and bird specimens instead arrived stored in barrels of liquor.[78] By the end of the French regime in Canada, however, at least some had arrived alive. Georges-Louis Leclerc, Comte de Buffon described a beaver that had been brought young from Canada and raised indoors. The animal was, he wrote, "tranquil enough, familiar enough, a little sad, even a little plaintive, without violent passions, giving itself only to little movements, making few efforts for anything, nonetheless seriously occupied with a desire for liberty."[79]

French authors on both sides of the Atlantic seem to have recognized that these animals had, at one time, also been indigenous to Western Europe and they acknowledged their own lack of experience with the animals. Detailed descriptions of the animal in the work of Buffon or the contemporary *Encyclopédie* project are reminiscent of how scholars of Native American cultures used ancient European histories to fill in gaps in their ethnographic and historical knowledge about newly discovered peoples.[80] The authors of the entry on *castor* in the *Encyclopédie* used observational and anatomical data on the beaver gathered in New France, for example, to refute the ancient story that male beavers would self-castrate to escape hunters, leaving behind them the testicles thought to possess the *castoreum* valued for its smell and putative medicinal properties.[81] A 1746 treatise on the beaver cited, among others, ancient authors such as "Dioscorides, Sextius, [and] Pliny," as well as Renaissance and early modern studies by "Rondelet, Bauhin, [and] Gesner."[82]

The study of beavers thus blended aspects of history, biology, and comparative ethnography. In the absence of any personal knowledge of the animal's ecology or habits, Buffon drew heavily from the accounts of missionaries, travellers, and naturalists who had seen the animal first hand in North America, most often with Indigenous guides.[83] He cited the surgeon Dièreville, who made his reliance on the knowledge of Indigenous hunters plain in his account of his travels to Acadia.[84] As this surgeon and others conjectured, fantastical beaver societies (some promised a beaver republic, while others promised that king beavers rule in a natural monarchy), Louis-Armand de Lom d'Arce, Baron de Lahontan similarly supplemented his own experience with that of Indigenous peoples whose knowledge he validated and even prioritized.[85] He explained, "I will begin by assuring you that these animals together form a decent society, that they seem to speak to each other, and reason with one another through certain unarticulated plaintive tones. The *Sauvages* say that they have an intelligible jargon, by the means of which they communicate their sentiments and their thoughts."[86] Even Sarrazin, less prone to this line of study, firmly rooted his scholarship in Indigenous worlds. In his 1704 anatomical study of the animal, he located specific types of beaver with specific Indigenous nations. Those among the Illinois and the Shawnee, for example, could be the colour of straw.[87] Even as he proceeded to a detail anatomical description, he made clear his evident reliance on the ecological and zoological knowledge of native peoples.

This reliance on Canadian experience and knowledge continues to this day. Throughout the twentieth century, as the exact relationship between the American *Castor canadensis* and the European *Castor fiber* remained unclear until the availability of molecular tools of identification, Canadian beavers were introduced both purposefully and accidentally into European territories where today they pose an invasive threat to native and reintroduced populations of the European beaver.[88] At the same time, since *Castor fiber* had been successfully eradicated from many of the territories in which its population is growing today, ecological observations of its American counterpart are translated to explain its relationships with its one-time native range. In a recent article that attempted to chart the "Comeback of the Beaver *Castor fiber*," for example, the authors wrote about the self-regulation of beaver populations that, "nearly all knowledge regarding this aspect stems from studies of *C. canadensis* in boreal forest systems in North America."[89]

If Europeans and Euro-Americans once looked to Indigenous peoples for knowledge about beaver, maple trees, and the other elements of the once-global northern hemisphere ecology that spanned the Bering Strait and Atlantic land bridges, this deference has long since ceased. Instead, on both sides of the Atlantic, Europeans and Euro-Americans expressed increasing certainty that Indigenous peoples and their knowledge belonged to the past. In the nineteenth-century, Hudson's Bay Company officials deliberately extirpated the beaver from much of its western range and overhunting reduced the animal to islands of its formerly extensive habitat.[90] Forced removals and residential schooling aimed to uproot Indigenous relationships with their land, threatening traditions that brought entire families to harvest maple syrup in the same decades that the federal government and business cooperatives brought the industry more fully under settler control.[91] Even in France, the future of beavers looked grim. By the end of the nineteenth century, one observer wrote about the remnants of local beaver populations in the Rhone Valley, that "The destruction of these beavers is very regrettable, but necessary and the administration finds it necessary to encourage it."[92]

Tracing out the histories of how these two symbols of Canadian identity in the twentieth century facilitated exchange between Indigenous peoples and Europeans and encouraged a broader consideration of the nature of New France suggests the promise of a more global early Canadian history. This is a perspective that we miss if we limit our temporal frame or conflate hydrology and geology with the entire early Canadian environment. If we do not understand how the environments of what is now Canada are the products of millions of years of movement and circulation, we will invariably fail to appreciate that these were not static environments that met Europeans or that existed as a sort of stage upon which the colonial drama would unfold. We miss this if we start in 1500 or even 14,000 years ago – when the non-human world is presented as a fait accompli – as something that was to be confronted, overcome, transformed. Instead, we can appreciate the emergence of a triangulated relationship between native, newcomers, and the non-human world and write early Canadian histories that challenge a national mythology that depeoples the landscape and its history, preferring an open wilderness to a mosaic of peoples and places.

NOTES

1 "Canada 150," Government of Canada, accessed 1 November 2020, https://www.canada.ca/en/canadian-heritage/services/anniversaries-significance/2017/canada-150.html.

2 Dani-Elle Dubé, "The Best and Worst of Canada: What Canadians Think of Their Own country," Global News, accessed 1 November 2020, https://global news.ca/news/3565640/the-best-and-worst-of-canada-what-canadians-think-of-their-own-country/.

3 Gavin Hewitt, "Canada 150: What Does it Mean to be Canadian Today." BBC News, https://www.bbc.com/news/world-us-canada-40416696.

4 "Uncertain Future: The State of Canadian Arctic Sovereignty," Northern Dawn, https://web.archive.org/web/20180911024911/http://northern-dawn.ca/2018/07/14/uncertain-future-the-state-of-canadian-arctic-sovereignty/.

5 "The Buffalo Declaration," https://buffalodeclaration.com/the-buffalo-declaration, 20 February 2020.

6 For examples of this process, see Binnema and Niemi, "'Let the Line be Drawn Now'"; Kheraj, *Inventing Stanley Park*; Sandlos, "Federal Spaces, Local Conflicts."

7 Meg Stanley and Tina Loo, "Getting into Hot Water: Racism and Exclusion at Banff National Park," NICHE: Network in Canadian History & Environment. https://niche-canada.org/2020/08/26/getting-into-hot-water-racism-and-exclusion-at-banff-national-park/.

8 Hurly, "Sleeping Bags, S'mores," 52–5.

9 Dick, *A Century of Parks Canada*, 378.

10 I realize that some readers may find the phrase "Canadian nature" suggestive of a settler-national attempt to nationalize the natural environment. However, here and throughout this chapter, I use the terms "Canada" and "Canadian" as a convenient shorthand to refer to northern North America. The complex interplay between the post-Confederation nation-state and nationalist ideologies surrounding it, on the one hand, and the natural environment on the other, is the subject of this essay.

11 Campbell, "The Wealth of Wilderness," 169.

12 For a broader discussion of whiteness and nature in Canada, see Baldwin, Cameron, and Kobayashi, *Rethinking the Great White North*.

13 Innis, *Fur Trade in Canada*, 33.

14 Ibid., 3.

15 Innis, *Cod Fisheries*, 470.

16 New, *A History of Canadian Literature*, 138.

17 Pageot, "Paysages, dépaysements," 287–305.

18 Watson, "Race, Wilderness, Territory," 278.

19   Gagnon, Létourneau, and Baril, "La peinture des années trente au Québec."

20   Wynn, "Nature and Nation," 33.

21   Newbigin, *Canada, the Great River*, 6.

22   Innis, *Fur Trade*, 383.

23   About Prince Edward Island, for example, Clark wrote that "We may assume that the natural characteristics of the island were but little affected by the Indians." Clark, *Three Centuries and the Island*, 17.

24   Quoted in Wynn, "W.F. Ganong," 10.

25   On the Laurentian School, see Berger, *Writing of Canadian History*, chapters 9 and 10.

26   Creighton, *A History of Canada*, 40.

27   For discussions of the "Laurentian Thesis" as it relates to Canadian environmental history, see MacDowell, *An Environmental History*, introduction; Dagenais and Cruikshank, "Gateways, Inland Deas, or Boundary Waters?" 413–24.

28   Creighton, *Commercial Empire of the St. Lawrence*, 25.

29   See also, Coates and Wynn, "Introduction."

30   Frye, *The Stubborn Structure*, 289.

31   Hammill, "'Death by Nature,'" 47–63.

32   Atwood, *Journals of Susanna Moodie*, 13.

33   Atwood, *Survival*, 49.

34   Wynn, "'Tracing One Warm Line," 7.

35   Harris and Warkentin, *Canada before Confederation*, xix.

36   Ibid., xx.

37   Harris, *Historical Atlas of Canada*, vol. 1: iv. The atlas is, in fact, dedicated to Innis and Clark.

38   Wynn, *Canada and Arctic North America*; Courville, *Le Québec*.

39   Richards, *The Unending Frontier*, 9.

40   Bolster, *The Mortal Sea*, 13. Cf., Bouchard, "The Newfoundland Fisheries," in this volume.

41   For an overview of this history, see Brown and Lomolino, *Biogeography*.

42   Serrano, "Molecular Phylogeography of the American Beaver," 9.

43   Jianhua Li et al., "Maple Phylogeny."

44   Graham, "The Tertiary History."

45   Tiffney, "The Eocene North Atlantic Land Bridge"; Tiffney, "Geographic and Climatic," 6.

46   Milne and Abbott, "The Origin and Evolution."

47 See also, Parsons, "Wildness without Wilderness."

48 Pielou, *After the Ice Age*, 5.

49 Hewitt, "The Genetic Legacy," 907.

50 Wynn, *Canada and Arctic North America*, 5.

51 Hewitt, "Genetic Legacy," 907.

52 Wynn, *Canada and Arctic North America*, 1.

53 McLachlan, Clark, and Manos, "Molecular Indicators of Tree Migration."

54 Jaramillo-Correa et al., "Inferring the Past."

55 Vargas-Rodriguez et al., "Large Scale Patterns."

56 Bemmels and Dick, "Genomic "Evidence."

57 Jaramillo-Correa et al., "Inferring the Past," 288.

58 Serrano, "Molecular Phylogeography of the American Beaver," 133, 136; Boudreau et al., "A Paleolimnological Record," 456.

59 Plint et al., "Giant Beaver Palaeoecology," 8.

60 Abrams and Nowacki, "Native Americans as Active and Passive Promoters"; Hart and Lovis, "Reevaluating What We Know."

61 Warren, "Ghosts of Cultivation," e0150707.

62 Springer et al., "Multiproxy Evidence from Caves," 281.

63 Barnosky et al., "Assessing the Causes," 70–5.

64 Morrissey, "The Power of the Ecotone," 671–2.

65 This has long been said but remains worth repeating. See Cook, *1492 and All That* and Denevan, "The Pristine Myth."

66 Oswald et al., "The Complex Relationship," 304.

67 Dittbrenner et al., "Modeling Intrinsic Potential," e0192538.

68 See, for example, Duhamel du Monceau, *Traité des arbres*, 1755.

69 "Observations botaniques," *Histoire de l'Académie*, 1730:65–6. [hereafter HMARS]

70 Buc'hoz, *Dictionnaire universel*, 557–61.

71 See Gerbi, *The Dispute of the New World*.

72 The best summary of this debate is Campeau, "Les origines du sucre d'érable," 53–66.

73 Quoted in ibid., 57.

74 Carstairs, "'Roots' Nationalism."

75 Quoted in Young, "Crown Agent," 416–33.

76 On Sarrazin's relationship with his patrons, see Vallée, *Un biologiste canadien*.

77 "Description anatomique d'un castor," HMARS, 1666–69: 3, part 1:137.

78 Parsons and Murphy, "Ecosystems Under Sail," 528.

79 Buffon, *Histoire naturelle*, 8:144.

80 See Pagden, *The Fall of Natural Man*, passim.

81 "CASTOR," in Morrissey, ed., *Encyclopédie*

82 Marius and Francke, *Traité du castor*, 6.

83 Buffon, *Histoire naturelle*, 8:144.

84 Dièreville, *Relation du voyage*, 254–9.

85 For an overview of these studies of beaver society, see Gagnon, *Images du castor*, chapter 3.

86 Lom d'Arce de Lahontan, *Oeuvres completes*, 699.

87 "Extrait d'une lettre de M. Sarrazin touchant l'Anatomie du Castor, luë à l'Academie par M. Pitton Tournefort," HMARS 1704:48.

88 Rouland and Migot, "La reintroduction du castor," 145–58.

89 Nolet and Rosell, "Comeback of the Beaver," 167.

90 Ott, "'Ruining' the River in the Snake Country," 166–95. See also, Müller-Schwarze, *The Beaver*, chapter 17.

91 See Huron, "Historical Roots of Canadian Aboriginal."

92 Saint-Hilaire, "Renseignements sur les castors du Rhone," 322.

Bibliography

ARCHIVES CONSULTED

Archives départementales de Charente-Maritime, France.
Archives départmentales Cote d'Armor, France.
Archives départementales de Seine-Maritime, France.
Archives départementales de Pyrénées-Atlantiques, France.
Archivos Historicos de los Protocolos de Guipúzcoa, Oñati, Spain.
Bayerische Staatsbibliothek, Munich, Germany.
Bibliothèque et archives nationales du Québec, Canada. [BANQ]
Biblioteca Estense, Modena, Italy.
Bibliothèque nationale de France, Paris, France. [BNF]
John Carter Brown Library, Brown University, Rhode Island, US.
Library and Archives Canada, Ottawa, Canada. [LAC]
National Archives, London, UK.
Rare Books and Special Collections, McGill University Libraries, Montreal, Canada.

PUBLISHED WORKS

Abel, Kerry. *Drum Songs: Glimpses of Dene History*. Montreal and Kingston: McGill-Queen's University Press, 2014.
Abel, Timothy J., David M. Stothers, and Jason M. Koralewski. "The Williams

BIBLIOGRAPHY

Mortuary Complex: A Transitional Archaic Regional Interaction Center in Northwestern Ohio." In *Archaic Transitions in Ohio and Kentucky Prehistory*, edited by Olaf H. Prufer, Sara E. Pedde, and Richard S. Meindl, 290–327. Kent, OH: Kent State University Press, 2001.

Abel, Timothy J., Jessica L. Vavrasek, and John P. Hart. "Radiocarbon Dating the Iroquoian Occupation of Northern New York." *American Antiquity* 84, no. 4 (2019): 748–61.

Abrams Marc D., and Gregory J. Nowacki. "Native Americans as Active and Passive Promoters of Mast and Fruit Trees in the Eastern USA." *The Holocene* 18, no. 7 (2008): 1123–37.

Abreu-Ferreira, Darlene. "Terra Nova through the Iberian Looking Glass: The Portuguese-Newfoundland Cod Fishery in the Sixteenth Century." *Canadian Historical Review* 79, no. 1 (March 1998): 100–17.

Abulafia, David. *The Discovery of Mankind: Atlantic Encounters in the Age of Columbus.* New Haven, CT: Yale University Press, 2008.

Acheson, James M. "Anthropology of Fishing." *Annual Review of Anthropology* 10, no. 1 (1981): 275–316.

Achilli, Alessandro, Ugo A. Perego, Hovirag Lancioni, Anna Olivieri, Francesca Gandini, Baharak H. Kashani, Vincenza Battaglia, Viola Grugni, Norman Anger-hofer, Mary P. Rogers et al. "Reconciling Migration Models to the Americas with the Variation of North American Native Mitogenomes." *Proceedings of the National Academy of Sciences* 110, no. 35 (27 August, 2013): 14308–13.

Adams, Julia. *The Familial State: Ruling Families and Merchant Capitalism in Early Modern Europe.* Ithaca, NY: Cornell University Press, 2005.

Agote, Xabier, and Argazkiak Jose Lopez. "Gure Itsasontziak." *Bertan* 23. Donostia–San Sebastián: Diputación Foral de Gipuzkoa, 2009.

Alden, John Eliot, with Dennis Landis. *European Americana: A Chronological Guide to Works Printed in Europe Relating to the Americas, 1493–1776*, 6 vols. New York: Readex Books, 1980.

Alfonse, Jean. *Les voyages auantureux dv capitaine Ian Alfonce, Sainctongeois auec priuilege du roy.* Poitou: Mellin de Saint-Gelais, 1559.

Allaire, Bernard. "Le commerce des fourrures à Paris et les pelleteries d'origine canadienne en France (1500–1632)." PhD diss., University de Laval, 1995.

– *Pelleteries, manchons et chapeaux de castor: les fourrures nord-américaines à Paris 1500–1632.* Septentrion: Québec, 1999.

– *La rumeur dorée: Roberval et l'Amérique.* Montreal: Les Éditions de la Presse, 2013.

Allaire, Bernard, and Donald Hogarth. "Martin Frobisher, the Spaniards, and a Sixteenth-Century Northern Spy." *Terrae Incognitae* 28 (1996): 46–57.

Allaire, Gratien, and Richard Jones. "Officiers et marchands: les sociétés de commerce des fourrures, 1715–1760." *Revue d'histoire de l'Amérique française* 40, no. 3 (1987): 409–28.

Allen, John L. "From Cabot to Cartier: The Early Exploration of Eastern North America, 1497–1543." *Annals of the Association of American Geographers* 82, no. 3 (1992): 500–21.

Allen, Robert S. "FIDLER, PETER." In *Dictionary of Canadian Biography*, vol. 6. University of Toronto/Université Laval, 2003.

Altschul, Jeffrey H., Keith W. Kintigh, Mark Aldenderfer, Elise Alonzi, Ian Armit, Juan Antonio Barceló, Christopher S. Beekman, Penny Bickle, Douglas W. Bird, Scott E. Ingram, Elena Isayev, Andrew W. Kandel, et al. "To Understand How Migrations Affect Human Securities, Look to the Past." *Proceedings of the National Academy of Sciences* 117, no. 34 (2020): 20342–5.

Ambler, Charles. "Alcohol and the Slave Trade in West Africa, 1400–1850." In *Drugs, Labor, and Colonial Expansion*, edited by W. Jankowiak and D. Bradburd, 73–87. Tucson: University of Arizona Press, 2003.

Anderson, Emma. *The Betrayal of Faith: The Tragic Journey of a Colonial Native Convert*. Cambridge, MA: Harvard University Press, 2007.

– "Blood, Fire, and 'Baptism': Three Perspectives on the Death of Jean de Brébeuf, Seventeenth-century Jesuit 'Martyr.'" In *Native Americans, Christianity, and the Reshaping of the American Religious Landscape*, edited by Joel W. Martin and Mark A. Nicholas, 145–7. Chapel Hill: University of North Carolina Press, 2010.

Andrews, Kenneth R. *Trade, Plunder, and Settlement: Maritime Enterprise and the Genesis of the British Empire, 1480–1630*. Cambridge: Cambridge University Press, 1984.

Andrews, Thomas D., Glen Mackay, Leon Andrew, Wendy Stephenson, Amy Barker, Claire Alix, and the Shúhtagot'ine Elders of Tulita. "Alpine Ice Patches and Shúhtagot'ine Land Use in the Mackenzie and Selwyn Mountains, Northwest Territories, Canada." *Arctic* 65, Supplement 1 (2012): 22–42.

Anghiera, Pietro Martire d'. *De Orbe Novo de Pietro Martire d'Anghiera*. Paris, 1587.

Anthony, David W. *The Horse, the Wheel and Language: How Bronze-Age Riders from the Eurasian Steppes Shaped the Modern World*. Princeton, NJ: Princeton University Press, 2007.

Archer, Gabriel. "The relation of Captain Gosnold's voyage to the north part of

Virginia, 1602." In *Collections of the Massachusetts Historical Society* vol. 3, no. 8. Boston: Published for the Society by Little, Brown, 1843.

Armitage, David. "Introduction to Grotius." In *The Free Sea*, by Hugo Grotius, xi–xx. Edited by David Armitage, translated by R. Hakluyt. Indianapolis, IN: Liberty Fund, 2004.

Armitage, David, and Michael J. Braddick, ed. *The British Atlantic World, 1500–1800*. Basingstoke, Hampshire: Palgrave Macmillan, 2009.

Armitage, Peter. *The Innu (The Montagnais-Naskapi)*. New York, Chelsea House Publishers, 1991.

Asher, George M., ed. *Henry Hudson the Navigator: The Original Documents in which his Career is Recorded*. London: Hakluyt Society, 1860.

Atwood, Margaret. *The Journals of Susanna Moodie*. Toronto: MacFarlane, Walter, & Ross, 1970.

– *Survival: A Thematic Guide to Canadian Literature*. Toronto: House of Anansi Press, 1972.

Auger, Réginald. *Labrador Inuit and Europeans in the Strait of Belle Isle: From the Written Sources to the Archaeological Evidence*. Québec: Centre d'études nordiques, 1991.

Azpiazu, José Antonio. *La empresa vasca de Terranova: Entre el mito y la realidad*. Donostia-San Sebastián: Ttarttalo. 2008.

– *Hielos y oceanos: Vascos por el mundo*. Donostia-San Sebastián: Ttarttalo, 2016.

Bahr, Arthur. *Fragments and Assemblages: Forming Compilations of Medieval London*. Chicago: University of Chicago Press, 2013.

Bailyn, Bernard. *Atlantic History: Concepts and Contours*. Harvard University Press, 2005.

Baker, J.H. *An Introduction to English Legal History*, 2nd ed. London: Butterworths, 1979.

Baldwin, Andrew, Laura Cameron, and Audrey Kobayashi, eds. *Rethinking the Great White North: Race, Nature, and the Historical Geographies of Whiteness in Canada*. Vancouver: UBC Press, 2011.

Barber, Peter. "Mapmaking in England, ca. 1470–1650." In *The History of Cartography*, edited by J.B. Harley and David Woodward, vol. 3 part 2. Chicago: University of Chicago Press, 1987.

Barkham, Michael. "French Basque 'New Found Land' Entrepreneurs and the Import of Codfish and Whale Oil to Northern Spain, C. 1580 to C. 1620: The Case of

Adam de Chibau, Burgess of Saint-Jean-de-Luz and Sieur de St. Julien." *New-foundland and Labrador Studies* 10, no., 1 (1994): 1–43.

Barkham, Selma Huxley. "The Basque Whaling Establishments in Labrador 1536–1632 – A Summary." *Arctic* 37, no. 4 (1984): 515–19.

– "The Mentality of the Men Behind Sixteenth-Century Spanish Voyages to Terra-nova." In *Decentring the Renaissance: Canada and Europe in Multidisciplinary Perspective, 1500–1700*, edited by Germaine Warkentin and Carolyn Podruchny, 110–24. Toronto: University of Toronto Press, 2001.

– "A Note on the Strait of Belle Isle During the Period of Basque Contact with Indians and Inuit." *Études/Inuit/Studies* 4, 1–2 (1980): 51–9.

Barkham, Selma Huxley, ed. *Los vascos en el marco del Atlántico Norte: Siglos XVI y XVII*. Itsasoa, vol. 3. Donostia-San Sebastián, Spain: Etor, 1988.

Barnosky, Anthony D., Paul L. Koch, Robert S. Feranec, Scott L. Wing, and Alan B. Shabel. "Assessing the Causes of Late Pleistocene Extinctions on the Continents." *Science* 306, no. 5693 (2004): 70–5.

Baron, Anne, Adrian L. Burke, Bernard Gratuze, and Claude Chapdelaine. "Characterization and Origin of Steatite Beads Made by Northern Iroquoians in the St. Lawrence Valley During the 15th and 16th Centuries." *Journal of Archaeological Science*: Reports 8 (2016): 323–4.

Barr, Juliana. "Geographies of Power: Mapping Indian Borders in the 'Borderlands' of the Early Southwest." *William and Mary Quarterly* 68, no. 1 (2011): 5–46.

Barrett, James H., and David C. Orton, eds. *Cod and Herring: The Archaeology and History of Medieval Sea Fishing*. Oxford & Philadelphia: Oxbow Books Ltd, 2016.

Baugh, Timothy G., and Jonathon E. Ericson, eds. *Prehistoric Exchange Systems in North America: Interdisciplinary Contributions to Archaeology*. Plenum Press, New York, 1994.

Bautier, Robert-Henri. *Sur l'histoire économique de la France médiévale*. Aldershot, UK: Variorum, 1991.

Beaulieu, Alain. "'L'on n'a point d'ennemis plus grands que ces sauvages:' l'alliance franco-innue revisitée (1603–1653)." *Revue d'histoire de l'Amérique française* 61, nos 3–4 (Winter–Spring 2008): 365–95.

Beckert, Sven. *Empire of Cotton: A Global History*. New York: Alfred A. Knopf, 2014.

Behringer, Wolfgang. *A Cultural History of Climate*. Cambridge: Polity, 2010.

Bélanger, René. *Les Basques dans l'estuaire du Saint-Laurent, 1535–1635*. Montreal: Les Presses de l'Université du Québec, 1971.

Bemmels, Jordan B., and Christopher W. Dick. "Genomic Evidence of a
  Widespread Southern Distribution During the Last Glacial Maximum for Two
  Eastern North American Hickory Species." *Journal of Biogeography* 45, no. 8
  (2018): 1739–50.
Bennett, Donna. "The Waters of Life and Death: A New Laurentian Thesis." In
  Acqua, realtà e metafora, edited by Caterina Ricciardi, Laura Ferri, Fabio
  Mugnaini. Rome: SEMAR, 1998.
Bennett, Herman Lee. *African Kings and Black Slaves: Sovereignty and Dispossession
  in the Early Modern Atlantic.* Philadelphia: University of Pennsylvania Press, 2019.
Bennett, Judith M. *History Matters: Patriarchy and the Challenge of Feminism.*
  Philadelphia: University of Pennsylvania Press, 2006.
Benson, Larry V., Michael S. Berry, Edward A. Jolie, Jerry D. Spangler, David W.
  Stahle, and Eugene M. Hattori. "Possible Impacts of Early-11th-, Middle-12th-,
  and Late-13th-Century Droughts on Western Native Americans and the Missis-
  sippian Cahokians." *Quaternary Science Reviews* 26 (2007): 336–50.
Benton, Lauren. *A Search for Sovereignty: Law and Geography in European Empires,
  1400–1900.* Cambridge: Cambridge University Press, 2010.
Benton, Lauren, and Richard Ross, eds. *Legal Pluralism and Empires, 1500–1850.*
  New York: New York University Press, 2013.
Berger, Carl. *The Writing of Canadian History: Aspects of English-Canadian Histori-
  cal Writing since 1900.* Toronto: University of Toronto Press, 1976.
Berkes, Fikret. *Sacred Ecology: Traditional Ecological Knowledge and Resource
  Management.* Philadelphia, PA: Taylor & Francis, 1999.
Bernard, Jacques. *Navires et gens de mer à Bordeaux (vers 1400-vers 1550).* Paris:
  S.E.V.P.E.N., 1968.
Bethencourt, Francisco, and Diogo Ramada Curto, eds. *Portuguese Oceanic Expan-
  sion, 1400–1800.* New York: Cambridge University Press, 2007.
Biggar, Henry Percival, ed. *A Collection of Documents Relating to Jacques Cartier
  and the Sieur de Roberval.* Ottawa: Public Archives of Canada, 1930.
– *The Early Trading Companies of New France, 1534–1632.* Toronto: University of
  Toronto Library, 1901.
– *An English Expedition to America in 1527.* Paris: F. Alcan, 1913.
– ed. *The Precursors of Jacques Cartier, 1497–1534: A Collection of Documents Relating
  to the Early History of the Dominion of Canada.* Ottawa: Government Printing
  Bureau, 1911.
Billinger, Michael S., and John W. Ives. "Inferring the Age Structure of AD 13th

Century Promontory Point Populations from Moccasin Size Data." *American Journal of Physical Anthropology* 156 no. 1 (2015): 76–89.

Binnema, Theodore. *Common and Contested Ground: A Human and Environmental History of the Northwestern Plains*. Norman: University of Oklahoma Press, 2001.

Binnema, Theodore, and Melanie Niemi. "'Let the Line be Drawn Now': Wilderness, Conservation, and the Exclusion of Aboriginal People from Banff National Park in Canada." *Environmental History* 11, no. 4 (2006): 724–50.

Birch, Jennifer. "Coalescent Communities: Settlement Aggregation and Social Integration in Iroquoian Ontario." *American Antiquity* 77, no. 4 (2012): 646–70.

– "Social Institutions and the Differential Development of Northern Iroquoian Confederacies." In *The Evolution of Social Institutions: Interdisciplinary Perspectives*, edited by D.M. Bondarenko, Stephen A. Kowalewski, and David S. Small, 419–35. New York: Springer, 2020.

Birch, Jennifer, Carley A. Crann, and Jean-Luc Pilon. "Chronological Modeling and Insights on European–St. Lawrence Iroquoian Interaction from the Roebuck Site, Ontario." *Canadian Journal of Archaeology* 40, no. 2 (2016): 332–47.

Birch, Jennifer, and John P. Hart. "Social Networks and Northern Iroquoian Confederacy Dynamics." *American Antiquity* 83, no. 1 (2018): 13–33.

Birch, Jennifer, and R.F. Williamson. *The Mantle Site: An Archaeological History of an Ancestral Wendat Community*. Lanham: Altamira Press, 2013.

Bird, Junius B. *Archaeology of the Hopedale Area, Labrador*. New York, Anthropological papers of the American Museum of Natural History, 39 (part 2), 1945.

Bishop, Charles A. *The Northern Ojibwa and the Fur Trade: An Historical and Ecological Study*. Toronto: Holt, Rinehart and Winston of Canada, 1974.

Blair, Susan E. "Ancient Wolastoq'kew Landscapes: Settlement and Technology in the Lower Saint John River Valley, Canada." PhD diss., Department of Anthropology, University of Toronto, 2004.

Blake, John W., ed. *Europeans in West Africa: 1450–1560: Documents to Illustrate the Nature and Scope of Portuguese Enterprise in West Africa, the Abortive Attempt of Castilians to Create an Empire There, and the Early English Voyages to Barbary and Guinea*. London: Hakluyt Society, 1942.

Blitz, John. "Adoption of the Bow in Prehistoric North America." *North American Archaeologist* 9 (1988): 123–45.

Blumenberg, Hans. *Shipwreck with Spectator: Paradigm of a Metaphor for Existence*. Translated by Steven Rendall. Cambridge, MA: MIT Press, 1997.

Bohaker, Heidi. "Nindoodemag: The Significance of Algonquian Kinship Networks in the Eastern Great Lakes Region, 1600–1701." *William and Mary Quarterly* 63, no. 1 (2006): 23–52.

Bolster, W. Jeffrey. *The Mortal Sea: Fishing the Atlantic in the Age of Sail.* Cambridge, MA: Belknap Press, 2014.

– "Putting the Ocean in Atlantic History: Maritime Communities and Marine Ecology in the Northwest Atlantic, 1500–1800." *American Historical Review* 113, no. 1 (February 2008): 19–47.

Bouchard, Jack. "Shetland Sheep and Azorean Wheat: Atlantic Islands as Provisioning Centers, 1400–1550." *Global Food History* (2020): 1–26.

– "Towards Terra Nova: The North Atlantic Fisheries and the Atlantic World, 1490–1600." PhD diss., University of Pittsburgh, 2018.

Boudreau, Robert E.A., Jennifer M. Galloway, R. Timothy Patterson, Arun Kumar, and Frederick A. Michel. "A Paleolimnological Record of Holocene Climate and Environmental Change in the Temagami Region, Northeastern Ontario." *Journal of Paleolimnology* 33, no. 4 (2005): 445–61.

Bradburd, Daniel, and William Jankowiak. "Drugs, Desire, and European Economic Expansion." In *Drugs, Labor, and Colonial Expansion*, edited by D. Bradburd and W. Jankowiak, 3–29. Tucson: University of Arizona Press, 2003.

Braddick, Michael J. *State Formation in Early Modern England: c. 1550–1700.* Cambridge: Cambridge University Press, 2000.

Brandão, José, ed. *Mémoires of Michilimackinac and the Pays d'en Haut: Indians and French in the Upper Great Lakes at the Turn of the Eighteenth Century.* East Lansing: Michigan State University Press, 2019.

Brandon, Pepijn. *War, Capital and the Dutch State (1588–1795).* Leiden: Brill, 2015.

Braudel, Fernand. *Civilization and Capitalism, 15th–18th Century*, vol. 1, *The Structures of Everyday Life.* New York: Harper & Row, 1982.

Braun, David P. "Midwestern Hopewellian Exchange and Supralocal Interaction." In *Peer Policy Interaction and Socio-Political Change*, edited by C. Renfrew and J. F. Cherry, 117–26. Cambridge: Cambridge University Press, 1986.

Bréard, Charles, and Paul Bréard, ed. *Documents relatifs à la marine normande et à ses armements aux XVIe Et XVIIe siècles pour le Canada, l'Afrique, les Antilles, le Brésil et les Indes.* Rouen: A. Lestringant, 1889.

Brewer, J.S., ed. *Letters and Papers, Foreign and Domestic, Henry VIII.* London: HM Stationery Office, 1867.

Brewster, Nathalie. *The Inuit in Southern Labrador: The View from Snack Cove.*

Occasional Papers in Northeastern Archaeology No. 15. St John's, NL: Copetown Press, 2006.

Brève relation du voyage de la Nouvelle France. Paris: Sébastien Cramoisy, 1632.

Brophy, Susan Dianne. *A Legacy of Exploitation: Early Capitalism in the Red River Colony.* Vancouver: UBC Press, 2022.

– "Reciprocity as Dispossession: A Dialectical Materialist Analysis of the Fur Trade." *Settler Colonial Studies* 9, no. 3 (3 July 2019): 301–19.

Brown James H., and Mark V. Lomolino. *Biogeography*, 2nd ed. Sunderland, MA: Sinauer Associates, 1998.

Brown, Jennifer S.H. *Strangers in Blood: Fur Trade Company Families in Indian Country.* Vancouver: UBC Press, 1980.

Brown, Vincent, and Joseph Calder Miller, eds. *The Princeton Companion to Atlantic History.* Princeton; Oxford: Princeton University Press, 2015.

Brugge, David M. "DNA and Ancient Demography." In *Climbing the Rocks, Papers in Honor of Helen and Jay Croty*, edited by Regge N. Wiseman, Thomas C. O'Laughlin, and Cordelia T. Snow, 49–56. Albuquerque: The Archaeological Society of New Mexico, 2003.

– "When Were the Navajos?" In *Southwestern Interludes, Papers in Honor of Charlotte J. and Theodore R. Frisbe*, edited by Regge N. Wiseman, Thomas C. O'Laughlin, and Cordelia T. Snow, 45–52. Albuquerque: The Archaeological Society of New Mexico, 2006.

Buc'hoz, Pierre-Joseph. *Dictionnaire universel des plantes, arbres et arbustes de la France.* Paris: Lacombe, 1770–71.

Buffon, Georges-Louis Leclerc de. *Histoire naturelle générale et particulière, avec la description du cabinet du roi.* Amsterdam: J.H. Schneider, 1767.

Bumsted, J.M. *The Peoples of Canada: A Pre-Confederation History*, 4th ed. Toronto: Oxford University Press, 2014.

Bunbury, J., and K. Gajewski. "Postglacial Climates Inferred from a Lake at Treeline, Southwest Yukon Territory, Canada." *Quaternary Science Reviews* 28, no. 3–4 (2009): 354–69.

Burden, Philip D. *The Mapping of North America: A List of Printed Maps, 1511–1670.* Rickmansworth, Herts.: Raleigh Publications, 1996.

Burke, Adrian L. "La provenance des matières premières lithiques et la reconstitution des réseaux d'interactions." In *Île aux Allumettes: L'Archaïque supérieur dans l'Outaouais*, edited by N. Clermont, C. Chapdelaine, and J. Cinq-Mars, 187–217.

Collection Paléo-Québec No 30. Montréal: Recherches amérindiennes au Québec, 2003.

– "Lithic Procurement and the Ceramic Period Occupation of the Interior of the Maritime Peninsula." PhD diss., Department of Anthropology, University at Albany-SUNY, Albany, NY, 2000.

– "Paleoindian Ranges in Northeastern North America Based on Lithic Raw Materials Sourcing." In *Notions de territoire et de mobilité: exemples de l'Europe et des premières nations en Amérique du Nord avant le contact européen. ERAUL 116 (Actes du Xe congrès annuel de l'Association Européenne des Archéologues, Lyon, 2004)*, edited by C. Bressy, A. Burke, P. Chalard, and H. Martin, 77–89. Liège: Études et recherches archéologiques de l'Université de Liège, 2006.

– "Stone Tool Raw Materials and Sources of the Archaic Period in the Northeast." In *The Archaic of the Far Northeast*, edited by D. Sanger and M.A.P. Renouf, 409–36. Orono: University of Maine Press, 2006.

– "Témiscouata: Traditional Maliseet Territory and Connections Between the St. Lawrence Valley and the St. John River Valley." In *Actes du trente-deuxième Congrès des Algonquinistes*, edited by John D. Nichols, 61–73. Winnipeg: University of Manitoba, 2001.

Burrage, Henry S. ed. *Early English and French Voyages, Chiefly from Hakluyt, 1534–1608*. New York: Scribner, 1906.

Butel, Paul. *The Atlantic*. London: Routledge, 1999.

Byers, Douglas S. "The Eastern Archaic: Some Problems and Hypothesis." *American Antiquity* 24, no. 3 (1959): 233–56.

Cadigan, Sean. *Hope and Deception in Conception Bay*. Toronto: University of Toronto Press, 1995.

Camenisch, Chantal, Kathrin M. Keller, Melanie Salvisberg, Benjamin Amann, Martin Bauch, Sandro Blumer, Rudolf Brázdil, Stefan Brönnimann, Ulf Büntgen, Bruce M.S. Campbell, Laura Fernández-Donado, Dominik Fleitmann, et al. "The 1430s: A Cold Period of Extraordinary Internal Climate Variability During the Early Spörer Minimum with Social and Economic Impacts in North-Western and Central Europe." *Climate of the Past* 12, no. 11 (December 2016): 2107–26.

Campbell, Bruce. *The Great Transition: Climate, Disease and Society in the Late-Medieval World*. Cambridge: Cambridge University Press, 2016.

Campbell, Claire. "The Wealth of Wilderness." In *The Nature of Canada*, edited by Colin Coates and Graeme Wynn. Vancouver: On Point Press, 2019.

Campbell, Wade. "Na'nilkad nee na'niltin – Learning from Herding: An Ethnoarchaeological Study of Historic Pastoralism on the Navajo Nation." *Kiva* 3 (2021): 295–315.

Campeau, Lucien, ed. *Monumenta Novae Franciae*, 9 vols. Rome: Monumenta Hist. Soc. Jesu, 1967–2003.

Campeau, Lucien. "Les origines du sucre d'érable." *Les Cahiers des dix* 45 (1990): 53–66.

Canny, Nicholas P., and Philip D. Morgan, ed. *The Oxford Handbook of the Atlantic World, c.1450-c.1850*. Oxford: Oxford University Press, 2013.

Carew, George, Earl of Totnes. *Calendar of the Carew Manuscripts: 1515–1574*. London: Longmans, Green, Reader & Dyer, 1867.

Carey, Daniel, and Claire Jowitt, eds. *Richard Hakluyt and Travel Writing in Early Modern Europe*. Hakluyt Society, Extra Series 47. Farnham, Surrey, England; Burlington, VT: Ashgate, 2012.

Carlos, Ann M, and Frank D Lewis. *Commerce by a Frozen Sea: Native Americans and the European Fur Trade*. Philadelphia: University of Pennsylvania Press, 2010.

Carpin, Gervais. *Histoire d'un mot: l'ethnonym 'canadien' de 1535 à 1691*. Québec: Septentrion, 1995.

Carr, Christopher, and D. Troy Case, eds. *Gathering Hopewell: Society, Ritual, and Ritual Interaction*. New York: Springer, 2005.

Carstairs, Catherine. "'Roots' Nationalism: Branding English Canada Cool in the 1980s and 1990s." *Histoire sociale / Social History* 39, no. 77 (2006): 235–55.

Carter, A.T. *History of English Legal Institutions*. London: Butterworths, 1902.

Cartier, Jacques. *Relations*. Edited by Michel Bideaux. Bibliothèque du nouveau monde. Montréal: Presses de l'Université de Montréal, 1986.

– *A Shorte and Briefe Narration of the Two Navigations and Discoveries to the Northweast Partes Called Newe Fraunce*. Translated by John Florio. London, 1580.

Castonguay, Daniel. "Les impératifs de la subsistance chez les Montagnais de la traite de Tadoussac (1720–1750)." *Recherches amérindiennes au Québec* 19, no. 1 (1989): 17–30.

Castro, Javi. "The Basque Seal Trade with Labrador in the Seventeenth Century." *Newfoundland and Labrador Studies* 33, no. 1 (2018): 63–82.

Ceci, Lynn. "The Value of Wampum Among the New York Iroquois: A Case Study in Artifact Analysis." *Journal of Anthropological Research* 38, no.1 (1982): 97–107.

Cell, Gillian T. *English Enterprise in Newfoundland, 1577–1660*. Toronto: University of Toronto Press, 1969.

Chakrabarty, Dipesh. *Provincializing Europe: Postcolonial Thought and Historical Difference*. Princeton, NJ: Princeton University Press, 2000.

Chalifoux, Éric. "Caractérisation des matières premières lithiques de l'île d'Anticosti." Unpublished report. Mi'gmawei Mawiomi Secretariat, Listuguj (Restigouche), Quebec, 2004.

Champlain, Samuel de. *Les Œuvres completes de Champlain*, 2 vols. Edited by Eric Thierry. Quebec City: Septentrion, 2019.

– *The Works of Samuel de Champlain*, 6 vols. Edited by H.P. Biggar. Toronto: University of Toronto Press, (1922–35) 1971.

Chapdelaine, Claude. "Cliche-Rancourt, un site du paléoindien ancien." In *Entre lacs et montagnes au Méganticois: 12000 ans d'histoire amérindienne*, edited by Claude Chapdelaine, 47–120. Montreal: Recherches amérindiennes au Québec, 2007.

– "The Early Paleoindian Occupation at the Cliche-Rancourt Site, Southeastern Quebec." In *Late Pleistocene Archaeology & Ecology in the Far Northeast*, edited by Claude Chapdelaine, 135–63. College Station: Texas A&M University Press, 2012.

– "L'analyse spatiale et le tissu social des maisonnées au site Droulers." In *Droulers-Tsiionhiakwatha: Chef-lieu iroquoien de Saint-Anicet à la fin du XVe siècle*, edited by Claude Chapdelaine, 415–38. Montreal: Recherches amérindiennes au Québec, 2019.

– *Le site de Chicoutimi: un campement préhistorique au pays des Kakouchacks*. Québec: Ministère des Affaires culturelles, 1984.

– "Le site Jacques à Saint-Roch-de-Richelieu: archaïque laurentien ou post-laurentien?" *Recherches amérindiennes au Québec* 17, no. 1–2 (1987): 63–80.

– *Le site Mandeville à Tracy: variabilité culturelle des Iroquoiens du Saint-Laurent*. Montreal: Recherches amérindiennes au Québec, 1989.

– "Saint Lawrence Iroquoians as Middlemen or Observers: Review of Evidence in the Middle and Upper Saint Lawrence Valley." In *Contact in the 16th Century: Networks among Fishers, Farmers and Foragers*, edited by Brad Loewen and Claude Chapdelaine, 149–70. Ottawa: University of Ottawa Press, 2016.

Chapdelaine, Claude, and Norman Clermont. "Adaptations, Continuity and Change in the Middle Ottawa Valley: A View from the Morrison and Allumettes Island Late Archaic Sites." In *The Archaic of the Far Northeast*, edited by D. Sanger and M.A.P. Renouf, 191–219. Orono: University of Maine Press, 2006.

Charles, Douglas K., and Jane E. Buikstra, eds. *Recreating Hopewell: New Perspectives on Middle Woodland in Eastern North America*. Gainesville: University Press of Florida, 2006.

Childs, Wendy R. "England's Icelandic Trade in the Fifteenth Century: The Role of the Port of Hull." *Northern Seas Yearbook* (1995): 11–31.

Chrestien, Jean-Pierre, and Daniel Dufournier. "Le grès béarnais au Canada." In *L'aventure maritime du golfe de Gascogne à Terre-Neuve*, edited by Jean Bourgoin and Jacqueline Carpine-Lancre, 251–70. Paris: Éditions du comité des travaux historiques et scientifiques, 1994.

Chrétien, Yves. "Les lames de cache du site Lambert et l'influence de la culture Meadowood dans la région de Québec." In *Archéologies québécoises*, edited by A.-M. Balac et al., 185–201. Montreal: Recherches amérindiennes au Québec, 1995.

Chrétien, Yves. "La manipulation stratégique des biens exotiques dans les contextes cérémoniels du Sylvicole inférieur: l'exemple de la région de Québec." *Anthropologie et Sociétés* 23 no. 1 (1999): 5–97.

Chrisomalis, Stephen, and Bruce G. Trigger. "Reconstructing Prehistoric Ethnicity: Problems and Possibilities." In *A Passion for the Past: Papers in Honour of James F. Pendergast*, edited by James V. Wright and Jean-Luc Pilon, 419–33. Mercury Series, Archaeology Paper No. 164. Gatineau, QC: Canadian Museum of Civilization, 2004.

Clark, Andrew Hill. *Acadia: The Geography of Early Nova Scotia to 1760*. Madison: University of Wisconsin Press, 1968.

– *Three Centuries and the Island: A Historical Geography of Settlement and Agriculture in Prince Edward Island, Canada*. Toronto, University of Toronto Press, 1959.

Clark, Jamie L., and John D. Speth. *Living and Dying on the Periphery. The Archaeology and Human Remains from Two 13th–15th Century AD Villages in Southeastern New Mexico*. Salt Lake City: The University of Utah Press, 2022.

Clermont, Norman. "L'augmentation de la population chez les Iroquoiens préhistoriques." *Recherches amérindiennes au Québec* 10, no. 3 (1980): 159–63.

– "Le Sylvicole inférieur au Québec." *Recherches amérindiennes au Québec* 20, no. 1 (1990): 5–17.

– "The Meaning of Early Late Woodland Pottery from Southwestern Quebec." *Northeast Anthropology* 49 (1995): 67–75.

– "The Origin of the Iroquoians." *The Review of Archaeology* 17, no. 1 (1996): 59–62.

Clermont, Norman, and Claude Chapdelaine. *Île Morrison: lieu sacré et atelier de l'archaïque dans l'Outaouais*. Montreal: Recherches amérindiennes au Québec, 1998.

– *Pointe-du-Buisson 4: quarante siècles d'archives oubliées*. Montreal: Recherches amérindiennes au Québec, 1982.

Clermont, Norman, Claude Chapdelaine, and Jacques Cinq-Mars, eds. *L'île aux Allumettes et l'Archaïque supérieur dans l'Outaouais.* Paléo-Québec No. 30. Montreal: Recherches amérindiennes au Québec, 2003.

Coates, Colin, and Graeme Wynn. "Introduction." In *The Nature of Canada*, edited by Colin MacMillan Coates and Graeme Wynn, 3–24. Vancouver: On Point Press, 2019.

Coates, Karen. "Walking into New Worlds. Native Traditions and Novel Discoveries Tell the Migration Story of the Ancestors of the Navajo and Apache." *Archaeology* 73 (2020): 38–43.

Cochrane, Timothy. *Gichi Bitobig, Grand Marais: Early Accounts of the Anishinaabeg and the North Shore Fur Trade.* Minneapolis: University of Minnesota Press, 2018.

Cohen, Margaret. *The Novel and the Sea.* Princeton, NJ: Princeton University Press, 2010.

Colpitts, George. "Accounting for Environmental Degradation in Hudson's Bay Company Fur Trade Journals and Account Books." *British Journal of Canadian Studies* 19, no. 1 (2006): 1–32.

– *North America's Indian Trade in European Commerce and Imagination, 1580–1850.* Leiden: Brill, 2014.

– *Pemmican Empire: Food, Trade, and the Last Bison Hunts in the North American Plains, 1780–1882.* New York: Cambridge University Press, 2014.

Condon, Margaret M., and Evan T. Jones. "William Weston: Early Voyager to the New World." *Historical Research* 91 (November 2018): 628–46.

Conrad, Margaret, Alvin Finkel, and Donald Fyson. *History of the Canadian Peoples*, vol. 1, *Beginnings to 1867*, 6th ed. Toronto: Pearson, 2015.

Cook, Ramsay. *1492 and All That: Making a Garden out of a Wilderness.* Toronto: Robarts Centre for Canadian Studies, 1993.

Cooper, Judith R. "Bison Hunting and Late Prehistoric Human Subsistence Economies in the Great Plains." PhD diss., Southern Methodist University, 2008.

Cormier, Louis, ed. *Jean-Baptiste Perrault, marchand voyageur, parti de Montréal le 28e de mai 1783.* Montreal: Boréal, 1978.

Cotton, William. *An Elizabethan Guild of the City of Exeter. An account of the proceedings of the Society of Merchant Adventurers, during the latter half of the sixteenth century.* Exeter: 1893.

Courville, Serge. *Le Québec: Genèses et mutations du territoire.* Ste. Foy: Presses de l'Université Laval, 2001.

Creel, D., R.F. Scott IV, and M.B. Collins. "A Faunal Record from West Central Texas and Its Bearing on Late Holocene Bison Population Changes in the Southern Plains." *Plains Anthropologist* 35, no. 127 (1990): 55–69.

Creighton, Donald. *The Commercial Empire of the St. Lawrence, 1760–1850.* Toronto: Ryerson Press, 1937.

– *The Empire of the St. Lawrence.* Toronto: Macmillan, 1956.

– *A History of Canada: Dominion of the North.* Boston: Houghton Mifflin, 1958.

Crompton, Amanda. "They Have Gone Back to their Country: French and Inuit Landscapes in 18th Century Southern Labrador." *Études/Inuit/Studies* 39, no. 1 (2015): 117–40.

Crowley, John E. "Empire versus Truck: The Official Interpretation of Debt and Labour in the Eighteenth-Century Newfoundland Fishery." *Canadian Historical Review* 70, no. 3 (1989): 311–36.

Cruikshank, Julie. "Oral Tradition and Oral History: Reviewing Some Issues." *Canadian Historical Review* 75 (1994): 403–18.

– *The Social Life of Stories: Narrative and Knowledge in the Yukon Territory.* Vancouver: UBC Press, 1998.

Cullen, L.M. *The Brandy Trade under the Ancien Régime: Regional Specialization in the Charente.* Cambridge: Cambridge University Press, 2002.

Cuningham, William. *The Cosmographical Glasse.* London, 1559.

Cunliffe, Barry W. *Facing the Ocean: The Atlantic and Its Peoples, 8000 BC–AD 1500.* New York: Oxford University Press, 2001.

Curtis, Jenneth E., and Pierre Desrosiers, eds. *Ramah Chert: A Lithic Odyssey.* Inukjuak, QC: Avataq Cultural Institute, 2017.

Dagenais, Michèle, and Ken Cruikshank. "Gateways, Inland seas, or Boundary Waters? Historical Conceptions of the St. Lawrence River since the 19th Century." *The Canadian Geographer / Le Géographe canadien* 60, no. 4 (2016): 413–24.

Dalby, David, and P.E.H. Hair. "'Le Langaige De Guynee': A Sixteenth Century Vocabulary from the Pepper Coast." *African Language Studies* V (1964): 174–91.

– "'Le Langaige Du Bresil': A Tupi Vocabulary of the 1540s." *Transactions of the Philological Society* 65, no. 1 (1966): 42–66.

Dalton, April S., Martin Margold, Chris R. Stokes, Lev Tarasov, Arthur S. Dyke, Roberta S. Adams, Serge Allard, et al. "An Updated Radiocarbon-Based Ice Margin Chronology for the Last Deglaciation of the North American Ice Sheet Complex." *Quaternary Science Reviews* 234 (2020): 1–27.

Dalton, Heather. *Merchants and Explorers: Roger Barlow, Sebastian Cabot, and Networks of Atlantic Exchange 1500–1560.* Oxford: Oxford University Press, 2016.

Dancey, William S. "The Enigmatic Hopewell of the Eastern Woodlands." In *North American Archaeology*, edited by T. Pauketat and D. DiPaolo Loren, 108–37. Oxford: Blackwell, 2005.

Daschuck, James. *Clearing the Plains: Disease, Politics of Starvation, and the Loss of Aboriginal Life*. Regina, SK: University of Regina Press, 2013.

Davies, K.G., and Hudson's Bay Company. *Northern Quebec and Labrador Journal and Correspondence, 1819–35*. London: Hudson's Bay Record Society, 1963.

Davis, John. *The Worldes Hydrographical Discription*. London, 1595.

Davis, Kathleen. *Periodization and Sovereignty: How Ideas of Feudalism and Secularization Govern the Politics of Time*. Philadelphia: University of Pennsylvania Press, 2008.

Davis, Ralph. *The Rise of the Atlantic Economies*. Ithaca, NY: Cornell University Press, 1973.

Deagan, Kathleen A., and José María Cruxent. *Columbus's Outpost among the Taínos: Spain and America at La Isabela, 1493-1498*. New Haven, CT: Yale University Press, 2002.

de Armas, Antonio Rumeo. "Las Pesquerías españolas en la costa de África (Siglos XV–XVI)." *Anuario de Estudios Atlánticos* no. 23 (28 March 2016): 349–72.

de Avilez Rocha, Gabriel. "The Pinzones and the Coup of the Acedares: Fishing and Colonization in the Fifteenth-Century Atlantic." *Colonial Latin American Review* 28, no. 4 (October 2019): 427–49.

– "Politics of the Hinterland: Taxing Fowl in and Beyond the Ports of Terceira Island, 1550–1600." *Early American Studies* 15, no. 4 (2017): 740–68.

Dechêne, Louise. *Habitants and Merchants in Seventeenth-Century Montreal*. Translated by Liana Vardi. Montreal and Kingston: McGill-Queen's University Press, 1992.

Dee, John. *General and Rare Memorials Pertayning to the Perfect Arte of Navigation*. London, 1577.

– *John Dee's Diary, Catalogue of Manuscripts and Selected Letters*. Edited by J.O. Halliwell-Phillipps, James Crossley, John Eglington Bailey, and M.R. James. Cambridge: Cambridge University Press, 2014.

Deen, Nicolaas G.H. *Glossaria duo Vasco – Islandica*. Amsterdam: H.J. Paris, 1937.

Delâge, Denys. *Bitter Feast: Amerindians and Europeans in Northeastern North America, 1600–64*. Vancouver: UBC Press, 1993.

– "La traite des pelletries aux XVIIe et XVIIIe siècles." *Les Cahiers des Dix*, no. 70 (2016): 343–89.

Delâge, Denys, and Étienne Gilbert. "Les Amérindiens face à la justice coloniale française dans le gouvernement de Québec, II – Eau de vie, traite des fourrures, endettement, affaires civiles." *Recherches Amérindiennes au Québec* 34 (2004): 31–41.

Delanglez, Jean. *Life and Voyages of Louis Jolliet, 1645–1700.* Chicago: Institute of Jesuit History, 1948.

Delmas, Vincent. "Indigenous Traces on Basque Sites: Direct Contact or Later Reoccupation?" *Newfoundland and Labrador Studies*, Papers on the Basques in Newfoundland and Labrador in the Seventeenth Century 33, no. 1 (2018): 20–62.

De Luca, Kelly. "Beyond the Sea: Extraterritorial Jurisdiction and English Law, c. 1575–c. 1640." PhD diss. Columbia University, 2008.

Denevan, William M. "The Pristine Myth: The Landscape of the Americas in 1492." *Annals of the Association of American Geographers* 82, no. 3 (1992): 369–85.

Dent, Joshua. "Community-Sourced Archaeology and Relinquishing the Inception of Research." *Canadian Journal of Archaeology/Journal canadien d'Archéologie* 44 (2020):48–65.

Denys, Nicolas. *Description geographique et historique des costes de l'Amerique septentrionale avec l'histoire naturelle du païs*, 2 vols. Paris: Claude Barbin, 1672.

Derry, David E. "Later Athapaskan Prehistory: A Migration Hypothesis." *The Canadian Journal of Anthropology* 5 (1975): 134–47.

Desbarats, Catherine, and Allan Greer. "Où est la Nouvelle-France?" *Revue d'histoire de l'Amérique française* 64, nos 3–4 (Winter/Spring 2011): 31–62.

Dessert, Daniel. *Les Montmorency: Mille ans au service des rois de France.* Paris: Flammarion, 2015.

Devine, Heather. *The People Who Own Themselves: Aboriginal Ethnogenesis in a Canadian Family, 1660–1900.* Calgary: University of Calgary Press, 2004.

Dick, Lyle. *A Century of Parks Canada, 1911–2011.* Calgary: University of Calgary Press, 2011.

Dickason, Olive Patricia. *Canada's First Nations: A History of Founding Peoples from Earliest Times*, third ed. Toronto: Oxford University Press, 2002.

Dièreville [first name unknown]. *Relation du voyage du Port Royal de l'Acadie ou de la Nouvelle France.* Edited by Norman Doiron. Montreal: Les Presses de l'Université de Montréal, 1999.

Dietler, M. "Alcohol: Anthropological/Archaeological Perspectives." *Annual Review of Anthropology* 35 (2006): 229–406.

Dieulefet, Gaëlle. "The Isle Aux Morts Shipwreck: A Contribution to Seventeenth-

Century Material Culture in Newfoundland." *Newfoundland and Labrador Studies*, Papers on the Basques in Newfoundland and Labrador in the Seventeenth Century 33, 1 (2018): 136–71.

Dieulefet, Gaëlle, and Brad Loewen. "Sur la route des pêcheurs malouins. Témoins céramiques des échanges entre la Méditerranée et l'Atlantique aux XVIIe et XVIIIe siècles." *Annales de Bretagne et des Pays de l'Ouest* 126, 3 (2019): 49–76.

Dillehay, T.D. "Late Quaternary Bison Population Changes on the Southern Plains." *Plains Anthropologist* 19 (1974): 180–96.

Dion, Roger. *Histoire de la vigne et du vin en France des origines au XIX siècle.* Paris: L'auteur, 1959.

Disney, A.R. *A History of Portugal and the Portuguese Empire: From Beginnings to 1807.* 2 vols. New York: Cambridge University Press, 2009.

Dittbrenner, Benjamin J., Michael M. Pollock, Jason W. Schilling, Julian D. Olden, Joshua J. Lawler, and Christian E. Torgersen. "Modeling Intrinsic Potential for Beaver (*Castor canadensis*) Habitat to Inform Restoration and Climate Change Adaptation." *PLOS ONE* 13, no. 2 (2018): e0192538.

Dodd, Christine F., Dona R. Poulton, Paul A. Lennox, David G. Smith, and Gary A. Warrick. "The Middle Ontario Iroquoian Stage." In *The Archaeology of Southern Ontario to A.D. 1650*, edited by C.J. Ellis and N. Ferris, 321–59. London: Ontario Archaeological Society, 1990.

Doering, Brian N., Julie A. Esdale, Joshua D. Reuther, and Senna D. Catenacci. "A Multiscalar Consideration of the Athabascan Migration." *American Antiquity* 85 (3) (2020): 470–91.

Donovan, Ken. "Precontact and Settlement: Ingonish and Northern Cape Breton from the Paleo Indians to the 18th century." *The Nashwaak Review* 22–3 (2009): 330–87.

Dove, Michael. "Plying the Northernmost Atlantic Trading Route to the New World: The Hudson's Bay Company and British Seaborne Empire." In *English Atlantics Revisited: Essays Honouring Professor Ian K. Steele*, edited by Nancy L. Rhoden, 174–205. Montreal and Kingston: McGill-Queen's University Press, 2007.

Dubois, Paul-André, and Maxime Morin. "La démographie amérindienne en Nouvelle-France. Sources historiques et herméneutique des chiffres." *Recherches amérindiennes au Québec* 48, no. 3 (2018): 113–23.

Duhamel du Monceau, Henri-Louis. *Traité des arbres et arbustes qui se cultivent en France en pleine terre.* Paris: H.L. Guerin & L.F. Delatour, 1755.

Duncan, T. Bentley. *Atlantic Islands: Madeira, the Azores, and the Cape Verdes in*

Seventeenth-Century Commerce and Navigation. Chicago: University of Chicago Press, 1972.

Dussel, Enrique. "Eurocentrism and Modernity (Introduction to the Frankfurt Lectures)." *Boundary* 2, 20 (1993): 65–76.

Du Voisin de La Popelinière, Henri Lancelot. *L'Amiral de France, et par occasion, de celuy des autres nations.* Paris: T. Périer, 1584.

Dyke, Arthur S. "An Outline of North American Deglaciation with Emphasis on Central and Northern Canada." *Developments in Quaternary Sciences* 2 (2004): 373–424.

Earle, Timothy, Clive Gamble, and Hendrik Poinar. "Migration." In *Deep History: The Architecture of Past and Present*, edited by Daniel Lord Smail and Andrew Shryock, 159–79. Berkeley: University of California Press, 2011.

Echebarria, Enrique Ayerbe, ed. *Los Vascos en el marco Atlántico Norte: Siglos XVI y XVII.* Gipuzkoa: Juan de Bilbao, 1989.

Echo-Hawk, Roger C. "Ancient History in the New World: Integrating Oral Traditions and the Archaeological Record in Deep Time." *American Antiquity* 65, no. 2 (2000): 267–90.

Édits, ordonnances royaux, déclarations et arrets du conseil d'état du roi concernant le Canada. Quebec: E.R. Frechette, 1854.

Edwards, Andrew David, Peter Hill, and Juan Neves-Sarriegui. "Capitalism In Global History." *Past & Present* 249, no. 1 (2020): 1–32.

Eiselt, Sunday. *Becoming White Clay: A History and Archaeology of Jicarilla Apache Enclavement.* Salt Lake City: University of Utah Press, 2012.

Ellis, Thomas. *A True Report of the Third and Last Voyage into Meta Incognita.* London, 1578.

Erlandson, Jon M., Michael Graham, and Bruce J. Bourque. "The Kelp Highway Hypothesis: Marine Ecology, the Coastal Migration Theory, and the Peopling of the Americas." *The Journal of Island and Coastal Archaeology* 2, no. 2 (2007): 161–74.

Escribano Ruiz, Sergio, and Saraí Barreiro Argüelles. "Travelling Ceramics: Basque Networks and Identities in the Gulf of Saint Lawrence." In *Contact in the 16th Century: Networks among Fishers, Farmers and Foragers*, edited by Brad Loewen and Claude Chapdelaine, 31–56. Ottawa: University of Ottawa Press, 2016.

Fagan, Brian M. *The First North Americans: An Archeological Journey.* London: Thames & Hudson, 2011.

Fagundes, Nelson J.R., Alice Tagliani-Ribeiro, Rohina Rubicz, Larissa Tarskaia,

Michael H. Crawford, Francisco M. Salzano, and Sandro L. Bonatto. "How Strong Was the Bottleneck Associated to the Peopling of the Americas? New Insights from Multilocus Sequence Data." *Genetics and Molecular Biology* no. 41, supplement 1 (2018): 206–14.

Farnsworth, Kenneth B., and Thomas E. Emerson, eds. *Early Woodland Archaeology.* Kampsville, IL: Center for American Archaeology Press, 1986.

Fay, Amelia. "Big Men, Big Women or Both? Examining the Coastal Trading System of the Eighteenth-Century Labrador Inuit." In *History and Renewal of Labrador's Inuit Métis,* edited by John C. Kennedy, 75–93. St John's, NL: Institute of Social and Economic Research, 2014.

– "Understanding Inuit-European Contact Along the Labrador Coast: A Case for Continuity." PhD diss., Memorial University, St John's, NL, 2016.

Fenn, Elizabeth A. *Pox Americana: The Great Smallpox Epidemic of 1775–82.* New York: Hill and Wang, 2001.

Fenton, William N. *The Great Law and the Longhouse: A Political History of the Iroquois Confederacy.* Norman: University of Oklahoma Press, 1998.

Ferland, Catherine. *Bacchus en Canada: boissons, buveurs, et ivresses en Nouvelle-France.* Quebec City: Septentrion, 2010.

– "Entre diplomatie et subversion: le rôle des boissons alcoolisées dans les rapports franco-amérindiens, XVIIe et XVIIIe siècles." In *Guerre et paix en Nouvelle-France,* edited by Alain Beaulieu. Ste-Foy, QC: Les Éditions Gid, 2003.

Fernandez-Armesto, Felipe. *Before Columbus: Exploration and Colonization from the Mediterranean to the Atlantic, 1229–1492.* Philadelphia: University of Pennsylvania Press, 1987.

– *The Canary Islands after the Conquest: The Making of a Colonial Society in the Early Sixteenth Century.* New York: Oxford University Press, 1982.

Fernandez de Navarrete, Martin, ed. *Colección de los Viages y descubrimientos que hicieron por mar los Españoles desde fines del siglo XV, con varios documentos inéditos concern. Á la historia de la marina Castellana y de los establecimientos españoles en Indias,* 5 vols. Madrid: Imprenta nacional, 1837–1880.

Ferris, Neal. *The Archaeology of Native-Lived Colonialism: Challenging History in the Great Lakes.* Tucson: The University of Arizona Press, 2009.

Fewkes, Jesse Walter. *Antiquities of the Mesa Verde National Park Spruce-Tree House.* Bureau of American Ethnology, Bulletin 41. Washington: Smithsonian Institution: 1909.

Fitzgerald, William. "Chronology to Cultural Process: lower Great Lakes Archaeology, 1500–1650." PhD diss., McGill University, 1990.

Fitzhugh, William. "After Red Bay: A Basque and Inuit Joint Venture on the Quebec
Lower North Shore." *Revue internationale des études basques* 59, 2 (2014): 320–48.

– "The Inuit archaeology of the Quebec Lower North Shore." *Études Inuit Studies*
39, no. 1 (2015): 37–62.

Fitzhugh, William, and Elizabeth Ward, eds. *Vikings: The North American Saga.*
Washington: Smithsonian Institution, 2000.

Flegontov, Pavel, N. Ezgi Altını ık, Piya Changmai, Nadin Rohland, Swapan
Mallick, Nicole Adamski, Deborah A. Bolnick, Nasreen Broomandkoshtbacht,
Francesca Candilio, Brendan J. Culleton, Olga Flegontova, T. Max Friesen, et al.
"Palaeo-Eskimo Genetic Ancestry and the Peopling of Chukotka and North
America." *Nature* 570 (June 2019): 236–40.

Flegontov, Pavel, N. Ezgi Altını ık, Piya Changmai, Nadin Rohland, Swapan
Mallick, Deborah A. Bolnick, Francesca Candilio, Olga Flegontova, Choongwon
Jeong, Thomas K. Harper, Denise Keating, Douglas J. Kennett, et al. *Paleo-Eskimo
Genetic Legacy Across North America.* Cold Spring Harbor: Cold Spring Harbor
Laboratory Press, 2017.

Fleming, R. Harvey, and E.E. Rich, eds. *Minutes of Council, Northern Department
of Rupert Land, 1821–31.* Toronto: Champlain Society, 1940.

Fonteneau, Jean. *La Cosmographie avec l'espère et régime du soleil et du nord par
Jean Fonteneau dit Alfonse de Saintonge.* Edited by Georges Musset. Paris: E.
Leroux, 1904.

Fortescue, Michael, and Edward J. Vajda. *Mid-Holocene Language Connections
between Asia and North America.* Leiden: Koninklijke Brill NV, 2022.

Fox, William. "Ethnogenesis in the Lower Great Lakes and the St. Lawrence
Region." *Ontario Archaeology* 95 (2016): 21–32.

Fox, William A., R.G.V. Hancock, and L.A. Pavlish. "Where East Met West: The
New Copper Culture." *The Wisconsin Archaeologist* 76 no. 3–4 (1995): 269–93.

Frake Charles, O. "Cognitive Maps of Time and Tide among Medieval Seafarers."
Man (London) 20, no. 2 (1985): 254–70.

Franchére, Gabriel. *Journal of a Voyage on the North West Coast of North America
during the Years 1811, 1812, 1813 and 1814.* Toronto: Champlain Society, 2013.

Francis, Daniel, and Toby Morantz. *Partners in Furs: A History of the Fur Trade in
Eastern James Bay, 1600–1870.* Montreal and Kingston: McGill-Queen's University
Press, 1983.

Freeman, M.R. "A Critical Review of Thule Culture and Ecological Adaptation." In *Thule Eskimo Culture: An Anthropological Retrospective*, edited by A.P. McCartney, 278–91. Archaeological Survey of Canada Mercury Series Paper No. 88. Ottawa: National Museum of Man, 1979.

Friesen, T. Max, and Charles D. Arnold. "The Timing of the Thule Migration: New Dates from the Western Canadian Arctic." *American Antiquity* 73, no. 3 (2008): 527–38.

Friesen, T. Max, and Owen K. Mason. "Pan-Arctic Population Movements: The Early Paleo-Inuit and Thule Inuit Migrations." In *The Oxford Handbook of the Prehistoric Arctic*, edited by T. Max Friesen and Owen K. Mason, 673–92. Oxford: Oxford University Press, 2016.

Fromhold, Joachim. *Western Cree (Pakisimotan Wi Iniwak) – the Canoecree, 1650–1770*. Morrisville, North Carolina: Lulu Press, 2010.

Frye, Northrop. *The Stubborn Structure: Essays on Criticism and Society*. Ithaca: Cornell University Press, 1970.

Fuller, Mary C. "Arthur and Amazons: Editing the Fabulous in Hakluyt's Principal Navigations." Special issue on Travel and Prose Fiction in Early Modern England, edited by Nandini Das. *The Yearbook of English Studies* 41, no. 1 (2011): 173–89.

– *Lines Drawn Across the Globe: Reading Richard Hakluyt's "Principal Navigations."* Montreal and Kingston: McGill-Queens University Press, 2023.

– "Missing Terms in English Geographical Thinking, 1550–1600." In *The State of Nature: Histories of an Idea*, edited by Mark Somos and Anne Peters, 28–60. Leiden and Boston: Brill, 2022.

– *Remembering the Early Modern Voyage: English Narratives in the Age of European Expansion*. New York: Palgrave Macmillan, 2008.

– "Richard Hakluyt's Foreign Relations." In *Travel Writing, Form, and Empire: The Poetics and Politics of Mobility*, edited by Julia Kuehn and Paul Smethurst, 38–52. New York: Routledge, 2009.

– *Voyages in Print: English Voyages to America 1576–1624*. Cambridge: Cambridge University Press, 1995.

Furst, Benjamin. "Suivre la voie fluviale. Politiques environnementales au Canada sous le régime français (1663–1760)." *Études rurales* 203 (2019): 62–81.

Gagnon, François-Marc. *Images du castor canadien, XVIIe–XVIIIe siècles*. Sillery: Septentrion, 1994.

Gagnon, François-Marc, Camille Létourneau, and Jean-Paul Baril. "La peinture des années trente au Québec / Painting in Quebec in the Thirties." *Journal of Canadian Art History / Annales d'histoire de l'art Canadien* 3, no. 1/2 (1976): 2–20.

Gallo, Tiziana. "Analyse comparative des témoins céramiques du site DcEp-2 et de la station A du site DcEp-5 à l'Anse à la Croix." Report on file, Département d'anthropologie, Université de Montréal, Montreal, 2013.

Gange, David. *The Frayed Atlantic Edge: A Historian's Journey from Shetland to the Channel*. Glasgow: William Collins, 2019.

Garcia, C.M. "Nuevos datos sobre bastimentos y envases en armadas y flotas de la carrera." *Revista de Indias* 64, no. 231 (2004): 447–84.

Gardiner, Mark. "The Character of Commercial Fishing in Icelandic Waters in the Fifteenth Century." In *Cod and Herring: The Archaeology and History of Medieval Sea Fishing*, edited by David Orton and James H. Barrett, 80–90. Oxford: Oxbow Books, 2016.

Gardiner, Mark, and Natascha Mehler. "English and Hanseatic Trading and Fishing Sites in Medieval Iceland: Report on Initial Fieldwork." *Germania* 85, no. 2 (2007): 385–427.

Gates, Charles M., ed. *Five Fur Traders of the Northwest: Being the Narrative of Peter Pond and the Diaries of John Macdonell, Archibald N. McLeod, Hugh Faries, and Thomas Connor*. St Paul: Minnesota Historical Society, 1933.

Gates St-Pierre, Christian. "Iroquoians in the St. Lawrence River Valley Before European Contact." *Ontario Archaeology* 96 (2016): 47–64.

– *Potières du Buisson. La céramique de tradition Melocheville sur le site Hector-Trudel*. Ottawa: University of Ottawa Press, 2006.

Gaudreau, Nathalie. "Stratégies de subsistance et identité culturelle des occupants de Seal Islands (FaAw-5) au Labrador méridional entre 1760 et 1820." MA thesis, département d'anthropologie, Université Laval, Quebec, 2011.

Gerbi, Antonello. *The Dispute of the New World: The History of a Polemic, 1750–1900*. Pittsburgh: University of Pittsburgh Press, 1973.

Gervais, Mélanie J. "If These Pots Could Talk: French Stoneware in Eastern Canada, circa 1540–1760." In *Tu sais, mon vieux Jean-Pierre: Essays on the Archaeology and History of New France and Canadian Culture in Honour of Jean-Pierre Chrestien*, edited by John Willis, 177–206. Ottawa: University of Ottawa Press, 2017.

Gespe'gewa'gi Mi'gmawei Mawiomi. *Nta'tugwaquanminen - Notre histoire. L'évolution des Mi'gmaqs de Gespe'gewa'gi*. Ottawa: Presses de l'Université d'Ottawa, 2018.

Gettler, Brian. *Colonialism's Currency: Money, State, and First Nations in Canada, 1820–1950*. Montreal and Kingston: McGill-Queen's University Press, 2020.

Gibson, James R., ed. *"Opposition on the Coast": The Hudson's Bay Company, American Coasters, the Russian-American Company, and Native Traders on the Northwest Coast, 1825–1846*. Toronto: The Champlain Society, 2019.

Gilbert, Humphrey. *A Discourse of a Discoverie for a New Passage to Cataia*. London, 1576.

Gilbert, M. Thomas P., Toomas Kivisild, Bjarne Grønnow, Pernille K. Andersen, Ene Metspalu, Maere Reidla, Erika Tamm, Erik Axelsson, Anders Götherström, Paula F. Campos, Morten Rasmussen, et al. "Paleo-Eskimo mtDNA Genome Reveals Matrilineal Discontinuity in Greenland." *Science* 320 no. 5884 (June 2008): 1787–9.

Gillis, John R. *Islands of the Mind: How the Human Imagination Created the Atlantic World*. New York: Palgrave Macmillan, 2004.

Gilmore, Kevin, John W. Ives and Derek Hamilton. "Franktown Cave, Colorado: A Promontory Culture Site on the Western Margin of the Great Plains." In *Holes in Our Moccasins, Holes in Our Stories. New Insights into Apachean Origins from the Promontory, Franktown, and Dismal River Archaeological Records*, edited by John W. Ives and Joel C. Janetski, 201–24. Salt Lake City: University of Utah Press, 2022.

Gilroy, Paul. *The Black Atlantic: Modernity and Double Consciousness*. Cambridge, MA: Harvard University Press, 1993.

Gimlette, John. *Theatre Of Fish: Travels through Newfoundland and Labrador*. New York: Knopf, 2005.

Giroux, Dalie. "Dette et colonisation. Analyse de quelques dispositifs de capture du travail indigène dans la traite des fourrures – XVIIe-XIXe siècles." *Politique et Sociétés* 37, no. 1 (2018): 133–56.

Goddard, Pliny E. "The Beaver Indians." *Anthropological Papers of the American Museum of Natural History* 10 (1916): 202–93.

Godinho, Vitorino Magalhães. *Os Descobrimentos e a economia mundial*. Lisbon: Editorial Presença, 1981.

Goldberg, Elizabeth A., Katherine J. Latham, and Edward A. Jolie. "The Local and the Distant Reflected in the Perishable Technologies from the Promontory Caves." In *Holes in Our Moccasins, Holes in Our Stories. New Insights into Apachean Origins from the Promontory, Franktown, and Dismal River Archaeological Records*, edited by John W. Ives and Joel C. Janetski, 163–77. Salt Lake City: University of Utah Press, 2022.

Gordon, Alan. "Heroes, History, and Two Nationalisms: Jacques Cartier." *Journal of the Canadian Historical Association/Revue de la Société historique du Canada* 10 (1999): 81–102.

Gordon, Bryan C. "The White River Ash Fall: Migration Trigger or Localized Event?" *Revista de Arqueología Americana* 30 (2012): 91–102.

Gosselin, Édouard-Hyppolite. *Nouvelles Glanes historiques normandes.* Rouen: Imprimerie de H. Boissel, 1873.

Grabowski, Jan. "French Criminal Justice and Indians in Montreal, 1670–1760." *Ethnohistory* 43 (1996): 405–29.

– "Le 'petit commerce' entre les Trifluviens et les amérindiens en 1665–1667." *Recherches Amérindiennes au Québec* 28 (1998): 105–21.

Graeber, David. *Debt : The First 5,000 Years.* Brooklyn, NY: Melville House, 2011.

Graham, Alan. "The Tertiary History of the Northern Temperate Element in the Latin American Biota." *American Journal of Botany* 86, no.1 (1999): 32–8.

Granger, Joseph E. Jr. *Meadowood Phase Settlement Pattern in the Niagara Frontier Region of Western New York State.* Anthropological Papers, Museum of Anthropology, University of Michigan No. 65. Ann Arbor, MI: Museum of Anthropology, 1978.

Green, Toby. *A Fistful of Shells: West Africa from the Rise of the Slave Trade to the Age of Revolution.* Chicago: University of Chicago Press, 2019.

Greene, Jack P., and Philip D. Morgan, eds. *Atlantic History: A Critical Appraisal.* Oxford: Oxford University Press, 2011.

Greer, Allan. "Canadian History: Ancient and Modern." *Canadian Historical Review* 77 (December 1996): 575–90.

– "La pêche, les communs maritimes et l'empire français en Amérique du Nord." In *La Nature en commun: Ressources, environnement et communautés (France et empire français XVIIe–XXIe siècles)*, edited by Fabien Locher, 169–86. Paris: Champ Vallon, 2020.

– *Peasant, Lord, and Merchant: Rural Society in Three Quebec Parishes, 1740–1840.* Toronto: University of Toronto Press, 1985.

– *The People of New France.* Toronto: University of Toronto Press, 1997.

– *Property and Dispossession: Natives, Empires and Land in Early Modern North America.* Cambridge: Cambridge University Press, 2018.

– "Settler Colonialism and Beyond." *Journal of the Canadian Historical Association* 30 (2020): 61–86.

– "Settler Colonialism and Empire in Early America." *William and Mary Quarterly*, third ser., vol. 76 (July 2019): 383–90.

Gregory, Chris A. *Gifts and Commodities*. London: Academic Press, 1982.

Grenier, Robert, Willis Stevens, and Marc-André Bernier, eds. *The Underwater Archaeology of Red Bay: Basque Shipbuilding and Whaling in the 16th century*, 5 vols. Ottawa: Parks Canada, 2007.

Grier, Colin. "The Organization of Production in Prehistoric Thule Whaling Societies of the Central Canadian Arctic." *Canadian Journal of Archaeology* 23, no. 1–2 (1999): 11–28.

Guimont, Jacques. *La Petite Ferme du cap Tourmente, un établissement agricole tricentenaire: De la ferme de Champlain aux grandes volées d'oies*. Sillery: Les Éditions du Septentrion, 1996.

Habib, Imtiaz. *Black lives in the English archives, 1500–1677: Imprints of the Invisible*. London: Routledge, 2008.

Hakluyt, Richard. *Divers Voyages*. London, 1582.

– *A Particuler Discourse Concerninge the Greate Necessitie and Manifolde Commodyties That Are like to Growe to This Realme of Englande by the Westerne Discoueries Lately Attempted, Written in the Yere 1584*, edited by David B. Quinn and Alison M. Quinn. London: Hakluyt Society, 1993.

– *The Principall Navigations, Voiages and Discoveries of the English Nation*. London, 1589.

– *The Principal Navigations, Voyages, Traffiques and Discoveries of the English Nation*, 3 vols. London: Bishop, Newberrie and Barker: 1598–1600.

Hakluyt, Richard, and Edmund Goldsmid. *The Principal Navigations, Voyages, Traffiques, and Discoveries of the English Nation*, 16 vols. Edinburgh: E. & G. Goldsmid, 1885–90.

Hale, Horatio. *Ethnography and Philology*, vol. 6 of *United States Exploring Expedition Under the Command of Charles Wilkes, U.S.N.* Philadelphia: Lea and Blanchard, 1846.

Hall, D. "Paleoenvironments, the Tsini'Tsini Site, and Nuxalk Oral History." In *Archaeology of Coastal British Columbia: Essays in Honour of Professor Philip M. Hobler*, edited by Roy L. Carlson and Philip M. Hobler, 13–28. Burnaby, BC: Department of Archaeology, Simon Fraser University, 2003.

Hall, Kim F. *Things of Darkness: Economies of Race and Gender in Early Modern England*. Ithaca, NY: Cornell University Press, 1998.

Hallson, Jennifer, and Courtney Lakevold. "Predicting Group Size and Structure Using Multiple Methods at Promontory Cave 1, Utah." In *Holes in Our Moccasins, Holes in Our Stories. New Insights into Apachean Origins from the Promontory,*

Franktown, and Dismal River Archaeological Records, edited by John W. Ives and Joel C. Janetski, 118–33. Salt Lake City: University of Utah Press, 2022.

Halsey, John R. "Without Forge or Crucible: Aboriginal Native American Use of Metals and Metallic Ores in the Eastern Woodlands." *The Michigan Archaeologist* 42, no. 1 (1996): 1–58.

Hämäläinen, Pekka, and Samuel Truett. "On Borderlands." *Journal of American History* 98, no. 2 (September 2011): 338–61.

Hammer, Paul. "Myth-Making: Politics, Propaganda and the Capture of Cadiz in 1596." *The Historical Journal* 40, no. 3 (1997): 621–42.

Hammill, Faye. "'Death by Nature': Margaret Atwood and Wilderness Gothic." *Gothic Studies* 5, no. 2 (2003): 47–63.

Hammond, G.P., and A. Rey. *Narrative of the Coronado Expedition 1540–1542*. Albuquerque: University of New Mexico Press, 1940.

Hanks, Christopher. "The Swampy Cree and the Hudson's Bay Company at Oxford House." *Ethnohistory* 29, no. 2 (Spring 1982) 103–15.

Hansen, Valerie. *The Year 1000: When Explorers Connected the World – and Globalization Began*. New York: Scribner, 2020.

Hare, P. Gregory, Christian D. Thomas, T.N. Topper, and Ruth M. Gotthardt. "The Archaeology of Yukon Ice Patches: New Artifacts, Observations, and Insights." *Arctic* 65 (Suppl. 1) (2012): 118–35.

Harris, Heather, and Kii7iljuus. "Tllsda Xaaydas K'aaygang.Nga: Long, Long Ago Haida Ancient Stories." In *Haida Gwaii: Human History and Environment from the Time of Loon to the Time of the Iron People*, edited by Daryl Fedje and Rolf W. Mathewes, 121–39. Pacific Rim Archaeology. Vancouver: UBC Press, 2005.

Harris, R. Cole, ed. *Historical Atlas of Canada*, 3 vols. Toronto: University of Toronto Press, 1987–93.

– *The Reluctant Land: Society, Space, and Environment in Canada before Confederation*. Vancouver: UBC Press, 2008.

– "The Saint Lawrence: River and Sea." *Cahiers de Géographie de Québec* 23 (1967): 171–9.

– *The Seigneurial System in Early Canada; a Geographical Study*. Madison: University of Wisconsin Press, 1966.

– "Strategies of Power in the Cordilleran Fur Trade." In *The Resettlement of British Columbia: Essays on Colonialism and Geographical Change*, 31–67. Vancouver: UBC Press, 1997.

Harris, R. Cole, and John Warkentin. *Canada before Confederation: A Study in Historical Geography.* Montreal and Kingston: McGill-Queen's University Press, 1974.

Harris, Ryan, and Brad Loewen. "A Basque Whaleboat: Chalupa no. 1." In *The Underwater Archaeology of Red Bay. Basque Shipbuilding and Whaling in the 16th Century*, edited by R. Grenier, M.-A. Bernier, and W. Stevens, vol. 4: 309–80. Ottawa: Parks Canada, 2007.

Harrisse, Henry. *Les Corte-Reals et leurs voyages au Nouveau-Monde.* Paris E. Leroux, 1883.

– *Découverte et évolution cartographique de Terre-Neuve.* Paris and London: H. Welter and Henry Stevens, Son & Stiles, 1900.

Hart, John P., Jennifer Birch, and Christian Gates St-Pierre. "Effects of Population Dispersal on Regional Signalling Networks: An Example from Northern Iroquoia." *Science Advances* 3 (2017): e1700497.

Hart, John P., and William A. Lovis. "Reevaluating What We Know about the Histories of Maize in Northeastern North America: A Review of Current Evidence." *Journal of Archaeological Research* 21, no. 2 (2013): 175–216.

Hart, John P., Susan Winchell-Sweeney, and Jennifer Birch. "An Analysis of Network Brokerage and Geographic Location in Fifteenth-Century AD Northern Iroquoia." *PLOS ONE* 14 no. 1 (2019): e0209689.

Hartery, Latonia. "The Cow Head Complex." MA thesis, University of Calgary, 2001.

Harvey, Barbara. *Living and Dying in England 1100–1540: The Monastic Experience.* Oxford: Clarendon Press, 1993.

Hatt, Gudmund. "Moccasins and Their Relation to Arctic Footwear." *Memoirs of the American Anthropological Association* 3, no. 3 (1916): 149–250.

Havard, Gilles. *Histoire des coureurs de bois: Amérique du Nord, 1600–1840.* Paris: Indes savantes, 2016.

Heidenreich, Conrad. *Huronia: A History and Geography of the Huron Indians, 1600–1650.* Toronto: McClelland and Stewart, 1971.

Heijmans, Elisabeth. *The Agency of Empire: Connections and Strategies in French Overseas Expansion (1686–1746).* Boston: Brill, 2019.

Henday, Anthony. *A Year Inland: The Journal of a Hudson's Bay Company Winterer.* Edited by Barbara Belyea. Waterloo, ON: Wilfrid Laurier University Press, 2001.

Hennepin, Louis. *Nouvelle découverte d'un tres grand pays situe dans l'Amérique, entre le Nouveau Mexique, et la mer glaciale.* Utrecht: Broedelet, Willem, 1697.

Henry, Alexander. *The Journal of Alexander Henry the Younger, 1799–1814.* Edited by Barry M. Gough. 2 vols. Toronto: Champlain Society, 1988.

Herzog, Tamar. *Frontiers of Possession: Spain and Portugal in Europe and the Americas.* Cambridge, MA: Harvard University Press, 2015.

Hewitt, Godfrey. "The Genetic Legacy of the Quaternary Ice Ages." *Nature* 405, no. 6789 (2000): 903–13.

Hickerson, Harold. "Fur Trade Colonialism and the North American Indian." *The Journal of Ethnic Studies* 1, no. 2 (Summer 1973): 15–44.

Histoire de l'Académie royale des sciences avec les mémoires de mathématique & de physique, pour la même année. Paris: La Compagnie des Libraires, 1666–69, 1702–97.

Hocquet, Jean-Claude. "Pêcheurs, hôtes et seigneurs." In *Histoire des pêches maritimes en France,* edited by Michel Mollat, 95-129. Toulouse: Privat, 1987.

Hodder, Ian. *Theory and Practice in Archaeology.* London; New York: Routledge, 1995.

Holm, Poul. "Climate Change, Big Data and the Medieval and Early Modern." In *Medieval or Early Modern: The Value of a Traditional Historical Division,* edited by Ronald Hutton, 70–84. Cambridge: Cambridge Scholars Publishing, 2015.

– *The North Atlantic Fisheries, 1100-1976: National Perspectives on a Common Resource.* Esbjerg: Fiskeri- og Søfartsmuseet, 1996.

Holm, Poul, Francis Ludlow, Cordula Scherer, Charles Travis, Bernard Allaire, Cristina Brito, Patrick W. Hayes, J. Al Matthews, Kieran J. Rankin, Richard J. Breen, Robert Legg, Kevin Lougheed, and John Nicholls. "The North Atlantic Fish Revolution (Ca. AD 1500)." *Quaternary Research* 98 (April 2019): 92–106.

Holm, Poul, John Nicholls, Patrick W Hayes, Josh Ivinson, and Bernard Allaire. "Accelerated Extractions of North Atlantic Cod and Herring, 1520–1790." *Fish and Fisheries* 23 (August 2021): 54–72.

Holyoke, Kenneth R. "Late Maritime Woodland Lithic Technology in the Lower Saint John River Valley." MA thesis, Department of Anthropology, University of New Brunswick, 2012.

Horodowich, Elizabeth. *Venetian Discovery of America: Geographic Imagination in the Age of Encounters.* Cambridge: Cambridge University Press, 2018.

Howley, James P. *The Beothucks or Red Indians, The Aboriginal Inhabitants of Newfoundland.* Cambridge: Cambridge University Press, 1915.

Hu, Di. "Approaches to the Archaeology of Ethnogenesis: Past and Emergent Perspectives." *Journal of Archaeological Research* 21 (2013): 371–402.

Hudson, Benjamin, ed. *Studies in the Medieval Atlantic.* New York: Palgrave Macmillan, 2012.

Huebner, J.A. "Late Prehistoric Bison Populations in Central and Southern Texas." *Plains Anthropologist* 36, no. 137 (1990): 343–58.

Hughes, Richard E., Phil R. Geib, and Courtney L.C. Ziska. "Investigating Dismal River Obsidian Use in Central Nebraska." *Plains Anthropologist* 64, no. 251 (2019): 257–74.

Hughes, Thomas L. "'The German Discovery of America': A Review of the Controversy over Pining's 1473 Voyage of Exploration." *German Studies Review* (2004): 503–26.

Humphries, Mark Osborne. "Working the Short-Haul Fur Trade: Voyageurs and the Family Economy at St-Benoît, 1796–1821." *Histoire Sociale / Social History* 54 (2021): 17–41.

Hurly, Jane. "Sleeping Bags, S'mores and the Great Outdoors: The Role of Nature-Based Leisure in Refugee Integration in Canada." MA thesis: Royal Roads University, 2015.

Huron, Ryan. "Historical Roots of Canadian Aboriginal and Non-Aboriginal Maple Practices." MA thesis: Wilfrid Laurier University, 2014.

Hutchinson, S.J., P.B. Hamilton, R.T. Patterson, J.M. Galloway, N.A. Nasser, C. Spence, and H. Falck. "Diatom Ecological Response to Deposition of the 833–850 CE White River Ash (East Lobe) Ashfall in a Small Subarctic Canadian Lake." *PeerJ* 7 (2019): e6269.

Huxley, Michael Barkham. "La Industria pesquera en el País Vasco peninsular al principio de la Edad Moderna: Una Edad de Oro." *Itsas Memoria. Revista de estúdios marítmos del País Vasco* 3 (2000): 29–75.

Ignace, Marianne, and Ronald Eric Ignace. *Secwépemc people, land, and laws = Yerí7 re Stsq'ey's-kucw.* Montreal and Kingston: McGill-Queen's University Press, 2017.

Innis, Harold A. *The Cod Fisheries: The History of an International Economy,* revised ed. Toronto: University of Toronto Press, 1954.

– *The Fur Trade in Canada.* New Haven, CT: Yale University Press, 1930.

– ed. *Select Documents in Canadian Economic History 1497-1783.* Toronto: University of Toronto Press, 1929.

Isham, James. *James Isham's Observations on Hudsons Bay, 1743, and Notes and Observations on a Book Entitled "A Voyage to Hudsons Bay in the Dobbs Galley," 1749.* Toronto: Champlain Society, 2013.

Ives, John W. "Alberta, Athapaskans and Apachean Origins." In *Archaeology in Alberta: a View from the New Millennium,* edited by J.W. Brink and J.F. Dormaar, 256–89. Medicine Hat, Alberta: Archaeological Society of Alberta, 2003.

– "Dene-Yeniseian, Migration, and Prehistory." In *The Dene-Yeniseian Connection*, edited by J. Kari and B. Potter, 324–34. Anthropological Papers of the University of Alaska: New Series 5. Fairbanks, AK: Department of Anthropology and Alaska Native Language Center, 2010.

– "Developmental Processes in the Pre-contact History of Athapaskan, Algonquian, and Numic Kin Systems." In *Transformations of Kinship*, edited by Maurice Godelier, Thomas R. Trautmann, and Franklin E. Tjon Sie Fat, 94–139. Washington: Smithsonian Institution Press, 1998.

– "Early Human History of the Birch Mountains." In *Alberta's Lower Athabasca Basin: Archaeology and Palaeoenvironments*, edited by Brian M. Ronaghan, 285–330. Edmonton: Athabasca University Press, 2017.

– "Resolving the Promontory Culture Enigma." In *Archaeology in the Great Basin and Southwest: Papers in Honor of Don D. Fowler*, edited by Nancy J. Parezo and Joel C. Janetski, 149–62. Salt Lake City: University of Utah Press, 2014.

– "Seeking Congruency – Search Images, Archaeological Records, and Apachean Origins." In *Holes in Our Moccasins, Holes in Our Stories. New Insights into Apachean Origins from the Promontory, Franktown, and Dismal River Archaeological Records*, edited by John W. Ives and Joel C. Janetski, 27–42. Salt Lake City: University of Utah Press, 2022.

– *A Theory of Northern Athapaskan Prehistory*. Boulder Colorado/Calgary, Alberta: Westview Press/University of Calgary Press, 1990.

Ives, John W., Michael Billinger, and Erika Sutherland. "The Promontory Moccasins and Footwear Landscapes in Late Period Western North America." In *Holes in Our Moccasins, Holes in Our Stories. New Insights into Apachean Origins from the Promontory, Franktown, and Dismal River Archaeological Records*, edited by John W. Ives and Joel C. Janetski, 85–96. Salt Lake City: University of Utah Press, 2022.

Ives, John W., Duane G. Froese, Joel C. Janetski, Fiona Brock, and Christopher Bronk Ramsey. "A High Resolution Chronology for Steward's Promontory Culture Collections, Promontory Point, Utah." *American Antiquity* 79 (2014): 616–37.

Ives, John W., and Joel C. Janetski. "Ways of Becoming – the Promontory Phenomenon." In *Holes in Our Moccasins, Holes in Our Stories. New Insights into Apachean Origins from the Promontory, Franktown, and Dismal River Archaeological Records*, edited by John W. Ives and Joel C. Janetski, 243–61. Salt Lake City: University of Utah Press, 2022.

Ives, John W., Joel S. Janetski, George R. Chournos. Jennifer Hallson, Lindsay

Johannson, and Gabriel Yanicki. "Promontory Revisited." In *Holes in Our Moccasins, Holes in Our Stories. New Insights into Apachean Origins from the Promontory, Franktown, and Dismal River Archaeological Records*, edited by John W. Ives and Joel C. Janetski, 57–81. Salt Lake City: University of Utah Press, 2022.

Jackson, Gordon. *The British Whaling Trade*. Oxford: Oxford University Press, 2017.

Jackson, Victoria. "Silent Diplomacy: Wendat Boys' 'Adoptions' at the Jesuit Seminary, 1636–1642." *Journal of the Canadian Historical Association / Revue de la Société historique du Canada* 27, 1 (2016): 139–68.

Jaramillo-Correa, Juan P., Jean Beaulieu, Damase P. Khasa, and Jean Bousquet. "Inferring the Past from the Present Phylogeographic Structure of North American Forest Trees: Seeing the Forest for the Genes." *Canadian Journal of Forest Research* 39, no. 2 (2009): 286–307.

James, Alan. *The Navy and Government in Early Modern France, 1572–1661*. London and Rochester, NY: Royal Historical Society and Boydell Press, 2004.

Jardine, Lisa, and William Sherman. "Pragmatic Readers: Knowledge Transactions and Scholarly Services in Late Elizabethan England." In *Religion, Culture, and Society in Early Modern Britain: Essays in Honour of Patrick Collinson*, edited by Anthony Fletcher and Peter Roberts, 102–24. Cambridge: Cambridge University Press, 1994.

Jensen, Anne M., and Glenn W. Sheehan. "Archaeology of the Late Western Thule/Iñupiat in Northern Alaska (A.D. 1300–1750)." In *The Oxford Handbook of the Prehistoric Arctic*, edited by T. Max Friesen and Owen K. Mason, 513–35. Oxford: Oxford University Press, 2016.

Jensen, Britta J.L., S. Pyne-O'Donnell, G. Plunkett, D.G. Froese, P.D.M. Hughes, M. Sigl, J.R. McConnell, M.J. Amesbury, P.G. Blackwell, C. van de Bogaard, C.E. Buck, D.J. Charman, J.J. Clague, et al. "Transatlantic Distribution of the Alaskan White River Ash." *Geology* 42 (2014): 875–8.

Jérémie, Nicholas. *Twenty Years of York Factory, 1694–1714: Jérémie's Account of Hudson Strait and Bay*, edited by R. Douglas and J.N. Wallace. Ottawa: Thorburn and Abbott, 1926.

Johansson, Lindsay D. "Promontory Culture: The Faunal Evidence." MA thesis, Department of Anthropology, Brigham Young University, 2013.

Johnson, Jessica Marie. *Wicked Flesh: Black Women, Intimacy, and Freedom in the Atlantic World*. Philadelphia: University of Pennsylvania Press, 2020.

Johnson, Lane B., Lee R. Johnson, Evan R. Larson, and Kurt F. Kipfmueller. "Culturally Modified Red Pine, Birch-Bark Canoes, and the Strategic Geography of the Fur Trade on Lake Saganaga, Minnesota, U.S.A." *Historical Archaeology* 52, no. 2 (2018): 281–300.

Jones, Eric E., and John L. Creese, eds. *Process and Meaning in Spatial Archaeology: Investigations into Precolumbian Iroquoian Space and Place.* Boulder: University Press of Colorado, 2016.

Jones, Evan T. "Alwyn Ruddock: 'John Cabot and the Discovery of America.'" *Historical Research* 81 (2008): 224–54.

– "England's Icelandic Fishery in the Early Modern Period." In *England's Sea Fisheries: The Commercial Sea Fisheries of England and Wales since 1300*, edited by Neil Ashcroft, David J. Starkey, and Chris Reid, 105–10. London: Chatham Publishing, 2003.

– "The Matthew of Bristol and the Financiers of John Cabot's 1497 Voyage to North America." *English Historical Review* 121, no. 492 (2006): 778–95.

Jones, Evan T., and Margaret M. Condon. *Cabot and Bristol's Age of Discovery.* Bristol: University of Bristol, 2016.

Jones, Siân. *The Archaeology of Ethnicity: Constructing Identities in the Past and Present.* London: Routledge, 1997.

Jong, Cornelis de. *Geschiedenis Van De Oude Nederlandse Walvisvaart.* 3 vols. Pretoria: University van Suid-Afrika te Pretoria, 1972.

Jordan, Richard and Susan A. Kaplan. "An archaeological view of the Inuit/European Contact Period in Central Labrador." *Études/Inuit/Studies* 4, no. 1–2 (1980): 35–45.

Kaplan, Susan. "Economic and Social Change in Labrador Neo-eskimo Culture." PhD diss., Bryn Mawr College, 1983.

– "European Goods and Socio-Economic Change in Early Labrador Inuit Society." In *Cultures in Contact: The Impact of European Contacts on Native American Cultural Institutions, A.D. 1000–1800*, edited by William W. Fitzhugh, 45–70. Washington: Smithsonian Institution Press, 1985.

– "Labrador Inuit Ingenuity and Resourcefulness: Adapting to a Complex Environmental, Social and Spiritual Environment." In *Settlement, Subsistence and Change Among the Labrador Inuit: The Nunatsiavummiut Experience*, edited by David C. Natcher, Lawrence Felt and Andrea Proctor, 15–42. Winnipeg: University of Manitoba Press, 2012.

Kaplan, Susan A., and James M. Woollett. "Challenges and Choices: Exploring the Interplay Between Climate, History and Culture on Canada's Labrador Coast." *Arctic, Antarctic and Alpine Research* 32 (2000): 351–9.

Karklins, Karlis. "Guide to the Description and Classification of Glass Beads Found in the Americas." *Beads* 24 (2012): 62–90.

Keith, Lloyd ed. *North of Athabasca: Slave Lake and Mackenzie River Documents of the North West Company, 1800–1821*. Montreal and Kingston: McGill-Queen's University Press, 2001.

Kenyon, Ian T., and Thomas Kenyon. "Comments on Seventeenth Century Glass Trade Beads from Ontario." In *Proceedings of the 1982 Glass Trade Bead Conference*, edited by Charles F. Hayes III, 59–74. Rochester, NY: Rochester Museum and Science Center, 1983.

Kerns, Virginia. *Scenes from the High Desert: Julian Steward's Life and Theory*. Urbana and Chicago: University of Illinois Press, 2003.

Kheraj, Sean. *Inventing Stanley Park: An Environmental History*. Vancouver: UBC Press, 2013.

Kidd, Kenneth E., and Martha Ann Kidd. *A Classification System for Glass Beads for the Use of Field Archaeologists*. Ottawa: Canadian Historic Sites, 1970.

King, James C. "Indian Credit as a Source of Friction in the Colonial Fur Trade." *Western Pennsylvania History*, (1966): 57–65.

King, Tiffany Lethabo. *The Black Shoals: Offshore Formations of Black and Native Studies*. Durham, NC: Duke University Press, 2019.

Kintigh, Keith W., and Scott E. Ingram. "Was the Drought Really Responsible? Assessing Statistical Relationships Between Climate Extremes and Cultural Transitions." *Journal of Archaeological Science* 89 (2018): 25–31.

Kleinschmidt, Harald. *Ruling the Waves: Emperor Maximilian I, the Search for Islands and the Transformation of the European World Picture c. 1500*. Goy-Houten: Hes & de Graaf, 2008.

Kocka, Jürgen. *Capitalism: A Short History*. Princeton, NJ: Princeton University Press, 2015.

Kohler, Timothy A., Scott G. Ortman, Katie E. Grundtisch, Carly M. Fitzpatrick, and Sarah M. Cole. "The Better Angels of Their Nature: Declining Violence through Time Among Prehispanic Farmers of the Pueblo Southwest." *American Antiquity* 79, no. 3 (2014): 444–64.

Kolodny, Annette. *In Search of First Contact: The Vikings of Vinland, the Peoples of the Dawnland, and the Anglo-American Anxiety of Discovery*. Durham, NC: Duke University Press, 2012.

Krauss, Michael E., and Victor Golla. "Northern Athapaskan Languages." In *Handbook of North American Indians*, vol. 6, *Subarctic*, edited by June Helm, 67–85. Washington: Smithsonian Institution Press, 1981.

Krech III, Shepard. *The Subarctic Fur Trade: Native Social and Economic Adaptations.* Vancouver: UBC Press, 1984.

– "The Trade of the Slavey and Dogrib at Fort Simpson in the Early Nineteenth Century." In *The Subarctic Fur Trade: Native Social and Economic Adaptations,* 99–146. Vancouver: UBC Press, 1984.

Kristensen, Todd J., Alwynne B. Beaudoin, and John W. Ives. "Environmental and Hunter-Gatherer Responses to a Volcanic Eruption in the Late Holocene Canadian Subarctic." *Arctic* 73, no. 2 (2020): 153–86.

Kristensen, Todd J., Gregory Hare, Ruth Gotthardt, Norman Easton, John W. Ives, Robert Speakman, and Jeff Rasic. "The Movement of Obsidian in Subarctic Canada: Hunter-Gatherer Social Networks and Responses to a Large Scale Volcanic Eruption." *Journal of Anthropological Archaeology* 56 (2019): 1–18.

Kristensen, Todd J., John W. Ives, and Kisha Supernant. "Power, Security, and Exchange: Impacts of a Late Holocene Volcanic Eruption in Subarctic North America." *North American Archaeologist* 42, 4 (2021): 425–72.

Kristensen, Todd J., Thomas D. Andrews, Glen MacKay, Ruth Gotthardt, Sean C. Lynch, M. John M. Duke, Andrew J. Locock, and John W. Ives. "Identifying and Sourcing Pyrometamorphic Artifacts: Clinker in Subarctic North America and the Hunter-Gatherer Response to a Late Holocene White River Ash East Volcanic Eruption." *Journal of Archaeological Science Reports* 23 (2018): 773–90.

Kuhn, T.S., K.A. McFarlane, P. Groves, A.O. Mooers, and B. Shapiro. "Modern and Ancient DNA Reveal Recent Partial Replacement of Caribou in the Southwest Yukon." *Molecular Ecology* 19, no. 7 (2010): 1312–23.

Kuitems, Margot, Birgitta L. Wallace, Charles Lindsay, Andrea Scifo, Petra Doeve, Kevin Jenkins, Susanne Lindauer, et al. "Evidence for European Presence in the Americas in AD 1021." *Nature* 601 (20 October 2021): 1–4.

Lacasse, Jean-Paul. *Les Innus et le territoire Innu Tipenitamun.* Québec: Septentrion, 2004.

Lainey, Jonathan C. *La 'monnaie des sauvages:' Les colliers de wampum d'hier à aujourd'hui.* Québec: Septentrion, 2004.

Langevin, Érik. "Un fjord, une rivière, un lac et des ruisseaux: variabilité culturelle paléohistorique sur le bassin hydrographique de la rivière Saguenay (Québec, Canada)." PhD diss., Université de Montréal, 2015.

Laudonnière, René de. *L'Histoire Notable de La Floride.* Paris, 1586.

– *A Notable Historie Containing Foure Voyages [...] unto Florida.* Translated by Richard Hakluyt. London, 1578.

La Vérendrye, Pierre Gaultier de Varennes. *Journals and Letters of Pierre Gaultier de Varennes de La Vérendrye and His Sons: With Correspondence between the Governors of Canada and the French Court, Touching the Search for the Western Sea.* Edited by Lawrence J. Burpee. Toronto: Champlain Society, 1927.

Laverdière, Charles-Honoré, ed. *Œuvres de Champlain*, 3 vols. Quebec City: Georges-Édouard Desbarats, 1870.

Le Blant, Robert. "La Compagnie de la Nouvelle-France et la restitution de l'Acadie (1627–1636)." *Revue d'histoire des colonies* 42 (1955): 69–93.

Le Blant, Robert, and René Baudry, eds. *Nouveaux documents sur Champlain et son époque.* Ottawa: Archives publiques du Canada, 1967.

LeBreton, Clarence, and Fidèle Thériault. *À la découverte de l'île de Caraquet.* Tracadie, NB: La Grande Marée, 2017.

LeClercq, Chrestien. *Nouvelle relation de la Gaspésie.* Paris: Chez Amable Auroy, 1691.

Lee Johnson, Jennifer. "Eating and Existence on an Island in Southern Uganda." *Comparative Studies of South Asia, Africa and the Middle East* 37 (2017): 2–23.

Lefebvre, Henri. *The Production of Space.* Malden, MA: Blackwell, 2004.

Le Jeune, Paul. *Relation de ce qui s'est passé en la Nouvelle France, en l'année 1633. Envoyée au R.P. Barth. Jacquinot, provincial de la compagnie de Jesus en la Province de France.* Paris: Sébastien Cramoisy, 1634.

– *Relation de ce qui s'est passé en la Nouvelle-France en l'année 1634 / Envoyée au R. Père [Barth. Jacquinot], provincial de la compagnie de Jésus en la Province de France / par le P. Paul le Jeune de la même compagnie, supérieur de la résidence de Kébec.* Paris: Sébastien Cramoisy, 1635.

– *Relation de ce qui s'est passé en la Nouvelle-France en l'année 1636/ Envoyée au R. Père provincial de la compagnie de Jésus en la Province de France / par le P. Paul le Jeune de la même compagnie, supérieur de la résidence de Kébec.* Paris: Sébastien Cramoisy, 1637.

– *Relation de ce qui s'est passé en la Nouvelle-France en l'année 1637/ Envoyée au R. Père Provincial De La Compagnie De Jésus En La Province De France / par le P. Paul le Jeune de la même compagnie, supérieur de la résidence de Kébec.* Rouen: Jean le Boulanger, 1638.

– *Relation de ce qui s'est passé en la Nouvelle-France en l'année 1638/ Envoyée au R. Père Provincial de la Compagnie de Jésus en la province de France/ par le P. Paul le Jeune de la même compagnie, supérieur de la résidence de Kébec.* Paris: Sébastien Cramoisy, 1638.

– *Relation de ce qui s'est passé en la Nouvelle-France en l'année 1639/ Envoyée au R. Père Provincial de la Compagnie de Jésus en la province De France / par le P. Paul le Jeune de la même compagnie, supérieur de la résidence de Kébec.* Paris: Sébastien Cramoisy, 1640.

Leonard, Kevin J.M. "Mi'kmaq Culture during the Late Woodland and Early Historic Periods." PhD diss., University of Toronto, 1996.

Lerbekmo, J.F. "The White River Ash: Largest Holocene Plinian Tephra." *Canadian Journal of Earth Sciences* 45 (2008): 693–700.

Léry, Jean de. *Histoire d'un voyage fait en la terre du Bresil, autrement dite Amerique.* La Rochelle, 1578.

Lescarbot, Marc. *Histoire de la Nouvelle France: contenant les navigations, découvertes, & habitations faites par les François és Indes Occidentales & Nouvelle-France souz l'avœu & authorité de noz Rois Tres-Chrétiens, & les diverses fortunes d'iceux en l'execution de ces choses, depuis cent ans jusques à hui : en quoy est comprise l'histoire morale, naturelle, & géographique de ladite province : avec les tables et figures d'icelle.* Paris: Chez Jean Milot, 1609.

Lespagnol, André. "État mercantiliste et littoral dans la France des XVIIe–XVIIIe siècles. Une première forme d'aménagement de l'espace littoral." In *Pouvoirs et littoraux du XVe au XXe siècle*, edited by Gérard Le Bouëdec, François Chappé and Christophe Cérino, 349–58. Rennes: Presses universitaires de Rennes, 2000.

Lestringant, Frank. *Le Huguenot et le sauvage: l'Amérique et la controverse coloniale, en France, au temps des guerres de religion (1555–1589).* Genève: Droz, 2004.

"Lettres et Mémoires de François-Madeleine-Fortuné Ruette d'Auteuil, procureur général du conseil souverain de la Nouvelle-France." In *Rapport de l'archiviste de la province de Québec,* 1922–23, 1–114. Quebec City: Ls-A. Proulx, 1923.

Li, Jianhua, Mark Stukel, Parker Bussies, Kaleb Skinner, Alan R. Lemmon, Emily Moriarty Lemmon, Kenneth Brown, Airat Bekmetjev, Nathan G. Swenson. "Maple Phylogeny and Biogeography inferred from Phylogenetic Data." *Journal of Systematics and Evolution* 57 (2019): 594–606.

Linebaugh, Peter, and Marcus Rediker. *The Many-Headed Hydra: Sailors, Slaves, Commoners, and the Hidden History of the Revolutionary Atlantic.* New York: Beacon Press, 2013.

Lints, Andrew, John W. Ives, and Hilary McDonald. "Art in the Time of Promontory Cave." In *Holes in Our Moccasins, Holes in Our Stories. New Insights into Apachean Origins from the Promontory, Franktown, and Dismal River Archaeological Records,* edited by John W. Ives and Joel C. Janetski, 134–45. Salt Lake City: University of Utah Press, 2022.

Lipman, Andrew. *The Saltwater Frontier: Indians and the Contest for the American Coast.* New Haven, CT: Yale University Press, 2015.

Litalien, Raymonde, Jean-François Palomino, and Denis Vaugeois. *La mesure d'un continent: Atlas historique de l'Amérique du Nord, 1492–1814.* Paris: Presses de l'université de Paris, Sorbonne, 2007.

Loewen, Brad. "Cultural Transmissions of the "Biscayne Shallop" in the Gulf of St. Lawrence, 1560–1750." In *The Archaeology of Vernacular Watercraft*, edited by Amanda M. Evans, 165–87. New York: Springer, 2016.

– "Glass and Enamel Beadmaking in Normandy, circa 1590–1635." *Beads* 31 (2019): 9–20.

– "Intertwined Enigmas: Basques and Iroquoians in the Sixteenth Century." In *Contact in the 16th Century: Networks among Fishers, Farmers and Foragers*, edited by Brad Loewen and Claude Chapdelaine, 57–76. Ottawa: University of Ottawa Press, 2016.

– "Sixteenth Century Beads: New Data, New Directions." In *Contact in the 16th Century: Networks among Fishers, Farmers and Foragers*, edited by Brad Loewen and Claude Chapdelaine, 269–86. Ottawa: University of Ottawa Press, 2016.

– "The World of Capitena Ioannis: Basque and Inuit in the Seventeenth Century." *Canadian Journal of Archaeology* 41, no. 2 (2017): 173–211.

Loewen, Brad, Sarai Barreiro Argüelles, and Catherine Cottreau-Robins. "S'adapter pour rester: continuités basques aux XVIIe et XVIIIe siècles." *Archéologiques* 34 (2021): 1–17.

Loewen, Brad, and Claude Chapdelaine, eds. *Contact in the 16th Century: Networks among Fishers, Foragers, and Farmers.* Mercury Series 176. Gatineau, QC: Ottawa, Ontario: Canadian Museum of History; University of Ottawa Press, 2016.

Loewen, Brad, and Vincent Delmas. "The Basques in the Gulf of St. Lawrence and Adjacent Shores." *Canadian Journal of Archaeology* 36 (2012): 351–404.

– "Les occupations basques dans le golfe du Saint-Laurent, 1530–1760. Périodisation, répartition géographique et culture matérielle." *Archéologiques* 24 (2011): 23–55.

Loewen, Brad, and Miren Egaña Goya. "Un aperçu des Basques dans la baie des Chaleurs. Le routier de Piarres Detcheverry, 1677." *Revue d'histoire de l'Amérique française* 29, no. 1–2 (2014): 125–51.

Lom d'Arce de Lahontan, Louis-Armand de. *Oeuvres complètes.* Montreal: Presses de l'Université de Montréal, 2000.

López Varela, Sandra L. ed. *The Encyclopedia of Archaeological Sciences.* Chichester: Wiley Blackwell, 2018.

Lorenzo d'Anania, Giovanni. *Lo scopremento dello stretto artico.* Naples, 1582.

Loring, Stephen. "Princes and Princesses of Ragged Fame: Innu Archaeology and Ethnohistory in Labrador." PhD diss., University of Massachusetts, Amherst, 1992.

Losier, Catherine, Brad Loewen, and Miren Egaña Goya. "In the Midst of Diversity: Recognizing the Seventeenth-Century Basque Cultural Landscape and Ceramic Identity in Southern Newfoundland and Saint-Pierre-et-Miquelon." *Newfoundland and Labrador Studies,* Papers on the Basques in Newfoundland and Labrador in the Seventeenth Century 33 (2018): 200–36.

Lozier, Jean-François. *Flesh Reborn: The Saint Lawrence Valley Mission Settlements through the Seventeenth Century.* Montreal and Kingston: McGill-Queen's University Press, 2018.

Lucas, Frederick W. *The Voyages of the Brothers Zeni.* London: Henry Stevens Son and Stiles, 1898.

Lucretius. *On the Nature of Things.* Translated by W.H.D. Rouse, revised by Martin F. Smith. Cambridge, MA: Harvard University Press, 1924.

Lynch, James. "The Iroquois Confederacy and the Adoption and Administration of Non-Iroquoian Individuals and Groups Prior to 1756." *Man in the Northeast* 30 (1985): 83–99.

MacDowell, Laurel Sefton. *An Environmental History of Canada.* Vancouver: UBC Press, 2012.

Mackay, Helen, Gill Plunkett, Britta Jensen, Thomas Aubry, Christophe Corona, Woon Mi Kim, Matthew Toohey, Michael Sigl, Markus Stoffel, Kevin Anchukaitis, Christoph Raible, Matthew Bolton, et al. "The 852/3 CE Mount Churchill Eruption: Examining the Potential Climatic and Societal Impacts and the Timing of the Medieval Climate Anomaly in the North Atlantic Region." *Climate of the Past* 18 (2022): 1475–508.

MacMillan, Ken, ed. *John Dee: The Limits of the British Empire.* Westport, CT: Praeger, 2004.

Mailhot, José, J.-P. Simard, and S. Vincent. "On est toujours ''Esquimau de quelqu'un." *Études/Inuit/Studies* 4, no. 1-2 (1980): 59–76.

Mailhot, José, and Sylvie Vincent. "Le droit foncier montagnais." *Interculture,* 15, no. 2–3 (1982): 65–74.

Malainey, Mary E. *A Consumer's Guide to Archaeological Science: Analytical Techniques*. New York: Springer, 2011.

Malhi, R., A. Gonzalez-Oliver, K.B. Schroeder, B.M. Kemp, J.A. Greenberg, S.Z. Dobrowski, D.G. Smith, A. Resendez, T. Karafet, M. Hammer, S. Zegura, T. Brovko. "Distribution of Y Chromosomes Among Native North Americans: A Study of Athapaskan Population History." *American Journal of Physical Anthropology* 137 (2008): 412–24.

Malhi, R.S., H.M. Mortensen, J.A. Eshleman, B.M. Kemp, J.G. Lorenz, F.A. Kaestle, J.R. Johnson, C. Gorodezky, and D.G. Smith. "Native American mtDNA Prehistory in the American Southwest." *American Journal of Physical Anthropology* 120 (2003): 108–24.

Mancall, Peter C. *Deadly Medicine: Indians and Alcohol in Early America*. Ithaca: Cornell University Press, 1995.

– *Hakluyt's Promise: An Elizabethan's Obsession for an English America*. New Haven, CT: Yale University Press, 2007.

Mancke, Elizabeth. "Early Modern Expansion and the Politicization of Oceanic Space." *Geographical Review* 89, no. 2 (1999): 225–36.

– "Empire and State." In *The British Atlantic World, 1500–1800*, 2nd ed., edited by David Armitage and Michael J. Braddick, 193–213. New York: Palgrave Macmillan, 2009.

– "Spaces of Power in the Early Modern Northeast." In *New England and the Maritime Provinces: Connections and Comparisons*, edited by Stephen J. Hornsby and John G. Reid, 32–49. Montreal and Kingston: McGill-Queen's University Press, 2005.

Mancke, Elizabeth, and John G. Reid. "Elites, States, and the Imperial Contest for Acadia." In *The "Conquest" of Acadia, 1710: Imperial, Colonial and Aboriginal Constructions*, edited by John G. Reid, 25–47. Toronto: University of Toronto Press, 2004.

Marius, Johannes, and Johann Francke. *Traité du castor, dans lequel on explique la nature, les propriétés et l'usage médico-chymique du castoreum dans la médecine*. Paris: David, 1746.

Marmol-Caravajal, Luys del. *Descripcion general de Affrica con todos los successos de guerras que a avido entre los infieles y el pueblo christiano ... hasta el ano de 1561*. N.p.: Rene Rabut, 1573.

Markham, Albert Hastings. *The Voyages and Works of John Davis, the Navigator*. London: Hakluyt Society, 1880.

Marques, António Henrique R. de Oliveira. *A Expansão Quatrocentista.* Lisbon: Editorial Estampa, 1998.

Marshall, Ingeborg. "Beothuk and Micmac: Re-examining Relationships." *Acadiensis* 17, 2 (1988): 52–82.

Marsters, Roger. "Approaches to Empire: Hydrographic Knowledge and British State Activity in Northeastern North America, 1711–1783." PhD diss., Dalhousie University, 2012.

Martijn, Charles A. "An Eastern Micmac Domain of Islands." In *Actes du vingtiéme congrés des algonquinistes,* edited by W. Cowan, 208–31. Ottawa: Carleton University Press, 1989.

– "Historic Inuit Presence in Northern Newfoundland Circa 1550-1800 CE." In *Painting the Past with a Broad Brush: Papers in Honour of James Valliere Wright,* edited by David L. Keenleyside and Jean-Luc Pilon, 65–101. Ottawa: University of Ottawa Press, 2009.

– "The Iroquoian Presence in the Estuary and Gulf of St. Lawrence River Valley: A Reevaluation." *Man in the Northeast* 40 (1990): 45–63.

– "La présence inuit sur la Côte-Nord du Golfe St-Laurent á l'époque historique." *Études/Inuit/Studies* 4, no. 1–2 (1980): 105–25.

Martijn, Charles, Selma Huxley Barkham, and Michael M. Barkham. "Basques? Beothuk? Innu? Inuit? or St. Lawrence Iroquoians? The Whalers on the 1546 Desceliers Map, Seen through the Eyes of Different Beholders." *Newfoundland and Labrador Studies,* 19, no. 1 (2003): 187–206.

Martin, Susan R. *Wonderful Power: The Story of Ancient Copper Working in the Lake Superior Basin.* Detroit: Wayne State University Press, 1999.

Martindale, Andrew. "Methodological Issues in the Use of Tsimshian Oral Traditions (Adawx) in Archaeology." *Canadian Journal of Archaeology / Journal Canadien d'Archéologie* 30, no. 2 (2006): 158–92.

Mary-Rousselière, Guy. *Qitdlarssuaq: The Story of a Polar Migration.* Translated by Alan Cooke. Winnipeg: Wuerz, 1991.

Maschner, Herbert, and Owen K. Mason. "The Bow and Arrow in Northern North America." *Evolutionary Anthropology: Issues, News, and Reviews* 22, no. 3 (2013): 133–8.

Mason, Owen. "The Context Between Ipiutak, Old Bering Sea and Birnik Polities and the Origin of Whaling During the First Millennium A.D. along the Bering Strait." *Journal of Anthropological Archaeology* 17 (1998): 240–325.

– "Flight from Bering Strait: Did Siberian Punuk/Thule Military Cadres Conquer

Northwest Alaska?" In *The Northern World* AD *900–1400*, edited by Herbert
Maschner, Owen Mason and Robert McGhee, 76–128. Salt Lake City: University
of Utah Press, 2009.

– "Thule Origins in the Old Bering Sea Culture: The Interrelationship of Punuk
and Birnirk Cultures." In *The Oxford Handbook of the Prehistoric Arctic*, edited by
T. Max Friesen and Owen K. Mason, 489–512. Oxford: Oxford University Press,
2016.

Masson, L.R. *Les bourgeois de la compagnie du Nord-Ouest: récits de voyages, lettres
et rapports inédits relatifs au nord-ouest canadien: publié avec une esquisse historique et des annotations*, 2 vols. Quebec City: A. Coté, 1889.

Mattoso, José. *História De Portugal*. Lisbon: Ed. Estampa, 1993.

Mauss, Marcel. "Essai sur le don: Forme et raison de l'échange dans les sociétés
primitives." *L'Année sociologique*, nouvelle série, 1 (1923–24): 30–186.

Mauss, Marcel. *The Gift*. Translated by Jane I. Guyer. Chicago: Hau Books, 2016.

McCaffrey, Moira. "Inventaire des sites archéologiques préhistoriques des Îles-de-
la-Madeleine, bilan: phase 1 (1988), phase 2 (1989), phase 3 (1990)." Report on file,
MRC des Îles-de-la-Madeleine. Quebec City: Ministère de la Culture et des
Communications, 1993.

McCartney, A.P. *Thule Eskimo Prehistory Along Northwestern Hudson Bay circa
1550–1800 C.E.* Mercury Series Archaeology Paper, No. 70. Ottawa: National
Museum of Man, 1977.

McCormack, Patricia Alice. *Fort Chipewyan and the Shaping of Canadian History,
1788–1920s: "We like to Be Free in This Country."* Vancouver: UBC Press, 2010.

McCusker, John J. "The Business of Distilling in the Old World and the New World
during the Seventeenth and Eighteenth Centuries: The Rise of a New Enterprise
and Its Connection with Colonial America." In *The Early Modern Atlantic Economy*, edited by John J. McCusker and Kenneth Morgan, 186–224. Cambridge:
Cambridge University Press, 2000.

McCusker, John J., and Kenneth Morgan, ed. *The Early Modern Atlantic Economy*.
Cambridge: Cambridge University Press, 2000.

McDermott, James. "The Company of Cathay: The Financing and Organization of
the Frobisher Voyages." In *Meta Incognita: A Discourse of Discovery*, vol. 1: *Martin
Frobisher's Arctic Expeditions, 1576–1578*, edited by Thomas H.B. Symons, Stephen
Alsford, and Chris Kitzan, 146–78. Ottawa: University of Ottawa Press, 1999.

– "Michael Lok, Mercer and Merchant Adventurer." In *Meta Incognita: A Discourse
of Discovery: Martin Frobisher's Arctic Expeditions, 1576–1578*, vol. 1: *Martin Fro-*

bisher's Arctic Expeditions, 1576–1578, edited by Thomas H.B. Symons, Stephen Alsford, and Chris Kitzan, 119–46. Ottawa: University of Ottawa Press, 1999.

– "'A Right Heroicall Heart': Sir Martin Frobisher." In *Meta Incognita: A Discourse of Discovery*, vol. 1: *Martin Frobisher's Arctic Expeditions, 1576–1578*, edited by Thomas H.B. Symons, Stephen Alsford, and Chris Kitzan, 55–118. Ottawa: University of Ottawa Press, 1999.

– *The Third Voyage of Martin Frobisher to Baffin Island 1578*. London: Hakluyt Society, 2001.

McGhee, Robert. *Ancient People of the Arctic*. Vancouver: UBC Press, 1996.

– *Canadian Arctic Prehistory*. Toronto, Van Norstrand Reinhold, 1978.

– *The Last Imaginary Place: A Human History of the Arctic World*. Toronto, Key Porter, 2004.

– "Paleoeskimo Occupations of Central and High Arctic Canada." *Memoirs of the Society for American Archaeology*, no. 31 (1976): 15–39.

– "The Peopling of Arctic Canada." In *Canada's Missing Dimension. Science and History in the Canadian Arctic Islands*, edited by C.R. Harrington, 666–76. Ottawa: Canadian Museum of Nature, 1990.

– "The Population Size and Temporal Duration of Thule Culture in Arctic Canada." In *On the Track of Thule Culture from Bering Strait to East Greenland*, edited by Bjarne Grønnow, 75–89. Copenhagen: National Museum of Denmark, 2009.

– "Radiocarbon Dating and the Timing of the Thule Migration." In *Identities and Cultural Contacts in the Arctic*, edited by Martin Appelt, Joel Berlund, and Hans Christian Gulløv, 181–91. Copenhagen: Danish Polar Center, 2000.

– "The Thule Prehistory of Canada." In *The Handbook of North American Indians*, vol. 5, *Arctic*, edited by David Damas, 369–75. Washington: Smithsonian Institution, 1984.

– "When and Why did the Inuit Move to the Eastern Arctic?" In *The Northern World AD 900–1400*, edited by Herbert Maschner, Owen Mason, and Robert McGhee, 155–63. Salt Lake City: University of Utah Press, 2009.

McGillivray, Duncan. *The Journal of Duncan M'gillivray of the North West Company at Fort George on the Saskatchewan, 1794–5*. Edited by Arthur S. Morton. Toronto: Macmillan Co. of Canada, 1929.

McGrath, Ann, and Mary Anne Jebb, eds. *Long History, Deep Time: Deepening Histories of Place*. Canberra: Australian National University Press, 2015.

McIntyre, Ruth. "William Sanderson: Elizabethan Financier of Discovery." *William and Mary Quarterly*, third series 13, no. 2 (1956): 184–201.

McKay, Ian. "The Liberal Order Framework: A Prospectus for a Reconnaissance of Canadian History." *Canadian Historical Review* 81 (December 2000): 616–45.

McLachlan, Jason S., James S. Clark, and Paul S. Manos. "Molecular Indicators of Tree Migration Capacity Under Rapid Climate Change." *Ecology* 86, no. 8 (2005): 2088–98.

McMillan, A.D. "When the Mountain Dwarfs Danced: Aboriginal Traditions of Paleoseismic Events along the Cascadia Subduction Zone of Western North America." *Ethnohistory* 49, no. 1 (2002): 41–68.

McNeill, J.R. "Peak Document and the Future of History." *American Historical Review* 125 (2020): 1–18.

McNiven, Ian J., and Lynette Russell. *Appropriated Pasts: Indigenous People and the Colonial Culture of Archaeology.* Lanham, MD: AltaMira Press, 2005.

McQuarrie, Aisling. "Running the Rivers: The North West Company and the Creation of a Global Enterprise, 1778–1821." PhD diss., University of Aberdeen, 2014.

Melançon, Robert. "La Nouvelle-France et la littérature." In *Éditer la Nouvelle France*, edited by Andreas Motsch and Grégoire Holtz. Laval: Presses Universitaires de Laval, 2011.

Meltzer, David J. "Was Stone Exchanged Among Eastern North American Paleoindians?" In *Eastern Paleoindian Lithic Resource Use*, edited by C.J. Ellis and J.C. Lothrop, 11–39. Boulder, CO: Westview Press, 1989.

Mensing, Scott, Jeremy Smith, Kelly Burkle Norman, and Marie Allan. "Extended Drought in the Great Basin of Western North America in the Last Two Millennia Reconstructed from Pollen Records." *Quaternary International* 188, no. 1 (2008): 79–89.

Mentz, Steve. *Shipwreck Modernity: Ecologies of Globalization, 1550–1719.* Minneapolis: University of Minnesota Press, 2015.

Mercator, Gerhard. *Atlas sive Cosmographicae meditationes de fabrica mundi et fabricati figura.* Duisburg, 1595.

Metcalfe, Jessica Z., John W. Ives, Sabrina Shirazi, Kevin Gilmore, Jennifer Hallson, Bonnie Clark, and Beth Shapiro. "Isotopic Evidence for Long-Distance Connections of the AD Thirteenth-Century Promontory Caves Occupants." *American Antiquity* 86, no. 3 (2021): 526–48.

Miglio, Viola. "'Go Shag a Horse!': The 17th–18th Century Basque–Icelandic Glossaries Revisited." *Journal of The North Atlantic* 1 (2008): 25–36.

Miller, Jay. "Tsimshian Ethno-Ethnohistory: A 'Real' Indigenous Chronology." *Ethnohistory* 45, no. 4 (1998): 657–74.

Miller, Shannon. *Invested with Meaning: The Raleigh Circle in the New World.* Philadelphia: University of Pennsylvania Press, 1998.

Mills, Barbara J., Matthew A. Peeples, W. Randall Haas, Jr, Lewis Borck, Jeffery J. Clark, and John M. Roberts, Jr. "Multiscalar Perspectives on Social Networks in the Late Prehispanic Southwest." *American Antiquity* 80, no. 1 (2015): 3–24.

Milne Richard I., and Richard J. Abbott. "The Origin and Evolution of Tertiary Relict Floras." *Advances in Botanical Research* 38 (2002): 281–314.

Miquelon, Dale. *New France, 1701–1744: A Supplement to Europe.* Toronto: McClelland and Stewart, 1987.

Miroff, Laurie E., and Timothy D. Knapp, eds. *Iroquoian Archaeology and Analytic Scale.* Knoxville: University of Tennessee Press, 2009.

Mitchell, A.R. "The European Fisheries in Early Modern Europe." In *The Cambridge Economic History of Europe*, vol. 5: *The Economic Organization of Early Modern Europe*, 133–84. Cambridge: Cambridge University Press, 1977.

Mitchell, Greg. "The Inuit of Southern Labrador and their Conflicts with Europeans to 1767." In *Exploring Atlantic Transitions: Archaeologies of Transience and Permanence in New Found Lands*, edited by Peter E. Pope with Shannon Lewis-Simpson, 320–30. Woodbridge: The Boydell Press, 2013.

Moccasin, Camina Weasel. "Continuing Writings on Stone." In *Archaeologies of Listening*, edited by Peter C. Schmidt and Alice B. Kehoe, 47–64. Gainsville: University of Florida Press, 2020.

Mollat, Michel. *Europe and the Sea.* Oxford: Blackwell, 1993.

– *Histoire des peches maritimes en France.* Toulouse: Privat, 1987.

– *Le Commerce maritime normand à la fin du moyen age: Étude d'histoire économique et sociale.* Paris: Plon, 1952.

Monroe, C., B.M. Kemp and D.G. Smith. "Exploring Prehistory in the North American Southwest with Mitochondrial DNA Diversity Exhibited by Yumans and Athapaskans." *American Journal of Physical Anthropology* 150 (2013): 618–31.

Moodie, D.W., A.J.W. Catchpole, and K. Abel. "Northern Athapaskan Oral Traditions and the White River Volcano." *Ethnohistory* 39 (1992): 148–71.

Mooney, James. *Calendar History of the Kiowa Indians.* 17th Annual Report of the Bureau of American Ethnology. Washington: Government Printing Office, 1898.

Morandière, Charles de la. *Histoire de la pêche française de la morue dans l'Atlantique septentrional*, 3 vols. Paris: Maisonneuve et Larose, 1962–66.

Morantz, Toby. "'Gift-Offerings to their Own Importance and Superiority': Fur Trade Relations, 1700–1940." In *Papers of the Nineteenth Algonquian Conference*, edited by William Cowan, 133–45. Ottawa: Carleton University Press, 1988.

– "'So Evil a Practice'; A Look at the Debt System in the James Bay Fur Trade."
In *Merchant Credit and Labour Strategies in Historical Perspective*, edited by
Rosemary E. Ommer, 203–22. Fredericton, NB: Acadiensis Press, 1990.

Moreau, Jean-François. "Des perles de la 'protohistoire' au Saguenay–Lac-Saint-
Jean?" *Recherches amérindiennes au Québec* 24, no. 1 (1994): 3–48.

Moreau, Jean-François, Érik Langevin, and François Guindon. "Saint Lawrence
Iroquoians as Middlemen or Observers: Review of Evidence in the Middle and
Upper Saint Lawrence Valley." In *Contact in the 16th Century: Networks among
Fishers, Farmers and Foragers*, edited by Brad Loewen and Claude Chapdelaine,
149–70. Ottawa: University of Ottawa Press, 2016.

Morgan, Lewis Henry. *The American Beaver and His Works*. Philadelphia: J.B.
Lippincott, n.d.

Morin, Eugène. "Early Late Woodland Social Interaction in the St. Lawrence River
Valley." *Archaeology of Eastern North America* 29 (2001): 65–100.

Morin, Michel. "Propriétés et territoires autochtones en Nouvelle-France, partie 2:
la gestion des districts de la chasse." *Recherches amérindiennes au Québec* 44, no. 1
(2014): 129–36.

Morison, Samuel Eliot. *The European Discovery of America: The Northern Voyages*.
New York: Oxford University Press, 1971.

Morrissey, Robert Michael. "The Power of the Ecotone: Bison, Slavery, and the Rise
and Fall of the Grand Village of the Kaskaskia." *Journal of American History* 102,
no. 3 (2015): 667–92.

Morrissey, Robert ed. *Encyclopédie, ou dictionnaire raisonné des sciences, des arts et
des métiers, ed. Denis Diderot and Jean le Rond D'Alembert*. University of Chicago:
ARTFL Encyclopédie Projet, Winter 2008 Edition,
http://encyclopedie.uchicago.edu/.

Moussette, Marcel. *Prendre la mesure des ombres: Archéologie du Rocher de la
Chapelle. Île aux Oies (Québec)*. Québec: Les Éditions GID, 2009.

– "Un univers sous tension: les nations amérindiennes du nord-est de l'Amérique
du Nord au XVIe siècle." *Les Cahiers des dix* 59 (2005): 149–77.

– "A Universe under Strain: Amerindian Nations in North-Eastern North America
in the 16th Century." *Post-Medieval Archaeology* 43, no. 1 (2009): 30–47.

Müller-Schwarze, Dietland. *The Beaver: Its Life and Impact*, 2nd ed. Ithaca: Cornell
University Press, 2011.

Murray, David. *Indian Giving: Economies of Power in Indian-White Exchanges*.
Amherst: University of Massachusetts Press, 2000.

Murton, James. *Canadians and Their Natural Environment: A History*. Toronto: Oxford University Press, 2021.

Nash, Ronald J. "Prehistory and Cultural Ecology – Cape Breton Island, Nova Scotia." In *Canadian Ethnology Society, Papers from the Fourth Annual Congress, 1977*, Mercury Series, Canadian Ethnological Service Paper 40, edited by R.J. Preston, 131–55. Ottawa: National Museum of Man, 1978.

Nash, Ronald J., ed. " Mi'kmaq: Economics and Evolution." *Curatorial Report* No. 57. Halifax: Nova Scotia Museum, 1986.

Nassaney, Michael S. *The Archaeology of the North American Fur Trade*. Gainesville, FL: University Press of Florida, 2017.

– "The North American Fur Trade in Historical and Archaeological Perspective." In *The Oxford Handbook of Historical Archaeology*, edited by James Symonds and Vesa-Pekka Herva. Online resource, 2014.

Nassaney, Michael S., and Kenneth E. Sassaman, eds. *Native American Interactions: Multiscalar Analyses and Interpretations in the Eastern Woodlands*. Knoxville: University of Tennessee Press, 1995.

Nelson, George. *My First Years in the Fur Trade: The Journals of 1802–1804*, edited by Laura L. Peers and Theresa M. Schenck. Montreal and Kingston: McGill-Queen's University Press, 2002.

Neuschel, Kristen B. "History and the Telescoping of Time: A Disciplinary Forum." *French Historical Studies* 34, no. 1 (2011): 47–55.

Newbigin, Marion. *Canada, the Great River, the Lands, and the Men*. London: Christophers, 1926.

New, W.H. *A History of Canadian Literature*. Montreal and Kingston: McGill-Queen's University Press, 2003.

Nicolas, Louis. *Histoire naturelle des Indes occidentales*. 3 vols. Edited by Daniel Fortin. Quebec City: GID, 2014.

Niellon, François. "S'Établir sur la terre de Caïn - Brador: une tentative canadienne au XVIIIe siècle." Report on file Ministère de la Culture et des Communications, Quebec, 1995.

Nolet, Bart, and Frank Rosell. "Comeback of the Beaver Castor fiber: An Overview of Old and New Conservation Problems." *Biological Conservation* 83, no. 2 (1998): 165–73.

Ogurtsov, M.G. "The Spörer Minimum Was Deep." *Advances in Space Research* 64, no. 5 (2019): 1112–16.

Oliver, Jennifer H. *Shipwreck in French Renaissance Writing*. Oxford: Oxford University Press, 2019.

Olson, Wes and Johanne Janelle. *The Ecological Buffalo: On the Trail of a Keystone Species*. Regina, SK: University of Regina Press, 2022.

Ommer, Rosemary E., ed. *Merchant Credit and Labour Strategies in Historical Perspective*. Fredericton, NB: Acadiensis Press, 1990.

Ortelius, Abraham. *Theatrum Orbis Terrarum*. Antwerp, 1570.

Ortman, Scott G., and Lynda McNeil. "The Kiowa Odyssey: Evidence of Historical Relationships Between Pueblo, Fremont and Northern Plains Peoples." *Plains Anthropologist* 63, no. 246 (2017): 152–74.

Osborne, Carolyn Miles. *The Wetherill Collections and Perishable Items from Mesa Verde*. Los Alamitos, California: [no publisher specified], 2004.

Oswald, Evan M., Jennifer Pontius, Shelly A. Rayback, Paul G. Schaberg, Sandra H. Wilmot, and Lesley-Ann Dupigny-Giroux. "The Complex Relationship between Climate and Sugar Maple Health: Climate Change Implications in Vermont for a Key Northern Hardwood Species." *Forest Ecology and Management* 422 (2018): 303–12.

Ott, Jennifer. "'Ruining' the River in the Snake Country: The Hudson Bay Company's Fur Desert Policy." *Oregon Historical Quarterly* 140, no. 2 (2003): 166–95.

Ouellet, Fernand. *Economic and Social History of Quebec 1760–1850: Structures and Conjonctures*. Toronto: Gage, 1980.

Ouellet, Jean-Christophe. "Préhistoire de la Moyenne-Côte-Nord: le chert de la Minganie et l'utilisation des ressources lithiques." Mémoire de maîtrise, Université de Montréal, 2010.

Ouellet, Réal, ed. *Chrestien Leclercq: Nouvelle relation de la Gaspésie*. Montréal: Presses de l'Université de Montréal, 1999.

Ouellet, Réal. *La Relation de voyage en Amérique (XVIe – XVIIIe siècles). Au carrefour des genres*. Sainte-Foy, QC: Presses de l'Université Laval, 2010.

Padrón, Ricardo. *The Indies of the Setting Sun: How Early Modern Spain Mapped the Far East as the Transpacific West*. Chicago: University of Chicago Press, 2020.

Pageot, Édith-Anne. "Paysages, dépaysements: La construction de mythes identitaires dans l'art canadien moderne et contemporain." *International Journal of Canadian Studies* 36 (2007): 287–305.

Pagden, Anthony. *The Fall of Natural Man: The American Indian and the Origins of Comparative Ethnology*. Cambridge: Cambridge University Press, 1986.

Pannekoek, Frits. *The Fur Trade and Western Canadian Society, 1670–1870*. Ottawa: Canadian Historical Association, 1987.

Parker, David. *La Rochelle and the French Monarchy: Conflict and Order in Seventeenth-Century France*. London: Royal Historical Society, 1980.

Parks, George B. "Tudor Travel Literature." In *The Hakluyt Handbook*, edited by David B Quinn, 97–132. London: Hakluyt Society, 1974.

Parker, James McPherson. *Emporium of the North: Fort Chipewyan and the fur trade to 1835*. Regina, SK: Alberta Culture and Multiculturalism/Canadian Plains Research Center, 1987.

Parsons, Christopher M. *A Not-So-New World: Empire and Environment in French Colonial North America*. Philadelphia: University of Pennsylvania Press, 2018.

– "Wildness without Wilderness: Biogeography and Empire in Seventeenth-Century French North America." *Environmental History* 22, no.4 (2017): 643–67.

Parsons, Christopher M., and Kathleen S. Murphy. "Ecosystems under Sail: Specimen Transport in the Eighteenth-Century French and British Atlantics." *Early American Studies* 10, no. 3 (2012): 503–29.

Pastore, Ralph. "The Collapse of the Beothuk World." Acadiensis 19, no. 1 (1989): 52–71.

Payne, Anthony. *Richard Hakluyt: A Guide to His Books*. London: Bernard Quaritch, 2008.

– "Richard Hakluyt and the Earl of Essex: The Censorship of the Voyage to Cadiz in the Principal Navigations." *Publishing History* 72 (2012): 7–52.

Payne, Anthony, and P.A. Neville-Sington. "An Interim Census of Surviving Copies of Hakluyt's 'Divers Voyages' and 'Principal Navigations.'" In *Richard Hakluyt and His Books*. London: Hakluyt Society, 1997.

Peck, Trevor R., and John W. Ives. "Late Side-Notched Projectile Points in the Northwestern Plains." *Plains Anthropologist* 46, no. 176 (2001): 163–93.

Peckham, Sir George. *A True Reporte, of the Late Discoveries, and Possession, Taken in the Right of the Crowne of Englande, of the New-Found Landes*. London, 1583.

Peers, Laura. *The Ojibwa of Western Canada, 1780 to 1870*. Winnipeg: University of Manitoba Press, 1994.

Peers, Laura L., and Carolyn Podruchny, eds. *Gathering Places: Aboriginal and Fur Trade Histories*. Vancouver: UBC Press, 2010.

Pendergast, James F., and Bruce G. Trigger. *Cartier's Hochelaga and the Dawson Site, Montréal*. Montreal and Kingston: McGill-Queen's University Press, 1972.

– "The Ottawa River Algonquin Bands in a St. Lawrence Iroquoian Context." *Canadian Journal of Archaeology* 23 (1999): 63–136.

– "Quelques notes sur la bande algonquine Ountchatarounounga (Onontchataronon) de la vallée de l'Outaouais." *Recherches amérindiennes au Québec* 29, no. 1 (1999): 27–39.

Pendergast, Russell Anthony. "The XY Company 1798 to 1804." PhD diss., University of Ottawa, 1957.

Pérez, Germán Santana. "Las Pesquerías en Berbería a mediados del siglo XVII." *Tebeto: Anuario del Archivo Histórico Insular de Fuerteventura*, no. 8 (1995): 13–30.

Perkins, Simeon. *The Diary of Simeon Perkins*, 5 vols. Toronto: Champlain Society, 1948.

Perrault, Jean-Baptiste. *Jean-Baptiste Perrault, marchand voyageur, parti de Montréal le 28e de mai 1783*, edited by Louis-P. Cormier. Montreal: Boréal, 1978.

Petersen, James B., and David Sanger. "An Aboriginal Ceramic Sequence for Maine and the Maritime Provinces." In *Prehistoric Archaeology in the Maritime Provinces: Past and Present Research*, edited by M. Deal and S. Blair, 121–78. Fredericton, NB: The Council of Maritime Premiers, Maritime Committee on Archaeological Cooperation, 1991.

Pettigrew, Stephanie, and Elizabeth Mancke. "European Expansion and the Contested North Atlantic." *Terrae Incognitae* 50, no. 1 (2018): 15–34.

Peyser, Joseph L. ed. *Jacques Legardeur de Saint-Pierre: Officer, Gentleman, Entrepreneur*. East Lansing: Michigan State University Press, 1996.

Phillips, Andrew, and J.C. Sharman. *Outsourcing Empire: How Company-States Made the Modern World*. Princeton, NJ: Princeton University Press, 2020.

Phillips Jr, William D. "Africa and the Atlantic Islands Meet the Garden of Eden: Christopher Columbus's View of America." *Journal of World History* (1992): 149–64.

Pielou, E. Chris. *After the Ice Age: The Return of Life to Glaciated North America*. Chicago: University of Chicago Press, 1991.

Radisson, Pierre-Esprit. *The Collected Writings*, 2 vols. Edited by Germaine Warkentin. Montreal and Kingston: McGill-Queen's University Press, 2012–14.

Pinkoski, Marc. "Julian Steward, American Anthropology, and Colonialism." *Histories of Anthropology Annual* 4 (2008): 172–204.

Pinsky, Valerie, and Alison Wylie, eds. *Critical Traditions in Contemporary Archaeology: Essays in the Philosophy, History, and Socio-politics of Archaeology*. New York: Cambridge University Press, 1989.

Pintal, Jean-Yves. *Aux frontières de la mer: la préhistoire de Blanc-Sablon*. Quebec City: Publications du Québec, 1998.

– "La rencontre de deux mondes." *Continuité* 92 (2002): 38–9.

Plint, Tessa, Fred J. Longstaffe, and Grant Zazula. "Giant Beaver Palaeoecology Inferred from Stable Isotopes." *Scientific Reports* 9, 7179 (2019).

Plourde, Michel. *L'exploitation du phoque à l'embouchure du Saguenay par les Iroquoiens de 1000 à 1534.* Ottawa: University of Ottawa Press, 2013.

– "Saint Lawrence Iroquoians, Algonquians, and Europeans in the Saint Lawrence Estuary between 1500 and 1650." In *Contact in the 16th Century: Networks among Fishers, Farmers and Foragers,* edited by Brad Loewen and Claude Chapdelaine, 119–48. Ottawa: University of Ottawa Press, 2016.

Plourde, Michel, and Christian Gates St-Pierre. "Les phocidés du secteur de l'embouchure du Saguenay: Modalités d'exploitation au sylvicole supérieur." *Recherches amérindiennes au Québec* 33 no. 1 (2003): 45–60.

Podruchny, Carolyn. *Making the Voyageur World: Travelers and Traders in the North American Fur Trade.* Toronto: University of Toronto Press, 2006.

Pope, Peter E. "Bretons, Basques and *Inuit* in Labrador and Northern Newfoundland: The Control of Maritime Resources in the Sixteenth and Seventeenth Centuries." *Études/Inuit/Studies* 39, no. 1 (2015): 15–36.

– "Fisher Men at Work: The Material Culture of the Champ Paya Fishing Room as a Gendered Site." In *Tu Sais, Mon Vieux Jean-Pierre: Essays on the Archaeology and History of New France and Canadian Culture in Honour of Jean-Pierre Chrestien,* edited by John Willis, 43–62. Ottawa: University of Ottawa Press, 2017.

– *Fish into Wine: The Newfoundland Plantation in the Seventeenth Century.* Chapel Hill, NC: University of North Carolina Press, 2004.

– *The Many Landfalls of John Cabot.* Toronto: University of Toronto Press, 1997.

– "Modernization on Hold: The Traditional Character of the Newfoundland Cod Fishery in the Seventeenth Century." *International Journal of Maritime History* 15, no. 2 (2003): 233–64.

– "Outport Economics: Culture and Agriculture in Later Seventeenth-Century Newfoundland." *Newfoundland and Labrador Studies* 19, no. 1 (2005).

– "Transformation of the Maritime Cultural Landscape of Atlantic Canada by Migratory European Fishermen, 1500–1800." In *Beyond the Catch: Fisheries of the North Atlantic, the North Sea and the Baltic, 900–1850,* edited by Louis Sicking and Darlene Abreu-Ferreira, 123–54. Leiden: Brill, 2009.

Pouliot, Laurence. "Étude de l'impact des interactions culturelles sur les occupants de l'Habitation 1 de Double Mer Point: Développement d'une nouvelle méthodologie pour l'étude des sites de contacts." MA thesis, Département des sciences historiques, Université Laval, 2020.

Power, Eileen, and M.M. Postan. *Studies in English Trade in the Fifteenth Century.* London: G. Routledge & Sons, 1933.

Powers, W.R., and R.H. Jordan. "Human Biogeography and Climate Change in Siberia and Arctic North America in the Fourth and Fifth Millennia BP." *Philosophical Transactions of the Royal Society of London, Series A, Mathematical and Physical Sciences* 330 no. 1615 (1990): 665–70.

Pritchard, James S. "Hydrography in New France." In *Charting Northern Waters: Essays for the Centenary of the Canadian Hydrographical Service*, edited by William Glover. Montreal and Kingston: McGill-Queen's University Press, 2004.

Promislow, Janna. "'Thou wilt not die of hunger ... for I bring thee Merchandise': Consent, Intersocietal Normativity and the Exchange of Food at York Factory, 1682–1763." In *Between Consenting Peoples: Political Community and the Meaning of Consent*, edited by Jeremy Webber and Colin Macleod, 77–114. Vancouver: UBC Press, 2010.

Prowse, D.W. *A History of Newfoundland from the English, Colonial, and Foreign Records with Numerous Illustrations and Maps.* London: Eyre and Spottiswoode, 1896.

Purchas, Samuel. *Hakluytus Posthumus, or Purchas His Pilgrimes.* 4 vols. London, 1625.

Quaife, Milo M., ed. *The John Askin Papers.* Detroit: Detroit Library Commission, 1928.

Quinn, Alison M., and David B. Quinn. "Contents and Sources of the Three Major Works." In *The Hakluyt Handbook*, edited by David Quinn, 2: 338–460. London: Routledge, 1974.

Quinn, David B. "GILBERT, Sir HUMPHREY," in *Dictionary of Canadian Biography*. Toronto and Quebec City: University of Toronto Press / les presses de l'Université Laval, 1966–.

– *The Hakluyt Handbook.* 2 vols. London: Hakluyt Society, 1974.

– ed. *Richard Hakluyt, Editor. A Study Introductory of the Facsimile Edition of Richard Hakluyt's Divers Voyages (1582) to which is Added a Facsimile of A Short and Briefe Narration of the Two Navigations to Newe Fraunce.* 2 vols. Amsterdam: Theatrum Orbis Terrarum, 1967.

– "The Voyage of Etienne Bellenger to the Maritimes in 1583: A New Document." *Canadian Historical Review* 43, no. 4 (1962): 328–43.

– *Voyages and Colonising Enterprises of Sir Humphrey Gilbert*, 2 vols. London: Hakluyt Society, 1940.

Quinn, David B., and Neil M. Cheshire, eds. *The New Found Land of Stephen*

Parmenius; the Life and Writings of a Hungarian Poet, Drowned on a Voyage from Newfoundland, 1583. Toronto: University of Toronto Press, 1972.

Quinn, David B., Alison M. Quinn, and Susan Hillier, eds. *New American World: A Documentary History of North America to 1612*. 4 vols. New York: Arno Press, 1978.

Raghavan, Maanasa, Michael DeGiorgio, Anders Albrechtsen, Ida Moltke, Pontus Skoglund, Thorfinn S. Korneliussen, Bjarne Grønnow, Martin Appelt, Hans Christian Gulløv, T. Max Friesen, William Fitzhugh, Helena Malmström, et al. "The Genetic Prehistory of the New World Arctic." *Science* 345, no. 6200 (2014).

Raff, Jennifer. *Origin: A Genetic History of the Americas*. New York: Grand Central Publishing, 2022.

Ramsden, Peter. "Becoming Wendat: Negotiating a New Identity around Balsam Lake in the Late Sixteenth Century." *Ontario Archaeology* 96 (2016): 121–32.

– "Sixteenth-Century Contact Between the Saint Lawrence Valley and the Upper Trent Valley." In *Contact in the 16th Century: Networks among Fishers, Farmers and Foragers*, edited by Brad Loewen and Claude Chapdelaine, 219–34. Ottawa: University of Ottawa Press, 2016.

– "The Use of Style in Resistance, Politics and the Negotiation of Identity: St. Lawrence Iroquoians in a Huron-Wendat Community." *Canadian Journal of Archaeology* 40, no. 1 (2016): 1–22.

Ramsden, Peter, and Lisa K. Rankin. "Thule Radiocarbon Chronology and Its Implications for Early Inuit-European Interaction in Labrador." In *Exploring Atlantic Transitions: Archaeologies of Transience and Permanence in New Found Lands*, edited by Peter E. Pope with Shannon Lewis-Simpson, 299–309. Suffolk: The Boydell Press, 2013.

Ramusio, Giovanni Batista. *Navigazioni et viaggi*. Venice, 1554.

Rankin, Lisa K. "Identity Markers: Interpreting Sod-House Occupation in Sandwich Bay, Labrador." *Études/Inuit/Studies* 39, no. 1 (2015): 91–116.

– "Inuit Settlement on the Southern Frontier." In *History and Renewal of Labrador's Inuit Métis*, edited by John C. Kennedy, 38–61. St John's, NL: Institute of Social and Economic Research, 2014.

– "Towards a Beothuk Archaeology: Merging Indigenous Agency with the Material Record." In *Tracing Ochre: Changing Perspectives on the Beothuk*, edited by Fiona Polack, 177–98. Toronto: University of Toronto Press, 2018.

Rankin, Lisa K., Matthew Beaudoin, and Natalie Brewster. "Southern Exposure: The Inuit of Sandwich Bay, Labrador." In *Settlement, Subsistence and Change*

Among the Labrador Inuit: The Nunatsiavummiut Experience, edited by David C. Natcher, Lawrence Felt, and Andrea Procter, 61–84. Winnipeg: University of Manitoba Press, 2012.

Rankin, Lisa K., and Amanda Crompton. "Kayaks and Chaloupes: Labrador Inuit and the Seascapes of Inter-Cultural Contact." In *Marine Ventures: Archaeological Perspectives on Human-Sea Relations*, edited by Hein Bjerck et al., 383–98. Sheffield: Equinox Publishing, 2016.

– "Meeting in the Straits: Intersecting Inuit and European Trajectories in Southern Labrador." In *Contact in the Sixteenth Century: Networks Among Fishers, Foragers and Farmers*, edited by Brad Loewen and Claude Chapdelaine, 11–29. Ottawa: University of Ottawa Press, 2016.

Rapport de l'archiviste de la province de Québec, 1922-23. Quebec City: Ls-A. Proulx, 1923.

Ray, Arthur J. *The Canadian Fur Trade in the Industrial Age*. Toronto: University of Toronto Press, 1990.

– "Indians as Consumers in the Eighteenth Century." In *Old Trails New Directions: Papers of the Third North American Fur Trade Conference*, edited by Carol M. Judd and Arthur J. Ray, 255–71. Toronto: University of Toronto Press, 1980.

– *Indians in the Fur Trade: Their Role as Trappers, Hunters, and Middlemen in the Lands Southwest of Hudson Bay, 1660-1870*, revised edition. Toronto: University of Toronto Press, 2005.

– ed. *Life and Death by the Frozen Sea: The York Fort Journals of Hudson's Bay Company Governor James Knight, 1714–1717*. Toronto: The Champlain Society, 2018.

Ray, Arthur J, and Donald B Freeman. *"Give Us Good Measure": An Economic Analysis of Relations between the Indians and the Hudson's Bay Company before 1763*. Toronto: University of Toronto Press, 1978.

Reid, John Phillip. *Patterns of Vengeance: Crosscultural Homicide in the North American Fur Trade*. Pasadena, CA: Ninth Judicial Circuit Historical Society, 1999.

Reilly, Aileen. "Women's Work, Tools, and Expertise: Hide Tanning and the Archaeological Record." MA thesis, Department of Anthropology, University of Alberta, 2015.

"Report of the Merchants of Montreal by their committee to the Honorable Committee of Council on Commercial Affairs and Police." *Michigan Historical Collections* 11 (1887): 473.

Restall, Matthew. "The New Conquest History." *History Compass* 10, no. 2 (2012): 151–60.

Reuther, J., B. Potter, S. Coffman, H. Smith, and N. Bigelow. "Revisiting the Timing of the Northern Lobe of the White River Ash." *Radiocarbon* 62, no. 1 (September 2020): 169–88.

Rhode, David. "Archaeobotanical Investigations in the Promontory Caves." In *Holes in Our Moccasins, Holes in Our Stories. New Insights into Apachean Origins from the Promontory, Franktown, and Dismal River Archaeological Records*, edited by John W. Ives and Joel C. Janetski, 146–62. Salt Lake City: University of Utah Press, 2022.

Ribaut, Jean. *The Whole and True Discoverye of Terra Florida.* London, 1563.

Rich, Edwin Ernest, ed. *Colin Robertson's Correspondence Book, September 1817 to September 1822.* Toronto: Champlain Society, 1939.

– *The History of the Hudson's Bay Company 1670–1870*, 2 vols. London: Hudson's Bay Record Society, 1958.

– ed. *Journal of Occurrences in the Athabasca Department, by George Simpson, 1820 and 1821, and Report.* Toronto: Champlain Society, 1938.

– "Trade Habits and Economic Motivation among the Indians of North America." *The Canadian Journal of Economics and Political Science/Revue canadienne d'économique et de science politique* 26, no. 1 (1960): 35–53.

Richards, John F. *The Unending Frontier: An Environmental History of the Early Modern World.* Berkeley: University of California Press, 2005.

Riley Sousa, Ashley. "Trapped? The Fur Trade and Debt Peonage in Central California." *Pacific Historical Review* 90, no. 1 (2021): 1–27.

Robichaud, Léon. "Habitants, autorités et délits en Nouvelle-France: les Montréalais et la traite des fourrures." In *Tu sais, mon vieux Jean-Pierre: essays on the archaeology and history of New France and Canadian culture in honour of Jean-Pierre Chrestien*, edited by John Willis, 207–26. Ottawa: Canadian Museum of History, 2017.

Robinson, Brian S., Jennifer C. Ort, William A. Eldridge, Adrian L. Burke, and Bertrand G. Pelletier. "Paleoindian Aggregation and Social Context at Bull Brook." *American Antiquity* 74, no.3 (2009): 423–47.

Robinson, Erick, Kyle Bocinsky, Darcy Bird, Jacob Freeman, and Robert L. Kelly. "Dendrochronological Dates Confirm a Late Prehistoric Population Decline in the American Southwest Derived from Radiocarbon Dates." *Philosophical Transactions of the Royal Society B: Biological Sciences* 376 (2021): 20190718

Robinson, S.D. "Extending the Late Holocene White River Ash Distribution, Northwestern Canada." *Arctic* 54, no. 2 (2001): 157–61.

Rochemonteix, Camille de, ed. *Relation par lettres de l'Amérique Septentrionalle (années 1709 et 1710)*. Paris: Letouzey et Ané, 1904.

Roper, L.H., and Bertrand Van Ruymbeke. "Introduction." In *Constructing Early Modern Empires: Proprietary Ventures in the Atlantic World, 1500–1750*, edited by L.H. Roper and Bertrand Van Ruymbeke, 1–10. Leiden: Brill, 2007.

Rouland, Patrick, and Pierre Migot. "La réintroduction du castor (Castor fiber) en France: Essai de synthèse et réflexions." *Revue d'écologie* 45 (1990): 145–58.

Roy, P.-G., ed. *Inventaire de pièces sur la côte de Labrador conservées aux archives de la province de Québec*, 2 vols. Quebec City: Archives de la province de Québec, 1940.

Roy, Susan. *These Mysterious People: Shaping History and Archaeology in a Northwest Coast Community*. Montreal and Kingston: McGill-Queen's University Press, 2010.

Royle, Stephen A. "A Human Geography of Islands." *Geography* (1989): 106–16.

Rubiés, Joan Pau. "From the 'History of Travayle' to the History of Travel Collections: The Rise of an Early Modern Genre." In *Richard Hakluyt and Travel Writing in Early Modern Europe*, edited by Daniel Carey and Claire Jowitt, 25–41. London: Routledge, 2016.

Ruggiu, François-Joseph. "Colonies, Monarchy, Empire and the French Ancien Regime." In *Crowns and Colonies: European Monarchies and Overseas Empires*, edited by Robert Aldrich and Cindy McCreery, 194–210. Manchester: Manchester University Press, 2016.

Ruggles, Richard I. "The Cartographic Lure of the Northwest Passage: Its Real and Imaginary Geography." In *Meta Incognita: A Discourse of Discovery*, vol. 1: *Martin Frobisher's Arctic Expeditions, 1576–1578*, edited by Thomas H.B. Symons, Stephen Alsford, and Chris Kitzan, 1: 179–256. Ottawa: University of Ottawa Press, 1999.

Rutherford, Douglas E. "Reconsidering the Middlesex Burial Phase in the Maine-Maritimes Region." *Canadian Journal of Archaeology* 14 (1990): 169–81.

Sahlins, Marshall D. *Stone Age Economics*. New York: Aldine, 1972.

Saint-Hilaire, Geoffroy. "Renseignements sur les castors du Rhone." *Bulletin de la société nationale d'acclimation de France* 4, no. 5 (1888).

Sanborn, Frederic R. *Origins of Early English Maritime Law*. New York: Century Co., 1930.

Sandlos, John. "Federal Spaces, Local Conflicts: National Parks and the Exclusionary Politics of the Conservation Movement in Ontario, 1900–1935." *Journal of the Canadian Historical Association* 16, no. 1 (2005): 293–318.

Sapir, Edward. "Internal Linguistic Evidence Suggestive of the Northern Origin of the Navaho." *American Anthropologist* 38 (1936): 224–35.

Savelle, James M. *Collectors and Foragers: Subsistence-Settlement Systems in the Central Canadian Arctic A.D. 1000–1960.* Oxford: British Archaeological Reports, 1987.

Savoie, Sylvie, and Jean Tanguay. "Le nœud de l'ancienne amitié: La présence abénaquise sur la rive nord du Saint-Laurent aux XVIIe et XVIIIe siècles." *Recherches amérindiennes au Québec* 33 (2003): 29–43.

Schledermann, Peter. "Ellesmere." In *Vikings: The North Atlantic Saga*, edited by William W. Fitzhugh and Elisabeth I. Ward, 248–56. Washington: Smithsonian Institution Press, 2000.

– "The Thule Tradition in Northern Labrador." MA thesis, Department of Anthropology, Memorial University of Newfoundland, 1971.

Schwindt, Dylan M., R. Kyle Bocinsky, Scott G. Ortman, Donna M. Glowacki, Mark D. Varien, and Timothy A. Kohler. "The Social Consequences of Climate Change in the Central Mesa Verde Region." *American Antiquity* 81, no. 1 (2016): 74–96.

Scott, Nancy. *Lake Nipigon: Where the Great Lakes Begin.* Toronto: Dundurn, 2015.

Seaver, Kirsten A. *The Frozen Echo: Greenland and the Exploration of North America, ca. A.D. 1000–1500.* Stanford, CA: Stanford University Press, 1996.

– "'A Very Common and Usuall Trade': The Relationship Between Cartographic Perceptions and 'Fishing' in the Davis Strait Circa 1500–1550." *British Library Journal* 22, no. 1 (1996): 1–26.

Seeman, Mark F. "The Hopewell Interaction Sphere: The Evidence of Inter-Regional Trade and Structural Complexity." *Indiana Historical Society, Prehistoric Research Series*, vol. 5, no. 2 (1979): 237–438.

Selkirk, Thomas Douglas. *A Sketch of the British Fur Trade in North America: With Observations Relative to the North-West Company of Montreal.* London: James Ridgway, 1816.

Serrano, Karla Pelz. "Molecular Phylogeography of the American Beaver (*Castor canadensis*): Implications for Management and Conservation." PhD diss., University of Arizona, 2011.

Settle, Dionyse. *A True Reporte of the Laste Voyage into the West and Northwest Regions &c., 1577, Worthily Atchieved by Capteine Frobisher of the Sayde Voyage the First Finder and Generall: With a Description of the People There Inhabiting, and Other Circumstances Notable.* London, 1577.

Sharpe, Christina. *In the Wake: On Blackness and Being.* Durham, NC: Duke University Press, 2016.

Sheehan, Glenn. "Whaling Surplus, Trade, War and the Integration of Prehistoric Northern and Northwestern Alaskan Economies, A.D. 1200–1826." In *Hunting the Largest Animals: Native Whaling in the Western Arctic and Sub Arctic,* edited by Alan P. McCartney, 185–206. Edmonton: Canadian Circumpolar Institute, 1995.

Sheehan, Jonathan. "Time Elapsed, Time Regained: Anthropology and the Flood." In *Sintflut und Gedächtnis: Erinnern und Vergessen des Ursprungs,* edited by Martin Mulsow and Jan Assmann, 321–35. Munich: Wilhelm Fink Verlag, 2006.

Sherman, William. *John Dee: The Politics of Reading and Writing in the English Renaissance.* Amherst: University of Massachusetts Press, 1995.

– *Used Books: Marking Readers in Renaissance England.* Philadelphia: University of Pennsylvania Press, 2008.

Shirazi, Sabrina, Nasreen Broomandkhoshbacht, Jonas Oppenheimer, Jessica Z. Metcalfe, Rob Found, John W. Ives, and Beth Shapiro. "Ancient DNA-Based Sex Determination of Bison Hide Moccasins Indicates Promontory Cave Occupants Selected Female Hides for Footwear by Promontory Cave Occupants." *Journal of Archaeological Science* 137 no. 1 (2022): 105533.

Shortt, Adam, William Smith, and Arthur R.M. Lower, eds. *Documents relatifs à la monnaie, au change et aux finances du Canada sous le régime français.* Ottawa: F.A. Acland, 1925.

Sicking, Louis, and Darlene Abreu-Ferreira, eds. *Beyond the Catch: Fisheries of the North Atlantic, the North Sea and the Baltic.* Leiden; Boston: Brill, 2009.

Sikora, Martin, Vladimir V. Pitulko, Vitor C. Sousa, Morten E. Allentoft, Lasse Vinner, Simon Rasmussen, Ashot Margaryan, Peter de Barros Damgaard, Constanza de la Fuente, Gabriel Renaud, Melinda A. Yang, Qiaomei Fu, et al. "The Population History of Northeastern Siberia Since the Pleistocene." *Nature* 570 (13 June 2019): 182–8.

Simpson, Leanne. "Looking after Gdoo-Naaganinaa: Precolonial Nishnaabeg Diplomatic and Treaty Relationships." *Wicazo Sa Review* 23, no. 2 (8 October 2008): 29–42.

Skelton, R.A. "Hakluyt's Maps." In *The Hakluyt Handbook,* 2 vols, edited by David Quinn, 1:48–69. London: Routledge, 1974.

Skinner, Claiborne. "The Einews of empire: The Voyageurs and the Carrying Trade of the pays d'en haut, 1681–1754." PhD diss., University of Illinois at Chicago, 1991.

Sleeper-Smith, Susan. *Indian Women and French Men: Rethinking Cultural En-*

counter in the Western Great Lakes. Amherst: University of Massachusetts Press, 2001.

Sloan, W.A. "The Native Response to the Extension of the European Traders into the Athabasca and Mackenzie Basin, 1770–1814." *Canadian Historical Review* 60, no. 3 (1979): 281–99.

Smail, Daniel Lord, and Andrew Shryock. "History and the 'Pre.'" *American Historical Review* 118, no. 3 (2013): 709–37.

Smandych, Russell, and Rick Linden. "Administering Justice without the State: A Study of the Private Justice System of the Hudson's Bay Company to 1800." *Canadian Journal of Law and Society* 11 (Spring 1996): 21–61.

Smith, David Chan. "The Hudson's Bay Company, Social Legitimacy, and the Political Economy of Eighteenth-Century Empire." *The William and Mary Quarterly* 75, no. 1 (2018): 71–108.

Smith, James G.E. "Chipewyan." In *Handbook of North American Indians*, vol. 6, *Subarctic*, edited by June Helm, 271–84. Washington: Smithsonian Institution, 1981.

Smith, Stefan Halikowski. "The Mid-Atlantic Islands: A Theatre of Early Modern Ecocide?" *International Review of Social History* 55, (2010): 51–77.

Snoek, Conor, Michaela Stang, and Sally Rice. "Linguistic Relationships between Apachean and Northern Athapaskan: On the possibility of 'Eastern Athapaskan.'" In *Holes in Our Moccasins, Holes in Our Stories. New Insights into Apachean Origins from the Promontory, Franktown, and Dismal River Archaeological Records*, edited by John W. Ives and Joel C. Janetski, 8–26. Salt Lake City: University of Utah Press, 2022.

Snow, C.P. *The Two Cultures and the Scientific Revolution*. Cambridge: Cambridge University Press, 1962.

Snow, Dean R. *The Iroquois*. Oxford: Blackwell, 1994.

Spence, Michael W., Robert H. Pihl, and Carl Murphy. "Cultural Complexes of the Early and Middle Woodland Periods." In *The Archaeology of Southern Ontario to A.D. 1650*, edited by C.J. Ellis and N. Ferris, 125–69. Occasional Publication of the London Chapter. London: Ontario Archaeological Society, 1990.

Spencer, Robert F. *The North Alaskan Eskimo: A Study in Ecology and Society*. Bureau of American Ethnology Bulletin No. 171. Washington: Smithsonian Institution, 1959.

Spielmann, Katherine A. "Coercion or Cooperation? Plains-Pueblo Interaction in the Protohistoric Period." In *Farmers, Hunters, and Colonists: Interaction between*

the Southwest and the Southern Plains, edited by Katherine A. Spielmann, 36–50.
Tucson: University of Arizona Press, 1991.

– "Late Prehistoric Exchange between the Southwest and the Southern Plains."
Plains Anthropologist 28 (1983): 257–72.

Spraakman, Gary. *Management Accounting at the Hudson's Bay Company: From
Quill Pen to Digitization.* 2015.

Springer, Gregory S., D. Matthew White, Harold D. Rowe, Ben Hardt, L. Nivanthi
Mihimdukulasooriya, Hai Cheng, and R. Lawrence Edwards. "Multiproxy Evidence from Caves of Native Americans Altering the Overlying Landscape During
the Late Holocene of East-Central North America." *The Holocene* 20, no. 2 (2010):
275–84.

Stanford, Dennis J. *The Walkpa Site, Alaska: Its Place in the Birnirk and Thule
Cultures.* Smithsonian Contributions to Anthropology No. 20. Washington:
Smithsonian Institution Press, 1976.

Starna, William A., and Ralph Watkins. "Northern Iroquoian Slavery." *Ethnohistory*
38 no. 1 (1991): 34–57.

Steele, C.R. "From Hakluyt to Purchas." In *The Hakluyt Handbook,* 2 vols, edited
by David Quinn, 1: 74–96. London: Routledge, 1974.

Steinberg, Philip E. "Lines of Division, Lines of Connection: Stewardship in the
World Ocean." *Geographical Review* 89, no. 2 (1999): 256–60.

– *The Social Construction of the Ocean.* Cambridge: Cambridge University Press,
2001.

Stern, Philip J. *The Company-State: Corporate Sovereignty and the Early Modern
Foundations of the British Empire in India.* New York: Oxford University Press,
2011.

Stevens-Arroyo, Anthony M. "The Inter-Atlantic Paradigm: The Failure of Spanish
Medieval Colonization of the Canary and Caribbean Islands." *Comparative
Studies in Society and History* 35, no. 3 (1993): 515–43.

Steward, Julian H. *Ancient Caves of the Great Salt Lake Region.* Bureau of American
Ethnology, Bulletin No. 115. Washington: Smithsonian Institution, 1937.

– "The Economic and Social Basis of Primitive Bands." In *Essays on Anthropology
in Honor of Alfred Louis Kroeber,* edited by Robert Lowie, 311–50. Berkeley:
University of California Press, 1936.

Stone, Anne C. "The Lineages of the First Humans to Reach Northeastern Siberia
and the Americas." *Nature* 570, no. 7760 (June 2019): 170–2.

Stopp, Marianne. "Faceted Inuit-European contact in southern Labrador." *Études/Inuit/Studies* 39, no. 1 (2015): 63–89.

– "Reconsidering Inuit presence in southern Labrador." *Études/Inuit/Studies* 26, no. 2 (2002): 71–106.

Stouraiti, Anastasia. "Talk, Script and Print: The Making of Island Books in Early Modern Venice." *Historical Research* 86, no. 232 (2013): 207–29.

Stout, Felicity. "'The Strange and Wonderfull Discoverie of Russia': Hakluyt and Censorship." In *Richard Hakluyt and Travel Writing in Early Modern Europe*, edited by Daniel Carey and Claire Jowitt, 153–63. London: Routledge, 2016.

Streuver, Stuart, and Gail L. Houart. "An Analysis of the Hopewell Interaction Sphere." In *Social Exchange and Interaction*, edited by Edwin N. Wilmsen. Anthropological Papers, Museum of Anthropology, University of Michigan, No. 46. Ann Arbor: University of Michigan Press, 1972.

Sturtevant, W.C. "The First Inuit Depiction by Europeans." *Études/Inuit/Studies* 4 (1980): 47–9.

Sumira, Sylvia. *The Art and History of Globes*. London: The British Library, 2014.

Symons, Thomas H.B., ed. *Meta Incognita: A Discourse of Discovery: Martin Frobisher's Arctic Expedition, 1576–1578*. 2 vols. Hull, QC: Canadian Museum of Civilization, 1999.

Szulman, Éric. *La Navigation intérieure sous l'ancien régime: Naissance d'une politique publique*. Rennes: Presses universitaires de Rennes, 2014.

Taché, Karine. *Structure and Regional Diversity of the Meadowood Interaction Sphere*. Ann Arbor: University of Michigan Press, 2011.

Tamm, Erika, Toomas Kivisild, Maere Reidla, Mait Metspalu, David Glenn Smith, Connie J. Mulligan, Claudio M. Bravi, Olga Rickards, Cristina Martinez-Labarga, Elsa K. Khusnutdinova, Sardana A. Fedorova, Maria V. Golubenko, et al. "Beringian Standstill and Spread of Native American Founders." *PLOS ONE* 2, no. 9 (September 2007): e829.

Tankersley, Kenneth B. "A Geoarchaeological Investigation of Distribution and Exchange in the Raw Material Economies of Clovis Groups in Eastern North America." In *Raw Material Economies among Hunter-Gatherers*, edited by A. Montet-White and S. Holen, 285–303. Lawrence: Department of Anthropology, University of Kansas, 1991.

Taylor, E.G.R. "A Letter Dated 1577 from Mercator to John Dee." *Imago Mundi* 13 (1956): 56–68.

Taylor, E.G.R., ed. *The Original Writings & Correspondence of the Two Richard Hakluyts*, 2 vols. 2nd series, nos. 76–7. London: Hakluyt Society, 1935.

Taylor, Garth. "The Inuit Middleman in the Labrador Baleen Trade." Paper presented at the 75th Annual Meeting of the American Anthropological Association. On File, Gatineau, QC: Canadian Museum of History, 1976.

– "Two Worlds of Mikak, Part I." *The Beaver* 31, no. 3 (1983): 4–13.

– "Two Worlds of Mikak, Part II." *The Beaver* 31, no. 4 (1984): 18–25.

Teit, James A. "Tahltan Tales." *The Journal of American Folklore* 34, no. 133 (1921): 223–53.

Thevet, André. *Les singularitez de la France antarctique*. Antwerp: Christophe Plantin, 1558.

Thierry, Eric. "La Paix de Vervins (1598) et les ambitions françaises en Amérique." In *Le Traité de Vervins*, edited by Jean-François Labourdette, Jean-Pierre Poussou, et Marie-Catherine Vignal, 373–89. Paris: Presses de l'Université de Paris-Sorbonne, 2000.

Thompson, David. *The Writings of David Thompson*. Edited by William Moreau, 2 vols. Montreal and Kingston: McGill-Queen's University Press, 2009-15.

Thorndike, Lynn. *The Sphere of Sacrobosco and Its Commentators*. Chicago: University of Chicago Press, 1949.

Thornton, John K. *A Cultural History of the Atlantic World, 1250–1820*. Cambridge, MA: Cambridge University Press, 2012.

Thwaites, Reuben, ed. *The Jesuit Relations and Allied Documents*. 73 vols. Cleveland, OH: Burrows Brothers, 1896–1900.

Tiffney, Bruce H. "The Eocene North Atlantic Land Bridge: Its Importance in Tertiary and Modern Phytogeography of the Northern Hemisphere." *Journal of the Arnold Arboretum* 66 (1985): 243–73.

– *Geographic and Climatic Influences on the Cretaceous and Tertiary History of Euramerican Floristic Similarity*. Prague: Karlova Universita, 2000.

Tomlins, Christopher L. *Freedom Bound: Law, Labor, and Civic Identity in Colonizing English America, 1580–1865*. New York: Cambridge University Press, 2010.

Tooker, Elisabeth. *An Ethnography of the Huron Indians, 1615–1649*. Washington: Government Printing Office, 1964.

– "The League of the Iroquois: Its History, Politics, and Ritual." In *Handbook of North American Indians*, vol. 15: *Northeast*, edited by B.G. Trigger, 418–41. Washington: Smithsonian Institution, 1978.

– "Northern Iroquoian Sociopolitical Organization." *American Anthropologist* 72 no. 1 (1970): 90–7.

Tough, Frank J. "Aboriginal Rights versus the Deed of Surrender: The Legal Rights of Native Peoples and Canada's Acquisition of the Hudson's Bay Company Territory." *Prairie Forum* 17 (1992): 225–50.

Tremblay, Roland. "Culture et ethnicité en archéologie: les aléas de l'identité conjuguée au passé." *Recherches amérindiennes au Québec* 29 (1999): 3–8.

– "La connexion abénaquise: quelques éléments de recherche sur la dispersion des Iroquoiens du Saint-Laurent orientaux." *Archéologiques* 10 (1996): 77–86.

– "Le site de l'anse à la Vache et le mitan du Sylvicole supérieur dans l'estuaire du Saint-Laurent." In *L'éveilleur et l'ambassadeur: essais archéologiques et ethnohistoriques en hommage à Charles A. Martijn*, edited by Roland Tremblay, 91–125. Montreal: Recherches amérindiennes au Québec, 1998.

– "A Middle Phase for the Eastern St. Lawrence Iroquoian Sequence: Western Influences and Eastern Practices." In *Taming the Taxonomy: Toward a New Understanding of Great Lakes Archaeology*, edited by R.F. Williamson and C.M. Watts, 83–100. Toronto: Eastendbooks and Ontario Archaeological Society, 1999.

– *Peuple du maïs: Les Iroquoiens du Saint-Laurent.* Montréal: Éditions de l'Homme, 2006.

Trigger, Bruce G. *The Children of Aataentsic: A History of the Huron People to 1660.* Montreal and Kingston: McGill-Queen's University Press, 1976.

– *A History of Archaeological Thought*, second edition. Cambridge: Cambridge University Press, 2006.

– *Natives and Newcomers: Canada's "Heroic Age" Reconsidered.* Kingston and Montreal: McGill-Queen's University Press, 1985.

– "Prehistoric Social and Political Organization: An Iroquoian Case Study." In *Foundations of Northeast Archaeology*, edited by D.R. Snow, 1–50. New York: Academic Press, 1981.

Trudel, François. "The Inuit of Southern Labrador and the Development of French Sedentary Fisheries (1700–1760)." In *Canadian Ethnology Society, Papers from the Fourth Annual Congress, 1977*, edited by Richard J. Preston, 99–120. Ottawa: Canadian Ethnology Service, 1978.

– "Les relations entre les Français et les Inuit au Labrador méridional, 1660–1760." *Études/Inuit Studies* 4, no. 1–2 (1980): 135–46.

Trudel, Marcel. *Histoire de la Nouvelle-France*, vol. 2, *Le comptoir, 1604–1627.* Montreal: Fides, 1966.

– "Un nouvel inventaire du Saint-Laurent, 1603." *Revue d'histoire de l'Amérique française* 16, no. 3 (1962): 313–47.

True, Micah. *Masters and Students: Jesuit Mission Ethnography in Seventeenth-Century New France.* Montreal and Kingston: McGill-Queen's University Press, 2015.

Tuck, James A. "Excavations at Red Bay, Labrador 1986." In *Archaeology in Newfoundland and Labrador 1986*, edited by J.S. Thomson and C. Thomson, 213–37. St John's, NL: Department of Tourism, Culture, and Recreation, Government of Newfoundland and Labrador, 1989.

– "The Iroquois Confederacy." In *New World Archaeology: Theoretical and Cultural Transformations*, edited by E.B.W. Zubrow, M.C. Fritz, and J.M. Fritz, 190–200. San Francisco: W.H. Freeman and Co., 1974.

Tuck, James A., and Robert Grenier, ed. *Red Bay, Labrador: World Whaling Capital A.D. 1550–1600.* St John's, NL: Atlantic Archaeology, 1989.

Turgeon, Laurier. "Basque-Amerindian Trade in the Saint Lawrence during the Sixteenth Century: New Documents, New Perspectives." *Man in the Northeast* 40 (1990): 81–7.

– "French Fishers, Fur Traders, and Amerindians During the Sixteenth Century: History and Archaeology." *William and Mary Quarterly* 55, no. 4 (1998): 585–610.

– "Pêches basques du Labourd en Atlantique nord (XVIe–XVIIIe siècle): ports, routes et trafics." In *Itsas memoria, Revista de estudios maritimos del Pais Vasco 3*, 163–78. Donostia-San Sebastián: Untzi Museoa-Museo Naval, 2000.

– "Pour redécouvrir notre 16e siècle: les pêches à Terre-Neuve d'après les archives notariales de Bordeaux." *Revue d'histoire de l'Amérique française* 39, no. 4 (1986): 523–49.

– "The Tale of the Kettle: Odyssey of an Intercultural Object." *Ethnohistory* 44, no. 1 (1997): 1–29.

– *Une histoire de la Nouvelle-France: Français et Amérindiens au XVIe siècle.* Paris: Belin, 2019.

– "Vers une chronologie des occupations basques du Saint-Laurent du XVIe au XVIIIe siècle: un retour à l'histoire." *Recherches amérindiennes au Québec* 24, no. 3 (1994): 3–15.

Turkel, William J. *The Archive of Place: Unearthing the Pasts of the Chilcotin Plateau.* Vancouver: UBC Press, 2014.

Turner, William W. "The Apaches." *Literary World* 20 no. 272 (1852): 281–2.

Tyrrell, J.B., ed. *Documents Relating to the Early History of Hudson Bay.* Toronto: Champlain Society, 2013.

– *Journals of Samuel Hearne and Philip Turnor between the Years 1774 and 1792.* Toronto: Champlain Society, 1934.

Umfreville, Edward. *The Present State of The Hudson's Bay Company.* Toronto: Ryerson Press, 1954.

Vachon de Belmont, François. *Histoire de l'eau-de-vie en Canada.* Quebec City: Literary and Historical Society of Quebec, 1840.

Vajda, Edward. "Dene-Yeniseian: Progress and Unanswered Questions." *Diachronica* 35, no. 2 (2018): 277–95.

– "A Siberian Link with Na-Dene languages." In *The Dene-Yeniseian Connection*, edited by J. Kari and B.A. Potter, 33–99. Fairbanks: University of Alaska, Department of Anthropology, 2011.

Valin, René-Josué. *Nouveau commentaire sur l'ordonnance de la marine du mois d'août 1681.* La Rochelle: Chez Jérôme Legier et Pierre Mesnier, 1760.

Vallée, Arthur. *Un biologiste canadien: Michel Sarrazin, sa vie, ses travaux et son temps.* Québec: Ls-A. Proulx, 1927.

Van Kirk, Sylvia. *Many Tender Ties: Women in Fur-trade Society in Western Canada, 1670–1870.* Winnipeg: Watson & Dwyer, 1980.

Vansina, Jan. *Oral Tradition as History.* Madison: University of Wisconsin Press, 1985.

Vargas-Rodriguez, Yalma L., William J. Platt, Lowell E. Urbatsch, and David W. Foltz. "Large Scale Patterns of Genetic Variation and Differentiation in Sugar Maple from Tropical Central America to Temperate North America." *BMC evolutionary biology* 15, no. 1 (2015): 1–14.

Vehik, Susan C. "Conflict, Trade, and Political Development on the Southern Plains." *American Antiquity* 67, no. 1 (2002): 37–64.

Viau, Roland. *Enfants du néant et mangeurs d'âme: Guerre, culture et société en Iroquoisie ancienne.* Montréal: Boréal, 1997.

Vickers, Daniel, and Vince Walsh. *Young Men and the Sea: Yankee Seafarers in the Age of Sail.* New Haven, CT: Yale University Press, 2005.

Vieira, Nina. "A Comparative Approach to Historical Whaling Techniques: Transfer of Knowledge in the 17th Century from the Biscay to Brazil." In *Cross-Cultural Exchange and the Circulation of Knowledge in the First Global Age*, edited by Amélia Polónia, Fabiano Bracht, Gisele Conceição, and Monique Palma, 125–44. Lisbon: Centro de Investigação Transdisciplinar Cultura, Espaço e Memória, 2018.

Vimont, Bartholemy P., Jérôme Lalemant, and Paul Le Jeune. *Relation de ce qui s'est passé en la Nouvelle France, en l'année 1640/ Envoyée au R. Père provincial de la compagnie de Jésus en la Province de France / Par Le P. Bartholemy Vimont de la même compagnie, supérieur de la résidence de Kébec.* Paris: Sébastien Cramoisy, 1641.

Wachuta, Joshua. "All and More than Was Owed: American Indians and Settler Capitalism on the Upper Mississippi, 1805–1890." PhD diss., Loyola University Chicago, 2019.

Wagner, Mike. "Asleep by a Frozen Sea or a Financial Innovator? The Hudson's Bay Company, 1714–63." *Canadian Journal of History* 49 (2014): 179–202.

Wallace, W. Stewart, ed. *Documents Relating to the North West Company.* Toronto: Champlain Society, 1934.

Wallis, Helen. "The First English Globe: A Recent Discovery." *Geographical Journal* 117 (1951): 275–90.

– "'Opera Mundi': Emery Molyneux, Jodocus Hondius and the First English Globe." In *Theatrum Orbis Librorum: Liber Amicorum Presented to Nico Israel on the Occasion of His Seventieth Birthday*, edited by Ton Croiset van Uchelen, Koert van der Horst, and Guenter Schilder, 94–104. Utrecht: HES Publishers, 1989.

Ward, Robin. *The World of the Medieval Shipmaster: Law, Business and the Sea, c.1350–c.1450.* Woodbridge: Boydell, 2009.

Warkentin, Germaine, ed. *Canadian Exploration Literature: An Anthology.* Toronto: Dundurn, 2007.

– *Pierre-Esprit Radisson: The Collected Writings*, 2 vols. Toronto: Champlain Society, 2012.

Warren, Robert J. "Ghosts of Cultivation Past: Native American Dispersal Legacy Persists in Tree Distribution." *PLOS ONE* 11, no. 3 (2016): e0150707.

Warrick, Gary, and Louis Lesage. "The Huron-Wendat and the St. Lawrence Iroquoians: New Findings of a Close Relationship." *Ontario Archaeology* 96 (2016): 133–43.

Waters, David W. *The Art of Navigation in England in Elizabethan and Early Stuart Times.* New Haven, CT: Yale University Press, 1958.

Waters, Michael R. "Late Pleistocene Exploration and Settlement of the Americas by Modern Humans." *Science* 365 (July 2019): eaat5447.

Watson, Scott. "Race, Wilderness, Territory, and the Origins of Modern Canadian Landscape Painting." In *Beyond Wilderness: The Group of Seven, Canadian Iden-*

tity, and Contemporary Art, edited by John O'Brian and Peter White. Montreal and Kingston: McGill-Queen's University Press, 2007.

Wey Gómez, Nicolás. *Tropics of Empire: Why Columbus Sailed South to the Indies.* Cambridge, MA: MIT Press, 2008.

Willan, Thomas Stuart. *The Muscovy Merchants of 1555.* Manchester: University of Manchester Press, 1953.

Wheat, David. *Atlantic Africa and the Spanish Caribbean, 1570–1640.* Chapel Hill: University of North Carolina Press, 2016.

Whelan, Mary K. "Dakota Indian Economics and the Nineteenth-Century Fur Trade," *Ethnohistory* 40 (1993): 246–76.

White, Bruce M. "The Fear of Pillaging: Economic Folktales of the Great Lakes Fur Trade." In *The Fur Trade Revisited*, edited by Jennifer S.H. Brown, W.J. Eccles, and Donald P. Heldman, 199–216. East Lansing: Michigan State University Press, 1994.

– "'Give Us a Little Milk': The Social and Cultural Meanings of Gift Giving in the Lake Superior Fur Trade." *Minnesota History* 48, no. 2 (1982): 60–71.

– *Grand Portage as a Trading Post: Patterns of Trade at "the Great Carrying Place."* Grand Marais, MN: Grand Portage National Monument, National Park Service, 2005.

– "A Skilled Game of Exchange: Ojibway Fur Trade Protocol." *Minnesota History* 50, no. 6 (1987): 229–40.

– "The Trade Assortment: The Meanings of Merchandise in the Ojibwa Fur Trade." In *Vingt Ans Après Habitants et Marchands Twenty Years Later: Lectures de l'histoire des XVIIe et XVIIIe siècles canadiens: Reading the History of Seventeenth- and Eighteenth-Century Canada*, edited by Sylvie Dépatie, Catherine Desbarats, Mario Lalancette, Danielle Gauvreau, and Thomas Wien, 115–37. Montreal and Kingston: McGill-Queen's University Press, 1998.

White, Richard. *The Middle Ground: Indians, Empires, and Republics in the Great Lakes Region, 1650–1815.* New York: Cambridge University Press, 1991.

White, Sam. *A Cold Welcome: The Little Ice Age and Europe's Encounter with North America.* Cambridge, MA: Harvard University Press, 2018.

Whitehead, Ruth H. "Navigation des Micmacs le long de la côte de l'Atlantique." In *Les Micmacs et la mer*, edited by C.A. Martijn, 224–32. Montréal: Recherches amérindiennes au Québec, 1986.

– *The Old Man Told Us: Excerpts from Micmac History, 1500–1950.* Halifax: Nimbus, 1991.

Whitridge, Peter. "Classic Thule [Classic Precontact Inuit]." In *The Oxford Hand-book of the Prehistoric Arctic,* edited by Max T. Friesen and Owen K. Mason, 827–49. Oxford: Oxford University Press, 2016.

– "The Construction of Social Difference in a Prehistoric Inuit Whaling Commu-nity." PhD diss., Arizona State University, Tempe. 1999.

– "Reimagining the Iglu: Modernity and the Challenge of the Eighteenth-Century Labrador Inuit Winter House." *Archaeologies* 4 (2008): 288–309.

Wien, Thomas. "Le Pérou éphémère: termes d'échange et éclatement du commerce franco-amérindien, 1645–1670." In *Vingt ans après habitants et marchands: Twenty Years Later: Lectures de l'histoire des XVIIe et XVIIIe siècles canadiens: Reading the History of Seventeenth- and Eighteenth-Century Canada,* ed. Sylvie Dépatie, Catherine Desbarats, Mario Lalancette, Danielle Gauvreau and Thomas Wien, 160–88. Montreal and Kingston: McGill-Queen's University Press, 1998.

Wilcocke, Samuel Hull, Edward Ellice, and Simon McGillivray. *A Narrative of Oc-currences in the Indian Countries of North America, since the Connexion of the Right Hon. the Earl of Selkirk with the Hudson's Bay Company, and His Attempt to Establish a Colony on the Red River: With a Detailed Account of His Lordship's Mil-itary Expedition to, and Subsequent Proceedings at Fort William, in Upper Canada.* London: B. McMillan, 1817.

Willerslev, Eske, and David J. Meltzer. "Peopling of the Americas as Inferred from Ancient Genomics." *Nature* 594 (June 2021): 356–64.

Williamson, Ronald F. "East–West Interaction among Fifteenth-Century St. Lawrence Iroquoian and North Shore of Lake Ontario Ancestral Wendat Com-munities." *Ontario Archaeology* 96 (2016): 104–20.

– *Legacy of Stone: Ancient Life on the Niagara Frontier.* Toronto: Eastendbooks, 1998.

Wilson, T.M., ed. *Drinking Cultures: Alcohol and Identity.* New York: Berg, 2005.

Wintroub, Michael. *The Voyage of Thought.* Cambridge: Cambridge University Press, 2017.

Witgen, Michael. *An Infinity of Nations: How the Native New World Shaped Early America.* Philadelphia: University of Pennsylvania Press, 2012.

Wolf, Eric R. *Europe and the People without History.* Berkeley: University of Califor-nia Press, 1982.

Workman, William B. "The Cultural Significance of a Volcanic Ash Which Fell in the Upper Yukon about 1400 years ago." In *International Conference on the Prehis-tory and Palaeoecology of Western North American Arctic and Subarctic,* edited by

S. Raymond and P. Schledermann, 239–61. Calgary: Archaeological Association, University of Calgary, 1974.

– *Prehistory of Aishihik-Kluane Area: Southwest Yukon Territory.* Archaeological Survey of Canada Paper Number 74. Ottawa: University of Ottawa Press, 1978.

– "The Significance of Volcanism in the Prehistory of Subarctic Northwest North America." In *Volcanic Activity and Human Ecology*, edited by Payson D. Sheets and Donald K. Grayson, 339–71. New York: Academic Press, 1979.

Wright, Edward. *Certaine Errors in Navigation.* London, 1599.

Wright, James V. "Before European Contact." In *Aboriginal Ontario: Historical Perspectives on the First Nations* edited by Edward S. Rogers and Donald B. Smith, 21–38. Toronto: Dundurn Press, 1994.

– *A History of the Native People of Canada*, 3 vols. Gatineau, QC: Canadian Museum of Civilization, 1995.

Wyatt, Michael. *The Italian Encounter with Tudor England: A Cultural Politics of Translation.* Cambridge: Cambridge University Press, 2005.

Wynn, Graeme. *Canada and Arctic North America: An Environmental History.* Santa Barbara, CA: ABC-CLIO, 2007.

– "Nature and Nation." In *The Nature of Canada*, edited by Colin Coates and Graeme Wynn, 25–50. Vancouver: On Point Press, 2019.

– "'Tracing One Warm Line through a Land so Wide and Savage': Fifty Years of Historical Geography in Canada." *Historical Geography* 30 (2012): 5–32.

– "W.F. Ganong, A.H. Clark and the Historical Geography of Maritime Canada." *Acadiensis* 10 (1981): 5–28.

Yanicki, Gabriel M. "Follow the Women: Ceramics and Ethnogenesis in the Intermontane West." In *Holes in Our Moccasins, Holes in Our Stories. New Insights into Apachean Origins from the Promontory, Franktown, and Dismal River Archaeological Records*, edited by John W. Ives and Joel C. Janetski, 97–117. Salt Lake City: University of Utah Press, 2022.

Yanicki, Gabriel M., and John W. Ives. "Mobility, Exchange and the Fluency of Games: Promontory in a Broader Sociodemographic Setting." *In Prehistoric Games of North American Indians: Subarctic to Mesoamerica*, edited by Barbara Voorhies, 139–62. Salt Lake City: University of Utah Press, 2017.

Yates, Frances A. *John Florio: The Life of an Italian in Shakespeare's England.* Cambridge: Cambridge University Press, 1934.

Yerbury, J. Colin. *The Subarctic Indians and the Fur Trade, 1680–1860.* Vancouver: UBC Press, 1986.

Young, Brian. *Patrician Families and the Making of Quebec: The Taschereaus and McCords*. Montreal and Kingston: McGill-Queen's University Press, 2014.

Young, Kathryn A. "Crown Agent – Canadian Correspondent: Michel Sarrazin and the Académie Royale des Sciences, 1697–1734." *French Historical Studies* 18, no. 2 (1993): 416–33.

Zeno, Niccolò. *De i Commentarii*. Venice: Francesco Marcolini, 1558.

Zolbrod, P.G. *Diné bahane`. The Navajo Creation Story*. Albuquerque: University of New of New Mexico Press, 1984.

Contributors

JACK BOUCHARD is assistant professor of history at Rutgers University, New Brunswick, New Jersey. He writes on the northwest Atlantic in the sixteenth century and is currently working on a book, *Terra Nova: Food, Water and Work in an Early Atlantic World* (Yale University Press, forthcoming).

ADRIAN L. BURKE is professor in the Département d'anthropologie at the Université de Montréal. His research interests include geoarchaeology of stone tool raw materials, circulation, and exchange of materials in the past, collaborative Indigenous archaeology in Canada and the USA.

SAMUEL DERKSEN is a doctoral candidate in history at McGill University. His dissertation is entitled, "Between Company and Corporation: An Examination of the North West Company's Legal Character and Corporate Strategy."

HELEN DEWAR is associate professor at the Université de Montréal. Her most recent publication is *Disputing New France: Companies, Law, and Sovereignty in the French Atlantic, 1598–1663* (McGill-Queen's University Press, 2022).

MARY C. FULLER is professor of literature at MIT. She just published *Lines Drawn Across the Globe: Reading Richard Hakluyt's Principal Navigations* (McGill-Queen's University Press, 2023).

CHRISTIAN GATES ST-PIERRE is associate professor at the Département d'anthropologie, Université de Montréal. His research interests include collaborative and Indigenous archaeology in northeastern North America, the study of ceramic and osseous artifacts, ancient foodways, archaeological heritage, and archaeological ethics.

ALLAN GREER is professor emeritus of history at McGill University. The author of, among other works, *Property and Dispossession: Natives, Empires and Land in Early Modern North America* (Cambridge University Press, 2018), he is currently working on an overview of Canada's deep history.

KATHERINE IBBETT is professor of French at the University of Oxford and tutorial fellow of Trinity College, Oxford; she is the author of *Compassion's Edge: Fellow-Feeling and its Limits in Early Modern France* (University of Pennsylvania Press, 2018) and is currently working on *Liquid Empire*, a book about French river writing, supported by a Leverhulme Research Fellowship.

JOHN (JACK) W. IVES is emeritus professor of anthropology, University of Alberta, where he founded the Institute of Prairie Archaeology (today, the Institute of Prairie and Indigenous Archaeology). He was most recently the editor (with Joel Janetski) of *Holes in Our Moccasins, Holes in Our Stories. Apachean Origins and the Promontory, Franktown and Dismal River Archaeological Records* (University of Utah Press, 2022).

BRAD LOEWEN is professor of anthropology at the Université de Montréal, focusing on historical and maritime archaeology. His most recent book is *Contact in the 16th Century: Networks Among Fishers, Foragers and Farmers* (University of Ottawa Press, 2016).

CHRISTOPHER PARSONS, associate professor of history at Northeastern University, is currently researching the early history of introduced epidemic diseases in what is now Canada and the United States. He is the author of *A Not-so-New World: Empire and Environment in French Colonial North America* (University of Pennsylvania Press, 2018).

LISA K. RANKIN is professor and Memorial University research chair in the Department of Archaeology at Memorial University of Newfoundland. She recently published "Tourism and Archaeology in Nunatsiavut," along with Laura Kelvin, Marjorie Flowers, and Charlotte Wolfrey in *The Inuit World*, edited by Pamela Stern (Routledge Press, 2022).

Index